THE CINEMATIC POLITICAL

In this book, Michael J. Shapiro stages a series of pedagogical encounters between political theory, represented as a compositional challenge, and cinematic texts, emphasizing how to achieve an effective research paper/essay by heeding the compositional strategies of films. The text's distinctiveness is its focus on the intermediation between two textual genres. It is aimed at providing both a conceptual introduction to the politics of aesthetics and a guide to writing strategies. In its illustrations of encounters between political theory and cinema, the book's critical edge is its emphasis on how to intervene in cinematic texts with innovative conceptual frames in ways that challenge dominant understandings of life worlds.

   The Cinematic Political is designed as a teaching resource that introduces students to the relationship between film form and political thinking. With diverse illustrative investigations, the book instructs students on how to watch films with an eye toward writing a research paper in which a film (or set of films) constitutes the textual vehicle for political theorizing.

Michael J. Shapiro is Professor of Political Science at the University of Hawai'i, Manoa. Among his recent publications are *Politics and Time: Documenting the Event* (2016); *Deforming American Political Thought*, 2nd edition (Routledge, 2016); *The Political Sublime* (2018); and *Punctuations: How the Arts Think the Political* (2019).

"The book is an excellent continuum of Shapiro's path breaking work on the relationship between political theory and film from his pivotal works, *Cinematic Political Thought* and *Cinematic Geopolitics*. Conceptually and methodologically this book is deepening and enhancing his approach of cinematic thinking in terms of advising the reader on, as he says, the 'how to' of relating political theory with cinema as epitomised in his cinematic writing style that problematizes the way we think about and view films."

—*Ian Fraser, Senior Lecturer in Politics,*
Loughborough University, UK

"Thanks to digital social media, we are all movie-makers now with global audiences. In this book, Michael J. Shapiro links the grammar of moving images to theorizing about politics in an authoritative and accessible way."

—*Terrell Carver, Professor of Political Theory,*
University of Bristol, UK

"This superb new book insightfully reimagines cinema as a vehicle for 'doing critically oriented political theory.' Much as Hayden White famously helped us to understand how the story of history is narrated (when written or when filmed), here Shapiro brilliantly illuminates how films can compose political theory. In this masterful, mature work, drawing on all his experience, his remarkable intellectual prowess fully in evidence, Shapiro gives political theory a vibrant cinematic dimension. The diverse examples provide accessible entrances for all readers—from Adam Smith to Deleuze and Guattari, from Bertolucci's *The Conformist* to *The Cats of Mirikitani*, *Sleep Dealer* and *Miss Bala* via *Hoop Dreams*. Most pertinently, the work's exploration of fascism has a stark relevance, if not warning, for our time."

—*Professor David Martin-Jones, Film and Television Studies,*
University of Glasgow, UK

THE CINEMATIC POLITICAL

FILM COMPOSITION AS POLITICAL THEORY

Michael J. Shapiro

NEW YORK AND LONDON

First published 2020
by Routledge
52 Vanderbilt Avenue, New York, NY 10017

and by Routledge
2 Park Square, Milton Park, Abingdon, Oxon, OX14 4RN

Routledge is an imprint of the Taylor & Francis Group, an informa business

© 2020 Taylor & Francis

The right of Michael J. Shapiro to be identified as author of this work
has been asserted by him in accordance with sections 77 and 78 of the
Copyright, Designs and Patents Act 1988.

All rights reserved. No part of this book may be reprinted or reproduced
or utilised in any form or by any electronic, mechanical, or other means,
now known or hereafter invented, including photocopying and recording,
or in any information storage or retrieval system, without permission in
writing from the publishers.

Trademark notice: Product or corporate names may be trademarks or
registered trademarks, and are used only for identification and explanation
without intent to infringe.

Library of Congress Cataloging-in-Publication Data
Names: Shapiro, Michael J., author.
Title: The cinematic political : film composition as political theory /
    Michael J. Shapiro.
Description: New York, NY : Routledge, 2020. | Includes
    bibliographical references and index.
Identifiers: LCCN 2019043541 (print) | LCCN 2019043542
    (ebook) | ISBN 9781138596160 (hardback) | ISBN
    9781138596177 (paperback) | ISBN 9780429487903 (ebook) |
    ISBN 9780429947339 (adobe pdf) | ISBN 9780429947315
    (mobi) | ISBN 9780429947322 (epub)
Subjects: LCSH: Motion pictures—Political aspects. | Motion
    pictures—Aesthetics. | Aesthetics—Political aspects. | English
    language—Rhetoric. | Report writing.
Classification: LCC PN1995.9.P6 S523 2020 (print) |
    LCC PN1995.9.P6 (ebook) | DDC 791.43/6581—dc23
LC record available at https://lccn.loc.gov/2019043541
LC ebook record available at https://lccn.loc.gov/2019043542

ISBN: 978-1-138-59616-0 (hbk)
ISBN: 978-1-138-59617-7 (pbk)
ISBN: 978-0-429-48790-3 (ebk)

Typeset in Galliard
by Apex CoVantage, LLC

For "Mom": Ruth Tavares-Toma

Contents

	List of Figures	*ix*
	Acknowledgments	*xi*
	Introduction	1
1	Extracting Political Theory From Lars von Trier: Conceptual Interferences With His *The Element of Crime*	26
2	Toward a Critical Assessment of "Now-Time": Contrasting *Hoop Dreams* With Kubrick's *Barry Lyndon*	52
3	Resituating Hiroshima	81
4	"The Light of Reason"	113
5	"Borderline Justice"	146
6	A Bi-City Cinematic Experience	178
7	The Phenomenology of the Cinema Experience	203
	Afterword: The Phenomenology of Watching and Writing	229
	Name Index	*235*
	Subject Index	*239*

Figures

0.1	A still from *The Conformist*: Marcello and Giulia dancing on their honeymoon	7
1.1	Psychiatrist with a monkey on his back	28
1.2	Fisher, Kim, and The Schmuck	35
1.3	VW in the junkyard	43
2.1	Estate image	67
2.2	Room full of portraits	68
2.3 and 2.4	Arthur and William, respectively, at St. Josephs	73
2.5	The shoe scene on the street	75
3.1	Charred figure of woman and baby	84
3.2	Crossed watches	91
3.3	Kolbowski lovers	98
3.4	Soccer ball	103
4.1	Café oven	115
4.2	The celestial group	115
4.3	Valuska and Eszter walking	125
4.4	Eclipse mimed on the building	127
5.1	Fordist factory	147
5.2 and 5.3	Del Rio Corporation and Casa Cruz	148
5.4	Laura wearing her crown	164
6.1	Kirchner Potsdamer Platz image	184
6.2	McCoy and Candy on metro car	185
6.3	Piggy and Shan on bus	186
6.4	Fat Man	190
7.1	Van Sant's *Psycho* victim	204
7.2	One of Marclay's clocks	206
7.3	A Grimonprez television still	214
7.4	McNamara off-center	222

Acknowledgments

I want to thank my editor, Natalja Mortensen, for her encouragement of the project at every stage. I also want to thank Bonnie Honig and Lori Marso for recruiting me as a participant in the Lars von Trier Political Theory and Film project, which helped inspire this book, and Davide Panagia deserves special thanks for his suggestions after reading a draft of the Introduction. I also want to thank those involved in Routledge's production process, especially Charlie Baker and Apex's Marie Louise Roberts for facilitating the final production process. This book is dedicated to "Mom," my mother-in-law, Ruth Tavares-Toma, who has lived a remarkably unselfish, hardworking, and giving life. No one I have ever known has done more to support her loved ones or who better exemplifies grace.

Introduction

PRESUPPOSITIONS: EVENT-DRIVEN LITERATURE

This monograph is a research handbook dedicated to methods for thinking and writing cinematically. It is organized as a series of demonstrations that feature the articulation of political theory with cinema. Much of the emphasis is on composition, on writing projects in which a film or of a set of films is a textual vehicle for political theorizing. The project is inspired by my recent participation in a collective effort to extract political theory from the films of Lars von Trier.[1] In the preface to that collection, Davide Panagia raises a question to which much of this monograph is a response: "Is there . . . a cinematic mode of political thinking?" His response is that it requires an "emphasis on political theorizing as a practice of invention and improvisation that allows us to imagine an affective constellation of worlds combining in aberrant forms. Such is at once the nature of cinema and politics."[2] The analysis throughout this book endorses what Panagia implies: Staging an encounter between political theory and cinema requires attention to the way thinking is a form of (aberrant) movement in both the media genres of political theory and cinema and to the selection of innovative conceptual frames to intervene in the cinematic text in ways that challenge dominant understandings of life worlds. The diverse chapters in Honig and Marso's collection provide such encounters with much of von Trier's film corpus. They compose political theory essays as they extract political theorizing from von Trier's cinematic compositions.

Heeding the importance of "composition," the undertaking to which I am referring as a cinematic mode of political theorizing presupposes a literary approach to political theory. Moreover, just as political theory is *composed*—its way of thinking emerges from the grammatical, figurative, and narrative dimensions that constitute literariness—filmmaking is also (among other things) a literary form. However, films are more complex than written texts. They are composed of narrative and non- (and antinarrative) forms, articulated through moving images (and isolated still ones in long take framing shots), montage

INTRODUCTION

sequences, soundtracks, and hues (color intensities or in the case of black-and-white films, the interaction between shadow and light). Following Gilles Deleuze and Felix Guattari's remarks about composition in general, one can infer that cinema, like other textual genres, involves a complex "aesthetic plane of composition."[3] That complexity imposes special demands. To heed the way a film thinks requires watching it multiple times, focusing each time on alternative aspects—for example watching a color film once by noting the chromatic sequence, then watching it with a focus on the soundtrack, watching it yet again with attention to the nature and sequence of shots, and finally watching it once more to note the alternative clashes and symbiotic resonances among the film's disparate aesthetic registers because a film's "clash of heterogeneous elements"[4] challenges traditional modes of comprehension and constitutes much of how it thinks and how it provokes thinking. Taking all those aspects into consideration, to stage an encounter between a film (in all its complexities) and a conceptually innovative mode of political theorizing is to treat a film as what Roland Barthes famously calls a "methodological field" in which one seeks to recover "its subversive force in respect to old classifications."[5] Put simply, to approach a film's potential political pedagogy is to concentrate on how it thinks as a text, where the thinking is lodged in the interrelations of images and their connections with the film's other expressive forms.

I want to draw from Barthes's remark about the "subversive force" to derive another implication—to reflect on a homology between the history of political theory and the history of cinema. Both political theory and cinema have been shaped by subversive "events," moments in which the relationships they seek to illuminate have become radically realigned. For an appreciation of such moments, there is doubtless no more decisive historical episode with respect to realigned relationships than the one Michel Foucault describes in his genealogical history of punishment. There he summarizes a dramatic shift in the official practice of punishment: "From an art of unbearable sensations, punishment became an economy of suspended rights."[6] That summarizing remark follows Foucault's description of a ghastly public torture scene in 1757 in which a would-be regicide is the target of the sovereign's revenge, a ritual through which the king's sovereign power is reactivated. He goes on to point out that subsequently ("[e]ighty years later"),[7] the accused, no longer the target of the sovereign's revenge, had become an object of knowledge within a radically different modality of power. Accordingly, by the mid-nineteenth century there emerges a new persona, "the criminal," whose career biography is assembled and interrogated by new knowledge agents, among whom are forensic psychiatrists. Whereas prior juridical processes had been concerned only with "offenses and penalties,"[8] governance had radically shifted its focus on life. No longer preoccupied with the life of the sovereign, the concern was with the life of the collective body. As a result, "modernity," according

INTRODUCTION 3

to Foucault, can be framed on the basis of the dramatic historical moment in which "political power assigned itself the task of administering life."[9]

To provide another illustration of a conceptually significant event, I want to evoke Gilles Deleuze's focus on shifts in the conceptual terrain of the history of philosophy. Among the most notable toward which he points is the Kantian moment, which radically revised the philosophical approach to experience. Whereas philosophy's pre-Kantian knowledge problem had been about the extent to which what appears to consciousness can be reliably observed, Kant's (self-described) "Copernican revolution" posits an active mode of consciousness in which a subject's structure of apprehension is the condition of possibility for experiential knowledge; as Deleuze puts it,

> [p]reviously philosophers spoke of phenomenon to distinguish what? Very broadly we can say that phenomenon was something like appearance . . . with Kant a radically new understanding of the notion of phenomenon emerges. Namely that the phenomenon will no longer at all be appearance. . . . There is [a Kantian] phenomenology from the moment that the phenomenon is no longer defined as appearance but as apparition. The difference is enormous because when I say the word apparition I am no longer saying appearance at all. . . . What does an apparition refer to? The appearance is something that refers to essence in a relation of disjunction, . . . which is to say either its appearance or its essence. The apparition is very different; it's something that refers to the conditions of what appears.

What then has that Kantian moment wrought? Deleuze adds, "The conceptual landscape has literally changed completely, the problem is absolutely no longer the same, the problem has become phenomenological."[10] "For the disjunctive couple appearance/essence, Kant will substitute the conjunctive couple, what appears/conditions of apparition."[11]

Political theory and cinema are therefore homologous in terms of the effects of the decisive historical moments to which Foucault and Deleuze refer. Over time, they have both been shaped and reshaped by ideational events that have intervened in the narratives of their developments. Critical writing that inter-articulates the two media genre practices must therefore be alert to key moments. To note one in the history of political theory, we can heed J. G. A. Pocock's identification of the "Machiavellian moment," which he describes as "a phrase to be interpreted in two ways . . . it denotes the moment, and the manner, in which Machiavellian thought made its appearance,"[12] and it points to its ongoing historical significance. The historical moment to which Pocock is referring is the emergence of Atlantic Republicanism, which ushered in a new temporality. Unlike the "theocentric" view of time as eternal, "[t]he republic

4   INTRODUCTION

was not timeless . . . it did not reflect by simple correspondence the eternal order of nature. . . . The thing most clearly known about republics was that they came to an end in time";[13] they were subject to historical rather than eternal time. Politically, the "Machiavellian moment" is articulated as a duty assigned to citizenship in the dominant political venue of the period, the city. If people are to be understood as historical beings rather than eternal ones, they have citizen responsibilities. Instead of merely exhibiting a morality that will guarantee their salvation (as they are required to exhibit within a theocratic understanding), they are enjoined within Machiavelli's embrace of republican historical time to exhibit civic virtue. That republican moment continued to reproduce itself beyond its Florentine period—for example, in eighteenth-century critiques of "a chaos of appetites" that compromised civic virtue.[14]

Similarly, the history of cinema has also had moments with such enduring effects. There is, for example, the "moment of psycho," initiated by the unforgettably violent shower scene in Alfred Hitchcock's *Psycho* (1960). "The moment of *Psycho*" is David Thomson's expression for Hitchcock's cinematic event, the graphic slaying of the victim, Marion Crane (Janet Leigh), by the psychotic killer, Norman Bates (Anthony Perkins). Thomson describes the scene typical of Hitchcock's approach to drama in which "the imaginary triumphs over the actual":

> [T]he audience is left to make sense of the gap between the ordinary and the absurd (the life on the road versus life in the Bates house). There's no doubt about the cinematic quality of the shower sequence. This is an old-fashioned montage, an impression of a lethal attack to which has been added the utmost expressiveness of Herrmann's music and the soundtrack[15] in which it is embedded. The total effect is delirium. . . . The question that remains [as the audience seeks comprehension] is not just who has killed Marion Crane, but what tempest has felt bound to overtake the film?[16]

As Thomson points out, that moment resulted in a new film genre, a form of noir violence that has encouraged other directors to follow the Hitchcock aesthetic, "bloodletting, sadism, and slaughter [came to be] taken for granted."[17] Among the films that have since exhibited *Psycho*'s cinematic legacy are Roman Polanski's *Repulsion* (1965), "a clever replay of the lovely blonde under duress,"[18] and David Lynch's *Blue Velvet* (1986), in which the audience is invited into "the soaring inwardness of a dream," after "a boy finds an ear and wonders where the rest of the body is [and comes to] realize that evil lurks in his hometown . . ."[19] As I have suggested in an analysis of the implications of that moment, "[a]fter Hitchcock everyday life's façade of innocence has become suspect."[20]

INTRODUCTION 5

ARTICULATING MOMENTS: HISTORICAL, THEORETICAL, AND CINEMATIC

Many have recognized that cinema has played a significant role in the creation of contemporary (collective) historical consciousness—for example, Jacques Ranciére, who suggests that "[c]inema [can] actually create the event . . . because of its specific power to make historic any apparition behind any window whatsoever."[21] It has been an important player in what can count as history. Accordingly, I want to reference a notable historical moment in the history of cinema in which it has been involved in constituting what is "historical" while at the same time opening itself to the intervention of political theory. The rise of fascism in the early and mid-twentieth century was one of the main conditions of possibility for the appearance of innovative thinking in academic and artistic genres, cinema among others. Subsequent to the defeat of Germany's National Socialist and Italy's Fascist dictatorship, the experience of fascism had a disproportion shaping effect on the post–World War II development of the social sciences, especially political psychology. As I have put it,

> [i]n the case of political psychology what was encouraged was a search for the fascist personality, understood to be a deviant type susceptible to authoritarian impulses or appeals [and among the inquiries undertaken were] . . . the authoritarian personality studies of Theodore W. Adorno and his associates, Milton Rokeach's work on open versus closed minds, and H. G. Eysenck's addition of a tender minded versus tough minded axis of opinion to the study of political ideology.[22]

In sum, for the social sciences in this period, to understand the emergent dangers of fascism, one was encouraged to inquire into what Adorno et al. referred to as the "*potentially fascistic* individual."[23] For Adorno et al., as was the case for Eysenck and Rokeach, fascism takes hold of susceptible mentalities. Those fascism-susceptible mentalities are treated by Eysenck as ideologies, a convergence of conservatism with tough-mindedness, articulated as a commitment to capital punishment and other harsh treatments for criminals, among other things, while Rokeach lumped the fascist mentality with orthodox Marxism-Leninism and rendered both mentalities as forms of dogmatic cognitive organization. The fascist moment also endured within the political science subdiscipline known as "comparative politics," which was shaped by a fear of instability. Its reigning presumption, developing in the post–World War II years, was that "a fascist-proof political system must institutionalize structural impediments to office-holding by partisans with extreme or marginal political agendas."[24]

The intellectual scene in Italy is especially instructive for purposes here because much of the response has been more aesthetic-oriented than psychological- or

6   INTRODUCTION

political system–oriented. The theorizing I want to identify is more a close up than a structural survey, and crucially, it turns our focus toward aesthetic or media genre-shaped forms of consciousness rather than toward a psychological framing of mentality. It is critically focused on the micropolitical dynamics of the fascist period, specifically on the way differently situated social types managed an unstable world. Carlo Lucarelli, for example, who had planned to write a doctoral thesis on the role of the police during the fascist period, was instead captivated by the career of a police detective who had eschewed allegiances and worked at his profession for political authorities on both fascist and antifascist sides during their alternating periods of political control. Lucarelli became so intrigued by the steadfastly maintained political neutrality of that career he abandoned his thesis and became a crime novelist, executing a trilogy with a protagonist that is a fictional version of that detective. In his preface (repeated in all three crime novels that form a trilogy), Lucarelli describes the difficult political choices at the moment during World War II on the Italian front when

> Italy splits in two as the German army occupies that part of the country not yet liberated by the advance of the Anglo-American forces [while Mussolini remains] in charge of the collaborationist government. . . . There is above all enormous moral and political confusion that combines the desperation of those who know they are losing, the opportunism of those ready to change sides, the guilelessness of those who haven't understood anything and the desire for revenge of those who are about to arrive.[25]

While Lucarelli's novels take leave of those precarious dynamics and invent a further career for his aesthetic subject, whom he names Commissario De Luca, an important moment in the history of cinema takes over to animate the "enormous moral and political confusion" to which Lucarelli refers in his prefaces. It is the moment of Italian Neorealism, a cinematic event that made the fraught choices under crisis during the fascist period and in the immediate post–World War II palpable to large audiences. The film theorist André Bazin, pointing to the way the genre generates "image-facts," describes the effect of that new film genre as "An Aesthetic of Reality" which provides "[a] fragment of concrete reality in itself multiple and full of ambiguity."[26] Elaborating the reality effect of Bazin's "image-facts," a commentator writes,

> This ambiguity is lessened to a degree when one image-fact is placed alongside another but they regain a certain autonomy and ambiguity regardless of this arrangement. They retain a materiality and weight beyond the use they are supposed to serve in regards [to] the narrative and the meaning the filmmaker wishes to elicit from the image. In Neorealism, there is a density to objects that allows them to retain an independence or integrity beyond their manipulation or use by the filmmakers.[27]

Among the most notable Neorealist cinematic treatments of the "moral and political confusion" that had intrigued Lucarelli and energized his novels is Bernardo Bertolucci's *The Conformist* (1970), which displays the "density of objects" characteristic of Neorealist cinema, as it looks back at the fascist period to evince an influential politics of aesthetics, using, among other devices, contrasting "binary pairs" of colors "to great expressive effect," characteristic of the way Neorealist films invited viewers into the intimacies of the historical moment.[28] Specifically, Bertolucci's *The Conformist* is composed with a dual temporality. One involves the personal story of the protagonist/assassin, Marcello Clerici, who, desirous of achieving an undiluted masculinity, struggles with repressing his homoerotic feelings as he plans the murder of his former antifascist professor, Luca Quadri, living in Paris. The film narrative manages that temporal layer with flashbacks that reveal the psychohistorical legacy of Marcello's disturbed masculinity, shown continually emerging in his present through a focus (using point-of-view shots) on the way he perceives his world. Within that aspect of the cinematic focus, much of the perceptual dynamic of the film would seem to render the plot as subject-centered and thus psychological. Accordingly, much of the time what the viewer sees is through Marcello's point of view. However, while Marcello's vexed desire structure continually attends and shapes his actions (e.g., arranging a loveless marriage; see Figure 0.1, "a carefully negotiated compromise with society,"[29] to enhance a heterosexual identity), he is nevertheless better understood as an aesthetic subject rather than a psychological one. The significance of displacing a psychological

FIGURE 0.1
A still from *The Conformist*: Marcello and Giulia dancing on their honeymoon. Source: Bernardo Bertolucci, *The Conformist*, Marianne Productions (1970).

8   INTRODUCTION

with an aesthetic reading is well illustrated in Leo Bersani and Ulysse Dutoit's analysis of Jean-Luc Godard's *Contempt* (1963), a film focused on a couple's growing estrangement as the wife, Camile's (Bridget Bardot) feelings for her husband Paul (Michel Piccoli) turn from love to contempt. Godard's film, unlike Bertolucci's, does not dwell on the psychological origins of the emotion. Instead, as Bersani and Dutoit point out, Godard's image sequences show contempt's "effect on the world," articulated through the mages that show what it does to "cinematic space."[30]

Similarly, although Marcello's psychosexual past is explored and its effects on his actions shape some of the film's imagery and the angles of vision of its shots, Bertolucci's narrative is also focused on the effects of a desire for normality at different levels. While the action is centered on an individual seeing to exhibit normality (Bertolucci says it is a film "about a man who conceives himself to be different from his fellows . . . and tries to hide this abnormality behind conformity to a social and political norm"),[31] the film is nevertheless concerned also with

> the parallel between, on the one hand, the way the bourgeoisie thinks about itself and the reality that hides behind that façade; and on the other, the complacent rhetoric of the fascist regime and the naked violence of the class war which the rhetoric is concealed.[32]

Apart from the psychodrama that Bertolucci's flashbacks lend to his film narrative, the Bersani/Dutoit insight about Godard's *Contempt* applies well to the way *The Conformist* is composed. As the plot unfolds, the desire for an appearance of normality shapes the film's cinematic space. For example, at one point in a conversation with his blind friend, Italo, as Marcello is explaining that he is marrying to appear to be a normal male, the scene is constructed with Marcello facing the camera while in the frame behind him is a window that looks out "onto a pavement where some people are walking past."[33] At the same time, Italo reinforces the normality theme. He "executes a 180 degree turn and stands next to Marcello [and] says that a normal man is one who turns his head to look at the backside of a beautiful woman walking past . . ."[34] That pervasive masculinity theme, which continually shapes the cinematic spaces around Marcello, is embedded in a second temporality, the historical moment in Italy's fascist period in which governance involves a longer-term normalizing, that of Italian collective identity. Succinctly put, the

> crucial problem [the film explores about] the impossible stability of the male identity that Marcello has constructed for himself . . . mirrors the similarly deceptive logic by which Fascism holds onto the illusion of a stable and unitary national body politic.[35]

INTRODUCTION 9

That temporality, which remains mostly off-screen, prompts not only the kind of assassination project taken on by Marcello in the film but also a wide variety of artistic endeavors, among which were government-funded film projects, mostly short documentaries aimed at providing fascism with a legitimating historical trajectory (after Mussolini had declared that "cinema was the regime's strongest weapon").[36] Given the deceptive illusion-creating use of the arts that Mussolini's government undertook (it went as far as to change the architecture of the city of Arezzo to materialize the myth that the Arentines were the original Italian race),[37] Neorealist cinema has served as a reality-sustaining counter-weapon.

For purposes of illustrating the structure of my investigations throughout the chapters that follow, it is important to recognize how the historical moment of fascism energized oppositional thinking in *both* political theory and cinema. The sexuality theme that Bertolucci summoned to frame the normality parallels in *The Conformist* is in part a legacy that what has been called "the Rossellini moment" lent to Neorealist cinema. As Christopher Wagstaff suggests, "Italian culture has, since the middle ages and under the influence of the Church, used sex as a political and moral code . . . [a] perspective most emphatically launched by Rossellini's film *Roma citta' aperta* [Rome Open City]."[38] It is a film that helped establish the Neorealist tradition within which Bertolucci's film operates. Rossellini's film articulates a sexually infused politics, which thereafter operated as a cinematic convention in the genre. As Wagstaff puts it, "Rossellini has to answer for initiating a whole Italian cinematic tradition."[39]

While as I suggest, Rossellini's film was an influential player in the historical negotiation of the way an event to be understood, it remains important to complement the film analysis with a conceptually developed political framing. Accordingly, I want to note that while focusing on the same period that inspired Rossellini's cinematic work, we can turn to Walter Benjamin's insights because he was as responsible as any thinker for developing aesthetically framed ideational weapons against fascism. His writings on both the arts and history represent one of the most significant legacies that the fascist period lent to political theory. With respect to his focus on the arts, while charging fascism with an aestheticization of politics that gives the masses only means of expression rather than material well-being, a politics that can only "culminate in one thing: war,"[40] Benjamin, although ambivalent (wary as he was of the symptoms of mass reception), regarded cinema as a potential counterforce, noting that "today's films can promote revolutionary criticism of social conditions."[41] They have that potential, he suggested, because they can afford "a deepening of apperception"[42] and are thus potential fields of analysis. "In comparison with the staged scene, the filmed behavior item lends itself more readily to analysis because it can be isolated more easily."[43]

INTRODUCTION

In addition, and crucially, for Benjamin, the "shock effect" of film disrupts the viewer's habitual practices of self-constitution by producing a "distraction" that encourages critical reflection.[44] Just as his views of cinema (and the arts, in general) were shaped by the moment of fascism, so was Benjamin's philosophy of history. Regarding the rise of fascism during his historical present (what he referred to as "now time" [*Jetztzeit*]) as a "state of emergency," Benjamin essentially flipped the temporal structure of Marxist historiography. He insisted that our critical historical sensibility must look to "a vanquished the past"[45] rather than exclusively tarrying with an eschatology of the future. In his most familiar remark about how the past is to be critically recovered, Benjamin writes, "To articulate the past historically does not mean to recognize it 'as it really was.' . . . It means to seize hold of a memory as it flashes up at a moment of danger."[46] Such historically attuned eruptions of memory lend themselves especially to cinematic treatment because, as Benjamin suggests, "most memories that we search for come to us as visual images."[47]

Resistance to fascism still inflects conceptions of history and solicits cinematic responses. Although it has been commonly assumed that fascism was a discrete and since surpassed historical moment, it persists (as Felix Guattari suggests) at the level of "the micropolitics of desire."[48] The continuing presence of fascism in a new form is a phenomenon that Deleuze and Guattari (effectively picking up Benjamin's conceptual intervention) have elaborated. It is a pervasive impulse that Deleuze describes:

> The new fascism is not the politics and economy of war. It is the global agreement on security, on the maintenance of peace—just as terrifying as war. All out petty fears will be organized in concert, all our petty anxieties will be harnessed to make micro-fascists of us; we will be called upon to stifle every little thing, every suspicious face, every dissonant voice, in our streets, in our neighborhoods, in our local theaters.[49]

Among the films that have addressed that micro-level of fascism are *Minority Report* (2002) and *Scanner Darkly* (2006), both based on science-fiction writer Philip Dick's novels, which address the kind of fascist future to which Deleuze's remarks refer.[50] Those films are "methodological fields" one can enter to theorize contemporary fascism.

SOME WORDS ON METHOD

Working with the presumption that cinema is an artistic practice that both shapes and often disturbs the grid of intelligibility within which political theory achieves a focus, I want to note that a primary presupposition that frames

INTRODUCTION 11

everything methodologically involved in the studies in this handbook is a commitment to intelligibility as an ambiguous achievement. Attunement to a society's or subculture's stock of common sense allows one to communicate effectively and share information. However, those who can merely communicate are (in the words of Deleuze and Guattari) "functionaries" able only to manage "ready-made thought."[51] They dwell in the realm of "opinions."[52] Locked within "the forces of recognition," they are unable to exercise an imagination of possibilities of "*terra incognita*."[53] What has enabled some creative writers to avoid the "sluggishness of the brain" and the "facilitating paths . . . of dominant opinions"[54] has been their resistance to "ready-made thought" with challenges to the reigning structures of intelligibility. To accomplish that resistance, one needs to investigate the contingent relationships between writing and reality.

Among the implications for approaching the texts of a political theorist that I derive from that presupposition is a writing strategy that mimics the compositional approach in many critically oriented films. Just as cinema works with juxtapositions among varying angles of vision, attention to the way critical cinema works encourages treating political theory as a writing practice and thereby not merely stating arguments but instead achieving critical thinking with juxtapositions among alternative intelligibilities. With a cinematic practice as a model for writing, we are encouraged to heed the way a political theorist *composes* a text—the narrative sequences and grammatical and rhetorical rhythms that constitute the imaginative invention of objects and relationships. Accordingly, developing an effective way for doing political theory critically implies being attentive to how theorists write, that is, being less concerned with what a theorist writes about than with how the theorist's language, the *form* of the writing, constitutes the "about." The Mexican film director Alfredo Cuarón makes a point about film language that applies to written texts as well:

> When critics equate "form" with appearance or "content" with plot, they're being facile, he said. And when people ask him what's more important: technique or story? "Then you say: They definitely don't understand what cinema is. Because what they're calling technique in film—and I'm not talking about commercial movies—isn't technique. It's language. When Tarkovsky makes decisions about framing and about how to move the camera, they're not technical decisions, or even stylistic ones. They're requirements of the language that he needs for his filmic experience.[55]

Similarly (with regard to political theory writing), working on the texts of Adam Smith (decades ago), I pointed out that "[i]n his treatment of value, as is the case in all his writing, Smith wrote with an eye cast outward on the world. Nevertheless, his domain of value is not so much a discovery as it is a textual production. It emerges in his language, his grammatical, rhetorical and narrative practices."[56] I went on to identify Smith's tendency to write legendary narratives or mythic plots, framed within a sensationalist epistemology in which subjects are constructed as passive observers afflicted by overwhelming impressions. As a result, my writing strategy involved situating the particularities of Smith's sensationalism by staging encounters between his sensationalist epistemology and alternatives that provide a more critically reflective way to construct a narrative of modernity (e.g., I found helpful models in the analyses of narrative by contemporary philosophers and literary theorists—Jean-François Lyotard, among the former, and Frank Kermode, among the latter).

Here I want to add that if one were to try stage "Adam Smith, the Movie," Smith himself would provide little help. Given that Smith's writing, as I noted, manifests a "tendency toward teleological narrative in which the natural order would coordinate individual striving to produce collective outcomes,"[57] he would have left the task of directing to that "natural order." And given Smith's tendency to "produce a temporal view of economic history that privileges the exemplary over the ordinary,"[58] there would be very little opening for a Neorealist approach that assembles "image-facts." In contrast, as Panagia has demonstrated, David Hume's writing is cinematically attuned. Without going into all the nuances of Panagia's convincing argument that Hume's philosophical empiricism, which "understands mental life, moral psychology, and civil society, to be about the assembly formation and the projection of appearances. . . . [It is] literally (*not* metaphorically) cinematographic . . . committed to the impression of moving images,"[59] I want to pick up a part of his demonstration that accords well with the political force of Neorealist cinema. Emphasizing the effects of cinematic discontinuities, Panagia writes,

> I claim that film matters to political theory because it offers political theorists an image of political thinking that emphasizes the stochastic serialization of actions, or what David Hume called 'broken appearances'[;] . . . the discontinuity . . . of moving images that films project make available an experience of resistance and change as a felt interruption of continuity.[60]

Hume's "broken appearances," an aspect of discontinuity that Panagia articulates with a politics of resistance, resonates with the Neorealist-influenced cinematic style of Michelangelo Antonioni. Using and applying color in some of his films to express ambivalence toward optimistic narratives of modernity, Antonioni draws on painting (and literally paints some scenes) to express ambiguity and contradiction. For example, the swatches of color added to the scenes in a film that explores industrial modernity in his *Red Desert* (1964) punctuate the film narrative and serve as interruptions of the continuity of the narrative sequences. As Antonioni has suggested (in a criticism of what he regarded as Hitchcock's unrealistic suspense narratives), "[l]ife is also made up of pauses."[61] Rather than creating Hitchcockian suspense, Antonioni continually suspends the dramatic action while organizing his filming to create an ambiguity as to whose or what point of view shapes the scene. Rather than a dramatic story, Antonioni's drama is a concatenation of visual moments (often seen from the point of view of a protagonist). As Deleuze puts it, "the whole of Antonioni's work, replaces 'traditional drama with a kind of *optical drama* lived by the character.'"[62] For purposes of regarding Antonioni's films as exemplars of critical compositional strategies that encourage thinking rather than consummated understandings, one has to observe how to interrupt, rather than fulfill, narrative expectations. As a result, such strategies are resistant to what Alexander Kluge calls "conceptual imperialism which colonizes its objects."[63]

For Antonioni and other filmmakers who "slow down the eye,"[64] the temporally extended shots that constitute cinematic punctuation are an antinarrative device that foregrounds objects and situations to interrupt sequences and call the viewer's attention to things that "call for thinking."[65] They create moments that shift the film from a "cinema of action" to a "cinema of seeing," where the latter bids the viewer to think about what he or she is seeing rather than being absorbed into an anticipation of what might come next.[66] Long takes that interrupt motion and rivet attention constitute much of the way Neorealist and other genres of critically oriented cinema think (a perspective I take up and elaborate both in the following chapter and in Chapter 7).

As a practitioner of nonnarrative film sequences, Roberto Rossellini helps us appreciate what is involved in the work of resisting simplistic narrative sequence:

> I hate the obligation which the story places upon me. The logical thread of the story is my enemy. Frankly I would like to shoot just episodes. . . . When I feel that the shot which I am setting up is only important for the logical thread of the story and not for what I really want to say. That is where I find myself impotent. . . . I have made films in episodes because I find myself at ease with them; because in that way I have been able to avoid those sequences that, as I said, are useful for a continuous narrative, but that, precisely because of their quality of being useful episodes, and not crucial ones. I find . . . supremely unpalatable.[67]

Those moments of extended focus (on what Rossellini regards as "crucial episodes" as opposed to narrative-facilitating ones) often provide the basis for an intermediation between genres. For example, the novelist and filmmaker

14   INTRODUCTION

Alain Robbe-Grillet, when asked how he translates literary forms into cinematic ones, responded, in part,

> In my work I don't begin with a preconceived story line. Objects give rise to thoughts, which become my novel or my film. A blue shoe, a broken bottle, and the sea inspired me, and became the point of departure and the evolutionary force for my film *Glissements progressifs du plaisir* [*Successive Slidings of Pleasure*].

Then in response to the follow-up question "Objects then, are often your creative point of departure. How else do they function in our work?" he says, "As punctuation. Punctuation devices, which denote transition in novels, such as commas and periods, have its cinematic counterpart."[68] Importantly, that "counterpart's" challenge to authority, which the intermediation enacts, constitutes the way the cinematic mode composes political theory. George Aichele, referring to Pasolini's film *The Gospel According to Saint Matthew* (1964), makes that point concisely: "the carrying across of the biblical text into a filmic medium . . . disrupts the boundaries of canonicity, interrupts the 'biblical' nature of the Gospel, and foregrounds the instability of authoritative claims about scriptural meaning."[69]

How then does one compose political theory by including encounters with the flows and pauses in cinematic texts while intervening with concepts to make sense of their narrative and nonnarrative moments? One of the methodological injunctions to which I adhere is that knowledge emerging in the theorizing encounter with a film results from a method that Cesare Casarino refers to as "philopoesis," the staging of an interference between a philosophical or theoretical set of concepts and an artistic text, which consists of affects and percepts (a method I illustrate in Chapter 1). As Casarino characterizes it, 'philopoesis' [as a method is a] "discontinuous and refractive interference between philosophy and literature."[70] What results is a mode of critical thinking that becomes available because the interference between genres opens up "emergent potentialities that disrupt the status quo of the history of forms."[71]

Casarino's philopoetic method is a version of genre intermediation that is inspired by Deleuze's approach to the encounter between philosophy and cinema, which he characterizes as interference. "Philosophical theory," Deleuze writes, "is itself a practice just as much as its object. It is a practice of concepts, and it must be judged in the light of the other practices with which it interferes."[72] Accordingly, as is the case with Casarino's approach to literary texts, the interference that Deleuze enacts in his cinema analysis is one among a critical genre, philosophy (which mobilizes concepts), and an artistic genre, cinema, (which mobilizes "affects and percepts").[73]

INTRODUCTION   15

Deleuze also provides guidance for another important methodological injunction I want to stress. It is about the grammar with which theoretical questions are raised. Addressing the temporal context of the concepts he brings to cinema readings, he suggests that concepts are historical dramas that yield themselves to a particular grammar. Specifically, in his remarks on "The Method of Dramatization," Deleuze states,

> It is not certain that the question *what is this?* is a good question concerning the essence of the idea. It may be that questions such as *Who? How much? Where? When* are better—as much for discovering the essence as for determining something more important about the idea.[74]

After having suggested that "[t]he idea responds only to the call of certain questions," Deleuze locates concepts in "dynamisms . . . which always presuppose a field in which they are produced."[75] What is thus crucial to the method Deleuze offers is what I want to characterize as attention to the grammar of agency. It is *not* the case that subjects use concepts but, rather, that the historical plane on which concepts emerge is the same plane on which subjects emerge, that is, subjectivity, I want to insist, is *an unstable set of historical events that theory aims at disclosing rather than being a fully formed locus of enunciation from which theory begins.* Accordingly, noting the historical contingency of subject formation, Deleuze suggests that subjects are in a process of becoming; they are "still only rough drafts, not yet, qualified or composed, rather patients than agents."[76] To figure that dynamic—the co-emergence of concepts and subjects—he treats it as a drama that takes place in what he calls "a 'strange theater'; what is staged, he says, is "a drama that corresponds to this or that concept"[77] and adds that "[g]iven any concept, we can always discover its drama."[78]

Deleuze's drama metaphor is inspired by his appreciation of Nietzsche's view of the grammar needed to capture subjectivities, which are contingent identities rather than reflections of essences:

> [W]hen Nietzsche asks *who,* or *from what perspective,* instead of *what,* he is not trying to complete the question *what is this?,* he is criticizing the form of this question and all its possible responses. When I ask *what is this?,* I assume there is an essence behind appearances, or at least something ultimate behind the masks. The other kind of question, however, always discovers other masks behind the mask, displacements behind every place, other 'cases' stacked up in a case.[79]

To pursue the "mask" imagery and illustrate a conceptual drama that actualizes the virtuality of the conceptual dynamism to which Deleuze refers, I recur

16   INTRODUCTION

to an example I have used elsewhere.[80] Edward Mussawir has applied the method of dramatization to jurisprudence, noting that justice "does not just reflect the stable social reality of the time but . . . 'dramatizes' it."[81] Edified by Deleuze's commitment to concepts as historical dramas, Mussawir resists the typical "what is justice" and "who is just" questions and provides a grammatically attuned aesthetic account of justice. For the stable subjects who reside in traditional juridical discourses, he substitutes personae (masks), asserting, "The person is not a 'subject' but a device or contrivance . . . [which makes possible] an aesthetic account of the masks that define civil and judicial existence."[82] To illustrate a particular historical moment in which a subject-as-contrivance is a result rather than an initiating agent, I have referred to the entry of "humanity" into a juridical space involved in the post–World War II war crimes trials. During the negotiations that led to the work of the IMT (International Military Tribunal), after World War II, the primary discursive condition of possibility for the Nuremberg war crimes trials was a new collective subject, "humanity." Because the international community needed to solicit a new collective subject to oppose the Nazi's necropolitical initiative, which was a hierarchical version of human nature (based on Alfred Hoche's notorious gloss on "life unworthy of life"),[83] the court needed what was a counter-anthropology that would enfranchise a collective plaintiff. What eventuated was "the conceptual development of a notion of "crimes against humanity'" so that "humanity as a whole," could be (re)established within legal discourse.[84]

Clearly, although the trial's collective subject/plaintiff, "humanity," was a contrivance (a mask), it was nevertheless one that served a noble ethico-political purpose. It enabled a juridical event that delivered a sense of justice to those who survived the Nazi atrocities and a post hoc justice for those who did not. The methodological question I want to raise, once we accept that subjectivities emerge as historical dramas, relates to how to use cinema to illustrate those dramas and, further, how to employ film analysis not only to deliver a pedagogy about the historical contingencies of subjectivity but also to practice an ethico-political commitment to justice by allowing for the appearance on the historical stage those who have failed to rise above the threshold of visibility. For that purpose, I reprise in Chapter 3 a variety of artistic endeavors (films among others) that recover the experiences associated with both the pretexts and aftermath of the nuclear bombs dropped on Japan in World War II.

Ultimately then, to appreciate the participation of cinema in subject formation, we must recognize that a film stages an encounter between two kinds of subjects, both of which should be understood as durations—the aesthetic subjects in the film whose dramas of self-fashioning develop during the cinematic sequences and the film's viewers, who are also durational subjects. They are located in a present that is continually subject to moments from the past (an aspect of the phenomenology of the film experience treated in Chapter 7)

INTRODUCTION   17

Therefore, to add a third methodological injunction: In order to theorize the embodied durational phenomenology of the film experience, two dimensions suggest themselves. One is experiential and the other conceptual. The Russian filmmaker Andrei Tarkovsky provides a way into the experiential dimension. His "saturated, long-take style [of filming] . . . relies on the audience as working participants in the act of film creation."[85] Criticizing the montage style of his fellow Soviet filmmaker Sergei Eisenstein, which he says, "deprives the person watching the screen of the prerogative of film . . . film's impact," he writes, "My own method [provides the audience with] "the opportunity to live through what is on the screen as if it were his own life, to take over the experience imprinted in time upon the screen . . ."[86] However, to lend the "audience" in Tarkovsky's account of "living through" an experiential duration, we have to take into account viewers' prior film experiences, heeding the way film images evoke film memories. As Kluge suggests, "spectators . . . constantly recreate cinema's experiential horizon . . . aided by the 'multitude of films' already in their 'minds'."[87]

It is again Walter Benjamin who helps us elaborate the conceptual part of the injunction. His analysis takes us beyond the personal experience of images, moving and still, to a conceptually rich politics of memory that elucidates the nature of the *collective* (and thus politically pregnant) moment in which images function. Noting "[w]hat distinguishes images from essences . . . is their historical index [which] . . . not only says that they belong to a particular time; it says above all, that they attain to legibility only at a particular time." Elaborating the implication, he adds, "Every present day is determined by the images that are synchronic with it: each 'now' is the now of a particular recognizability."[88] In short, Benjamin's concept of an image's "historical index" bids us to theorize the political resonances of cinema by locating its images within the forces at work in the "now." He takes us from the experiential to the conceptual by locating image culture within a critical politics of history. In Chapter 2, I undertake a comparative film reading oriented (after Benjamin) toward disclosing a politics of "now-time."

The primary aesthetic presupposition I want to foreground is that the cinematic media genre recommends itself as a vehicle for doing critically oriented political theory not only because, as Walter Benjamin noted, it has "a moral shock effect," evoking sensibilities that have slumbered, either because many of the social and political world's most violent effects are veiled or because of the dulling effects of other genres[89] but also because of the way cinema (as Siegfried Kracauer suggests) "inscribes the image with moments of temporality and contingency that *dis*figure the representation" and subjects the viewer to "encounters with contingency, lack of control and otherness."[90] Similarly, as Jacques Rancière points out, cinema is the genre best suited to rendering judgments on the facticity of events unstable because much of its critical capacity

18   INTRODUCTION

arises from "la contradiction que le visible y apporte a la signification narrative [the contradiction that the visible brings to narrative signification]."[91] Those aspects of cinema's critical capacity for animating political theory shape all of the book's chapters. However, this is not strictly speaking a "film book." Each chapter features intermediations between cinematic texts and other textual genres—philosophy, political theory, literature, and other artistic media genres. The ultimate pedagogical aim is to alter the "aesthetic landscape"[92] in order to broaden and render more critical the frames within which political theory can be composed.

NOTES

1. See Bonnie Honig and Lorie Marso eds., *Politics, Theory, and Film: Critical Encounters with Lars Von Trier* (Oxford: Oxford University Press, 2016).
2. *Ibid.*, xvii.
3. Gilles Deleuze and Felix Guattari, *What is Philosophy?*, trans. Hugh Tomlinson and Graham Burchell (New York: Columbia University Press, 1994), 196.
4. Jacques Rancière applies the expression, "clash of heterogeneous elements" to Jean Luc Godard's film *Histoire du Cinema*, crediting that effect with the film's critical political pedagogy: see Jacques Rancière, *The Future of the Image*, trans. G. Elliot (New York: Verso, 2007), 55.
5. Roland Barthes, "From Work to Text," in *Image, Music, Text*, trans. Stephen Heath (New York: Hill and Wang, 1978), 157.
6. Michel Foucault, *Discipline and Punish: The Birth of the Prison*, trans. Alan Sheridan (New York: Pantheon, 1977), 11.
7. *Ibid.*, 6.
8. See Michel Foucault, "About the Concept of the 'Dangerous Individual' in 19th-Century Legal Psychiatry," *Journal of Law and Psychiatry* 1: 1 (1978), 1–18.
9. Michel Foucault, *The History of Sexuality*, Vol. 1, trans. Robert Hurley (New York: Pantheon, 1978), 138. For a review of the Foucault's relevant conceptual contributions, see Michael J. Shapiro, "Foucault and Method," in *Foucault and the Modern International*, eds. Philippe Bonditti et al. (London: Palgrave, 2017).
10. The phenomenology of the cinema experience is the subject of Chapter 7.
11. The quotations are from Deleuze's web lectures: http://deleuzelectures.blogspot. com/2007/02/on-kant.html.
12. J. G. A. Pocock, *The Machiavellian Moment: Florentine Political Thought and the Atlantic Republican Tradition* (Princeton, NJ: Princeton University Press, 1975), vii.
13. *Ibid.*, 53.
14. *Ibid.*, 486.
15. For analyses of soundtracks, see Larry Sider, Diane Freeman, and Jerry Sider eds. *Soundscape* (New York: Wallflower, 2003).
16. David Thomson, *The Moment of Psycho: How Alfred Hitchcock Taught America to Love Murder* (New York: Basic Books, 2010), 63.
17. *Ibid.*, 67.
18. *Ibid.*, 120.

INTRODUCTION   19

19. *Ibid.*, 130.
20. Michael J. Shapiro, *The Political Sublime* (Durham: Duke University Press, 2018), 171.
21. The quotation is from Jacques Rancière, *Figures of History*, trans. Julie Rose (Cambridge: Polity, 2014), 30.
22. I review those approaches in the introduction to Michael J. Shapiro and Hayward Alker eds. *Challenging Boundaries* (Minneapolis: University of Minnesota Press, 1996), xix.
23. See Theodor W. Adorno, et al. *The Authoritarian Personality*, Parts One and Two (New York: John Wiley & Sons, 1964).
24. See Michael J. Shapiro, *Studies in Trans-Disciplinary Method: After the Aesthetic Turn* (London: Routledge, 2012), 5.
25. I am quoting from the Preface to the last novel in the series: Carlo Lucarelli, *Via Delle Oche*, trans. Michael Reynolds (New York: Europa Editions, 2008), 12.
26. Andre Bazin, "An Aesthetic of Reality: Cinematic Realism and the Italian School of Liberation," in *What is Cinema, Volume Two*, trans. High Gray (Berkeley: University of California Press, 1971).
27. Sam Ishii-Gonzales, "The 'Image-Fact' in Bazin and Bresson," On the web at: https://lesiecledelumiere.wordpress.com/2012/05/25/the-image-fact-in-bazin-and-bresson/.
28. The quotations are from Christopher Wagstaff, *Il Conformista* (London: BFI, 2007), 14.
29. The phrase belongs to Sergio Rigoletto, "Contesting National Memory: Masculine Dilemmas and Oedipal Scenarios in Bernardo Bertoclucci's *Strategia del ragno* and *Il conformist*," *Italian Studies* 67: 1 (2012), On the web at: https://rl.uoregon.edu/2013/03/24/rigoletto-2/.
30. Leo Bersani and Ulysses Dutoit, *Forms of Being* (London: BFI, 204), 21–22.
31. Bertolucci's remarks are noted in Wagstaff, *Il Conformista*, 80.
32. *Ibid.*
33. The quotations are from Rigoletto, "Contesting National Memory."
34. *Ibid.*
35. *Ibid.*
36. See D. Medina Lassansky, *The Renaissance Perfected: Architecture, Spectacle, & Tourism in Fascist Italy* (University Park: Pennsylvania University Press, 2004), 99.
37. *Ibid.*, 214–215.
38. Wagstaff, *Il Conformista*, 81.
39. *Ibid.*
40. Walter Benjamin, "The Work of Art in the Age of Mechanical Reproduction," in *Illuminations*, ed. Hannah Arendt, trans. Harry Zohn (New York: Schocken, 1969), 241.
41. *Ibid.*, 231.
42. *Ibid.*, 235.
43. *Ibid.*, 136.
44. The quotations are drawn from Rodolphe Gasché, "Objective Diversions: On Some Kantian Themes in Benjamin's 'The Work of Art in the Age of Mechanical Reproduction'," in *Walter Benjamin's Philosophy: Destruction and Experience*, eds. Andrew Benjamin and Peter Osborne (London: Routledge, 1994), 197.

45. I am borrowing the quoted expression from Ronald Beiner, "Walter Benjamin's Philosophy of History," *Political Theory*, 12: 3 (August, 1984), 426.
46. Walter Benjamin, "Theses on the Philosophy of History," in Arendt, ed. *Illuminations*, 255.
47. Walter Benjamin, "The Image of Proust," in Arendt ed. *Illuminations*, 214.
48. See Felix Guattari, "Everybody Wants to Be a Fascist," in *Chaosophy: Texts and Interviews 1972–1977* (New York: Semiotext(e)), 154–175.
49. Gilles Deleuze, *Two Regimes of Madness* (New York: Semiotext(e), 2006), 138.
50. For an analysis of those films see my chapter, "For an Anti-Fascist Aesthetics," in *Studies in Trans-Disciplinary Method: After the Aesthetic Turn*, ed. Michael J. Shapiro (London: Routledge, 2012).
51. Deleuze and Guattari, *What is Philosophy?*, 51.
52. *Ibid.*, 145.
53. The latter quotations are from Gilles Deleuze, *Difference and Repetition*, trans. Paul Patton (New York: Columbia University Press, 1994), 136.
54. Deleuze and Guattari, *What is Philosophy?*, 49,
55. See the Marcela Valdes interview with Cuarón In *The New York Times Magazine*, December 16, 2018, On the web at: www.nytimes.com/2018/12/13/magazine/alfonso-cuaron-roma-mexico-netflix.html?rref=collection%2Fsectioncollection%2Fmagazine&action=click&contentCollection=magazine&region=rank&module=package&version=highlights&contentPlacement=3&pgtype=sectionfront.
56. Michael J. Shapiro, *Reading "Adam Smith": Desire, History, and Value*, 2nd ed. (Lanham, MD: Rowman & Littlefield, 2002), 46.
57. *Ibid.*, xix.
58. *Ibid.*
59. Davide Panagia, *Impressions of Hume: Cinematic Thinking and the Politics of Discontinuity* (Lanham, MD: Rowman & Littlefield, 2013), 48.
60. *Ibid.*, 23.
61. Antonioni quoted in Joe McElhaney, *The Death of Classical Cinema: Hitchcock, Lang, Minelli* (Albany, NY: SUNY Press, 2006), 239.
62. The outer quotation is from Deleuze, *Cinema 2: The Time Image*, trans. Hugh Tomlinson and Robert Galeta (Minneapolis: University of Minnesota Press, 1989), 9. (He draws the inner quotation from Claude Ollier.) On Antonioni's cinematic style, see also Pier Paolo Pasolini, "The Cinema of Poetry," in *Heretical Empiricism*, trans. Ben Lawson and Louise K. Barnett (Bloomington: Indiana University Press, 1988).
63. Alexander Kluge, "On Film and the Public Sphere," trans. Thomas Y. and Miriam Hansen *New German Critique*, No. 24/25 (Autumn 1981–Winter 1982), 211.
64. I am borrowing that expression from Jean-François Lyotard, *Discourse, Figure*, trans. Anthony Hudek and Marry Lyndon (Minneapolis: University of Minnesota Press, 2011), 212.
65. The phrase is in quotation marks because I am adopting Martin Heidegger's expression *Was Heist Denken*, which translates as either "what is called thinking or "what calls for thinking": see Martin Heidegger, *What Is Called Thinking*, trans. J. Glenn Gray (New York: Harper, 1968).
66. The distinction is Gilles Deleuze's in *Cinema 2: The Time Image*, trans. Hugh Tomlinson and Robert Galeta (Minneapolis: University of Minnesota Press, 1989), 272.

INTRODUCTION 21

67. Rossellini quoted in Christopher Wagstaff, *Italian Neorealism: An Aesthetic Approach* (Toronto: University of Toronto Press, 2007), 85–86. Some of the best Rossellini analysis is in David Forgacs, Susan Lutton, et al., *Roberto Rossellini: Magician of the Real* (London: BFI, 2001).

68. Godelieve Mercken-Spaas, "An Interview with Alain Robbe-Grillet and Lillian Dumont," *The French Review* 50: 4 (March, 1977), 653.

69. George Aichele, "Translation as De-canonization: Matthew's Gospel According to Pasolini," *Crosscurrents* 51 (2002), paraphrased in Elizabeth A. Castelli, "Introduction: Translating Pasolini Translating Paul," in *St Paul: A Screenplay*, ed. Pier Paolo Pasolini (London: Verso, 2013), ebook, loc, 133.

70. Cesare Casarino, "Philopoesis: A Theoretico-Methodological Manifesto," *boundary 2* (2002), 86.

71. The quotation is from Gilles Deleuze, *Foucault*, trans. Sean Hand (Minneapolis: University of Minnesota Press, 1988), 86.

72. Deleuze, *Cinema 2*, 280.

73. See Deleuze and Guattari, *What Is Philosophy*, 163–199.

74. Gilles Deleuze, "The Method of Dramatization," in *Desert Islands and Other Texts 1953–1974*, trans. Michael Taomina (New York: Semiotext(e), 2004), 94.

75. *Ibid.*, 96–97.

76. *Ibid.*, 97.

77. *Ibid.*, 98.

78. *Ibid.*

79. *Ibid.*, 113–114.

80. Michael J. Shapiro, *War Crimes, Atrocity, and Justice* (Cambridge: Polity, 2015), 162.

81. Edward Mussawir, *Jurisdiction in Deleuze: The Expression and Representation of the Law* (New York: Routledge, 2011), 22.

82. *Ibid.*, 22–23.

83. See Alfred Hoche's, *Arztliche Bemerkungen* in Karl Binding and Alfred Hoche, *De Freigabe der Vernichtung Lebensunwerten Lebens: Ihr Mass und ihre Form* (Leipzig, 1920), 61–62.

84. The quotations are from Roberto Esposito, *Third Person*, trans. Zakiya Hanafi (Cambridge: Polity, 2012), 64. I say "re-established" because the notion of crimes against humanity actually predated the pretrial Nuremberg negotiations. It was originally evoked in 1906 by E. D. Morel in reference to the atrocities in the "The Congo Free State." In his *History of the Congo Reform Movement*, he refers to King Leopold II of Belgium's conduct in the Congo as "a great crime against humanity" (the quotation is from William Roger Louis and Jean Stengers, eds. *E. D. Morel's History of the Congo Reform Movement* [Oxford: The Clarendon Press, 1968], 167).

85. I am quoting from Elizabeth Zelensky, "Tarkovsky, Science and Faith," *Religions: A Scholarly Journal* (2014), 17, On the web at: www.qscience.com/doi/abs/10.5339/rels.2014.science.17.

86. Andrei Tarkovsky, *Sculpting in Time*, trans. Kitty Hunter-Blair (London: Faber and Faber, 1989), 183.

87. Kluge, "Film and the Public Sphere," 207.

88. Walter Benjamin, *The Arcades Project*, trans. Howard Eiland and Kevin McLaughlin (Cambridge, MA: Harvard University Press, 1999), 462–463.

22 INTRODUCTION

89. Benjamin's remark about the moral shock effect of film is in his "The Work of Art in the Age of Mechanical Reproduction," in *Illuminations*, ed. Hannah Arendt, trans. Harry Zohn (New York: Schocken, 1968), 238.
90. These concise representations of Siegfried Kracauer's ideas on film belongs to Hansen, "Introduction" to Siegfried Kracauer's *Theory of Film* (Princeton: Princeton University Press, 1997), xv and xiii respectively.
91. Jacques Rancière, *La Fable Cinematographique* (Paris: Editions Du Seuil, 2001), 22.
92. The phrase belongs to Hans Breder, who established an interdisciplinary "intermedia" program at the University of Iowa: See his "Intermedia: Enacting the Liminal," *Performing Arts Journal* 17: 2/3 (May–September, 1995), 114.

REFERENCES

Adorno, Theodor W., et al. (1964) *The Authoritarian Personality*, Parts One and Two, New York: John Wiley & Sons.

Barthes, Roland (1978) 'From Work to Text,' in *Image, Music, Text*, trans. Stephen Heath, New York: Hill and Wang.

Bazin, Andre (1971) 'An Aesthetic of Reality: Cinematic Realism and the Italian School of Liberation,' in *What is Cinema*, Vol. 2, trans. High Gray, Berkeley: University of California Press.

Beiner, Ronald (1984) 'Walter Benjamin's Philosophy of History,' *Political Theory*, Vol. 12 (3), pp. 423–434.

Benjamin, Walter (1968) 'The Image of Proust,' in *Illuminations*, ed. Hannah Arendt, New York: Schocken, pp. 201–215.

Benjamin, Walter (1968) 'Theses on the Philosophy of History,' in *Illuminations*, ed. Hannah Arendt, trans. Harry Zohn, New York: Schocken, pp. 253–264.

Benjamin, Walter (1968) 'The Work of Art in the Age of Mechanical Reproduction,' in *Illuminations*, ed. Hannah Arendt, trans. Harry Zohn, New York: Schocken.

Benjamin, Walter (1999) *The Arcades Project*, trans. Howard Eiland and Kevin McLaughlin, Cambridge, MA: Harvard University Press.

Bersani, Leo and Dutoit, Ulysses (2004) *Forms of Being*, London: BFI.

Boelhower, William (1998) 'Inventing America: A Model of Cartographic Semiosis,' *Word and Image*, Vol. 4 (2), pp. 475–496.

Breder, Hans (1995) 'Intermedia: Enacting the Liminal,' *Performing Arts Journal*, Vol. 17 (2/3), pp. 112–120.

Casarino, Cesare (2002) 'Philopoesis: A Theoretico-Methodological Manifesto,' *boundary 2*, Vol. 29 (1), pp. 65–96.

Castelli, Elizabeth A. (2013) 'Introduction: Translating Pasolini Translating Paul,' in *St Paul: A Screenplay*, ed. Pier Paolo Pasolini, London: Verso.

Deleuze, Gilles (1988) *Foucault*, trans. Sean Hand, Minneapolis: University of Minnesota Press.

Deleuze, Gilles (1989) *Cinema 2: The Time Image*, trans. Hugh Tomlinson and Robert Galeta, Minneapolis: University of Minnesota Press.

Deleuze, Gilles (1994) *Difference and Repetition*, trans. Paul Patton, New York: Columbia University Press.

Deleuze, Gilles (2004) 'The Method of Dramatization,' in *Desert Islands and Other Texts 1953–1974*, trans. Michael Taomina, New York: Semiotext(e), pp. 94–116.

Deleuze, Gilles (2006) *Two Regimes of Madness*, New York: Semiotext(e).

INTRODUCTION   23

Deleuze, Gilles (2007) 'Lectures on Kant,' at: http://deleuzelectures.blogspot. com/2007/02/on-kant.html.

Deleuze, Gilles and Guattari, Felix (1994) *What is Philosophy?* trans. Hugh Tomlinson and Graham Burchell, New York: Columbia University Press.

Esposito, Roberto (2012) *Third Person*, trans. Zakiya Hanafi, Cambridge: Polity.

Forgacs, David, Lutton, Susan, et al. (2001) *Roberto Rossellini: Magician of the Real*, London: BFI.

Foucault, Michel (1977) *Discipline and Punish: The Birth of the Prison*, trans. Alan Sheridan, New York: Pantheon.

Foucault, Michel (1978) 'About the Concept of the "Dangerous Individual" in 19th-Century Legal Psychiatry,' *Journal of Law and Psychiatry*, Vol. 1 (1), pp. 1–18.

Foucault, Michel (1978) *The History of Sexuality*, Vol. 1, trans. Robert Hurley, New York: Pantheon.

Gasché, Rodolphe (1994) 'Objective Diversions: On Some Kantian Themes in Benjamin's "The Work of Art in the Age of Mechanical Reproduction",' in *Walter Benjamin's Philosophy: Destruction and Experience*, eds. Andrew Benjamin and Peter Osborne, London: Routledge.

Guattari, Felix (1995) 'Everybody Wants to Be a Fascist,' in *Chaosophy: Texts and Interviews 1972–1977*, New York: Semiotext(e), pp. 154–175.

Heidegger, Martin (1968) *What is Called Thinking*, trans. J. Glenn Gray, New York: Harper.

Honig, Bonnie and Marso, Lorie, eds. (2016) *Politics, Theory, and Film: Critical Encounters with Lars Von Trier*, Oxford: Oxford University Press.

Ishii-Gonzales, Sam (2012) 'The "Image-Fact" in Bazin and Bresson,' at: https:// lesiecledelumiere.wordpress.com/2012/05/25/the-image-fact-in-bazin-and-bresson/.

Jameson, Fredric (2013) *The Antinomies of Realism*, New York: Verso.

Kluge, Alexander (1982) 'On Film and the Public Sphere,' trans. Thomas Y. and Miriam Hansen, *New German Critique*, No. 24/25, pp. 53–74.

Kracauer, Siegfried (1997) *Theory of Film*, Princeton: Princeton University Press.

Lassansky, Medina D. (2004) *The Renaissance Perfected: Architecture, Spectacle, & Tourism in Fascist Italy*, University Park: Pennsylvania University Press.

Louis, William Roger and Stengers, Jean, eds. (1968) *E. D. Morel's History of the Congo Reform Movement*, Oxford: The Clarendon Press.

Lucarelli, Carlo (2008) *Via Delle Oche*, trans. Michael Reynolds, New York: Europa Editions.

Lyotard, Jean-François (2011) *Discourse, Figure*, trans. Anthony Hudek and Marry Lyndon, Minneapolis: University of Minnesota Press.

McElhaney, Joe (2006) *The Death of Classical Cinema: Hitchcock, Lang, Minelli*, Albany: SUNY Press.

Mercken-Spaas, Godelieve (1977) 'An Interview With Alain Robbe-Grillet and Lillian Dumont,' *The French Review*, Vol. 50 (4), pp. 653–655.

Mussawir, Edward (2011) *Jurisdiction in Deleuze: The Expression and Representation of the Law*, New York: Routledge.

Panagia, Davide (2013) *Impressions of Hume: Cinematic Thinking and the Politics of Discontinuity*, Lanham: Rowman & Littlefield.

Pasolini, Pier Paolo (1988) 'The Cinema of Poetry,' in *Heretical Empiricism*, trans. Ben Lawson and Louise K. Barnett, Bloomington: Indiana University Press.

Pocock, J. G. A. (1975) *The Machiavellian Moment: Florentine Political Thought and the Atlantic Republican Tradition*, Princeton: Princeton University Press.

Ranciere, Jacques (2001) *La Fable Cinematographique*, Paris: Editions Du Seuil.

Rancière, Jacques (2007) *The Future of the Image*, trans. G. Elliot, New York: Verso.

Rancière, Jacques (2014) *Figures of History*, trans. Julie Rose, Cambridge: Polity.

Rigoletto, Sergio (2012) 'Contesting National Memory: Masculine Dilemmas and Oedipal Scenarios in Bernardo Bertolucci's *Strategia del ragno* and *Il conformist*,' *Italian Studies*, Vol. 67 (1), at: https://rl.uoregon.edu/2013/03/24/rigoletto-2/.

Shapiro, Michael J. (2002) *Reading "Adam Smith": Desire, History, and Value*, 2nd ed., Lanham: Rowman & Littlefield.

Shapiro, Michael J. (2012) *Studies in Trans-Disciplinary Method: After the Aesthetic Turn*, London: Routledge.

Shapiro, Michael J. (2015) *War Crimes, Atrocity, and Justice*, Cambridge: Polity.

Shapiro, Michael J. (2017) 'Foucault and Method,' in *Foucault and the Modern International*, eds. Philippe Bonditti et al., London: Palgrave.

Shapiro, Michael J. (2018) *The Political Sublime*, Durham: Duke University Press.

Shapiro, Michael J. and Alker, Hayward, eds. (1996) *Challenging Boundaries*, Minneapolis: University of Minnesota Press.

Sider, Larry and Freeman, Diane, eds. (2003) *Soundscape*, New York: Wallflower.

Tarkovsky, Andrei (1998) *Sculpting in Time*, trans. Kitty Hunter-Blair, London: Faber and Faber.

Thomson, David (2010) *The Moment of Psycho: How Alfred Hitchcock Taught America to Love Murder*, New York: Basic Books.

Wagstaff, Christopher (2007) *Il Conformista*, London: BFI.

Wagstaff, Christopher (2007) *Italian Neorealism: An Aesthetic Approach*, Toronto: University of Toronto Press, pp. 85–86.

Zelensky, Elizabeth (2014) 'Tarkovsky, Science and Faith,' *Religions: A Scholarly Journal*, Vol. 17, at: www.qscience.com/doi/abs/10.5339/rels.2014.science.17.

SUGGESTED READING

For additional insights from Rancière on film, see his *Film Fables*, trans. Emiliano Battista (New York: Berg, 2006) and Paul Bowen ed., *Ranciere and Film* (Edinburgh: Edinburgh University Press, 2013).

For a review of the Foucault's relevant conceptual contributions, see Michael J. Shapiro, 'Foucault and Method,' in *Foucault and the Modern International*, eds. Philippe Bonditti et al. (London: Palgrave, 2017).

For further treatments of Hitchcock see Slavoj Žižek ed., *Everything You Always Wanted to Know About Lacan: (But Were Afraid to Ask Hitchcock)* (New York: Verso, 2010).

For critical analyses of contemporary fascism, see Brad Evans and Julian Reid eds., *Deleuze & Fascism: Security, War, Aesthetics* (London: Routledge, 2013).

For reviews of the Italian cinematic tradition, see Giorgio Bertellini and Gian Piero Brunetta eds., *The Cinema of Italy* (New York: Wallflower, 2004).

For analyses of Deleuze on cinema, see David N. Rodowick, *Gilles Deleuze's Time Machine* (Durham: Duke University Press), and *The Virtual Life of Film*

(Cambridge, MA: Harvard University Press, 2007) and David Deamer, *Deleuze's Cinema Books: Three Introductions to the Taxonomy of Images* (Edinburgh: Edinburgh University Press, 2016).

For more on Benjamin's approach to the shock effect see Susan Buck-Morss, "Aesthetics and Anaesthetics: Walter Benjamin's Artwork Essay Reconsidered," *October*, 62 (Fall, 1992), 3–41.

CHAPTER **1**

Extracting Political Theory From Lars von Trier

Conceptual Interferences With His The Element of Crime

THE WRITING OCCASION

It is often the case that to compose a political theory essay while engaging a cinematic text, one selects a political theory problem first and then decides to explore a particular film or set of films for purposes of amplification and illustration. For example, to theorize interethnic antagonisms during the Euro-America's westward expansion, an appropriate cinematic engagement would be with John Ford's classic westerns, from *Stagecoach* (1939), a pro–white settler film, to *Cheyenne Autumn* (1964), one quite critical of the Euro-American "ethnogenesis"[1] However, in this case the film selection came first. I was invited to choose one of von Trier's films to make a contribution to political theory while analyzing it. Although it is usually the case that the cinematic text I select is one I have already seen, in this case I selected von Trier's *The Element of Crime* sight unseen. Even though I had watched a number of von Trier's films, I decided to let this one affect me before I determined how to frame my engagement with it. Having written about detective stories in novels and films, I was led by the synopses of von Trier's *Element* to expect that the previous work I had done on detective fiction would provide some entry points for the analysis. As many have discovered, detective fiction is a promising genre to which one can turn for purposes of theorizing because detectives are among other things epistemologically oriented aesthetic subjects. As they seek to discover the agents or pattern of agency responsible for a crime, they also uncover aspects of the sociopolitical order.

Why von Trier? My hosts for the project, Bonnie Honig and Lori J. Marso, provide an intriguing rationale. Looking at von Trier's cinematic corpus as a whole, they

> see von Trier's films as intensifying clichés of gender, power, and politics that ironize them and may usefully press democratic and feminist theory in new directions, perhaps even releasing them from the ennui that is often associated with the practice of theory today.[2]

THE CINEMATIC CLICHÉ IN *THE ELEMENT OF CRIME*

That conceptual hint provides the opening for my reading of von Trier's *The Element of Crime*.

Although here I approach von Trier's *The Element of Crime* by drawing on the chapter I contributed to the Honig–Marso volume, I want to begin by heeding the conceptual gesture I quoted above, the Honig–Marso phrase that refers to the way von Trier's films intensify the "clichés of gender, power, and politics that ironize them and may usefully press democratic and feminist theory in new directions, perhaps even releasing them from the ennui that is often associated with the practice of theory today." Recalling my remarks in the Introduction about the critical value of resisting institutionalized modes of intelligibility, the Honig–Marso reference to the cliché encourages me to recall Gilles Deleuze's gloss on the cliché in his reading of the canvasses of Francis Bacon and to pursue a critical intermediation between painting and cinema. Deleuze locates Bacon's strategy in a phenomenological frame, suggesting that to understand what Bacon does in executing a painting is to presume that he does not work on a blank white surface. Rather, "everything he has in his head or around him is already on the canvass, more or less virtually before he begins his work."[3] "In order to resist the 'psychic clichés' and 'figurative givens' that have governed artistic practices, Bacon had to 'transform' or 'deform' what was always-already on the canvas."[4] Bacon's own account of how that is accomplished invokes the concept of distortion: "what I want to do is to distort the thing beyond the appearance, but in the distortion to bring it back to a recording of appearance."[5] With the word *recording*, Bacon provides a conceptual bridge from painting to cinema. What his canvasses show, he suggests, is the *process* by which something appears. Deleuze is helpful with respect to that aspect of Bacon's painting as well. As I noted in the Introduction, in his lecture on Kant Deleuze suggests that what the Kantian revolution in philosophy turns on is a dramatic change in approaching the phenomenon of appearance. To repeat that quotation, "with Kant a radically new understanding of the notion of phenomenon emerges. Namely that the phenomenon will no longer at all be appearance." Rather, what Kant lends to epistemology is a concern with "the conditions of what appears."[6] Accordingly, as is the case with interpreting Bacon's canvasses, the analysis of cinematic texts requires a consideration of *the epistemology of the image as it emerges*, that is, inquiry into the conditions of possibility for its appearance. And given Deleuze's account of Bacon's struggles with the "psychic clichés and "figurative givens," which are already symbolically there on his canvasses, we must also concern ourselves with the epistemic significance of cinematic clichés.

FIGURE 1.1
Psychiatrist with a monkey on his back. Source: Lars von Trier, *The Element of Crime*, Det Danske Filminstitut (1984).

In contrast to the Deleuzian account of the clichés that Bacon strove to resist on his canvases is the Honig–Marso account of von Trier's intensification of them. Although the two strategies appear to be radically opposed, the effects are similar. Von Trier's intensifications, like Bacon's deformations, serve to call attention to one's tendency to be absorbed unreflectively into common sense, into the prevailing systems of intelligibility through which one (uncritically) shares the world with others. Thus, in the opening scene of *Element*, where the protagonist, Fisher (Michael Elphick), is under hypnosis and being sent in a dream state back to Europe to solve a crime (while actually sitting in Egypt in the office of the psychiatrist who has hypnotized him), the psychiatrist has a monkey on his back (Figure 1.1).

The literal presence of the cliché, having a "monkey on your back" has the effect of distancing us from psychiatric practice. Instead of unreflectively accepting its protocols, we are encouraged to recognize its weight of ideational baggage. The monkey on the psychiatry's back is what weighs him down; it stands (or, better, sits in) for an accumulation of professionally protected protocols.

THE FILM NARRATIVE

Before mobilizing concepts to engage the rest of the film, I need to provide readers with a brief synopsis, one that serves as a threshold to the conceptual work on the film. At a minimum, that implies identifying protagonists.

The film opens with the previously noted Fisher living in Cairo as an expatriate. He is undergoing hypnosis in order to recall his last case. The hypnosis serves as a frame with which to present Europe as a dreamscape, a Europe that ultimately serves as the film's main protagonist. My primary theoretical move is therefore to suggest that Europe-as-dreamscape displaces the film narrative's murder story by calling the viewer's attention to the land- and cityscapes through which Fisher moves. At the beginning of the film, we learn that the case Fisher is undergoing hypnosis to recall is his last one, the pursuit of a killer known as the "Lotto Murderer," who had been strangling and mutilating young girls selling lottery tickets. The Europe he encounters as he picks up the pursuit again has become dystopic. It is dark, decaying, and subject to violent policing practices. As Fisher undertakes the investigation, he employs the controversial method of his former mentor, Osborne (Esmond Knight), which is described in Osborne's book *The Element of Crime*. Joined eventually in his search by a prostitute named Kim, who had allegedly been involved with the murderer (and has borne his child), Fisher takes on additional aspects of his quarry as well because Osborne's method requires the detective to identify with the mind of the killer. As Fisher's mind merges with that of the killer, his behavior becomes increasingly like that of his quarry.

CINEMATIC CARTOGRAPHIES

Having identified Europe as a main protagonist, a crucial step requires coordinating cinematic and historical space. Once Fisher takes leave of the psychiatrist (but actually remains in his dream state) and the scene shifts from Egypt to Europe, the film's spatial context is foregrounded. Drawing conceptually on Tom Conley's analysis of cinematic cartography (in which he states that a film's first shots initiate "the spaces of the cinematic story"),[7] I wrote in my original analysis of the film, "Two cartographic migrations shape the narrative of von Trier's *The Element of Crime*." The first migration is oneiric; it is Fisher's dream state migration from Egypt to Europe when he begins narrating his story: "I'm a policeman. I've finally been called back to Europe to solve a murder case." We can thus see von Trier's human protagonist as an exile and border crosser whose movements inscribe the film's double terrain, a cartographic journey of detection and an extended dystopic representation of Europe, which Fisher's self-description reinforces at the point where he characterizes himself as "the last European."

As the film narrative progresses and we learn that Fisher has translated his former mentor's book into Arabic, he emerges as an aesthetic figure who bridges two domains (to translate is to "bridge" in most Northern European languages). Consequently, we have to recognize that the film's initiating geography is not merely functional; that is, it is not there simply to provide the viewers with a route map of a protagonist's journey. On one hand (in terms of the film narrative), Fisher's journey follows his investigation, as he "moves" (in his dream state) from Egypt to Europe. On the other (in terms of the film's symbolism), the two places, Egypt and Europe (specifically Germany), are historical imaginaries, where Egypt seems to stand for an anachronistic historical space. It represents the beginning of the kind of complex social and political system that receives its consummation in the contemporary European nation-state. Michel Foucault provides a conceptual intervention to characterize that historical fantasy. Quoting Nietzsche, he refers to "Egyptianism, the obstinate 'placing of conclusions at the beginning,' of 'making last things first.'"[8] The Europe with which the psychiatrist tells Fisher he is obsessed is thus a long-standing obsession, articulated as a mythic narrative in which Europe is the epitome of a progressive modernity. Jacques Derrida also provides us with a critique of that story. He treats that view of Europe as the self-centered fantasy that it is "the universal essence of humanity." He suggests that there are other possible "headings."[9]

As for the second cartography, which articulates the film narrative, it emerges as a geographic odyssey that follows a "tailing report" created by Fisher's mentor, Osborne who had preceded him as the investigator on the case. The report refers to an H-shape that is supposed to show the trajectory of Harry Grey's (the alleged "Lotto Murderer") murders. Guided by the report, Fisher draws an H on a wall to serve as a map of the crimes, so that he can anticipate the location of the killer's cartographic progress and prevent his next murder. However, the H-map is effectively trumped by a different map, a cognitive map in which, following Osborne's famous but since discredited method (elaborated below), Fisher uses what is *elemental* in his subjectivity, that part of his mentality that he shares with the killer.

We can therefore locate the cognitive Fisher in a Kantian frame as (among other things) a transcendental rather than psychological subject because his unconscious is Kantian rather than Freudian. That insight turns the intellectual framing of von Trier's crime story in a philosophical rather than psychological direction. While von Trier is often seen as one who is playing randomly with images and narratives (at one point he says, "I am a simple masturbator of the cinema. . . . The only thing I have in mind when I make a film is my own enjoyment"),[10] close attention to the ways in which "element" functions in the film reveals that he is not just "jerking off" (or jerking us around, the surmise of some reviewers); he's made a film worthy of philosophical analysis. The film's enigmas, I suggest, respond to a philosophical approach, which forms the main part of the analysis I initially undertook.

THE PHILOSOPHICAL APPROACH: PHILOPOESIS

Here is the primary conceptual intervention (which I preview in the Introduction): In the conclusion of his *Cinema 2*, Gilles Deleuze summons the concept of "interference" to characterize his philosophical engagement with cinema. "Philosophical theory," he writes, "is itself a practice just as much as its object. It is a practice of concepts, and it must be judged in the light of the other practices with which it interferes."[11] The interference that Deleuze enacts in his cinema books is one between a critical genre, philosophy (which mobilizes concepts), and an artistic genre, cinema, (which mobilizes "affects and percepts").[12] As I also noted in the Introduction, inspired by Deleuze's concept of interference, Cesare Casarino, analyzing novels, develops the concept of "philopoesis," which "names a certain discontinuous and refractive interference between philosophy and literature."[13] What results, according to Casarino, is a mode of critical thinking that becomes available because the interference between genres opens up "emergent potentialities that disrupt the status quo of the history of forms."[14] As Deleuze has elaborately demonstrated, that philopoetic method applies to cinema as well. Accordingly, I suggest that it is an especially propitious method with which to approach von Trier's films because they feature provocative engagements among a variety of artistic genres: film, poetry, literature, television, and the history of cinema. More specifically in the case of *Element*, the interference, conveyed primarily by images (but also by dialogue, monologue, and narrative), involves the concept of "element."

To elaborate the way that interference articulates the way the film thinks while heeding Deleuze's treatment of cinema *as* philosophy, I deploy two philosophical frames within which von Trier's film can be elucidated, one Kantian and the other Nietzschean. Although for von Trier the concept of "element" refers primarily to natural elements inasmuch as the scenes are pervaded by water and sand, I render element as a philosophical concept as well, drawing on Kant's concept of transcendental subjectivity (an *elemental* subjectivity), which applies well to the identification between the film's protagonist, the former police detective, Fisher, and the suspected perpetrator he is pursuing, Harry Grey, the alleged serial killer of young girls. I also draw on Nietzsche's concept of truth as metaphorically imposed to treat the films mobilized figuration in which the primary natural "elements" in play operate as figuration meant to shape inferences about subjects, places, and the historical moment.

To begin explicating the Kantian aspect of my analysis, I turn to a passage in a novel that alerted me to the relevance of Kant's transcendental subject to the film. Without naming him, Holocaust survivor Imre Kertesz in his novel *Kaddish for an Unborn Child* unerringly glosses Kant's transcendental subject.

The novel's protagonist/narrator, like von Trier's, articulates a Kantian unconscious. Seeking to understand a seemingly irrational choice by "Teacher," a fellow internee in a concentration camp who imperils his own survival by not absconding with the helplessly immobilized narrator/protagonist's food allotment, he remarks, "there is a pure concept, untrammeled by any foreign material, whether our body, our soul, our wild beasts, a notion which lives as a uniform image in our minds, yes, an ideal."[15]

Given Kertesz's post camp investment in Kantian philosophy (he read Kant and translated Kantian texts into Hungarian), when he describes Teacher's choice, we can take the terms *pure* and *untrammeled* to refer to the Kantian concept of transcendence. What is enjoined in the quotation is Teacher's noumenal self. Kertesz's narrator says that Teacher is "*unable* to live without preserving this concept intact in its pure, untrammeled openness to scrutiny," a concept for which

> there is no explanation for, since it is not rational as compared with the tangible rationality of an issue of food rations, which in the extreme situation called a concentration camp might serve to avoid the ultimate end, if it would serve that purpose, if that purpose did not run up against the resistance of an immaterial concept which sweeps even vital interests to the side.[16]

The pure concepts of the understanding that Kant develops in his *Critique of Pure Reason* and reinflects to generate an ethical transcendence in his *Critique of Practical Reason* help to situate Kertesz's Teacher, who, despite the perils he faces in a situation of violent incarceration, manifests his freedom. Without dwelling at length on Kant's philosophy of experience, suffice it to say for the purposes here, that his philosophy articulates a tension between two noumenal realities—pure concepts of the understanding and pure objects (things in themselves)—and that to resolve the tension, Kant privileges the knower a choice that creates the conditions of possibility for what is required for morality, *freedom*. For Kant, it is ultimately our separation from the noumenal realm, which is always beyond our reach, which creates the possibility for freedom and thus morality (our inability to close the gap between appearance and reality instantiates our freedom). Moreover, that condition of possibility for our freedom and thus our morality is a subjective necessity. Untrammeled by experience, it is *elemental* and thus simultaneously fundamental to subjectivity and fundamentally intersubjective.

Where then do the natural elements come in to Kant's picture of "man's" (*das Mann's*) freedom? In his analytic of the sublime, Kant's version of mind, which is represented as harmonious in his analytic of the beautiful, experiences "discord" in response to something—for example, a violent storm or anything so "absolutely large" that because it is beyond our ordinary conceptual determinations, creates a "feeling of purposiveness quite independent of nature." The fit between the mind and nature (this "marriage . . . this betrothal proper to the beautiful," as Jean-François Lyotard puts it, "is broken by the sublime."[17] Specifically, in his invocation of what he calls the "dynamically sublime," Kant's subject recognizes that nature is fearsome without fearing it. As a result, the experience of the sublime elevates the imagination:

> Insofar as it incites fear [nature] . . . calls up that power in us (which is not nature [and] . . . nature is here called sublime merely because it elevates the imagination to a presentation of those cases in which the mind can make felt the proper sublimity if its destination, in comparison with nature itself.[18]

Nevertheless, Kant frets that although the experience of the sublime results in the recognition of one's freedom, the "subjective necessity" that must predicate a shared moral sense is threatened: "in respect to our judgment upon the sublime in nature, we cannot promise ourselves . . . the accordance with others."[19] As I have noted elsewhere, "to finesse the seeming recalcitrance of the experience of the sublime to the 'subjective necessity' that [his Third Critique] is designed to establish, Kant turns to a concept of "culture," which he had treated in his *Critique of Practical Reason*, a culture that "has its root in human nature." It is a shared moral sensibility, a "presupposition of a moral feeling."[20] With that as philosophical framing, we can observe that, in effect, von Trier's *Element* inverts the Kantian subject's intersubjectivity. He renders it as a shared evil sensibility, which creates the conditions of possibility for the Osborne method (elaborated later) that Fisher attempts to implement.

While Kantian philosophy provides a framing that helps us discern the cognitive map (in effect, the "untrammeled" mentality) which Fisher follows to catch the killer—it helps us understand the film's primary aesthetic subject, for the truth of the crime is to be discovered within the mentality of the detective—it is Nietzschean philosophy that provides a discernment of how the film thinks with images and juxtapositions, that is, with an elaborate metaphoricity. Specifically, an approach to the "truth" of the "crime" and the larger historical space and moment within which it is portrayed in the film is suggested in Nietzsche's remarks on truth:

> Truth is a mobile army of metaphors, metonyms, anthropomorphisms, in short a sum of human relations which have been subjected to poetic and rhetorical intensification, translation and decoration [. . .]; truths are illusions of which we have forgotten that they are illusions, metaphors which have become worn by frequent use and have lost all sensuous vigor [. . .].

Yet we still do not know where the drive to truth comes from, for so far we have only heard about the obligation to be truthful which society imposes in order to exist.[21]

We can appreciate how Nietzsche's remark applies to the moving images in von Trier's film if we recognize that contrary to the traditional mimetic version of the functioning of metaphors (the presumption, going back to Aristotle, that "To produce a good metaphor is to see a likeness" or equivalence),[22] the Nietzschean view suggests that metaphors *impose* a likeness or equivalence. On this view, the metaphoricity in *Element* is an argument rather than a discovery. To situate the way the argument unfolds cinematically, we can heed the similarity between the way von Trier's film thinks metaphorically and the way a cinematic master of metaphorical montage works, by noting the way Jean-Luc Godard's films work. In a remark about Godard's *Histoire(s) du Cinema*, which can be applied without modification to von Trier's *Element*, Jacques Rancière writes,

> The cinema that he recounts to us appears as a series of appropriations of other arts. . . . And in this tangle the very notion of image . . . emerges as that of a metamorphic operativeness, crossing the boundaries between the arts and denying the specificity of materials.[23]

And crucially, Godard's appropriations constitute the set of equivalences his *Histoire(s) du Cinema* evokes: The film contains a "clash of heterogeneous elements that provide a common measure." It creates an equivalence between "two captivations,"[24] that of the "German crowds by Nazi ideology" and that of the "film crowds by Hollywood."[25] Similarly, von Trier's *Element* creates a "clash of heterogeneous elements" as it draws on a wide variety of the arts and combines cinematic aesthetics familiar in the films of Herzog, Hitchcock, and Tarkovsky, as well as Godard (among others). Once we articulate the Nietzschean gloss with Kantian one, we have both a cinematic and a prepolitical framing and can then inquire into the kind of politics to which the film gestures. While Kant helps us appreciate the complex mentalities in the film, Nietzsche helps us appreciate the films concatenation of images.

SORTING PROTAGONISTS AND FACTICITIES WHILE HEEDING IMAGES

Recognizing that Europe is effectively a major protagonist in von Trier's film, we can observe how *Element* challenges the presumption that Europe is the essence of a progressive historical narrative. Through the film's image narrative,

EXTRACTING POLITICAL THEORY FROM VON TRIER

Europe is anything but a fulfillment of a progressive civilizational narrative. Instead, it is represented as a degenerated terrain—for example, as a retrograde junkyard (represented in an automobile junkyard in the area where Fisher and Police Chief Kramer (Jerold Wells) are inspecting a crime scene. There as elsewhere von Trier makes his argument with images. Throughout the film, rather than resorting to concepts and philosophemes, von Trier creates his symbolic geography with imagery of "elements," primarily sand and water. These two elements challenge both mythical narratives. Egypt, as Fishers says, is being "sanded over"; that element is effacing "Egyptianism." And Europe is a sinkhole rather than the realization of a progressive life world. The wetness pervading Germany contrasts markedly with the sand-swept dryness of Egypt. It is drowning in water ("Water water everywhere and not a drop to drink" intones Fisher when he arrives). Like Coleridge's Ancient Mariner, von Trier's Fisher is sadder but wiser. He is functioning in a story in which von Trier's "elements" belong to a nature that mocks rather than affirms the progressive story of western civilization and its so-called enlightenment. That mocking is also enacted by von Trier himself as the character "The Schmuck of Ages," who serves as a hotel desk clerk who grudgingly discloses clues about the brief hotel stay of the murderer, Harry Grey, whom Fisher is pretending to be when he checks in (Figure 1.2). The Schmuck's name is doubtless a reference to

FIGURE 1.2
Fisher, Kim, and The Schmuck. Source: Lars von Trier, *The Element of Crime*, Det Danske Filminstitut (1984).

36   EXTRACTING POLITICAL THEORY FROM VON TRIER

"The Rock of Ages," an eighteenth-century religious hymn in which nature, in the form of a mountain with an overhang, affords protection from harsh elements (metaphorically represented as Christ's protection: "The Lord is my Rock, and my Fortress, and my Deliverer," Psalm 18:2). Rather than a protecting Christ figure, The Schmuck is an unreliable prick.[26] And the elements afford no protection; von Trier's "nature" is akin to Nietzsche's version. It has "no opinion of us" but is nevertheless, in von Trier's words, a "force . . . that intrudes upon and somehow invades people's morals."[27]

What kind of political sensibility can one discern from von Trier's collection of shards, loosely held together by a dreamlike noir narrative? Rather than a mere politics of crime, the film's politics of aesthetics emerges from the unexpected equivalences it creates. The artist Jean Dubuffet provides a relevant insight about the politics of aesthetics involved in generating such equivalences: "Why shouldn't we group sharp-tailed swallows with 'knives' (both pointed and piercing) rather than lump them with ostriches, etc. as birds? Artists and poets should dislocate such conventions."[28] Similarly we are encouraged to explore von Trier's dislocations with which he imposes a wide variety of unexpected equivalences, which taken as a whole, yield a critique of European modernity (one that he continues in his subsequent films, *Epidemic* and *Europa*, which together with *Element*, constitute his "Europa trilogy"). Presuming that to appreciate how von Trier's film thinks we have to note how he mobilizes and refigures artistic genres, it is imperative to focus first on the way he dislocates detective fiction and its realization in the film noir genre.

POLICING METHODS

Von Trier's film apes the hardboiled version of detective fiction, which was a departure from the classic version (for example in Conan Doyle's Sherlock Holmes crime stories). For Conan Doyle, crime was a temporary aberration, a disruption of a culturally cohesive social order. His dramas imply therefore that solving of the case pulls the social order back to its proper normative functioning. In contrast for the hardboiled detective, most famously invented by Dashiell Hammett and Raymond Chandler, "the idea of a common culture seems both profoundly appealing and ultimately unbelievable."[29] Exemplary is Hammett's Sam Spade, who evinces no redemptive sentiments. At the end of *The Maltese Falcon*, his secretary, Efie, commends his solving of a case but feels his presence as an insult to moral decency. He has solved the crime but has heartlessly turned in Bridget O'Shaunessy, who was his client. Spade functions in an order whose relations are radically contingent rather than culturally cohesive, a perspective that Hammett provides in the story by having Spade tell a parable about a man named Flitcraft who suddenly reinvents his life after a traumatic moment to the story's client/perpetrator, O'Shaunessy.

While the hardboiled detective does not function in a cohesive social order, he (most often "he") is an unsentimental servant of clients, not of the society; he has a good grasp of social relations, which he shares with the classic detective. Elsewhere, I've referred to "two epistemic dimensions of crime solving, "forensics and metis," where the former involves technologies of information gathering—featured, for example, in recent decades on television crime dramas in which victims' bodies are scrutinized and crime scenes are scanned for pieces of evidence—and the latter involves the practical reasoning of detectives who use their experience of people's constraints, desires, and motives, in short their sensitivity to the dynamics of interpersonal interactions, to imagine the trajectory of the perpetrators of crime and their subsequent evasions. Moreover, that reasoning is contextualized for the canny detective by their understanding of the city, which as Amin and Thrift succinctly put it, is "a kind of force field of passions that associate and pulse bodies in particular ways."[30]

The Cuban crime novelist Leonardo Padura effectively captures both epistemic dimensions of crime scene in a conversation in which his police detective, Mario Conde (aka "The Count") evinces both a keen forensic-related observation and an "urban metis" in response to his assistant's assumption that the murder victim, a strangled transvestite who had bled from the rectum and showed no signs of having struggled, died as a result of an angry client's murderous rage:

> This is fishy. . . . Nobody lets himself be strangled without scratching back. And you tell me, what can you hide in your rectum? Drugs? A jewel? And how come the other fellow knew he had to search there of all places? . . . Well, because obviously they knew each other. . . . And what about the red dress, which must be from somewhere special? And why's such an elegant transvestite carrying his identity card. Don't you think it's incongruous?[31]

The epistemology of detection in *Element* is wholly different. Although "practical reasoning" is involved, that reasoning is constituted as a structurally transcendent mentality that reflects a moral (in this case evil) *sensus communis* rather than the social canniness of the detectives in the hardboiled crime genre. The "method" is articulated in Osborne's book, *The Element of Crime*, which Fisher takes as his guide, a method in which the detective must evince the same mentality as the fugitive. Following the method's protocols, Fisher follows the killer's route; stays in the same hotels; wears a hat with the killer, Harry Grey's, name on it; and has sex with the woman, Kim, with whom Grey had been involved.

38 EXTRACTING POLITICAL THEORY FROM VON TRIER

It is clear that von Trier drew on detective literature as well as films, for there is a novelistic prototype of his crime story, which doubtless shaped the film narrative. In Friedrich Dürrenmatt's *The Pledge* (1958), the detective, Matthäi, disbelieves the coerced confession of a suspect and searches for the actual serial killer of young girls who is rumored to be dead so that the case is never solved. And as is the case with von Trier's Fisher, obsession is involved; once Matthäi has made a pledge to the parents of one of the victims, he is relentlessly motivated in his search, even as a psychiatrist warns him that the killer he is seeking is a product of his obsession rather than a real perpetrator. Also like von Trier's Fisher, Matthäi uses a young girl as bait, a housekeeper's daughter, Annemarie, who matches the profile of the killer's victims. However, von Trier includes a twist. In *Element*, Fisher, who is using Osborne's method to simulate the mentality of the killer, inadvertently kills the young girl he dangles as bait (in a struggle to quiet her screaming and her attempt to flee). That act deepens the match between his and the killer's persona.

AN OTHERNESS IN EUROPE

As I have suggested, although an unusual crime genre drives the narrative of *Element*—a shared mentality between the killer and the detective—the film's political register becomes available when we focus on locating Europe as a self-forgetful dystopia rather than as an exemplar of a progressive modernity. The film's political register is more available as a critique of European culture than it is a critical intervention into perspectives on crime and justice. To recover that aspect of the film, I have to highlight a moment that has been neglected in reviews and critiques, one that speaks to a temporal trajectory involving Europe's debts for its intellectual and cultural heritage, which I repeat in this version. That moment is Fisher's first gesture as he greets his former mentor, Osborne. He shows up with a gift for Osborne, an Arab translation of his mentor's book, *The Element of Crime*. When rather than thanking Fisher, Osborne remarks that the translation was done without his permission, we have to see that response as something other than ingratitude. Osborne's reaction resonates as an allegory of historical denial. Europe owes much of its intellectual and cultural heritage—indeed, much of its so-called enlightenment—to Arab thinkers. For example, it was thanks to the commentaries of Ibn Rushd (Averroës), among which were his commentaries on Aristotle's Nicomachean Ethics and on Plato's Republic in the twelfth century, that Europeans became familiar with much of ancient Greek thought and subsequently incorporated the Hellenism that shaped much of their intellectual culture. Ultimately, Fisher's delusional quest, guided by Osborne's method, is a narrative thread that pales in comparison with Europe's delusions about itself. The truth that the

EXTRACTING POLITICAL THEORY FROM VON TRIER

film pursues is not about a perpetrator of serial murders but of European culture, which von Trier offers as a cinematic actualization of Nietzschean truth (quoted earlier): "a mobile army of metaphors, metonyms, anthropomorphisms, in short a sum of human relations which have been subjected to poetic and rhetorical intensification, translation and decoration."

FILM FORM AS POLITICAL CRITIQUE

Part of *Element*'s "poetic and rhetorical intensification, translation and decoration" is expressed in the interactions between Fisher and the prostitute, Kim. At one point, in a remark that inter-articulates violence and Eros, Fisher tells Kim that he is going to "fuck her back to the Stone Age" (an appropriation of General Curtis LeMay's infamous remark during the Vietnam War, urging the United States to bomb Vietnam back to the Stone Age). Kim's body is compliant with Fisher's simulation of Grey as her lover. However, her discourse is resistant. She tries to derail Fisher's delusional quest, asking him at one point if he will stop now that he has found what he wanted (where "what he wanted" remains ambiguous). And when Fisher talks about figuring out Grey's motives, she says, "Bad men don't have motives." Later she promotes a version of reality that Fisher is increasingly ignoring, telling him, "[Y]ou're not Harry Grey, you're Fisher," and adding that pursuing Grey "is not our work."

Kim's resistance to Fisher's delusion, his "obsession with Europe" articulated as a pursuit of a serial killer, situates her as an "attendant" who focuses the film's facticity. It is a persona figured, developed, and analyzed by Deleuze in his interpretations of Francis Bacon's paintings, a figure that has no narrative relationship with the painting's central character(s). Deleuze nominates that figure as an attendant, a "spectator" who seems to "subsist, distinct from the [main] figure" and provides the basis for determining the facticity of the scene. In his words, it indicates "the relation of the Figure to its isolating place," or "what takes place."[32] In short, Kim's resistance to Fisher's quixotic quest renders the crime genre incidental to the film's primary political register. It bids us to focus on the Europe-as-problematic-obsession in which Fisher's detection is taking place rather than on the investigative drama.

To evoke another Deleuzian insight (noted in the Introduction), which guides us away from the crime drama and toward the spatiotemporal context in which it takes place, as the film narrative progresses we should assume that von Trier has created a cinema of seeing rather than a cinema of action. As viewers, our question should be what are we seeing rather than what is going to happen next.[33] For example, animals show up in a variety of scenes, each time with a different intertextual reference. One in particular evokes one of Franz Kafka's many animal allegories. In his story "A Report to an Academy," Kafka has an ape giving a fluent account of his life. It has been "nearly five years," he states, "since I was an ape."[34] He reports that he "observed everything quietly" (while caged) and succeeded eventually in achieving "the cultural level of the average European."[35] The ape's report is both a challenge to the radical separation of human from animal and a riposte to Europe's smug assumption about its cultural superiority. That smug assumption is something Derrida has also addressed in a treatment of the human–animal separation but with a different take on the division. He notes that the separation has been essential to the human "autobiography." What is involved, he writes, is

> the presentation of self to human life, the autobiography of the human species, the whole history of the self that man recounts to himself . . . the thesis of rupture or abyss between those who say "we men," "I, a human," and what this man among men who say "we," what he *calls* the animal or animals.[36]

Instead of an autobiographical story, von Trier's *Element* reflects on the human (or, more specifically, European "man's") separation from the animal with moving images. And instead of a story about an animal reaching for a higher-evolutionary niche, it is one about a collective Europe moving in reverse evolution. There are no apes in *Element*, but there are two primates. In addition to the opening scene with the Egyptian psychiatrist who has a monkey sitting on his shoulder is a later scene in which Fisher opens the lid on a drainpipe and sees a lemur stuck and shivering. Fisher, confined in a state of hypnosis from which he cannot escape, is mimed by the animal. The lemur is both a reflection of himself and a sign that his humanity has not evolved beyond that of the primate.

FISHER AND SPACE

Throughout *Element*, the viewer sees Fisher's dreamscape while hearing his narration. Aware that he is hypnotized, we are inclined to think that what we are witnessing is a product of the protagonist's mentality, that is, that what is expressed throughout the film emerges from Fisher's inner space. However, given that Fisher is a character in a film, he should be understood as an aesthetic rather than as a cognitive subject (even though his mentality is the "method" of detection). His role involves "articulate[ing] and mobiliz[ing] thinking . . . .[he is one] whose movements and dispositions are less significant in terms of what they reveal about [an] inner life than what they tell us about the world to which [the subject] belong[s]."[37] Addressing himself to why we cannot simply heed a speaker's inner space, Vilém Flusser puts it well: "The speaker's inner space, just behind the vocal cords and just prior to speaking out, cannot be understood as a private space because it is filled with words that have an inherently public character and stem from the public sphere."[38] Inasmuch as Fisher as an aesthetic subject is a cinema character as well as a speaker whose "inner space" is always already an outer space, we must heed *what* von Trier is saying about that outer space, which the camera provides, and *how* he is saying it, with a montage of images as well as with monologue and dialogue.

CINEMATIC POLITICAL THOUGHT: VON TRIER'S TEMPORAL CONTEXT

I am now ready to address the "what" of von Trier's cinematic thinking, which become available when we recognize that the film, produced at a particular moment in Euro-modernity, is oriented as critique and is drawn from critical intellectual currents. Briefly, the historical moment of von Trier's cinematic statement comes in a period when the moribund development and modernization narratives of the mid-twentieth-century social sciences have been subject to critical questioning. It is a time (characterized by Robert Young) of "European culture's [growing] awareness that it is no longer the unquestioned and dominant center of the world."[39] Moreover, that critical questioning has gone well beyond the "no longer" to reflect on Europe's past colonial abuses. Rather than simply valorizing European enlightenment (characterized in Immanuel Kant's famous essay in which Euro-Enlightenment's "reason" is cast as a form of maturity), what is engaged is a serious reconsideration of the colonial experience and its aftermath. Referring to the Enlightenment's critical return two centuries after Kant's characterization, Foucault notes the "movement by which, at the end of the colonial era, people began to ask the West what rights its culture, its science, its social organization and finally its rationality itself could have to laying claim to a universal validity." "Is it not a mirage," he adds, "tied to an economic domination and a political hegemony?" Insofar Enlightenment reason returns, he insists, it is

> not at all a way for the West to take cognizance of its present possibilities and of the liberations to which it can accede, but as a way of interrogating it on its limits and on the power which it has abused. Reason as despotic enlightenment.[40]

To appreciate the "what" of von Trier's film therefore is to recognize that he wants to challenge the story in which Europe's dominant autobiography places it at the center of the world. And to elaborate the "how," we can liken his approach to that of Thomas Mann's in his deconstruction of a similar self-centered story, in his case the biblical Joseph's fantasy that *his* story is at the center of history. Like von Trier, Mann makes use of montage, in his case a literary montage. At the beginning of the third volume of his novelistic tetralogy, *Joseph and his Brothers*, Mann has Joseph remark (to the nomadic Ma'onites who pull him from the pit where his brothers had left him to die), "Where are you taking me." One of them, Kedeema, responds, "You have a way of putting yourself in the middle of things," and goes on to point out that they are headed somewhere and that Joseph happens to be with them; they have no reason to regard themselves as part of his story: "Do you suppose that we are journeying simply so that you may arrive somewhere your god wants you to be."[41] Edified by Kedeema's remarks, Joseph admits that "the world has many middle points"[42] but insists nevertheless that at least he stands in the center of *his* circle.

As I have noted elsewhere, the form of Mann's novel comports well with critical cinematic approaches.[43] Having constructed his approach to the Joseph story as a literary montage, Mann reports that his novelistic treatment of the biblical Joseph allowed him to gloss a world of diverse styles (what he calls "lyricisms") and positions that were in the process of merging from the many to the one. Specifically describing that distribution of lyricisms, he states that "all that is Jewish, throughout the work, is merely foreground, only one style element among others, only *one* stratum of its language which strangely fuses the archaic world and the modern, the epical and the analytic," and adds that the poem in the last volume, "the song of annunciation" sung by a child to the aged Jacob, is an old composition of psalter recollections and little verses of the German romantic type, a musical fusion that is an example of the character of the whole work, which seeks to blend a great many things, and because it images everything human as a unity, it borrows motives, memories, and allusions, as well as linguistic sounds from many spheres.[44]

Like Mann, von Trier creates his story with available cultural and artistic texts (extant in *his* historical moment) while at the same time displacing his character, Europe, from the center. However, unlike Mann, he is seeking to disturb rather than "blend." His pastiche of textual references (from cinema, television, and diverse historical episodes) constitutes a cinematic version of the questioning of Euro-modernity to which Foucault refers in his reinflection of the enlightenment to a "despotic enlightenment." Inasmuch as "enlightenment" is a heliotrope, a light-based figure, one of von Trier's most significant ripostes to Europe's enlightenment presumption is the dark tone maintained throughout *Element*. The film is shot in dark shades, achieved with dark, yellowish sodium lights, which render his Europe as a world in darkness is In one register, the darkness is appropriate to the genre within which von Trier constructs the film narrative, a noir crime story. In another, it expresses a counter-Enlightenment statement about Europe.

As for the "despotic" dimension, that adjectival modifier of enlightenment is conveyed by Fisher's superior, the police chief Kramer (Jerold Wells), a character who, with his shaved bullet-shaped head and leather coat, is seemingly copied from Telly Savalas's eponymous character in the American television detective series, Kojak, a police procedural drama (1973–1978) that was popular in many counties, including Germany, among others. In his first appearance, Chief Kramer is at a crime scene standing on the partially caved-in roof of a wrecked automobile, which is sitting among many other seemingly abandoned cars (in what looks like an automobile graveyard). Holding a megaphone, he is shouting in a stentorian voice at his detectives: "Nobody move, Nobody Move." Once again, if we regard the crime story is incidental, we can surmise that Kramer is characterizing Europe (or, more specifically, Germany) as static, a clue the film provides by having Fisher remark as he approaches the scene, "Europe lies dormant." Moreover, and tellingly, one of the cars is a historical trope. Fisher arrives in a VW Beetle, and before that, he is hit in the foot with a toy version of it, played with by a small boy at Osborne's home. The toy version implies that the VW is an innocent object inasmuch as it is attached to a young "innocent." However, once we recall the origin of the car, it loses its innocence. The VW Beetle is a product of Germany's National Socialist past. Having learned about Henry Ford's production system, Hitler, once he became chancellor in 1933, declared at a Berlin auto show that he wanted to motorize Germany by facilitating the mass production of an affordable car. That car, the prototype of the VW Beetle, came to be designated as a "people's car" (Volkswagen). Hitler later delivered the design to Ferdinand Porsche, whose company ultimately manufactured it (Figure 1.3).[45]

FIGURE 1.3
VW in the junkyard. Source: Lars von Trier, *The Element of Crime*, Det Danske Filminstitut (1984).

Significantly, as Kramer is shouting his directions, a now-static "motorized Germany" is a backdrop for police brutality, a brutality existing on a historical trajectory from National Socialist Germany (where the automobiles provide the linkage). That historical narrative of brutality is emphasized as a group of Kramer's detectives are observed beating a man who has been spread-eagled against one of the abandoned cars. The police chief, Kramer, once dismounted from the old car, mentions to Fisher that he, Kramer, had become chief even though he had much less talent as a detective than Fisher. He then proceeds to fire his gun wildly in various directions, including at a retreating young woman. Kramer's immediate story, one of an unexpected career advancement that effectively impugns the conceit that Europe/Germany is committed to meritocracy, is less important than the symbolic story, in which Kramer is an icon of a brutal Europe. That brutality is lent a temporal trajectory by Fisher, who interrupts Kramer's gunplay, shouting, "Have you lost your mind," implying that the European mind, once allegedly civilized and humane, has devolved into a level of primal and mindless violence.

That Europe had degenerated into an anachronistic past rather than progressing economically and culturally is signaled soon after Fisher arrives from Egypt. Among his first words as he approaches Osborne's home are "Where's the stairs? You've moved the fucking stairs." And while he is in Germany, there are catastrophes (literally downward tropes) in the form of descending, falling, and diving bodies. At the crime scene, the body of the murder victim is lowered by a crane, and later, people dive from the crane leaning over a lake with a rope around their ankles (in response to which Kramer remarks, "They call it a ritual. I call it crime"). At a minimum, it appears to be a suicidal impulse, repeated in gory detail at the end of the film, when the jumper has a spray of blood vomited from his mouth after the rope goes taut.

Ultimately, *Element* abounds in madness rather than enlightenment with its characters evincing primal drives of sexual and physical aggression (enacted by, among other things, the way Fisher's sex with Kim is akin to a violent rape) in a Europe, which, like the characters, has regressed. Shortly after Fisher arrives in Germany, we see a horse-drawn apple cart driven by an elderly man (it is toppled, animating another of von Trier's intensified clichés, in this case "upsetting the applecart"). Such an obvious animation of a cliché has to alert us to the borrowing in other image moments, many of which are drawn from intellectual and artistic texts. They become the film's thought vehicles as Europe's regressing culture is engaged through critical cultural materials, especially the filmmakers whom von Trier admires. For example, the opening Cairo scene is reminiscent of German director Werner Herzog's *The Enigma of Kasper Hauser* (1975), which features a young idiot savant who showed up in Nuremberg in 1828, having been disabled by being kept in a dungeon for most of his life. A virtually feral person by the time of his appearance, he is almost

EXTRACTING POLITICAL THEORY FROM VON TRIER

unable to speak or walk. Impervious to civilizational codes, he is nevertheless haunted by images of Cairo. There are a host of others cinematic references, at least two of which refer to Tarkovsky's films: A donkey struggling to regain his footing in an early scene in Germany recalls a similar shot of a wounded horse in his *Andrei Rublev* (1966), and the water-saturated scenes clearly reference his *Stalker* (1979). Moreover, as one critic has pointed out, "von Trier's references don't extend merely to his filmmaking forebears." Drawing from "Western cultural output taken as a whole," the film is

> littered with dozens of quotes that range from children's nursery rhymes like "Oranges and Lemons" and "This is the house that Jack built" to serious poetry like Ludwig Uhland's melancholic war remembrance "I Had a Comrade" (partially recited within the film by Osborne, in its original German) and a section of "In the Greenest of the Valleys" by Edgar Allen Poe: . . . "In the monarch thought's dominion. It stood there. Never seraph spread a pinion over fabric half so fair." [And] At one point, Trier even has Fisher quoting James Joyce's modernist landmark, "Finnegan's Wake."[46]

CONCLUSION: VON TRIER'S (AND OTHER'S) EUROPE

As I have implied, there is significant homology between conceptual orientations that seek to decenter and deprivilege the conceits that an individual or collective have about their centrality to the story of their epoch and the decentering effect of film form. Influenced in part by Henri Bergson's philosophy of embodiment, Deleuze makes a strong case for the decentering capacity of cinema. While Bergson saw the body as a center of perception, his centered body is nevertheless a center of indetermination inasmuch as its perceptions are always partial. The brain for Bergson is a particularizing and evacuating mechanism.[47] Turning to cinema's capacity to restore what perception evacuates, Deleuze renders the cinematic body as a center of indetermination whose perceptual incapacities are exceeded by cinema's capacity. Through its camera work—cuts and juxtapositions and the varied kinds of focus—it generates perspectives that depart from the control exercised by perception. Accordingly, Deleuze insists that "cinema does *not* have subjective perception as its model because the mobility of its centers and the variability of its framings always lead it to restore vast acentered and deframed zones."[48]

In *Element* von Trier effectively inter-articulates two forms of mobility to offer a "truth" of Euro-modernity: the earlier-noted Nietzschean approach to figuration (a "mobile army of metaphors, metonyms, anthropomorphisms . . .

46 EXTRACTING POLITICAL THEORY FROM VON TRIER

which have been subjected to poetic and rhetorical intensification, translation and decoration") and the "mobility of [cinema's] centers and the variability of its framings" to challenge Europe's autobiographical conceit that its story is at the center of world history. That Europe is von Trier's obsession (like his character Fisher's) becomes evident in his filmography. He follows *Element* with two more Europe-focused films, *Epidemic* (1987) and *Europa* (1991), which, like *Element*, treat postwar European cultural crises with a resort to the same heavily allegorical figuration. In *Epidemic*, a film whose narrative genre is a medical catastrophe, the focus is on a self-defeating attempt by a young doctor to prevent the spread of a plague but who manages only to exacerbate it. In *Epidemic*, von Trier again summons the mechanism of hypnosis and displays his emphasis on misguided individuals trying to do good but achieving evil. However, an obsession with Germany frames much of the film. Its moving frames explore the same dissolute postwar Germany that appears in *Element*, reflected in this film by its industrial core, its *Ruhrgebiet*, during the 1980s. And in *Europa*, where once again hypnosis is used to reflect a diminished cognition of reality, von Trier takes German history back to 1945 and features a character whose new vocation as a conductor reveals the way the railroad system, seemingly now innocent as it transports war veterans around, has an evil past; it was formerly used to transport Jews to concentration camps.

Just as doing critical political theorizing requires distantiation, it is evident that what von Trier has sought to achieve cinematically, beginning with his *Element* and continued through the next two films of his "Europa Trilogy" was distantiation, what both Foucault and Blanchot famously refer to as a "thought from outside,"[49] which is facilitated by his use of the cinematic art's capacity to decenter European conceits about its story. In the case of *Europa*, von Trier's avoidance of a single perspective is achieved by combining "two images filmed with different lenses."[50] However, rather than a further elaboration of von Trier's technical innovations, I want to conclude by invoking another thought from outside, that belonging to Aimé Césaire, a Francophone poet from Martinique. Like von Trier, Césaire has challenged the popular development and modernization discourses of the social sciences. However, his challenge goes well beyond von Trier's Germany obsession and indicts all of "Western Man."

As I have pointed out elsewhere (partly repeated in the Introduction), much of the character of twentieth-century comparative politics "has been dominated by a fear of instability and, accordingly, a disparagement of those multiparty systems that allow for the aggregation of extreme or marginalized voices and interests" and that the assumption has been that "[a] safe 'civic culture' [is] one that would never allow a Hitler to emerge. . . . Such was the anxiety of the imperial center as it produced many of the conceptual commitments of postwar political science." I go on to ask, "How else one might construct the Hitler question," and summon the perspective of Aimé Césaire, who, rather

EXTRACTING POLITICAL THEORY FROM VON TRIER 47

than treating the Hitler phenomenon as a historical aberration, viewed it as of a piece with what he called "Western European barbarism . . . a truth that the peoples of Europe have hidden from themselves."[51] What they have failed to understand about the Hitler phenomenon, according to Césaire, is "that it is barbarism . . .

> but before they were its victims, they were its accomplices; that they toler-ated Nazism before it was inflicted on them, that they absolved it, shut their eyes to it, legitimized it, because, until then, it had been applied only to the non-European peoples; that they cultivated that Nazism, that they were responsible for it.[52]

NOTES

1. For use of the expression and analysis of the dynamic, see William Boelhower, "Inventing America: A Model of Cartographic Semiosis," *Word and Image* 4: 2 (April–June, 1998).
2. Bonnie Honig and Lori J. Marso, "Introduction," in *Politics, Theory, and Film: Critical Encounters with Lars Von Trier*, eds. Bonnie Honig and Lori J. Marso (Oxford: Oxford University Press, 2016), 1–2.
3. Gilles Deleuze, *Francis Bacon: The Logic of Sensation*, trans. Daniel W. Smith (Minneapolis: University of Minnesota Press, 2003), 71.
4. *Ibid.*, 71–72.
5. Francis Bacon, quoted in David Sylvester, *The Brutality of Fact: Interviews With Francis Bacon* (New York: Thames and Hudson, 1981), 40.
6. See Gilles Deleuze, "Kant, Synthesis and Time," On the web at: http://deleuzelectures. blogspot.com/2007/02/on-kant.html.
7. Tom Conley, *Cartographic Cinema* (Minneapolis: University of Minnesota Press, 2007).
8. Michel Foucault, "Nietzsche, Genealogy, History," in *Language, Counter-Memory, Practice*, ed. Donald Bouchard (Ithaca: Cornell University Press, 1977).
9. Jacques Derrida, *The Other Heading: Memories, Responses and Responsibilities*, trans. Michael B. Nass (Bloomington: Indiana University Press, 1992), 48.
10. The quotation is from Nigel Andrews, "Maniacal Iconoclast of Film Convention," in *Lars von Trier: Interviews*, ed. Jan Lumholdt (Jackson: University Press of Mississippi, 2003), 82.
11. Gilles Deleuze, *Cinema 2: The Time Image*, trans. Hugh Tomlinson and Robert Galeta (Minneapolis: University of Minnesota Press, 1989), 280.
12. See Gilles Deleuze and Felix Guattari, *What Is Philosophy*, trans. Hugh Tomlinson and Graham Burchell (New York: Columbia University Press, 1994), 163–199.
13. Cesare Casarino, "Philopoesis: A Theoretico-Methodological Manifesto," *boundary 2* (2002), 86.
14. The quotation is from Gilles Deleuze, *Foucault*, trans. Sean Hand (Minneapolis: University of Minnesota Press, 1988), 86.
15. Imre Kertesz, *Kaddish for an Unborn Child*, trans. Tim Wilkinson (New York: Random House, 1990), 42.

48 EXTRACTING POLITICAL THEORY FROM VON TRIER

16. *Ibid.*, 44.
17. Jean-François Lyotard, "After the Sublime: The State of Aesthetics," in *The Inhuman*, trans. Geoffrey Bennington and Rachel Bowlby (Stanford: Stanford University Press, 1991), 137.
18. Immanuel Kant, *The Critique of Judgment*, trans. J. H. Bernard (Amherst: Prometheus Books, 2000), 126.
19. *Ibid.*, 119.
20. Michael J. Shapiro, *Cinematic Geopolitics* (London: Routledge, 2009), 97.
21. Friedrich Nietzsche, "On Truth and Lie in a Non-Moral Sense," in *The Portable Nietzsche*, trans. Water Kaufman (New York: Penguin, 1977), 46–47.
22. The quotation is from Jacques Derrida, "White Mythologies," in *Margins of Philosophy*, trans. Alan Bass (Chicago: University of Chicago Press, 1984), 237.
23. Jacques Rancière, *The Future of the Image*, trans. G. Elliot (New York: Verso, 2007), 55.
24. *Ibid.*
25. *Ibid.*, 53.
26. *Schmuck* derives from the Yiddish *smok* (penis) and has come to denote a contemptible, shameful, or foolish person.
27. Von Trier, quoted in von Trier's Eclecticism Right from the Start in *Mossy World*, June 26, 2011: On the web at: http://amossyworld.tumblr.com/post/6922322015/von-triers-eclecticism-right-from-the-start.
28. The quotation is from H. Gilonis's commentary, "Re-invented from Scratch: Dubuffet and Gulevich's *Les Murs*," in *Dubuffet's Wall: Lithograph for Les Murs* (Paris: Les Editions du Livre, 1950), 14.
29. The quotation is from Sean McCann, *Gumshoe America* (Durham: Duke University Press, 2000), 4.
30. The quotation is from Ash Amin and Nigel Thrift, *Cities: Reimaging the Urban* (Cambridge: Polity, 2002), 86.
31. Leonardo Padura, *Havana Red*, trans. Peter Bush (London: Bitter Lemon Press, 1997), 26.
32. Gilles Deleuze, *Francis Bacon: The Logic of Sensation*, trans. Daniel W. Smith (Minneapolis: University of Minnesota Press, 2003), 14.
33. Deleuze, *Cinema 2*, 272.
34. Franz Kafka, "Report of an Academy," in *Kafka: The Complete Stories* (New York: Schocken, 1976), 250.
35. *Ibid.*, 255.
36. Jacques Derrida, *The Animal That Therefore I Am*, trans. David Wills (New York: Fordham University Press, 2008), 9.
37. I am quoting from one of my texts: Michael J. Shapiro, *Studies in Trans-Disciplinary Method: After the Aesthetic Turn* (London: Routledge, 2012), 11.
38. Vilém Flusser, *Gestures*, trans. Nancy Ann Roth (Minneapolis: University of Minnesota Press, 2014), loc 633–642. Similarly, as Martin Nitsche argues, Husserl's phenomenological philosophy discredits the separation between inner and outer space; see his *The Methodological Precedence of Intertwining: An Introduction to Transitive-Topological Phenomenology* (Wuzburg: Konigshausen & Neumann, 2018).
39. Robert Young, *White Mythologies: Writing History and the West* (New York: Routledge, 1990), 19–20.

EXTRACTING POLITICAL THEORY FROM VON TRIER   49

40. The quotations are from Michel Foucault's preface to Georges Canguilhem, *The Normal and the Pathological*, trans. Carolyn R. Fawcett (New York: Zone Books, 1989), 12.
41. Thomas Mann, *Joseph and his Brothers*, trans. John E. Woods (New York: Alfred A. Knopf, 2005), 541.
42. *Ibid.*
43. Shapiro, *Cinematic Geopolitics*, 7.
44. Thomas Mann, *The Theme of the Joseph Novels*, Speech delivered at the Library of Congress (Washington, DC: Library of Congress, 1942), 11.
45. Go to www.volkswest.co.uk/beetle_history.html for the history of the VW Beetle.
46. The quotation is from "Film Walrus Reviews," Jan 26, 2008, On the web at: www.filmwalrus.com/2008/01/review-of-element-of-crime.html.
47. See Henri Bergson, *Creative Evolution*, trans. Keith Ansel-Pearson (London: Palgrave, 2007).
48. Gilles Deleuze, *Cinema 1*, trans. Hugh Tomlinson and Barbara Habberjam (Minneapolis: University of Minnesota Press, 1986), 64.
49. See *Foucault/Blanchot*, containing Michael Foucault, "Maurice Blanchot: The Thought From Outside," and Maurice Blanchot, "Michel Foucault as I Imagine Him," trans. Jeffrey Mehlman (New York: Zone Books, 1987).
50. The quotation is from an interview with von Trier: Toby Rose, "Lars von Trier, Director," in *Lars von Trier: Interviews*, ed. Jan Lumholt (Jackson: University Press of Mississippi, 2003), 87.
51. See Michael J. Shapiro, "Introduction," in *Challenging Boundaries*, eds. Michael J. Shapiro and Hayward Alker (Minneapolis: University of Minnesota Press, 1996), xix.
52. Aimé Césaire, *Discourse on Colonialism*, trans. Joan Pinkham (New York: Monthly Review Press, 1972), 14.

REFERENCES

Amin, Ash and Thrift, Nigel (2002) *Cities: Reimaging the Urban*, Cambridge: Polity.

Andrews, Nigel (2003) 'Maniacal Iconoclast of Film Convention,' in *Lars von Trier: Interviews*, ed. Jan Lumholdt, Jackson: University Press of Mississippi, pp. 81–83.

Bergson, Henri (1986) *Creative Evolution*, trans. Keith Ansel-Pearson, London: Palgrave.

Casarino, Cesare (2002) 'Philopoesis: A Theoretico-Methodological Manifesto,' *boundary 2*, Vol. 29 (1), pp. 65–96.

Césaire, Aimé (1972) *Discourse on Colonialism*, trans. Joan Pinkham, New York: Monthly Review Press.

Conley, Tom (2007) *Cartographic Cinema*, Minneapolis: University of Minnesota Press.

Deleuze, Gilles (1986) *Cinema 1*, trans. Hugh Tomlinson and Barbara Habberjam, Minneapolis: University of Minnesota Press.

Deleuze, Gilles (1988) *Foucault*, trans. Sean Hand, Minneapolis: University of Minnesota Press.

Deleuze, Gilles (1989) *Cinema 2: The Time Image*, trans. Hugh Tomlinson and Robert Galeta, Minneapolis: University of Minnesota Press.

Deleuze, Gilles (2003) *Francis Bacon: The Logic of Sensation*, trans. Daniel W. Smith, Minneapolis: University of Minnesota Press.

Deleuze, Gilles (2007) 'Kant, Synthesis and Time,' at: http://deleuzelectures.blogspot.com/2007/02/on-kant.html.

Deleuze, Gilles and Guattari, Felix (1994) *What is Philosophy*, trans. Hugh Tomlinson and Graham Burchell, New York: Columbia University Press.

Derrida, Jacques (1984) 'White Mythologies,' in *Margins of Philosophy*, trans. Alan Bass, Chicago: University of Chicago Press, pp. 207–272.

Derrida, Jacques (1992) *The Other Heading: Memories, Responses and Responsibilities*, trans. Michael B. Nass, Bloomington: Indiana University Press.

Derrida, Jacques (2008) *The Animal That Therefore I Am*, trans. David Wills, New York: Fordham University Press.

Flusser, Vilém (2014) *Gestures*, trans. Nancy Ann Roth, Minneapolis: University of Minnesota Press.

Foucault, Michel (1977) 'Nietzsche, Genealogy, History,' in *Language, Counter-Memory, Practice*, ed. Donald Bouchard, Ithaca: Cornell University Press.

Foucault, Michel (1989) 'Preface,' in *The Normal and the Pathological*, ed. Georges Canguihem, trans. Carolyn R. Fawcett, New York: Zone Books, pp. ix–xx.

Gilonis, Harry (1950) 'Re-invented From Scratch: Dubuffet and Gulevich's *Les Murs*,' in *Dubuffet's Wall: Lithograph for Les Murs*, Paris: Les Editions du Livre, pp. 14–17.

Honig, Bonnie and Marso, Lori J. (2016) 'Introduction,' in *Politics, Theory, and Film: Critical Encounters with Lars Von Trier*, eds. Bonnie Honig and Lori J. Marso, Oxford: Oxford University Press, pp. 1–19.

Kafka, Franz (1976) 'Report of an Academy,' in *Kafka: The Complete Stories*, New York: Schocken, pp. 250–261 .

Kant, Immanuel (2000) *The Critique of Judgment*, trans. J. H. Bernard, Amherst: Prometheus Books.

Kertesz, Imre (1990) *Kaddish for an Unborn Child*, trans. Tim Wilkinson, New York: Random House.

Lyotard, Jean-François (1991) 'After the Sublime: The State of Aesthetics,' in *The Inhuman*, trans. Geoffrey Bennington and Rachel Bowlby, Stanford: Stanford University Press, pp 89–107.

Mann, Thomas (1942) *The Theme of the Joseph Novels*, Speech delivered at the Library of Congress, Washington, DC: Library of Congress.

Mann, Thomas (2005) *Joseph and His Brothers*, trans. John E. Woods, New York: Alfred A. Knopf.

McCann, Sean (2000) *Gumshoe America*, Durham: Duke University Press.

Nietzsche, Friedrich (1977) 'On Truth and Lie in a Non-Moral Sense,' in *The Portable Nietzsche*, trans. Water Kaufman, New York: Penguin, pp. 46–47.

Nitsche, Martin (2018) *The Methodological Precedence of Intertwining: An Introduction to Transitive-Topological Phenomenology*, Wuzburg: Konigshausen & Neumann.

Padura, Leonardo (1997) *Havana Red*, trans. Peter Bush, London: Bitter Lemon Press.

Rancière, Jacques (2007) *The Future of the Image*, trans. G. Elliot, New York: Verso.

Rose, Toby (2003) 'Lars von Trier, Director,' in *Lars von Trier: Interviews*, ed. Jan Lumholt, Jackson: University Press of Mississippi, pp. 86–87.

Shapiro, Michael J. (1996) 'Introduction,' in *Challenging Boundaries*, eds. Michael J. Shapiro and Hayward Alker, Minneapolis: University of Minnesota Press, pp. xv–xxiii.

Shapiro, Michael J. (2009) *Cinematic Geopolitics*, London: Routledge.

Shapiro, Michael J. (2012) *Studies in Trans-Disciplinary Method: After the Aesthetic Turn*, London: Routledge.

Sylvester, David (1981) *The Brutality of Fact: Interviews With Francis Bacon*, New York: Thames and Hudson.

Young, Robert (1990) *White Mythologies: Writing History and the West*, New York: Routledge.

SUGGESTED READING

For other analyses of von Trier's films, see Emma Bell, "The Passions of Lars von Trier," in *New Readings in Nordic Cinema*, ed. C. Claire Thomson (Norwich, UK: Norvik Press, 2006), 205–216; and Linda Badley, *Lars von Trier* (Urbana: University of Illinois Press, 2009). And for commentary and interview with von Trier, see Jan Lumholdt ed., *Lars von Trier: Interviews* (Jackson: University Press of Mississippi, 2003).

For critical analyses of the animal–human divide, as it is articulate artistic genres, see Anat Pick, *Creaturely Poetics: Animality and Vulnerability in Literature and Film* (New York: Columbia University Press, 2011).

CHAPTER **2**

Toward a Critical Assessment of "Now-Time"

Contrasting Hoop Dreams *With Kubrick's* Barry Lyndon

INTRODUCTION

This chapter draws from an article and a book chapter that originated in draft form as a paper delivered at a conference on the relationship between time and value.[1] The original impulse was to analyze cinematic texts in order to explore the temporalities characteristic of particular historical periods while assessing their implications for the value attributed to the subjects who belong to those periods. As I prepared for the conference and contemplated the compositional strategy of my contribution, I was struck by a contemporary event that revealed the value attached to a moving African American body, a defensive tackle on the New York Giants team in the National Football League. My reflection on that event dictated the cinematic choices I made to elaborate the analysis. Here's the original introduction:

> On Monday, October 28, 1996, sports journalist Mike Freeman's report on the Sunday Giants-Lions game, in *The New York Times*, featured a pass interception by the Giant's Ray Agnew:
>
> > This is an image that might endure in the minds of the Lions for months to come: Giants defensive lineman Ray Agnew, after picking off a pass, rumbling 34 yards for a touchdown, his 285 pound body running so slowly it seemed the feat couldn't be captured on an hour long highlight show.[2]

I saw two kinds of time-related value articulated in that passage. The first involves the modern mediascape within which sports reports are situated. The television broadcast to which the journalist refers has a temporal structure that limits the amount of time that can be allocated to the coverage of a particular moment in a sporting contest. The second involves the value attached to the

TOWARD A CRITICAL ASSESSMENT OF "NOW-TIME"

performance of the bodies involved in the sporting contest. Accordingly, I wrote,

> If the phenomenon of professional football is confined to the playing field, the value of Ray Agnew's performance was 6 points, added to the Giant's score. However, it is clear to the reporter, Freeman, that the spatio-temporality of contemporary sports exceeds what occurs during playing time. In extending the temporal boundaries of the Agnew event into a post-game media future, Freeman offers in a remarkably efficient sentence a sophisticated reading of how sports are now experienced. He recognizes that the media value of Agnew's interception is contingent on its duration. To be re-experienced as publicity, it must compete with several other key sporting moments to fit within an hour-long episode of sports television at the end of the day.[3]

It became evident as I sought to shape an essay that would provide a critical perspective on the time–value implications of such an event, I would have both to locate Freeman's insights in a broader field of events and to heed Agnew's identity as a black athlete (the latter in part because discrimination blocked the entry of black athletes into professional sports for decades, so that the appearance of a Ray Agnew involves a temporal lag). Two kinds of phenomenology therefore had to be addressed. One involved the historically peculiar situation of the contemporary experience of sports, the other the more general experience of the time–value relationships of the present, especially in terms of how those relationships are articulated in the value of particular moving/performing bodies.

The first inquiry-related task, aimed at a critical apprehension of the peculiarity of the present, necessitates a historical genealogy of sport (which is undertaken in the below). The second requires a sorting through of philosophies of the event, with an eye toward a propitious way to characterize the present or what Walter Benjamin called *Jetztzeit* ("now-time")[4] To locate Ray Agnew's performance as an event in now-time, that is, to analyze the event conceptually and critically, implies illuminating the present from an *uncommon* perspective, where I refer to the "uncommon" in anticipation of a philosophical intervention to come, specifically a resistance to Immanuel Kant's commitment to the way events provoke a universal common sense. I suggest that Kant's theorizing of a timeless common sense (a *sensus communis*) obviates a critical appreciation of the specific historical forces at work in alternative historical periods.

Having evoked the idea of the "critical," as well as having challenged the notion of common sense, it became clear that the next theoretical gesture in the composition of the essay required both an appreciation and a critique of

54   TOWARD A CRITICAL ASSESSMENT OF "NOW-TIME"

the master of critique, Immanuel Kant. In the original version of the essay I put that gesture this way:

> Why turn to Kant, who was among other things a philosopher of common sense, when what is sought is an uncommon sense? Although I will argue that Kant's commitment to a universalistic model of thought is ultimately disenabling for thinking the present, I want to argue as well that it is Kant who also creates the conditions of possibility for an uncommon, critical encounter with the present. Kant addressed the relevant question. He asked not only about the certainty of knowledge but also, as Benjamin aptly put it, about "the integrity of an experience that is ephemeral."[5]

The ambiguity in Kant's contribution to a critical analysis inspired an extended reflection on the advantages and disadvantages of Kantian temporality for an understanding of the event, which I include here with only slight modification. In his approach to the integrity of ephemeral experiences, Kant overturned the simplistic narrative of experience that privileges objects. Denying that things in themselves can command the structure of experience, his narrative of understanding has a subject's representing faculty implicated in the constitution of phenomena. And most significantly for treating the event in question, that faculty, in the form of a productive understanding, constitutes phenomena with a sensibility that involves "relations of time."[6] Thus, the Agnew event begins to make sense if we turn to Kant's philosophy of experience, which inaugurates a critical view of the kind of exemplary experience that Freeman describes. Kantian critique (articulated in his First Critique) is initially aimed at asking how it is that an intelligible experience is possible, given our lack of access to things in themselves. By the time he had executed his third critique, he had mobilized a variety of metaphors to figure the role of the faculty of judgment. However, his most persistent figuration is governmental. He suggests that the achievement of intelligibility requires an integration of the various faculties through which phenomena are constituted, with judgment as the mediating mechanism that provides "transitions" among the various domains over which the different faculties exercise their respective legislative authorities.[7]

At a philosophical level, the Kantian construction of experience is critical, both because it recognizes that the raw matter involved in the flow of events does not by itself add up to a meaningful experience—what is required is what Kant calls a subject engaged in a "representational activity"[8]—and because that representational activity does not achieve a natural closure. The (nonclosural) narrative structure of the Kantian account of experience (presented most comprehensively in his Third Critique, but also developed elsewhere, especially in his Anthropology) is as follows: First there is "organic sensation";[9] however,

TOWARD A CRITICAL ASSESSMENT OF "NOW-TIME"

because sensation generates a disordered set of disparate perceptions, the cognitive faculty becomes activated to order them. Sense perception is prior to an integrated understanding: "sense perceptions certainly precede perceptions of the understanding."[10] It is the stage in which the subject is merely affected by the world. There follows an "understanding," as the cognitive faculty "joins perceptions and combines them under a rule of thought by introducing order into the manifold."[11]

Yet this active aspect of perception has not finished its task until it universalizes itself and goes public, where going public is not a process of social communication. The communication part of the narrative of experience is what Kant designates as enlightenment at the level of the subject, whose consciousness is engaged in reflection. On reflection, the judging faculty of taste contains the assumption of a "universal voice," which is an "idea" whose confirmation must be postponed.[12] Finally, because that same reflecting faculty contains a prior estimate of its universal communicability,[13] the movement of reflective consciousness gives rise to the public sphere (in a strictly formal sense) in that what begins with matter and is then given form ultimately becomes common or social. The ultimate part of the narrative is the movement of what Kant calls a "universal communicability," which he says is something that "everyone expects and requires from everyone else."[14]

The enlightenment achieved in this Kantian narrative is a process by which the subject, as a form of reflective consciousness, becomes larger than experience. Throughout his three critiques, Kant's solution to the *aporias* of experience is to make the subject larger than the world. That enlargement is effected by letting go of the sensible world: The subject's experience realizes its universality and communicability, Kant states, by virtue of the subject's "letting go the element of matter,"[15] thereby accomplishing *"enlarged* thought."[16] Kant's narrative of experience is a story of judgment, which moves the subject toward a *sensus communis* "without the mediation of a concept"[17] and without actual social communication. Instead of an expansion involving communicative dissemination, what increases is the size and coherence of the subject's comprehension.

We have to look elsewhere in Kant's writings to discover social as opposed to cognitive expansion. The social analogue to the individual enlightenment narrative is available in Kant's political writings. His hoped-for global enlightenment is a process that is structurally homologous with the process of enlargement he attributes to the enlightened subject. Just as the individual process of enlightenment aims, through the exercise of the faculty of judgment, to produce a harmony among the various spheres of the intellect and thereby achieve experience that is universalizable and universally communicable, the publicity achieved by important events (an exemplar for Kant is the French Revolution) must lead to a globally shared experience and ultimately a moral

56   TOWARD A CRITICAL ASSESSMENT OF "NOW-TIME"

sensus communis, embodying a global harmony. People everywhere, reading the "signs of the times," would move, Kant proposed toward a universal, cosmopolitan tolerance:

> The peoples of the earth . . . have entered in varying degrees into a universal community, and it has developed to the point where a violation of rights in *one* part of the world is felt *everywhere*.[18]

Kant's reading of the "signs of the times" was influenced both by a current event, the French Revolution, and a more general, teleological commitment about the historical tendency of humanity: his prognostication that it was moving toward a more peaceful epoch. To discern a moral purpose in history, he thought, it is necessary to read historical signs, in particular to search for an important event, which would allow us to conclude that "mankind is improving."[19]

Kantian temporality is thus divided into two structurally isomorphic enlightenment stories, one at the level of the subject and one at the level of international society. To what extent does the Kantian story of experience at both levels fit the event in question? Certainly, Ray Agnew's event, both the on-field performance and its potential futurity as a highlight on sports television, is public. And the temporality of experiencing the event more or less fits the Kantian enlightenment narrative. There is the raw experience (a large body in motion), then there is the imposition of form on the experience (it results in a score that is calculated in a way that integrates it within the prescribed protocols of the sport), and finally, because it involves a performance whose singularity stands out, it becomes (barely) appropriate for summarizing the action in subsequent publicity (it can be featured on televisual and printed media with almost global distribution). Just as certainly, however, Kant's mental formalism—his story of the individual subject's enlightenment through enlargement, which characterizes the later stages of the event within Kantian temporality—is inadequate for treating how the event achieves meaning and value, commonly or uncommonly. Moreover, Kant's model of enlightenment at the social level hardly allows for an appreciation of how the description of the event can produce a critical reading of modernity.

Leaving aside for the moment the uncommon sense needed to capture the event as a political insight, by which I mean the sense in which one can recognize what is special about today as opposed to yesterday (as regards the control implications of the spatiotemporality of sports), the Kantian reliance on mental faculties and his construction of the public sphere based on a shared mentality fail to adequately illuminate the event's intelligibility. "We" (sports fans) know what Mike Freeman means; we can share his coding of the event-as-experience, not because of a shared structure of apprehension, in which time is internal to our mentality, but because familiar *practices* of temporality govern the event.

Such practices shape the organization of sports, of media, and of our structures of sociality in general. To the extent that we experience an event together as the same kind of event—although there are certainly diverse cultures of reception—we do so because of the way a complex set of spatiotemporal practices, which articulate the rhythms of our present life world, shape the event and its reception. Furthermore, the more social dimension of Kant's model of enlightenment, his conception of the effects of reading the signs of the times, cannot render the event in critical political terms because the boundaries of events is mediated by structures and technologies of dissemination, not merely by perceiving faculties, made coherent by the exercise of judgment.

Nevertheless, while Kant's notion of a *sensus communis* is ultimately cognitive and formal rather than social and cultural, failing to account for the complex process by which experiences are encoded in general and how they are reinflected critically by those who seek to render them from different angles of vision, his introduction of a critical attitude toward modernity remains instructive. By asking what is special about the present, he provided an avenue for locating the value of Ray Agnew's performance in a more critical horizon of contemporary values.

ALTERNATIVES TO KANTIAN TEMPORALITY

Having addressed what is gained versus lost with respect to a comprehension of the Agnew event within the Kantian framework of judgment, the next compositional step is to suggest a more adequate philosophical framing. There are two contemporary thinkers, Michel Foucault and Gilles Deleuze, who are edified by Kant's contribution to critique but depart from Kantian philosophy in ways relevant to my analysis. In the case of Foucault, the relevant thought vehicle is his genealogical approach to the events of the present. In the case of Deleuze, the vehicle is a demonstration of the way that contemporary cinema provides a mode of thought about time and events that encodes the peculiarities of the present. Both thinkers are influenced by Nietzsche's insistence that access to an uncommon sense derives not from the way consciousness legislates but from what can be discerned from creative conceptual practices. Accordingly they both resist Kant's commitment to a universalistic legislative power inherent in the shared common sense of mental faculties and instead heed Nietzsche's attack on the canonical philosophical tradition, which has yielded a mode of thinking merely able "to take everything that has hitherto happened and been valued, and make it clear, distinct, intelligible and manageable."[20] In short, both Nietzsche-inspired thinkers resist institutionalized modes of intelligibility. What must therefore be the next step in the analysis are the specifics of what they contribute to a critical perspective on the event.

THE FOUCAULDIAN GLOSS ON THE EVENT

To situate the contrast between Foucault's and Kant's way of framing events for purposes of achieving a philosophically adequate basis for the analysis, we have to heed Kant's political writings in which his philosophical search for a way to capture experience is rendered through a specific set of commentaries on what for him were contemporary events. Here, Heidegger is helpful in his analysis of the grammar with which Kant posed questions. As I note in Chapter 1, to analyze a theorist, one must heed the *form*—grammar, figuration, narrative structure, etc.—of the theorist's thinking, not merely its objects of analysis. As Heidegger puts it, grammatically speaking, Kant changed the question from "What is a thing?" to "Who is man?" That is, Kant's philosophical revolution is a change in focus from the object of experience to the universally shared subjective structure of apprehension.[21] Yet at the same time, in his political writings, Kant deployed his approach to value and judgment on his own historical period. Shifting from a universalistic concern with subjective experience to historical specificity, he sought a politically perspicuous understanding of his historical moment. Thus, with one mind, he constructed a universalistic, timeless narrative, while with another, he resisted that universalistic narrative and operated at the level of the historical example.[22]

Kant's attention to his own historical time is especially evident in his text on enlightenment, where, as Foucault suggests, "he is not seeking to understand the present on the basis of a totality or of a future achievement. He is looking for difference: What difference does today introduce with respect to yesterday."[23] Instead of encouraging a transcendental attitude toward value, which encourages us to ask *what* it is, given how subjects can, in a universalistic sense, make experience coherent, Kant ultimately sets the stage for a "historico-critical attitude."[24] As Foucault summarizes the implications, Kant's specific question about the significance of his time and place

> entails an obvious consequence: that criticism is no longer to be practiced in the search for formal structures with universal value, but rather as a historical investigation into the events that have led us to constitute ourselves and to recognize ourselves as subjects of what we are doing, thinking, saying.[25]

The consequence entailed is therefore a reorientation of approaches to value and intelligibility. A critical approach to those questions asks about the modalities of value and meaning, about how valued aspects of life are shaped and represented, and about the time of the shaping and expression— in short, about *when* a difference with respect to value and meaning is articulated.

In Foucault's genealogical frame the "events" that have (for example) produced the modern body, as it is understood in institutionalized interpretations, are arbitrary. Foucault, like Kant, rejects the iconic thing in itself, but rather than displacing the privileging of the thing with a "productive understanding," responsible for the shape and temporal extension of phenomena, Foucault substitutes a genealogical practice of historical sensibility. His history of sensibility substitutes "the haphazard play of domination"[26] for a model in which what exists arises from a (Kantian) cognitively internal progressive process of discovery as understandings become historically enlarged.

To render Foucault's genealogical perspective relevant to the sporting event with which the analysis began, we have to turn to a genealogy of the sporting experience. Ray Agnew's slowly moving body is not something that the evolution of wisdom can discover; it is "slow" on the basis of the ways in which particular media, articulated with various other modern institutions, affect the duration of representations. Seeing the body and the interpretations imposed on its motions as a product of complex structures of power and authority is afforded by a genealogical reading of the history of bodies and the spatiotemporalities in which they are situated.

It should be noted as well that this way of seeing bodies in motion implies a different answer to the question, "What is critique?"[27] from that supplied by Kant. For the Kantian concern with knowledge and legitimation, Foucault substitutes a concern with "power and eventualization."[28] Paying attention to what he thinks German critical thought has neglected, "the coercive structure of the signifier,"[29] Foucault locates political effects in imbalances among forces, such that events achieve their intelligibility at the expense of alternative modes of intelligibility. To examine "eventualization"[30] is therefore to inquire into the "mechanisms of coercion"[31] that hover around the contemporary coding of events as experience. That Foucauldian focus encourages us to locate Agnew's performance as a peculiarly contemporary event, shaped by the forces now controlling the sporting experience, which can be retrieved critically by considering a genealogy of sports.

A BRIEF GENEALOGY OF THE EXPERIENCE OF SPORTS

If we heed both the Kantian critical approach to the present and Foucault's reorientation of the question of critique, we can deepen our appreciation of the power-related temporality of sports. The first step must involve a focus on the temporal legacy of sports. What we now regard as sports evolved from what were once regarded as "pastimes." Although there are various different places at which the narrative could begin in order to locate the significant ruptures that distinguish today's sporting experiences, the departure of sport from "ritual"[32] and from sport's more ludic dimensions stand out. For the former, the practices of the ancient Greeks provide an exemplary initiating venue, while for the latter, one would do well by investigating the changing balance of forces between play and display that Johan Huizinga famously observed. Writing at roughly midcentury, Huizinga argued that "with the increasing systematization and regimentation of sport, something of the pure play-quality is inevitably lost."[33]

We need not develop a historically extended genealogy to capture the critical implications of the Agnew event. We can restrict our attention to the relatively recent historical dynamics that Huizinga had in mind. The "systematization and regimentation" of which he spoke have been grouped and summarized by Norbert Elias as "sportization,"[34] a historical process through which leisure time activities, whose structures had been controlled by (nonprofessional) participants, became subject to various rules and regulations, which altered their structures and the conditions shaping participation eligibility. Elias points out that the current strictures on duration, participation, and venue resulted from all the forces associated with the commercialization of modern life, with time control and budgeting as the most significant dimensions.

The temporal dimensions of the sports themselves came to be experienced in the context of the temporal practices of spectators, as the time for watching sporting events expanded with changes in the structures of work and leisure. In the earlier part of the twentieth century, sports had their seasons, and spectators came to associate their trips to various sporting arenas with the time of year as well as with the leisure time of the weekend. However, the weekend as a structuring time of experience is a relatively recent invention. Parallel to a history of the sportization of pastimes is the historical production of the sporting spectator who emerged as the result of two historic victories. The first was the victory of secular authorities over church authorities. Over approximately three centuries, Puritanism and other religious assemblages that sought to preserve nonworking times for religious observance lost out to the pressures from political leaders, entrepreneurs, and the population at large to institutionalize a weekend in which leisure and sporting activities and spectatorship became dominant.[35] But the weekend itself could only achieve its temporal specificity as leisure after a second kind of victory, the historic victory of labor to shorten the working week. In sum, "although play and games have been part of every known society, leisure institutions as a segregated part of life available to the masses required a change in both organizational and cultural values."[36]

Without dwelling on all of the recent changes associated with the commercialization of sport and the proliferation of the various commodities—both things and persons associated with this stage—the role of media has to be considered as primary. Two analysts of the sport–media relationship make that

TOWARD A CRITICAL ASSESSMENT OF "NOW-TIME"

point unequivocally: "The single most dominant influence on the way sport is experienced in American society is that of the mass media, particularly television."[37] Recalling Ray Agnew's (slowly) hurtling body, one might say that for a relatively brief moment, *he* had the game under control. However, if Lever and Wheeler's attribution about the dominance of television in the production of the sporting experience is correct, the issue of Agnew's control over the game and, indeed, over his own moving body at other moments becomes more complex.

It is certainly the case that television broadcast of professional sports has displaced other forms of institutional control over nonwork time. It was a sign of the times, for example, when an ESPN's advertisement for its Sunday football game (in the 1980s) showed Oakland Raiders' cornerback Lester Hayes kneeling in a prayerful pose in the Los Angeles Coliseum accompanied by the lines: "Join our Congregation every Sunday for an inspirational experience." The ad plays with an interesting anachronism. The "Congregation" will not physically congregate in church or at the game; it consists rather of remote viewers watching, for the most part within the confines of their separate dwellings. And, of course, the substitution of sports viewing for church attendance (as well as live stadium attendance) has economic correlates. The secularization of formerly religiously affiliated colleges has led among other things to more influence over the symbolism of the schools by sport shoe manufacturers than by denominational religious leaders.

The influence of sports clothing manufacturers is, of course, closely tied to the media–college sports relationship. At the college level, the importance of revenues from television has skewed athletic programs toward a heavy emphasis on athletic recruitment and has altered the goals of the sports program. A winning season must include postseason participation; the necessary recruitment involved in the success of a collegiate sports program requires the chance of a postseason appearance in a bowl or tournament. A college team must be "bowl-bound" to be "telegenic" and thereby be able to raise the revenues and acquire the talent to have its program remain competitive, hence its susceptibility to inducements to exclusive sports clothing and shoe contracts. The media-related economic forces behind sports publicity now have a more pervasive effect than the older forms of social publicity, religious and political, that participated in shaping the social body.

If we go back to the Kantian model of experience, we can recognize that the ultimate stage, that of publicity, must be understood differently from what is implied in Kant's notion of expanding shared cognition. The conditions of possibility for publicity involve a complex organization of space, time, economic value, and ultimately social meaning that shape the prior stages of how events are experienced at the level of cognition. The mere matter—moving bodies— and the more immediate consequences of those bodies in motion (the question of which moves count as valuable contributions) are significantly affected by the structures of publicity.

For example, football and basketball are among the sports that have changed their rules to hold the interest of present and remote spectators. And unregulated moves *in* such sports by players are affected by the future publicity of the contest. Accordingly, a professional basketball player, Scottie Pippen of the Chicago Bulls, when asked during a postgame interview why he had not contested an opponent's shot at a particular moment in the contest, responded that he did not want his futile defensive gesture to be a postgame highlight. At that moment, Pippen, a black athlete functioning in a media-inspired, commercial environment, had seized momentary control over his value by controlling his movements. Similarly, as Giants' tackle Ray Agnew, another black athlete, hurtled toward the end zone, his movement and the value that would result were under his control, even though the ultimate value of the experience, which would include its potential for postgame exposure, was not. The compelling value questions are therefore condensed in Ray Agnew's run. How are the power implications of the time-value relationship, immanent in moving black athletic bodies, to be mapped, and furthermore, how does an approach to this question help us understand "now-time" more generally?

To approach those questions, we have to broaden our gaze so that it takes in what precedes, as well as what follows from, a particular set of movements. More specifically, to appreciate more critically the relationship between moving African American bodies and value, one must extend the game not only into its futurity in media reproductions but also backward into the dynamics of recruitment and beyond that analyze the activities engendered by the search for "black gold"[38] being mined by the sports establishment, from high school to professional levels. Recognizing that the value of the black athlete extends from the games and their media representations to the marketing of game-related products—Michael Jordan was, at one point, arguably the most globally recognized marketing icon as well as athlete[39] (aspects of his uniform style persist)—we must pursue the implications of how various forces that feed off games also participate in inducing movement and producing containment of moving bodies in the process of collecting them.

Viewed from the perspective of potential professional athletes, the temptation to dream of a professional athletic career, no matter how the odds are stacked against success, is obvious. And given the enormous gap between black social mobility, in general, and the relative successes of black athletes in sports, the dream of a successful athletic career energizes the sporting play of many young black males in the poor neighborhoods of U.S. cities. Athletic success is seen as a "last shot,"[40] as a way out. The effects of those dreams, that is, the mobilization of the bodies that they evince, are portrayed in Steve James, Feeder Marx, and Peter Gilbert's film version (1994; and in Ben Joravsky's

TOWARD A CRITICAL ASSESSMENT OF "NOW-TIME"

subsequent book version, 1995) of *Hoop Dreams*, which follows the high school basketball careers of Arthur Agee and William Gates, two gifted players from a Chicago housing project. The emphasis here is on the film rather than the book version of the story because in important respects the cinematic practice—the assemblage of camera shots in *Hoop Dreams*—captures both the motion requirements of the game of basketball and the social mobility requirements for athletic and monetary success imposed on Arthur and William, the primary personae of the docudrama. However, to understand how cinematic practice relates to such movement, we must preface a consideration of the film with a treatment of the intimate relationship between cinematic time/movement and modernity. This requires a consideration of another gloss on Kant, that of Gilles Deleuze.

THE DELEUZIAN GLOSS

Like Foucault, Deleuze extracts himself from Kant patiently, giving him his due at each juncture. From the point of view of the problem of temporality, Deleuze recognizes that Kant's contribution, beyond introducing a more active subject, involves the introduction of "time into thought."[41] Because for Kant time is not intrinsic to the world but rather to the productive understanding, Deleuze credits him with supplying a resistance to a progressive model of history. Understanding is a constitutive event, not a form of recognition of events that preexist the modalities of their conceptual capture. Nevertheless, Deleuze finds it necessary not only to depart from the Kantian formalism, where time is intrinsic to a universalizing mental faculty, but also from the Kantian emphasis on productive understanding as a mode of *representation*. For Deleuze, one constitutes events politically, not merely cognitively. Elaborating on the necessity for leaving Kant's emphasis on epistemology behind, Deleuze notes,

> We must then break with the long habit of thought which forces us to consider the problematic as a subjective category of our knowledge or as an empirical moment which would indicate only the imperfection of our method and the unhappy necessity for us not to know ahead of time—a necessity which would disappear once we acquire knowledge.[42]

Events have no determined actuality for Deleuze; they are formed neither in the world nor by structures of subjectivity. Rather, they have a virtual structure that is never captured in any particular determination.[43] Because they offer no natural points of division, they emerge as a result of an imposition. But what is involved in those impositions in which the actuality of the event emerges? It is not as Kant would have it the imposition of a universalizing intellect.

64 TOWARD A CRITICAL ASSESSMENT OF "NOW-TIME"

It is rather the imposition of what Deleuze and Guattari call "order-words."[44] Temporally, at the level of the virtual, the event is continuous. For example, bodies grow old. But for a given actualization of the body, there must be specific impositions, expressed in such order-words as "you are no longer a child."[45]

Whereas Kant supplies a universalizing cognitive status to the ordering faculty or intellect, Deleuze and Guattari's order-words should be understood normatively rather than cognitively; they function within a pragmatics and politics of language. To resist a cognitive rendering of the temporality of events-as-actualizations is to resist "dogmatism." But Deleuze's resistance to dogmatism is different from Kant's. The dogmatic image of thought, according to Deleuze, is the very idea that "thought has an affinity with the true."[46] Thought for Deleuze is not aimed toward a Kantian *sensus communis*, it is aimed at achieving an uncommon sense. It does not seek "the truth" but seeks instead to provide vehicles for experiencing the world differently. Accordingly, thought expresses events rather than representing them. Deleuze rejects a commitment to the epistemic authority of common sense because it rests on the presupposition that "thought is the natural exercise of a faculty," which has an "affinity with the true" if we assume "*good will on the part of the thinker* and an *upright nature on the part of thought*."[47] Deleuze regards this exercise of "common sense" as recognition rather than thought; it, along with "good sense" (the contribution of faculties), constitutes the doxa, the unreflected—on acceptance of the world of actualities that exist in everyday discourses.

As a contribution to critical political thinking, then, Deleuzian "thought," insofar as it resists representation and mere recognition ("common sense"), supplies an *uncommon sense*. By supplying conceptualizations that (in Deleuze's terms) counter-actualize events, it situates us in a place to both map and treat critically the current forces shaping relations of time and value. The question becomes one of the vehicles for the production of thinking-as-uncommon-sense, and among the places toward which Deleuze turns for critical thought vehicles is cinema, which, in its modern realization, is a mode of articulation that thinks the politics of time and value. It is a critical and disruptive thought enterprise rather than a mechanism of representation that unreflectively participates in the production of a *sensus communis*.

STILLS AND MOVEMENT IMAGES

According to Deleuze, as cinema evolved the mobile camera ultimately led to the "emancipation of the viewpoint" and, most significantly, to a privileging of time over space. With the use of montage (among other

TOWARD A CRITICAL ASSESSMENT OF "NOW-TIME"

cinematic practices, e.g., the depth of focus shot), "[t]he shot would then stop being a spatial category and become a temporal one."[48] In Deleuze's neo-Kantianisms experiencing events critically in the present is afforded not by the exercise of a faculty of judgment, which can integrate the domains controlled by disparate mental faculties, but by a cinematic apparatus. Deleuze notes that whereas the meaning of movement in antiquity involved the idea of transition—"movement refers to intelligible elements, Forms or Ideas which are themselves eternal or immobile"[49]—modernity is an epoch without privileged instants. Movement is understood as a matter of assembling "any-instant-whatever."[50] Therefore, contemporary cinema enacts modernity's construction of time and movement as "the system which produces movement as a function of any-instant-whatever that is, as a function of equidistant instants, selected so as to create an impression of continuity."[51]

The modern cinema of the "time-image" according to Deleuze constituted a break; it is a way of reading events that is more critical than mere perception.[52] As long as the camera merely followed action, the image of time was indirect, presented as a consequence of motion. But the new "camera consciousness" is no longer defined by the movements it is able to follow. Now, "even when it is mobile, the camera is no longer content to follow the character's movement."[53] It employs the time image to think cinematically about the time and value of the present. The homology that Deleuze posits between cinematic practice and our (critically thoughtful) experience of time movement of the present—"thinking in cinema through cinema"[54]—is best observed when we distance ourselves from the present both historically and cinematically, the former to make the present peculiar and the latter to observe how a time-sensitive camera consciousness can render any period critically. Accordingly, to launch such an observation as the next compositional step, I sought a more static historical epoch and analyzed a cinematic practice capable of capturing it. For that, I selected Stanley Kubrick's film version of Thackeray's *Barry Lyndon*, having noticed his tendency to fix his camera and use mostly framing shots to let the action unfold within a static sociopolitical culture, the "estate space" of English aristocracy in the eighteenth century, a period in which the order was almost wholly ascriptive in structure and thought to be a creation of divine will.[55] Various mechanisms were in place to defeat attempts to alter or penetrate that order. And, to complete the contrast, Kubrick, cinematically sensitive to the fixity of the eighteenth-century order not only immobilized his camera but also made his scenes more painterly and photographic than cinematic. In constructing a camera consciousness that fit the period, he explicitly acknowledged his understanding of the social-cinematic homology by referring to his cinematographer (in the credits) as a "photographer."

BARRY LYNDON

The novel on which the film is based, William Makepeace Thackeray's *The Memoirs of Barry Lyndon, Esq.*, derives much of its critical edge from the narrative voice of its protagonist. Observing a tale told by Barry Lyndon that does not ring true, readers are encouraged to reflect on the boundary between truth and fiction. Making problematic the interrelationship of text and reader while at the same time satirizing the seriousness with which one would-be social climber faces the value of heritage or pedigree, the novel distances the reader from its protagonist's world. Written a century after its subject matter, the tale seems as much directed toward illuminating the ambiguities of telling tales and distinguishing that telling from history as it is involved in illuminating a particular historical period.[56]

In Kubrick's film version, "the power of the false"[57] is also enlisted but in the service of a different aim. The protagonist's voice is displaced from narrative control by a narrative voice of one of Barry Lyndon's contemporaries, and more important, the oral text is superseded by the visual, cinematic text. Rather than being subjected to an unreliable narrator, the film viewers experience what Deleuze calls a "crystalline regime," which he juxtaposes to an organic one.[58] In organic film narration, the objects of cinematic attention are assumed to be independent. The camera simply follows the action. Organic narration is therefore "truthful narration," even if it follows the action of a fictional story.[59]

In contrast, in crystalline film narration, cinematic attention creates its objects. Chronological time—that which is imposed by following the actors—is displaced by "non-chronological time," and movements, which are "necessarily 'abnormal' are "essentially false."[60] The experience of the viewers is shaped by the ensemble of camera shots. Instead of composing movement images to treat the tensions explicitly acknowledged by the actors, the camera creates time images that respond to the critical thinking of the cinematic apparatus rather than the particular forms of awareness of the actors. As for what kind of awareness is offered to the viewer, who is situated in the present, Kubrick's camera renders the eighteenth century from the point of view of the present. The scenes are situated to suggest that while modernity is cinematic, the eighteenth century was more painterly or photographic, which implies that modernity is to the eighteenth century as the film genre is to those of painting and photography.

Frank Cossa provides supporting insights to such a comparison. Discerning the pervasiveness of art-historical referents of eighteenth-century life in the film, he writes,

> Lady Lyndon (Marisa Berenson) . . . is dressed and coiffed like the ladies
> in Gainsborough portraits . . . the famous candlelit interiors in the film
> resemble those of Joseph Wright of Derby. . . . The crystal grey tonalities in many of the daylight interiors call to mind the genre paintings of

both Chardin and Greuze [and] when a groom trots out a horse that Barry (Ryan O'Neal) will buy for his son, groom and horse strike a pose reminiscent of George Stubbs' portraits of famous racehorses of the day.[61]

Insofar as Kubrick is establishing a homology between technologies of representation and modalities of sociability, it is inapposite to complain, as one reviewer did, that *Barry Lyndon* is "a triumph of technique over any human content."[62] It is precisely Kubrick's cinematic "technique" that constitutes the content. The deceptions of Kubrick's *Barry Lyndon* are less significant than the aristocratic practices of time and space that the camera work constructs while Redmond Barry (Ryan O'Neill), an Irishman with a questionable pedigree, attempts to insinuate himself in English estate society.

The camera presents that society with an emphasis on its forms and slow, ritualistic pacing. Even the battle scenes, which on the basis of body count are very bloody, come across as rigidly organized death rituals. What one observes is an order that preserves its static structures of privilege by absorbing and defeating movement. Kubrick's camera articulates that stasis as his film, with framing and zoom shots, explores massed armies, large estates, ornate interiors, and wall paintings, capturing them with a series of *tableaux vivants*. Through the ensemble of shots, the animate is continually inhibited by the inanimate.

The estates in *Barry Lyndon* are shot frontally; they are made to appear as they do in eighteenth-century engravings (Figure 2.1). Pedigree is represented through various still portraits. And in the midst of the stasis and restraint of eighteenth-century English society, an ambitious Barry Lyndon tries to move in and upward,

FIGURE 2.1
Estate image. Source: Stanley Kubrick, *Barry Lyndon*, Hawk Films (1975).

aiming to achieve an aristocratic status. However, because he is ill attuned to his new social milieu, he fails "to acquire aristocratic restraint,"[63] an inability that ultimately defeats him. Unable to manage the slow, ritualistic decorum of the society to which he seeks admission, Barry Lyndon is finally stopped by a bullet in a duel with his stepson, Lord Bullington, and is physically immobilized after he loses the wounded leg. Thereafter, his body mimes the structural inhibitions to status movement.

All the structural elements leading to Barry Lyndon's failure are captured cinematographically. Most of the shots are taken with a static camera. While the framing shots and zooms are wholly appropriate for representing the stasis of the social order, even the use of montage reflects a lack of motion in that order. Rather than conveying action in the form of movement through time, montage in Barry Lyndon is "referential" as many scenes refer to earlier ones.[64] For example, dueling scenes occur at the beginning and end of the film, the latter recalling the former. Highly stylized scenes of kissing and embracing at many points throughout the film, more than a dozen of which involve Barry Lyndon, have the effect of demonstrating the perseverance of ceremonial forms rather than the social progress of the protagonist. Although Barry Lyndon does manage to rise up the social ladder temporarily, ultimately his inability to adopt the correct gestural economy leads to his fall. He fails to fit correctly within the frames of his century, well represented figuratively in a scene in which the film-as-still-pictures focuses on Barry Lyndon's attempt to acquire pictures (at exorbitant prices according to the voice-over narration). At a point at which he ambles slowly through a room with many elegantly framed paintings, the room's array of portraits seems to reflect the spatiotemporal zone, English estate society, in which he is striving for a peerage (Figure 2.2).

FIGURE 2.2
Room full of portraits. Source: Stanley Kubrick, *Barry Lyndon*, Hawk Films (1975).

TOWARD A CRITICAL ASSESSMENT OF "NOW-TIME"   69

Although Barry Lyndon has married into wealth—to Lady Honoria Lyndon (Marisa Berenson)—the film shows that in the eighteenth-century aristocratic world, money alone will not produce the desired status movement. Movement and time are ordered by a moral economy that helps preserve the connection between birth and fortune. Nothing testifies better to that static arrangement than a scene in which the aristocratic Bullington family, into which Barry Lyndon has married, is going over its accounts. Seated with them is their friend and confidante, the Reverent Runt, who is beside Lady Lyndon, along with Lord Bullington, Barry's stepson, the rightful heir, while she signs her bills in a *tableau vivant*, captured by a still camera.

Nevertheless, Kubrick's immobilized camera does not immobilize thought. It participates in providing a politics of time. For example, the frequent resort to a depth-of-field shots, in which current action is unfolding in front of enduring residences, ancestral paintings, and managed estate grounds, has the effect of showing those things that have time on their side as the more effectual background against which the mere striving motion of a Barry Lyndon is futile.[65] More generally, as Deleuze points out, even when a shot remains immobile, it can fracture the illusion that space is wholly separate from time, a mere container of actions and the illusion that time simply chronologically records the process of evoking and resolving the tensions, which are explicitly acknowledged by those who participate in them.[66] The camera has access to what the characters do not, a thinking of time not in terms of its derivation from the chronology of action but in terms of the juxtapositions necessary to render problematic the forces at work and the intersections of those forces as they emanate from different layers in time.[67] To highlight the homologies between cinematic practice and the forces tied to the temporal structures of historical periods, we need a radical contrast, which is available in the film to which the analysis now turns.

HOOP DREAMS

In contrast with the cinematic forms in Kubrick's *Barry Lyndon*, the documentary film *Hoop Dreams* contains frequent panning and tracking shots as the viewer watches the attempts of Arthur Agee and William Gates to use their basketball skills to escape from their impoverished housing project and realize their shared dream of playing professional basketball. Speed rather than restraint and decorum is demanded of them. To appreciate the prescribed movements they must achieve to realize their goals, we have to be attentive not only to their particular biographies, on which the film focuses, but also to the movement demands of modernity in general. The opening shots, while the credits are run, show the rapid motion demands of the present. Chicago's moving traffic—trains, cars, trucks, and buses—crisscross our view of the city.

70   TOWARD A CRITICAL ASSESSMENT OF "NOW-TIME"

The movement of vehicles with which the film begins is the beginning of a camera consciousness that operates throughout *Hoop Dreams* to provide a gloss on the politics of the collection of African American bodies for professional sports. Because the camera consciousness deployed in *Hoop Dreams* is very different from its realization in *Barry Lyndon*, it supplies a political reading of contemporary time–value relationships when so juxtaposed.

What must be understood to situate that reading is that power manifested itself differently in the twentieth century from the way it did in the eighteenth. Centuries after the French Revolution, the structures of domination had changed their modalities. If we recognize that the French Revolution was the most dramatic assault on the aristocracy's management of the stasis governing the European society of the eighteenth century, Paul Virilio's gloss on the events beginning in 1789 become especially apropos. He asserts that the revolution, far from ending subjection, in general, was rather a revolution against the *"constraint to immobility."*[68] Thereafter, with the birth of the modern state, the *"freedom of movement"*[69] of the early days of the revolution had been turned by the exercise of state power to an *"obligation to mobility,"*[70] as the state involved itself in, among other things, the recruitment and mobilization of a citizen army.

Of course, modernity's commercial forces have been at least as involved in the mobilization of bodies as the state and certainly more so in the case of the movement that nourishes sporting franchises. What we have to add to this picture of mobilization are the moving frames within which the movements constituting modernity are witnessed. The motion of the sporting bodies—from recruitment to performance and subsequent publicity—are to be understood in the context of the way that motion is apprehended through modern media, which Oliver Wendell Holmes well understood. Observing the early photographic stages of the cinematic society, he glossed modernity-as-experience in an idiom that summons Kant's categories but appropriately revised the relationship between the form-imposing faculties and the matter they apprehend:

> Form is henceforth divorced from matter. In fact matter as a visible object is of no great use any longer, except as the mold on which form is shaped. Give us a few negatives of a thing worth seeing, taken from different points of view, and that is all we want of it.[71]

As Holmes recognized, "modernity" is a new kind of structure of experience. The modern city, as a venue of hyper-stimuli, places pressures on the Kantian reliance on faculties that tend toward a universal common sense. Jonathan Crary affirms that observation: "Since Kant . . . part of the epistemological dilemma of modernity has been about the human capacity for synthesis amid fragmentation and atomization of a cognitive field."[72] Whereas Crary's remark renders the issue in Kantian, cognitive terms, we must rather presume (as Crary does in other observations) that the experience to which he refers is owed to technologies of representation and reproduction.

Whatever the relative contributions of human cognition and technology-induced forms in the constitution of experience, there is a strong homology between the structure of cinematic representation and modern life. No one has recognized that homology more profoundly than Walter Benjamin:

> The film corresponds to profound changes in the apparatus of apperception—changes that are experienced on the scale of private existence by each passerby in big city traffic, and on the scale of world history by each fighter against the present social order.[73]

With Benjamin's insight in mind, we can better appreciate the contemporary experience of sports, both from the point of view of those seeking entry into the rewards of playing for a high level of remuneration and those who watch games and enact their connection with them by buying sports shoes and clothing. Benjamin recognized that as exhibition value displaces ritual value in a variety of contexts,[74] market considerations intervene and wrest control over the meaning of a performance, whether it is enacted in a feature film or a sporting contest.[75]

We are now in a position to locate the value derived from what Virilio called the modernity's "obligation to mobility" as it applies to Arthur Agee and William Gates in *Hoop Dreams*. At a minimum, the contemporary demands on mobility and the correlative demands on "apparatuses of apperception" are so familiar to us it is easy to miss the extent to which *Hoop Dreams* captures the modern experience of sports as much with its camera work as with its storyline. At a thematic level the story has a familiar theme. Arthur and William see their basketball skills as their opportunity to be part of the American dream; they hope to make it all the way into the status of professionals as players in the National Basketball Association (NBA). And because a black recruiter, with contacts in a white private high school with big-time basketball aspirations, has a similar view of their skills, they end up enrolling in the school. The film is, among other things, an ethnography of both the venues in which they reside and those they must traverse and enter in their quest. It effectively maps the spaces and living relationships in their impoverished black neighborhood, in white suburbia, and in the competitive basketball venues of high schools and colleges, all of which participate in the structural recruitment of black athletes.

There is pressure for Arthur and William to move rapidly, not only on the basketball court but also in the process of moving through discordant social spaces. The normalizing pressures that exist within their black neighborhood are quite different from those that structure performances in the white high school they attend after being recruited for their basketball skills. That structural story, told by the camera, can be missed if one simply follows the drama associated with Arthur and William's attempts to achieve the status of professional basketball players.[76] For example, Jillian Sandell's highly politicized reading of the film fails to appreciate how it works because her reading is wholly thematic. The problem of neglecting cinematic form surfaces early in an otherwise effective gloss of the story:

> Spotted by talent scouts when they are 14, Arthur and William are offered scholarships to attend St. Joseph's College—a predominantly white, Catholic private school in suburban Westchester and the alma mater of Detroit Pistons' star, Isaiah Thomas . . . the central conceit of *Hoop Dreams* is whether Arthur and/or William will become "the next Isaiah Thomas." Both boys must get up at 5:30 A.M. to make the three-hour round trip to St. Joseph's . . . and this is a testament to the work ethic and sense of sacrifice that the film valorizes.[77]

Sandell may be correct that the pleasure the film delivers to white audiences derives from their witnessing of a story about two young African Americans seeking a piece of the American dream, but in addition to the "organic narrative," which follows the striving of Arthur and William, is the "crystalline narrative" assembled by the various camera shots. Sandell neglects that narrative because her focus is on representational space rather than cinematically thought time. She notes that the black urban experience provides a *space* for filmmakers to treat issues of cultural life in the ghetto,[78] for example, but fails to treat the way the mobile camera renders movements through space and provides a critical, nonchronological view of time. By cutting from the time of basketball games to the temporalities of family life to the temporalities of the educational process and emphasizing both conjunctures and disjunctions, the camera consciousness in *Hoop Dreams* "invents," in Deleuze's terms, a "transverse continuity of communication" between different temporal layers.[79] Rather than merely representing a sequence of events, the film seizes Arthur and William's experiences and connects them to a politics and ethics of modernity. While it shows spaces and bodies, it thinks time and value.

The film can therefore be seen as an effective event when it is thought of as rendering aspects of mobility rather than merely exploring spaces. If we follow the filming's montage structure, particularly the tracking shots and cuts and juxtapositions, we learn that success is denied to Arthur and William because they cannot move fast enough. On one hand, the American dream, reflected through the promotion of a narrative about playing your way into the NBA, produces an incitement to mobility, but on the other, the need to move rapidly through discordant social spaces obviates the realization of that dream.

There is the travel time required to get to St. Joseph's, there is the difficulty of learning the kind of articulations demanded in the classroom and on the court in dealing with white culture, and there are the academic demands on young men without cultural capital. All those barriers to rapid motion impede their progress (Figures 2.3 and 2.4).

FIGURES 2.3 AND 2.4
Arthur and William, respectively, at St. Josephs. Source: Steve James, *Hoop Dreams*, Kartemquin Films (1994).

74   TOWARD A CRITICAL ASSESSMENT OF "NOW-TIME"

Arthur is also faced with another aspect of time; he is frustrated by his biological clock because he fails to gain height rapidly enough to impress St. Joseph's coach, who ultimately allows his scholarship to be cut to the point where he must drop out of the school. Thereafter, Arthur manages to move rapidly enough through academic space in the city school and on the court to push his inner-city, predominantly black high school to the finals of the state championships. However, all his rapid motion on the court is ultimately inadequate because he is unable to achieve the social mobility necessary to place him in a more visible trajectory through the sporting establishment.

The fate of William Gates, who appears more promising to the white basketball establishment at St. Joseph's, bears a striking resemblance to the fate of Barry Lyndon. William manages to stay at St. Joseph's and is recruited by Marquette University, a major college basketball power, but he is ultimately defeated because a knee injury slows him. Barry Lyndon's loss of his leg is allegorical. *His* immobility reflects the immobility of the aristocratic structure. After his moving fails to penetrate the stasis of eighteenth-century English society, his final immobility is ironic and allegorical. In contrast, William's loss of mobility is substantive; it handicaps him in the race to achieve an NBA level of playing ability. Despite a diminution in his mobility, he shows just enough promise to acquire help from the white establishment in moving over the academic hurdles and manages to qualify for a basketball scholarship. He moves well enough to constitute "black gold," that is, to be a potential resource in the marketing of a basketball program, but the potential is never fully realized.

Most significantly, *Hoop Dreams*'s narrative, conveyed by a cinematic practice, does not at all valorize the "American dream." The framing shots in *Barry Lyndon* are to the structure of power and authority in the eighteenth century as the tracking shots in *Hoop Dreams* are to that structure in modernity. Barry Lyndon, the marginal Irishman without pedigree, is defeated by stasis, while the marginal, black would-be basketball stars, Arthur and William, without cultural and economic capital, are defeated by their inability to get up to speed in modernity's implacable "obligation to mobility." Finally, in terms of the comparison of the cinematic articulation of the way the respective centuries are to be politically thought, while the montage effects in *Barry Lyndon* are referential, serving to underscore the perseverance of static structures, the montage effects in *Hoop Dreams* provide a lesson in the political economy of modern sports. For example, a rapid cut from Arthur watching professional basketball on television to Arthur on the playground seeking to mimic the movement he has seen shows the way the exhibition of sports motivates and thereby mobilizes a would-be star. And equally significant is the cut from scenes of playing basketball and watching basketball to one of the most telling scenes in the film: The camera suddenly captures a group of young black males walking down the street in new, expensive basketball shoes (Figure 2.5). That pool of black gold is far larger than the one containing would-be basketball stars.

TOWARD A CRITICAL ASSESSMENT OF "NOW-TIME"

FIGURE 2.5
The shoe scene on the street. Source: Steve James, *Hoop Dreams*, Kartemquin Films (1994).

NOTES

1. "Time and Value," Institute for Cultural Research, Lancaster University, 10–13 April 1997.
2. See Mike Freeman, "Pontiac, Michigan, Oct. 27: Giants Crush Inept Lions in the Dome," *New York Times*, October 28, 1996, p. B7.
3. See the original article: Michael J. Shapiro, "Toward a Politics of Now-Time: Reading *Hoop Dreams* with Kubrick's *Barry Lyndon*," *Theory & Event* 2: 2 (1998), On the web at: http://muse.jhu.edu.eres.library.manoa.hawaii.edu/article/32511.
4. See Walter Benjamin, "On the Program of the Coming Philosophy," in *Benjamin: Philosophy, History, Aesthetics*, ed. Gary Smith (Chicago: University of Chicago Press, 1989), 1.
5. *Ibid.*
6. Immanuel Kant, *Critique of Pure Reason*, trans. J. M. D. Meiklejohn (London: George Bell and Sons, 1876), 99.
7. See Kant's use of a geopolitical/governmental metaphor to describe the separation of powers and territorial jurisdictions between different cognitive faculties in the introduction to his third critique: *The Critique of Judgment*, trans. James Creed Meredith (Oxford: Clarendon Press, 1952), 12.
8. *Ibid.*, 151.
9. This expression is used in Immanuel Kant, *Anthropology From a Pragmatic Point of View*, trans. Victor Lyle Dowdell (Carbondale: Southern Illinois University Press, 1978), 40.

10. That sequence appears both in Kant's *Critique of Judgment* and in his *Anthropology from a Pragmatic Point of View*.
11. *Ibid.*
12. Kant, *Critique of Judgment*, 56.
13. *Ibid.*, 154.
14. *Ibid.*, 155.
15. *Ibid.*,151.
16. *Ibid.*,152.
17. *Ibid.*, 153.
18. See Immanuel Kant, "Perpetual Peace," in *Political Writings*, trans. H. B. Nisbet (New York: Cambridge University Press, 1991), 107–108.
19. Immanuel Kant, "The Contest of Faculties," in *Political Writings*, 181.
20. The quotation is from Friedrich Nietzsche, *Beyond Good and Evil*, trans. R. J. Hollingdale (Baltimore: Penguin, 1974), # 211.
21. See Martin Heidegger, *What Is a Thing?* trans. W. B. Barton, Jr. and Vera Deutsch (Chicago: Henry Regnery, 1970).
22. As David Lloyd points out, although much of Kant's *Critique of Judgment* was aimed at providing a universalistic and timeless basis for understanding, his approach to judgment was also very much influenced by his reflection on his particular historical location, "the disintegrating post-feudal condition of late eighteenth-century Germany." And, as Lloyd adds, Kant's turn to examples often undercut the universal model of experience he sought to provide. See David Lloyd, "Kant's Examples," *Representations* 28 (1989), 34.
23. Michel Foucault, "What Is Enlightenment?" in *Interpretive Social Science: A Second Look*, eds. Paul Rabinow and William Sullivan (Berkeley: University of California Press, 1987), 159.
24. *Ibid.*, 171.
25. *Ibid.*, 170.
26. Michel Foucault, "Nietzsche, Genealogy, History," in *The Foucault Reader*, ed. Sherry Simon I Paul Rabinow, trans. Donald Bouchard (New York: Pantheon, 1984), 83.
27. See Michel Foucault, "What Is Critique?" in *The Politics of Truth*, eds. Sylvere Lotringer and Lysa Hochroth, trans. Lysa Hochroth (New York: Semiotext(e), 1997), 23–24.
28. *Ibid.*, 59.
29. *Ibid.*, 42.
30. *Ibid.*, 49.
31. *Ibid.*, 50.
32. That history is treated in Allen Guttman, *From Ritual to Record* (New York: Columbia University Press, 1978).
33. Johan Huizinga, *Homo Ludens* (Boston: Beacon Press, 1955), 197.
34. Norbert Elias, "Sport as a Sociological Problem," in *Quest for Excitement*, eds. Norbert Elias and Eric Dunning (Oxford: Basil Blackwell, 1986), 126–149.
35. That process is chronicled in in Denis Brailsford, *Sport, Time, and Society* (New York: Routledge, 1991), 52.
36. The quotation is from Janet Lever and Stanton Wheeler, "Mass Media and the Experience of Sport," *Communication Research* 20 (1993), 126.

37. *Ibid.*, 125.
38. The expression belongs to John Hoberman, *Darwin's Athletes* (New York: Houghton Mifflin, 1996).
39. For an analysis of the Jordan phenomenon, see the monograph issue of the *Sociology of Sports Journal* 13: 1 (1996).
40. See Darcey Frey's ethnography of the aspirations of black athletes and their families in the Coney Island section of Brooklyn: "The Last Shot," *Harpers*, No. 286 (1993), 37–60 and *The Last Shot* (New York: Simon & Schuster, 1994).
41. Gilles Deleuze, *Difference and Repetition*, trans. Paul Patton (New York: Columbia University Press, 1994), 87.
42. Gilles Deleuze, *The Logic of Sense*, trans. Mark Lester (New York: Columbia University Press, 1990), 54.
43. See Gilles Deleuze and Felix Guattari, *What Is Philosophy?*, trans. Hugh Tomlinson and Graham Burchell (New York: Columbia University Press, 1994).
44. *Ibid.*
45. *Ibid.*
46. Deleuze, *Difference and Repetition*, 131.
47. *Ibid.*
48. Gilles Deleuze, *Cinema 1*, trans. High Tomlinson and Barbara Habberjam (Minneapolis: University of Minnesota Press, 1986), 3.
49. *Ibid.*, 4.
50. *Ibid.*
51. *Ibid.*, 5.
52. Gilles Deleuze, *Cinema 2*, trans. Hugh Tomlinson and Robert Galete (Minneapolis: University of Minnesota Press, 1989), 24.
53. *Ibid.*, 23.
54. *Ibid.*, 165.
55. For a treatment of this aspect of estate space see Donald Lowe, *History of Bourgeois Perception* (Chicago: University of Chicago Press, 1982).
56. These observations about the novel have been aided by Robert P. Fletcher's reading of it: "'Proving a Thing Even While You Contradict It': Fictions, Beliefs, and Legitimation in *The Memoirs of Barry Lyndon Esq*," *Studies in the Novel* 27 (1995), 493–514.
57. This part of the analysis is edified by Deleuze's observations on "the powers of the false" in *Cinema 2*, 126–155.
58. Deleuze, *Cinema 2*, 126.
59. *Ibid.*, 127.
60. *Ibid.*, 129.
61. Frank Cossa, "Images of Perfection: Life Imitates Art in Kubrick's *Barry Lyndon*," *Eighteenth Century Life* 19 (1995), 79.
62. The quotation is from Benjamin Ross, "Eternal Yearning," *Sight & Sound* (October, 1995), 42.
63. Cossa, "Images of Perfection," 81.
64. I owe the expression "referential montage" and the insights into its use in various parts of the film to John Engell's analysis: "*Barry Lyndon*, a Picture of Irony," *Eighteenth Century Life* 19 (1995), 83–88.
65. See Deleuze's discussion of the critical thought effects of the depth of field shot: *Cinema 2*, 108ff.

TOWARD A CRITICAL ASSESSMENT OF "NOW-TIME"

66. *Ibid.*, 128.
67. In his analysis of the time-image, Deleuze points out how the camera "instead of composing movement images . . . decomposes the relations in a direct time-image in such a way that all possible movements emerge from it," *Ibid.*, 130.
68. See Paul Virilio, *Speed and Politics*, trans. Mark Polizzotti (New York: Semiotext(e), 2006), 29.
69. *Ibid.*, 30.
70. *Ibid.*
71. Oliver Wendell Holmes, "The Stereoscope and the Stereograph," in *Essays in Photography*, ed. Alan Trachtenberg (New Haven: Leete's Island Books, 1980), 80.
72. Jonathan Crary, "Unbinding Vision: Manet and the Attentive Observer in the Late Nineteenth Century," in *Cinema and the Invention of Modern Life*, eds. Leo Charney and Vanessa R. Schwartz (Berkeley: University of California Press, 1995), 47.
73. Walter Benjamin, "The Work of Art in the Age of Mechanical Reproduction," in *Illuminations*, ed. Hannah Arendt, trans. Harry Zohn (New York: Schocken, 1968), 25.
74. *Ibid.*, 223.
75. *Ibid.*, 231.
76. My characterization of movement through "discordant social spaces" is inspired by the analysis of the disjunctive performance demands on "stone butches" in their movement through the social network by Judith Halberstam, "Lesbian Masculinities: or Even Stone Butches Get the Blues," *Women and Performance* 8 (1996), 61–63.
77. Jillian Sandell, "Out of the Ghetto and into the Marketplace: *Hoop Dreams* and the Commodification of Marginality," *Socialist Review* 25: 2 (1995), 59.
78. *Ibid.*, 57.
79. Deleuze, *Cinema 2*, 123.

REFERENCES

Benjamin, Walter (1968) 'Theses on the Philosophy of History,' in *Illuminations*, ed. Hannah Arendt, trans. Harry Zohn, New York: Schocken, pp. 253–264.
Benjamin, Walter (1968) 'The Work of Art in the Age of Mechanical Reproduction,' in *Illuminations*, ed. Hannah Arendt, trans. Harry Zohn, New York: Schocken, pp. 217–252.
Benjamin, Walter (1989) 'On the Program of the Coming Philosophy,' in *Benjamin: Philosophy, Aesthetics, History*, ed. Gary Smith, Chicago: University of Chicago Press, pp. 1–12.
Brailsford, Denis (1991) *Sport, Time, and Society*, New York: Routledge.
Cossa, Frank (1995) 'Images of Perfection: Life Imitates Art in Kubrick's *Barry Lyndon*,' *Eighteenth Century Life*, Vol. 19 (1), pp. 77–89.
Crary, Jonathan (1995) 'Unbinding Vision: Manet and the Attentive Observer in the Late Nineteenth Century,' in *Cinema and the Invention of Modern Life*, eds. Leo Charney and Vanessa R. Schwartz, Berkeley: University of California Press.
Deleuze, Gilles (1986) *Cinema 1*, trans. High Tomlinson and Barbara Habberjam, Minneapolis: University of Minnesota Press.

TOWARD A CRITICAL ASSESSMENT OF "NOW-TIME"   79

Deleuze, Gilles (1989) *Cinema 2*, trans. Hugh Tomlinson and Robert Galeta, Minneapolis: University of Minnesota Press.

Deleuze, Gilles (1990) *The Logic of Sense*, trans. Mark Lester, New York: Columbia University Press.

Deleuze, Gilles (1994) *Difference and Repetition*, trans. Paul Patton, New York: Columbia University Press.

Deleuze, Gilles and Guattari, Felix (1994) *What is Philosophy?* trans. Hugh Tomlinson and Graham Burchell, New York: Columbia University Press.

Elias, Norbert (1986) 'Sport as a Sociological Problem,' in *Quest for Excitement*, eds. Norbert Elias and Eric Dunning, Oxford: Basil Blackwell, pp. 126–149.

Engell, John (1995) '*Barry Lyndon*, a Picture of Irony,' *Eighteenth Century Life*, Vol. 19 (1), pp. 83–88.

Fletcher, Robert P. (1995) '"Proving a Thing Even While You Contradict It": Fictions, Beliefs, and Legitimation in *The Memoirs of Barry Lyndon Esq*,' *Studies in the Novel*, Vol. 27 (4), pp. 493–514.

Foucault, Michel (1984) 'Nietzsche, Genealogy, History,' in *The Foucault Reader*, ed. Paul Rabinow, trans. Donald Bouchard and Sherry Simon, New York: Pantheon, pp. 76–100.

Foucault, Michel (1987) 'What Is Enlightenment?,' in *Interpretive Social Science: A Second Look*, eds. Paul Rabinow and William Sullivan, Berkeley: University of California Press, pp. 157–176.

Foucault, Michel (1997) 'What Is Critique?,' in *The Politics of Truth*, trans. Sylvere Lotringer and Lysa Hochroth, New York: Semiotext(e), pp. 41–82.

Freeman, Mike (1996) 'Pontiac, Michigan, Oct. 27: Giants Crush Inept Lions in the Dome,' *New York Times*, October 28, 1996, p. B7.

Frey, Darcey (1994) *The Last Shot*, New York: Simon & Schuster.

Guttman, Allen (1978) *From Ritual to Record*, New York: Columbia University Press.

Halberstam, Judith (1996) 'Lesbian Masculinities: or Even Stone Butches Get the Blues,' *Women and Performance*, Vol. 8 (2), pp. 61–73.

Heidegger, Martin (1970) *What is a Thing?*, trans. W. B. Barton, Jr. and Vera Deutsch Chicago: Henry Regnery.

Hoberman, John (1996) *Darwin's Athletes*, New York: Houghton Mifflin.

Holmes, Oliver Wendell (1980) 'The Stereoscope and the Stereograph,' in *Essays in Photography*, ed. Alan Trachtenberg, New Haven: Leete's Island Books, pp. 79–85.

Huizinga, Johan (1955) *Homo Ludens*, Boston: Beacon Press.

Kant, Immanuel (1876) *Critique of Pure Reason*, trans. J. M. D. Meiklejohn, London: George Bell and Sons.

Kant, Immanuel (1952) *The Critique of Judgment*, trans. James Creed Meredith, Oxford: Clarendon Press.

Kant, Immanuel (1978) *Anthropology From a Pragmatic Point of View*, trans. Victor Lyle Dowdell, Carbondale: Southern Illinois University Press.

Kant, Immanuel (1991) 'The Contest of Faculties,' in *Political Writings*, New York: Cambridge University Press, pp. 174–183.

Kant, Immanuel (1991) 'Perpetual Peace,' in *Political Writings*, trans. H. B. Nisbet, New York: Cambridge University Press, pp. 93–108.

Lever, Janet and Wheeler, Stanton (1993) 'Mass Media and the Experience of Sport,' *Communication Research*, Vol. 20 (1), pp. 124–143.

80 TOWARD A CRITICAL ASSESSMENT OF "NOW-TIME"

Lloyd, David (1989) 'Kant's Examples,' *Representations*, No. 28, pp. 34–54.
Lowe, Donald (1982) *History of Bourgeois Perception*, Chicago: University of Chicago Press.
Nietzsche, Friedrich (1974) *Beyond Good and Evil*, trans. R. J. Hollingdale, Baltimore: Penguin.
Ross, Benjamin (1995) 'Eternal Yearning,' *Sight & Sound*, No. 42, pp. 42–43.
Sandell, Jillian (1995) 'Out of the Ghetto and into the Marketplace: *Hoop Dreams* and the Commodification of Marginality,' *Socialist Review*, Vol. 25, pp. 54–66.
Shapiro, Michael J. (1998) 'Toward a Politics of Now-Time: Reading *Hoop Dreams* with Kubrick's *Barry Lyndon*,' *Theory & Event*, Vol. 2 (2), at: http://muse.jhu.edu.eres.library.manoa.hawaii.edu/article/32511.
Virilio, Paul (2006) *Speed and Politics*, trans. Mark Polizzotti, New York: Semiotext(e).

SUGGESTED READING

For More on the Temporality-Event Relationship, See

Brian Massumi, "Perception Attack: Brief on War Time," *Theory & Event* 13 (3) (2010);
Michael J. Shapiro, *Politics and Time: Documenting the Event* (Cambridge, UK: Polity, 2016).

For More on Stanley Kubrick, See

Michel Ciment, *Stanley Kubrick*, trans. Gilbert Adair (New York: Holt, Rinehart and Winston, 1983); Mario Falsetto, *Stanley Kubrick: A Narrative and Stylistic Analysis* (Westport: Greenwood Press, 1994); Vincent LoBrutto, *Stanley Kubrick: A Biography* (New York: Fine Books, 1997); Thomas Allen Nelson, *Kubrick: Inside a Film Artist's Maze* (Bloomington: Indiana University Press, 2000).
Sandro Bernardi, *Le Regard esthetique selon Kubrick* (Vincennes: Presses Universitaires de Vincennes, 1994).
For more on Kant's Third Critique, see Rodolphe Gasché, *The Idea of Form: Rethinking Kant's Aesthetics*; Michael J. Shapiro, *The Political Sublime* (Durham: Duke University Press, 2018).

CHAPTER 3

Resituating Hiroshima

INTRODUCTION: HIROSHIMA'S WILL-HAVE-BEEN

This chapter continues with the temporality theme developed in Chapter 2. Its initial inspiration was an invitation to contribute to a monograph issue of the journal *Thesis Eleven* on the 70th anniversary of the World War II atomic bombings of Hiroshima and Nagasaki. What began as an article migrated into a book on politics and time, an exploration of the temporal grammars through which one can capture the endurance of events. The book's main argument is that an event's endurance is best understood through a future-perfect (often cited as the future-anterior) verb tense, the "will have been."[1] That grammatical choice implies that every event is subject to reinterpretation in light of what comes afterward. Two conceptual tasks occupy the discussion in this version: The first involves bringing theory to a critical focus on events; the second involves analyses of the way cinema can contribute to an event's historical endurance, its openness to continual reinterpretation.

The cinematic dimension of this chapter, to which new material is added from other cinema analyses, focuses on two Hiroshima-related films, the Marguerite Duras–Alain Resnais feature film *Hiroshima Mon Amour* (1959) and Linda Hattendorf's documentary *The Cats of Mirikitani* (2006). Added to those is a video remediation of the Duras–Resnais film, refocusing it on the last Iraq war, and a documentary that treats a more recent bombing atrocity, the drone killings of Pakistani civilians, which was part of the continuing "War on Terror" that the Obama administration inherited from the Bush presidency. Much of the inspiration for the structure of the essay's remediation theme is Rosalyn Deutsche's studies in her *Hiroshima After Iraq: Three Studies in Art and War*, which I referenced in my submission to the monograph issue under the title "The Presence of Hiroshima:

82   RESITUATING HIROSHIMA

Temporality, Plasticity, and Grammar." The aspirational abstract for my submission reads,

> As is made evident in Rosalyn Deutsche's recent book *Hiroshima After Iraq*. Hiroshima keeps returning through the way diverse artistic genres evoke parallels between the bombing of Hiroshima and more recent atrocities. Drawing on Walter Benjamin's concept of temporal plasticity and at the same time heeding the relationship between presence and grammar, this essay will ponder the future anterior of Hiroshima, its continuous will-have-been, as artistic genres continue to restage its significance.

Once underway, the article and the subsequent book chapter emerged with the title "Hiroshima Temporalities" and had become an analysis of the continuing presence of Hiroshima-as-event through the many artistic media genres through which the bombing of Hiroshima has been rendered. To initiate the essay version, I drew on recollections of two media events, one, a feature film I attended and, the other, a television news broadcast I watched (both of which I reprise with slight modification here): In August 1966, I saw two media events that occurred at roughly the same time. The first was shown as "the late show" at the Nippon, a Honolulu movie house that showed Japanese films, a sentimental genre (e.g., stories about beloved elementary school teachers) in the early evening and a (soft) pornography genre around midnight. That evening the late show was Hiroshima native Kaneto Shindo's *Lost Sex*, which features "the Master," Hideo Kanze, a Noh theater director as the protagonist. He has been rendered impotent by the nuclear fallout of the Hiroshima bombing. The film narrative is mainly concerned with his sexual functioning. In an initiating scene, the Master's potency has been regained as he is lying in a hospital bed. It has seemingly been restored by the hand manipulations of a young nurse (the scene is shown while being narrated to the Master's housekeeper in a flashback). While concerning itself with the problem of sexual potency, the film provides a window into one aspect of the adversities that were an immediate legacy of the bombing, the physical and mental traumas that disrupted intimate relations. The story does not end well for the Master. After a failed marriage, when his potency has once again become fugitive, his 37-year-old housekeeper, a war widow, is able briefly to restore his sexual efficacy by staging erotic scenes in which she is the main actor. However, because he misinterprets the stagings (she solicits other seducers to simulate him), he breaks off the relationship out of jealousy, only to learn after her death that the seduction scenes were for his benefit. The film ends with the Master as a lonely, unloved man, watching the snow fall from a window at his mountain residence.

The second media event had a quite different ending. It was a televised showing of *military* potency, a simulated bombing run staged on the August 6 anniversary of the Hiroshima atomic bombing. Featured during a newscast on a local Hawaii television station, the staging's setting was an open field at a military base on the island of Oahu. While a group of military families are seated in temporary bleachers flanking the field, an air force bomber did a flyover and dropped a smoke bomb. As the smoke rose, a voice on installed loudspeakers announced, "There's the bomb that ended the war." The people in the bleachers applauded for several minutes. For them, as for many participating in U.S. collective memory, the bombing was the end of the Hiroshima event.

REMEDIATING THE EVENT

The original aim of the chapter was to remediate the event, emphasizing the point of view of the victims for whom the event's effects and implications endure. Its secondary aim was to focus on the contributions of cinema, which I foreground here because of the chapter's location in a pedagogical framing of the cinema-political theory relationship. To proceed, I pick up where I followed the media experiences I described with the suggestion that the two different endings I have glossed testify to radically different experiences of the bombing, two different practices of historico-cultural memory in Japan and the United States. I want to note especially that the turn to cinema (among other media genres) in this chapter is part of this book's focus on the ways that cinematic time engages historical time.

Since the dropping of the atom bomb on Hiroshima, the event has been interpreted officially and in most popular culture genres in the United States as a distant, increasingly abstract, and now-historically superseded event. Out of touch with the Japanese experience after Hiroshima, much of the historical emphasis in diverse U.S. media genres (and, to a large extent, in academic security studies) has been on futuristic imaginings of nuclear apocalypses. An examination of Japanese media genres tells a different kind of story, one in which the event remains current. For example, in Kenzaburo Oe's *Hiroshima Notes* (prepared after several returns to Hiroshima, roughly two decades after the bombing), the event is described as emotionally vivid and enduring for those who were on the scene. As Oe, puts it (while observing people visiting "the Memorial Cenograph for the Atomic Bomb Victims"), "How often have I seen . . . people standing still and silently in Hiroshima. On that fateful day in 1945, they saw hell unleashed here. Their eyes are deep, darkened, fearful."[2] Other perspectives articulating the Japanese experience are available in a collection of drawings by Hiroshima survivors, turned over to an exhibition, "Unforgettable Fire," inspired after "one survivor brought a hand-drawn picture to the NHK's, the Nippon Hoso Kyokai's Japanese Broadcasting Corporation's Hiroshima office" in 1975.[3] Among the drawings is one by a young "schoolgirl" who describes the scene she saw (and then drew) at 7:30 a.m., the morning after the bombing, which she witnessed while headed from school toward her home:

> I passed by Hijiyama. There were few people to be seen in the scorched field. I saw for the first time a pile of burned bodies in a water tank by the entrance to the broadcasting station. Then I was suddenly frightened by the terrible sight on the street 40 to 50 meters from Shukkeien Garden. There was a charred body of a woman standing frozen in a running posture with one leg lifted and her baby tightly clutched in her arm. (Figure 3.1)[4]

FIGURE 3.1
Charred figure of woman and baby. Source: A drawing from Yasuko Yamagata's "Unforgettable Fire," Japan Broadcast Company (1977).

RESITUATING HIROSHIMA 85

Japanese victims of the Hiroshima bombing have been largely invisible in the United States, where the allocation of the event to a distant past has rendered public exposure to the event as a closed and static story. It is mainly treated as the apex of the U.S. war strategy, glossed in war history books and in a museum display at the Aeronautical and Space Museum (part of the Smithsonian complex) in Washington, D.C. Congressional lobbying has continually blocked public displays about the bombing that would testify to the experiences of its victims. As a result, the Smithsonian's version of the event eschews Japanese experiences and perspectives and locates it within the history of military flight. The Smithsonian narrative celebrates the U.S. war victory, framing the bombing within a discourse that "attributes national security to air power."[5] To intervene conceptually in the Hiroshima event (the method to which I refer in the Introduction and Chapter 1 as "philopoesis") I enlist Walter Benjamin's concept of "temporal plasticity," a time "wholly without direction,"[6] which he discerns in a reflection on the poetry of Friedrich Hölderlin.

To apply Benjamin's concept, the focus is on creative acts in some of the more critically oriented artistic genres that engage the atomic bombing of Hiroshima with "plastic structure of thought,"[7] a mode of thinking that opens events to future interpretations. That conceptual gesture helps us to recognize that Hiroshima is a never-ending event. It endures through the interventions of a variety of artistic and cultural texts that reflect on it with an emphasis on the effects on the lives of those who have confronted its consequences directly—for example, Oe's, who wrote that "the Hiroshima within me does not come to an end with this publication [of his *Hiroshima Notes*]."[8] Oe's subjects have lived perpetually with their experiences of the bombing. They are subjects whose traumas exist in "an impossible temporality—it has happened; it is always about to occur—and inasmuch as it impinges in every aspect of the subject—defines the subject as a post-traumatic subjectivity."[9]

OTHER RETURNS TO HIROSHIMA

Rosalyn Deutsche's analysis of how Hiroshima—variously refigured in three media engagements—is (re)interpreted after the Iraq War encourages artists to return to the Hiroshima event. She activates the implications of Benjamin's concept of plastic temporality by articulating the event of the bombing with a more recent historical episode, the second Iraq War. As a result, her analysis is in accord with the grammar I have suggested as most appropriate for capturing the endurance of events, the future anterior. Foregrounding that grammar, she shows how three returns to Hiroshima contribute to the event's will-have-been. Notably for example, in her treatment of Silvia Kolbowski's video *After Hiroshima Mon Amour*, she suggests that the video "returns to Hiroshima. . .

confront the legacy of the atomic bombing, linking it to the present invasion and occupation of Iraq."[10] Specifically, Kolbowski's video recasts the Duras–Resnais film *Hiroshima Mon Amour* with a different temporal pacing and with a different mode of oral address as it intersperses images from the Iraq war and other recent events. The video creates a heterogeneous temporal association of the two wars as it gives both the past and the present different interpretive significance.

HIROSHIMA MON AMOUR, YET AGAIN

To situate critically Kolbowski's intervention and creative play with the temporality of the Duras–Resnais film, I first revisited the temporal play in both the screenplay that Duras and Resnais wrote and the cinematic realization of their script. Because in the film much of the camera's attention is on the character known as "Elle," one reading of the film narrative construes it as "a documentary on Emmanuel Riva [the actress who plays Elle], a French woman who is having a post bombing affair with a Japanese man, *Lui* (Eiji Okada)]."[11] However, the film goes well beyond its emphasis on Elle's war experience. As it foregrounds her slow, rhythmic narration, it is deployed simultaneously on the Hiroshima event, on Elle's recollections, and on the more general conditions of possibility for coming to reliable terms with one's own experience of the bombing. Elle's experience is therefore rendered allegorically as the film achieves a critical reading that renders its narrative general and universal. The film is primarily about relationships between personal memory and historical time.

By way of a brief summary, the film opens with two lovers in bed. We see body parts whose morphology is indistinct because they are too close and the scene is too cropped to allow the viewers certainty of what they are seeing. Duras describes the opening:

> As the film opens, two pairs of bare shoulders appear little by little. All we see are these shoulders—cut off from the body at the height of the head and hips—in an embrace, and as if drenched with ashes, rain, dew, or sweat, whichever is preferred. The main thing is that we get the feeling that this dew, this perspiration, has been deposited by the atomic "mushroom" as it moves away and evaporates. It should produce a violent, conflicting feeling of freshness and desire.[12]

With its focus on bodies, first those of the two lovers and then on documentary scenes of bombing victims, the film narrative is a radical contrast with a geopolitical security story in which the bodies of Japanese victims are rendered in an abstract war discourse as "casualties." It frames the bombing biopoliti-cally, positioning bodies in two experiential registers, the bombing's effects on relations of intimacy and its material signature on victim's bodies. Combining the event time of the devastating bombing and the micro-temporality of the rhythms of intimacy, the initial scene of the film shows the lovers seeming at first "to be under a rain of ash" and subsequently to have skin that looks clear and smooth with a light glistening of the sweat of erotic effort. In a few brief cinematic moments, the lovers' skin registers moments of "both pleasure and pain."[13] The close-up shots of bodies throughout the film constitute its primary challenge to the various narratives of the Hiroshima bombing that have shaped U.S. collective memory (which usually includes a persistent "visuality of the atom bomb"),[14] rendered as a mushroom cloud. In the absence of images of the specific devastation to bodies and dwellings, that iconic shape serves as a sublime image-reference to U.S. national security. Seen by most as a still picture radically cut off from event time, it is a still image that effaces the pro-cesses and marks of devastation that occurred on the ground during and after the explosion and persisted thereafter. To set the context for an elaborating of the film's composition structure, I want to cut away from its way of inter-articulating temporalities and turn to an account that, like the film, substitutes the drama of unfolding, catastrophic experiences for the stasis of the pervasive U.S. renderings of the bombing.

MUSHROOMS AND JELLYFISH

In contrast with the iconic "mushroom cloud" that pervades the U.S. repre-sentations of the atomic attacks on Hiroshima and Nagasaki is Masuji Ibuse's classic novelistic account of the Hiroshima bombing in his *Black Rain*. In the novel, the narrator/protagonist Shigematsu Shizuma describes the aftermath of the explosion not only as a "mushroom cloud" but also as a "jellyfish cloud."[15] That latter imagery is a stunning alert because Ibuse's aesthetic subject, Mr. Shizuma, who provides a trenchant witnessing of the aftermath of the bombing throughout the novel, is seeing the cloud in real time. As a result, the scenes he reports are cinematic rather than photographic. He sees the "cloud" as a mass of undulating motion whose color, he reports, was changing before his eyes. Mr. Shimizu has both personal and public tasks throughout the novelistic drama. At the same time that he is managing difficult familial intimacy issues, he is collecting and interpreting the scenes of the devastated cityscape awash in dead, dying, and sick bodies. That latter public task mirrors the experience of the novelist. Ibuse himself, who was at the scene of the bombing's aftermath. Before he wrote the novel, he collected diaries and did interviews with victims and other residents. Mimicking Ibuse's actual experience of the aftermath of

88   RESITUATING HIROSHIMA

the bombing, his character Mr. Shizuma performs the novel's narrative as his "journal of the bombing," written with a "Chinese brush and ink."[16]

As comprehensively as any text on Hiroshima, Ibuse's *Black Rain* delivers the temporalities of the bombing's aftermath, both through its descriptions of the dynamics of the visuals (images of the cloud as an undulating jellyfish, of bodies in various stages of morbidity and decrepitude, and of buildings destroyed or in the process of falling apart) and with details of the developing discourses with which those victimized and/or in the vicinity of the bombing came to terms with their experience. One of those discourses is about the bomb as a weapon. Over time, as Mr. Shizuma reports on-the-ground descriptions of what had been dropped on Hiroshima, it undergoes redescriptions. At first it is called a "new weapon," then a "new-type bomb," followed by a "high-capacity bomb," and finally, once more information has become available, an "atomic bomb."[17]

The novel also delivers moments that speak to a bureaucratic temporality. It narrates the way various aspects of the management of everyday life unfold as resources become scarce. For example, despite there being a post bombing state of emergency, which required rapid restoration of services, bureaucracies continued to function at their usual slow pace. In response to the coal shortage brought to the attention of the "Control Station" by a petition from Mr. Shizuma, a lieutenant in charge states, "Concerning coal as I have said many times already . . . we must hold a conference before we can come to any conclusion . . . I'm afraid you'll have to wait until we've held our conference."[18]

The novel also recovers the damage to traditional cultural practices, recording the way the rhythms of everyday life are disturbed. In great detail, it reviews the changes in culinary practices, which had to be radically altered because of severe shortages, and it also treats the way nonmaterial aesthetic practices are compromised. At one point, Mr. Shizuma describes his aesthetic deprivation: "Emerging from the main gate of the Clothing Depot, I'm struck by the desolation of the lotus pond." He adds that he misses his former daily enjoyment of the surroundings: "the glossy black sheen of the crows' plumage in the morning blends well with the green of the rice plants, and equally well with the rice fields after they have started to turn yellow."[19]

The novel also treats disturbances to intimacy patterns as it comments on the disruption of traditional courtship and marriage practices, exemplified in a narrative thread involving Mr. Shizuma's niece, Yasoku, on whom atom-polluted black rain has fallen. She has intermittent bouts of radiation sickness, which give rise to rumors that make her a dubious marriage prospect. While that part of the narrative is the major way in which the novel treats the disruption of intimacies, it references other intimacy effects as well. Mr. Shizuma reports, for example, that he has heard two characters say that "those injured by the bomb, even if only slightly hurt, had lost all interest in sex."[20]

Ultimately, as the translator of Ibuse's *Black Rain* puts it, the novel "lays the small human preoccupations and foibles . . . against the mighty purposes of the state . . . against the threat of universal destruction, he sets a love form and sense of wonder at life in all its forms."[21] And I would add, the novel is a life-affirming micro-politics of the Japanese social world as it explores the destruction and disruption of the vital rhythms of Japanese life that resulted from the necropolitics of state antagonisms. Appalled by that reality, Ibuse's Mr. Shizuma makes the case for a continuing ethical reflection on the event. In remarks that help me connect the novel to the text to which I return, the Duras–Resnais film *Hiroshima Mon Amour*, he says that what has happened to the inhabitants is "moral damage" that will persist well into the future: "In olden times, people used to say that in an area badly damaged by war it took a century to repair the moral damage done to the inhabitants."[22]

HIROSHIMA MON AMOUR AND THE MORALITY OF FORMS

Mr. Shizuma's remark about the moral damage wrought by the bombing of Hiroshima provides for a propitious return to Duras–Resnais's film. In accord with the focus of both Ibuse's *Black Rain* and Kaneto Shindo's *Lost Sex* on the bombing's disruption of the forces of desire and intimacy, *Hiroshima Mon Amour* constructs a transversality between a love story and the material and social destruction of the city. The main film narrative is a story of a love affair between an unnamed French actress from the city of Nevers, referred to as "Elle," and an unnamed Japanese architect from Hiroshima referred to as "Lui." However, the love affair functions within an interpretation-estranging context. At the outset of the film's focus on the lovers' intimacies, a critical disconnection attends their interactions. As their bodies connect in mutual passion, their conversation is dissensual.

While they are caressing each other, the conversation begins with Lui saying, "You saw nothing in Hiroshima. Nothing." Elle responds, "I saw everything. Everything." A visual disjuncture attends the dissensual conversation. There is a thematic separation between what Elle narrates and what the viewer sees. For example, Elle reports that by the 15th day, a vast profusion of blooming flowers are visible, poking up through the ashes, "unheard of in flowers before then," she adds. However, at the moment she is talking about the new vitality represented by the flowers, what is shown onscreen is morbidity rather than vitality. The viewer is treated to the sight of damaged, grotesque bodies to which a medical staff is administering. The musical score heightens the dissensus with a rapid, frenetic pace that accompanies the observable tension between Elle's statements about what she sees and what is shown. In contrast, Lui's rebuttals to Elle's recollections are backed by a contrapuntal, single instrument (seemly to be a woodwind), which contrasts with the flute and string accompaniment to Elle's insistences.

The disjunctive juxtapositions and other aspects of the film form of *Hiroshima Mon Amour* establish a temporal trajectory that articulates what *Black Rain*'s Mr. Shizuma calls "moral damage." The film puts flesh on that expression as it animates the process of bodily disintegration observable in the film's historical footage. And while it creates a diremption between witnessing and knowing, it tracks processes of witnessing. Provoked by Lui's frequent assertions that she saw nothing, Elle reports the evidence of her eyes: "I saw the hospital, I'm sure of it . . . how could I not have seen it." However, while stating that she saw what was in the museum in Peace Square "four times," she introduces uncertainty into that witnessing by evoking the concept of lack; she refers to how the museum reconstructs the Hiroshima event and calls it a "reconstruction for lack of anything else."

Those moments, along with several others, indicate that the film evokes a distrust of fixed images and iconic representations. Throughout the film narrative, an epistemology of the gaze gives way to an epistemology of interpretive ambiguity, as the film articulates sense memory with a grammatical framing of history that extends into an uncertain and contingent future. As it inter-articulates cinematic and historical time, it discounts immediate perception in order to value a dynamic of an unending ethical negotiation, a strategy made apparent in its treatment of the fragile interface between narrative and image. For example, as Elle's remarks about the knowledge gained from seeing what is in the museum, what is made visible is a tracking shot of a mother and children approaching the museum, followed by further tracking shots that explore the outside and inside of the building. What one can we make of those cinematic moments is supplied by Jean Luc Godard's provocative suggestion that the aesthetic and moral aspects of the film coincide. Asked about whether the film is jarring aesthetically or morally, he replies, "Tracking shots *are* a question of morality."[23]

Affirming Godard's observation, the film incessantly juxtaposes the memory of the Hiroshima bombing to the movement of bodies involved in war tourism, especially by cutting from tracking shots of the memorial venues in Peace Square to hands caressing skin. It is a contrast between a fixed institutionalized realization of the bombing (a fetishizing of the event in buildings, posters and glass cases) and a dynamic bodily sense memory, as the two lovers caress each other's skin while at the same time verbally negotiating their different loci of enunciation and the experiential trajectories that have brought them together.

Lest there be any doubt about the film's focus on alternative temporalities— for example, between the war experience of Elle, who is shamed in her city of Nevers because of an affair with a German soldier, and of Lui, who has resided

RESITUATING HIROSHIMA

FIGURE 3.2
Crossed watches. Source: Alain Resnais, *Hiroshima Mon Amour*, Argos Films (1959).

in Hiroshima but was not near ground zero during the bombing—one of the most telling shots is an overhead of the night table by the bed, which shows their two wristwatches on the nightstand crossed over each other (Figure 3.2).

To pursue Godard's observation about the morality of tracking shots, we can attend to the way other aspects of the film's form articulate a morality, for example through montage, a cutting back and forth between the scenes of devastation and the lovers, cuts between the instantaneous destruction of bodies and the slow rhythms of intimacy through which the film makes its primary moral statement. The film, like Ibuse's *Black Rain*, is revealing the bombing's disruption of the temporal rhythms of the life world. Observing that disruption with images, the film has exemplary cuts between moments that articulate ordinary biological time and moments that testify to event time. For example, in the same moment that the lovers are engaged in a slow caressing of each other's smooth, unblemished skin, Elle mentions that when the bomb dropped, there were 200,000 dead and 80,000 wounded in nine seconds. And earlier, as the camera tracks the displays in the museum, there is a long take of glass containers with (what Elle's voice-over refers to as) "human flesh, suspended, as if still alive—it's agony still fresh." Subsequently, we see "anonymous masses of hair that the women upon waking, would find had fallen out," followed by the

92   RESITUATING HIROSHIMA

badly burned flesh of a man's back. The moments that combine instantaneous and rapid morbidity are followed by scenes of the lovers slowly caressing each other's smooth skin. That contrast between the slow indulgence with which healthy skin is appreciated and the suddenly damaged flesh resulting from the bombing is also obliquely referenced with a display of scorched metal, which Elle describes as looking as vulnerable as flesh.

The discursive and imagistic focus on flesh, along with the foregrounding of an erotic relationship between Elle and Lui (both of whom are married), effectively lends the film a counter-Pauline morality. As is well known, Pauline theology juxtaposes the spirit to the flesh. Denigrating the flesh, Saint Paul mentions, among other things, "fornication, impurity, licentiousness . . . drunkenness, carousing" (Galatians 5:19–21), anything that involves the carnal sins," which are associated with a sensual enjoyment involving "the flesh." In contrast, Elle virtually celebrates what she calls her "dubious morals." In accord with Elle's indulgence in an erotic *jouissance*, the film suggests that enjoyment of the flesh—of the intimate rhythms of bodily exchange—is what the bombing, specifically, and the war, as a whole, have disrupted. In place of the slow, intimate rhythms of life, the war has produced an accelerated decrepitude.

Ultimately, through both its cinematic form and discursive narration, the film suggests that Hiroshima (in contrast to the way it is rendered in abstract policy discourses and treatises on apocalypse) is an atrocity that began with instantaneous destruction and was followed by the accelerated morbidity. At one point, Elle provides a brief phenomenology of the war's attack on the body. After looking in a mirror, she wistfully exclaims that she was young once. That observation calls to mind another instance of atrocity-imposed decrepitude. Imre Kertesz's fictional character Gyuri Köves, a young Hungarian concentration camp survivor, offers a more prolix account of the phenomenology of the accelerated decrepitude wrought by that war (with a Duras-like emphasis on smooth skin). While he is in the Buchenwald *lageri*, Gyuri says,

> I can safely say there is nothing more painful, nothing more disheartening than to track day after day, to record day after day, yet again how much of one has wasted away. Back home, while paying no great attention to it, I was generally in harmony with my body: I was fond of this bit of machinery, so to say. I recollect reading some exciting novel in our shaded parlor one summer afternoon, the palm of my hand meanwhile caressing with pleasing absentmindedness the golden-downed, pliantly smooth skin of my tautly muscular sunburned thigh. Now that same skin was drooping in loose folds, jaundiced and desiccated.[24]

In the film, decrepitude is referenced along with other dangers, the destruction of memory. Dwelling on the ethics of memory, which through Elle's

RESITUATING HIROSHIMA   93

narration is articulated as a primary aspect of the film's morality, the film has Elle continually remarking on the importance of not forgetting Hiroshima— as important, she says at one point as never forgetting either her former love for a German soldier in Nevers (here the city name has special resonance) or the current one in Hiroshima (even though that second love bids to efface the memory of the first). Cinematically constructing the theme of forgetting in the present and doing it with a Proustian emphasis on sense memory, the film suggests an equivalence between the two objects of forgetting: lovers and historical events. Elle notes that she had been "under the illusion I would never forget Hiroshima," and she laments her forgetting of her first love, the German soldier:

> I was unfaithful to you tonight with this stranger. I told our story. It was, you see, a story that could be told. For fourteen years I hadn't found . . . the taste of an impossible love again since Nevers. Look how I'm forgetting you. . . . Look how I've forgotten you.

That lyrical inter-articulation of intimacy and memory with an emphasis on its ethical implications sets up a return Silvia Kolbowski's video *After Hiroshima Mon Amour*, which simultaneously counters the forgetting of the bombing's devastation of the Japanese lifeworld and suggests an equivalence with the Iraq war.

KOLBOWSKI'S AND ANOTHER AFTER

To appreciate the way Kolbowski returns to and grammatically refigures *Hiroshima Mon Amour,* we have to heed the grammatical play in Duras's screenplay. For example, at one point, Elle switches to a future tense: "Asphalt will melt; chaos will prevail . . . an entire city will be lifted off the ground—then will fall back to earth in ashes." And in another part of the screenplay (but not ultimately in the film version), she shifts to the future anterior, as Elle says to Lui, "You will have seen me." No doubt Inspired by those passages, Carol Mavor, analyzing the film, plays with the grammar as well. She suggests, "Hiroshima contains the ashes of Proust's memory of future wars."[25]

Kolbowski is similarly inspired, especially by the "you will have seen me" grammar. As Rosalyn Deutsche points out, as she reviews Kolbowski's artistic intervention, which summons the Duras–Resnais version of the Hiroshima bombing and rethinks it in the context of the Iraq invasion and occupation, "[t]he word *after* in Kolbowski's title raises the question of time and therefore of history, which is to say of the meaning of past events."[26] In accord with Duras's grammatical imposition through Elle's narration, Kolboswki's "after"

94   RESITUATING HIROSHIMA

is also governed by the future anterior or will have been. That grammar is the analytic with which she reinserts Hiroshima in the present and thereby rethinks both events.

Crucially, inasmuch as the vehicles for animating the "after" in Kolboswki's video are bodies involved in intimacy and the exercise of sense memory (instead of the geo-strategic concerns and the technological preoccupations that have shaped U.S. collective memory), her story is a critical intervention into the way that cultural memory will be incessantly renegotiated. Deutsche puts Kolboswki's temporal intervention in clear perspective: "Kolbowski's *After Hiroshima Mon Amour* has a kind of flashforward structure, one that suggests what Hiroshima 'will have been' by substituting a movement forward to the present for Resnais's movement backward from narrative present to the past."[27]

The Cats of Mirikitani

Heeding the critical political effect of Kolbowski intervention (to which I return later in this chapter), I want to point to another "after"—Hiroshima after 9/11 as its will have been is altered in another artistic event, Linda Hattendorf's documentary film *The Cats of Mirikitani* (2006). Hattendorf lived in Lower Manhattan, very near where a homeless street artist, Jimmy Mirikitani, made and occasionally sold his drawings. Passing him frequently and fascinated by his drawings of cats, she decided to do a short film interview with him, with the thought of ultimately creating a documentary of a street artist:

> It was January 2001, and bitterly cold. He was wrapped in so many hats, coats, and blankets that I could barely see his face. Despite the cold, he was proudly exhibiting his artwork under the shelter of a Korean deli. A picture of a cat caught my eye and we struck up a conversation. It was soon apparent that he was not just selling his artwork, but homeless and living on the street. He seemed so old and frail, and yet full of spirit and life. I was curious and concerned—and I like cats. He gave me the drawing, but asked me to take a picture of it for him. I came back the next day with a small video camera. I asked if he could tell me the stories in some of his pictures. And he had many stories to tell! That's how it began.[28]

The "stories to tell" turned out to powerfully inflect an event that took place during Hattendorf's documentary. Born in Sacramento, California, and raised in Hiroshima, Jimmie and his family experienced two kinds of war atrocity. Despite being American citizens, he and his sister, like many Americans of Japanese ancestry, were sent to an internment camp. In Jimmie's case, after being held there for three-and-a-half years, he was forced to sign a document renouncing his citizenship and was then held for brief periods in two other

RESITUATING HIROSHIMA 95

places—effectively forced labor camps—before he ended up in New York and in the street after the man for whom he worked as a domestic servant died. Added to his being victimized with his illegal incarceration is the Hiroshima bombing which wiped out much of his family in Japan.

Jimmie, who was effectively a practicing archivist, recorded the atrocities visited on him and his family in his drawings. They constitute a vernacular archive. Depicted in some of the drawings is the Tule Lake, California, detention site where Jimmie and his family were interned and in others the Hiroshima bombing. His artistic commentary on both atrocities achieved public exposure when Hattendorf's documentary allowed him and his work to rise above the threshold of recognition. Once merely located in the street, where his contribution to the Hiroshima archive was part of a hidden world, it exploded onto many screens as Hattendorf's film migrated from diverse film festivals (where it won several prizes) to theater chains, where it achieved an expanding publicity. The animation of Jimmie's war archive contrasts markedly with the Smithsonian's Enola Gay exhibition, which sits in a building, a "privileged topology" for archives that frieze historical events.[29] As Achille Mbembe points out, traditionally "the term archives refers to a building, a symbol of a public institution" and to "a collection of documents—normally written documents—kept in this building." Accordingly, "the status and power of the archive derives from this entanglement of building and documents."[30] It is the material presence of archive buildings that effects the power-invested identification and consolidation of the diverse documents constituting the archive, which Derrida refers to as its "consignation."[31]

In contrast, Jimmie's archive, prior to the documentary, had been in the street, a place that has often provided spaces of contestation and renegotiation of the meanings of events. His mobile vernacular archive constituted a political challenge to the sedentary fixity of official archives. As Hattendorf's documentary proceeded, the location of the Mirikitani counter-archive became perilous. The September 11, 2001, destruction of the World Trade Center's Twin Towers took place. As a result, the documentary's temporal and spatial focus shifted. To save Jimmie from the toxic air in the Lower Manhattan streets, Hattendorf took him into her apartment. While the two of them resided together in the apartment (and Hattendorf became a character in the documentary, often appearing in front of the camera), they watched the television news together, which she edited to select out aspects of the post 9/11 "War on Terror." Near the beginning of Jimmie's stay in the apartment, President Bush's first public utterance about the destruction of the Twin Towers is aired. Referring to the event as "despicable acts of terror," he goes on to say, "America was targeted because we're the brightest beacon for freedom and opportunity in the world." Thereafter, much of what Hattendorf edits in from television news comes from CNN's version of events, which they offer with a possessive grammar, "America's New War."

96   RESITUATING HIROSHIMA

As the "new war" takes the form of the invasion of Afghanistan, on the domestic front, the profiling of alleged domestic subversion enters the news, which Hattendorf splices into her film. A voice on her television says, "[U]nder the circumstances a measure of racial profiling is inevitable." And as the domestic war on terror and the invasion of Afghanistan proceed, Jimmie provides commentaries, for example, "Can't make war, everything ashes," and "same old story." Meanwhile, Hattendorf supplies her own commentary with a montage of documentary footage. There are historical shots of old notices posted here and there about the demand for Japanese Americans to report to internment centers; there are scenes of attacks on Middle Eastern Americans by vigilantes (e.g., a Middle Eastern face is shone behind a store window that is riddled with bullet holes); and, ultimately, Jimmie's commentary, which had been daily etched, is shown as the camera focuses on his two versions of his experience of the war—several drawings of the Tule Lake internment camp where he was incarcerated (and where, Jimmie points out, many died due to sickness) and one of the Hiroshima bombing that wiped out his family and most of his former schoolmates: "Everything ashes—just like moon . . . killed babies, children, women, and may old people," as Jimmie puts it.

To situate the politics of temporality that Jimmie's story discloses, I have referred to the critical temporality that belongs to the capacity of the cinema, inspired by Gilles Deleuze's analysis of the temporality of the cinema genre. As a Deleuzian analysis implies, in the films of directors like Alain Resnais, "sheets of the past coexist and confront each other"[32] "to produce a critical temporal multiplicity that challenges . . . models of unitary time."[33] However, what is delivered in Hattendorf's film goes beyond mere multiplicity. By interconnecting the atrocities experienced by Japanese Americans in the United States and Japanese civilians in Hiroshima with targets of the War on Terror at home and abroad, the film enacts an ethico-political statement through the equivalence its juxtaposition creates.

In Hattendorf's *Cats*, the ethical emerges from the aesthetic. The politics of aesthetics that her film articulates is in accord with one that Jacques Rancière has theorized and illustrated in an analysis of Jean-Luc Godard's film *Histoire(s) du Cinema*. That film, according to Rancière, contains a "clash of heterogeneous elements that provide a common measure." It creates an equivalence between "two captivations,"[34] that of the "German crowds by Nazi ideology" and that of the "film crowds by Hollywood."[35] Similarly, by activating *its* historical equivalence, *The Cats of Mirikitani* effectively shifts the focus from CNN's and other historical narratives that foreground the "mission" of "America's war" (recall President George W. Bush's "mission accomplished" speech on the deck of a U.S. aircraft carrier) to the war's innocent victims. The film displaces the media's accounts of the temporal rhythms of a war's strategies, with a mapping of the temporal rhythms of exemplary victims' life worlds (in the United States and Japan). In addition, the temporal rhythms of Hattendorf's documentary illuminate the personal and historical times that constituted Jimmie Mirikitani's experience while at the same time articulating the politics of *Jetztzeit* or "now-time," discussed in Chapter 2's evocation of Walter Benjamin's sense of historical time, which incorporates the past into the way the present can be experienced.[36]

MEDIA, THE ETHICS OF ATTENTION, AND ANOTHER HIROSHIMA

As Ibuse's *Black Rain* and other treatments have made evident, apart from Hiroshima's continual return as it is evoked in comparison with later atrocities, the effects of the bombing were both instantaneous and slow: killing "about 100,000 (instantly) . . . 95,000 of them civilians . . . another 100,000, most of those civilians [who] experienced . . . drawn out deaths from the effects of radiation."[37] And since, many have died over a longer extended period through mortal injuries and radiation sickness. The depleted uranium left in the Iraqi environment is a legacy that is shared with a host of other forms of what Rob Nixon refers to as "slow violence."[38] Nixon's analysis of slow violence is focused on the gradual forms of deadly attrition that receive either no or very brief coverage in the mainstream media—for example, the environmental degradation caused by unregulated capitalism, starvation owed to both structures of inequality and violent conflicts that destroy food sources, and the lethal zones left with toxicities, mines, and other unexploded military ordinance in the aftermath of wars.

However, in addition to identifying the relevant temporalities, my concern is with the genres through which victims of atrocity can be allowed to become part of public history. For that purpose, there are artistic media genres that supplement the effects of cinema. One relevant artistic intervention is the sculptural assemblages of Doris Salcedo, treated by Jill Bennett in her analysis of "empathic" forms of vision. Rather than making direct images of people suffering, Salcedo creates images that testify to their disappearance, for example, her "Widowed House," which is represented by "partially dismantled furniture . . . dispersed around the gallery space."[39] As these exhibitions grab the viewers' attention, they evoke an obligation to recognize "the ethical weight of others,"[40] whose fates tend to fade rapidly from public consciousness. Such installations, which reframe the past by bringing it into the present and (like the films I have analyzed) open it to a perpetual future, show us that "the temporality of justice is not linear but symphonic . . . both retrospective and prospective"; it is an "elegant temporality [that is] also redemptive; if the past cannot literally be changed, it can imaginatively be reclaimed for the benefit of society."[41]

With the redemptive aspect of such a justice in mind, I want to acknowledge once more the attention-summoning approach to Hiroshima afforded by Silvia Kolbowski's video installation, *After Hiroshima Mon Amour* because it points to Hiroshima as memory and as an enduring present and future. Kolbowski's 22-minute installation redoes the film as a video installation and photographic exhibition that reconstitutes the film as a trauma that migrates into the present. The video begins very much like the Duras–Resnais screenplay with a close-up sequence of bodies, which, in this case, are ambiguously involved either in an erotic encounter or in a death scene. However, the scene is quickly interrupted by a night-vision scene in which members of the U.S. military, wielding automatic weapons are intimidating Iraqis. As other scenes are inter-articulated with a miming of the Duras–Resnais film (displaced on different ethnic bodies), the theme that emerges is the official United States' lack of guilt over its indifference to human suffering in Hiroshima and in subsequent events, notably the Iraq War and Hurricane Katrina (which is sometimes referred to as "our Hiroshima"). Kolbowski seals the connection between Hiroshima and Katrina with video clips of the aftermath of Hurricane Katrina (taken from news clips of the devastated city) and with a more subtle reference to both Iraq and Katrina. Recognizing that the Katrina event disproportionately victimized African American bodies, the erotic scene that Kolbowski invents to mime the Duras–Resnais version of lovers in *Hiroshima Mon Amour* is between a Middle Eastern man and a black woman (Figure 3.3).

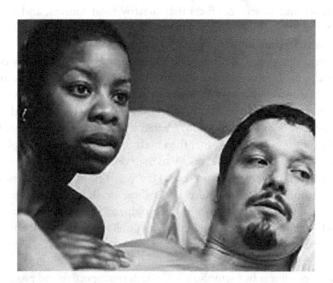

FIGURE 3.3
Kolbowski lovers. Source: Silvia Kolbowski, *After Hiroshima Mon Amour*, Independent Video Film (2008).

A NEW KIND OF WAR AND ANOTHER "NEW WEAPON"

When Linda Hattendorf's film had the events after 9/11 recall Hiroshima, the Japanese internment, and the life of Jimmie Mirikitani, it turned a story about a street artist into a critical analysis of the contemporary "War on Terror." What can be said about the way the emergence of "now-time"? How can we have the past in the present since her documentary bears on the way we can recover Hiroshima's significance? There's a strong hint in a recent observation about contemporary history: "We have unprecedented electronic surveillance . . . [and] as with war photography, the technology that testifies coevolves with, and is set along side the technology that kills."[42]

We can go further than suggesting a mere coevolution of the technologies of recording and killing. In the case of the atomic bomb dropped on Hiroshima, there was an instantaneous recording of some of the bodies and objects obliterated. The bomb itself was a photographic technology as well as a weapon. Because the radiation from the bomb spread out horizontally in straight lines, the objects in its path absorbed some of the energy. As a result, anything behind those objects—for example, walls—ended up being either lighter or darker where the objects had blocked the radiation as they were being obliterated. Thus, in various places, some of the people of Hiroshima and some of their objects absorbed the bomb's thermal energy, leaving shadows on the walls behind them. John Hersey famously supplied and creatively figured specifics; for example, "a painter on a ladder was monumentalized in a kind of bas-relief on the stone façade of a bank building on which he was working, in the act of dipping his brush into his paint can."[43]

Ironically, while the military gaze involved in planning the bombing articulated a distancing anthropological discourse—a macro-political view of a collectivity known as the Japanese "population"—the technological realization of that gaze, the bomb itself, provided a different, more fined-tuned ethnographic gaze. It created a micropolitical view of the consequences. As a result, we are encouraged to inquire into the way contemporary weapons, the current relays of the current military gaze, see and record? Of late that question has evoked comparisons between the Hiroshima bombing and contemporary drone warfare.[44]

The drone is a new kind of weapon for a new kind war, "a war that [according to former president George W. Bush] requires us to be on an international manhunt."[45] Breaking with conventional warfare, the "manhunt," operates in a new topology. Instead of entering battlefields that involve an encounter between two armed opponents, "it is more like a vast campaign of extrajudicial executions."[46] From the dubious perspective of U.S. official policy, the drone contrasts markedly with the Hiroshima bombing and other bombing events that killed thousands of civilians. It is represented as a weapon that singles out enemies and avoids killing civilians. Moreover, along with official apologists (in the Whitehouse, the Pentagon and the Central Intelligence Agency [CIA]), the weapon as a realization of the contemporary military gaze, has support from "certain professors of moral philosophy [who are] recycled as military consultants" [to] provide a legitimating perspective that assures that the "weapons are *ethical in themselves*,"[47] rather than being a source of what Ibuse's Mr. Shizuma called "moral damage."

In order to legitimate the humanitarian reticence that is attributed to Drones, the weapon itself has to be understood as ethically sensitive because the military gaze is relayed through the weapons themselves—from rifles with scopes through armored vehicles to drones. Under the rubric of "what does a weapon see," However, as I have suggested elsewhere, in the case of the current weapons *dispositif* (the human–weapons assemblages and their supervising agencies that program enmities, deciding what kinds of subjects get targeted), the likelihood of a neglect of the military rules of engagement designed to protect noncombatants increases.[48]

In the case of drones, the "pilots" are dealing with a more traumatic scopic field than was the case of the pilot of the Enola Gay. While the latter was too distant to observe the specific human consequences of dropping his bomb, drone operators, looking through their weapon, see their human targets (often monitoring them for days and becoming familiar with their social and familial habitus) and have to fire on the basis of deliberations in which they do not get to participate (an issue I treat later). Who decides on targeting, and what are the criteria that relayed by the military gaze through the weaponized drones? Although during President Barack Obama's administration, the targeting decisions were shifted from the White House to the Pentagon, it has remained the case (continuing to be operative within the administration of President Donald Trump) that the criteria usually come from the CIA's security-oriented anthropology. In early uses of weaponized drones, specific persons were targeted after deliberations by a decision-making group that often included the president and his staff. However since then, under the direction of the CIA, the warrants for killing have turned from "personality" targeting to "signature" targeting, where the latter strikes are against "men believed to be militants associated with terrorist groups, but whose identities aren't always known."[49] The "knowledge" on which the CIA has been relying to develop what I have elsewhere called necro biographies (brief biographical sketches used to justify targeting killing) has often been contributed by a war-friendly social science. The cultural aspect of the war zone, designated with the abstract, distancing expression, "Human Terrain System," has been mapped with the assistance of recruited "knowledge agents" at meetings of the American Anthropological Association.[50]

RESITUATING HIROSHIMA 101

Official spokespersons from the president on down have legitimated targeted killings by resorting to what Michel Foucault famously calls a "truth weapon," asserting that it is very rare for anyone other than actual enemy combatants to get killed. However doubtless, as Foucault points out, "given that the relationship of dominance works to their advantage, it is certainly not in their [the government's] interest to call any of *this* [my emphasis] into question."[51] The truth weapon has nevertheless been challenged. Systematic ethnographic work has called "this" into question. A joint Stanford–New York University investigation of the use of drones in Pakistan concluded that while in the United States the dominant narrative about their use is of a surgically precise and effective tool that avoids killing innocents by enabling "targeted killing of terrorists with minimal downsides or collateral impacts," what they found was an alarming level of atrocity visited on innocent civilians: "From June 2004 through mid-September 2012, available data indicate that drone strikes killed 2,562–3,325 people in Pakistan, of whom 474–881 were civilians, including 176 children."[52] Despite official denials, a similar pattern has been discovered in Yemen. For example, "[a] drone attacked a wedding procession [the second time a drone hit a wedding party] in al Bayda province, killing up to 12 reported civilians." After the organization Human Rights Watch

> raised concerns about multiple civilian deaths . . ., [t]he US has said it has investigated the claims but has found no evidence of civilian casualties. Yet earlier [that] month, New York Times reporter Mark Mazzetti, author of a book on drones, wrote that JSOC had been barred from carrying out drone strikes in the country because of 'botched' strikes.[53]

Under such circumstances, it is not surprising that critical responses to the U.S. drone strategy evoke comparisons with the atomic bombing of civilians in Hiroshima. After the first atom bomb struck Hiroshima, killing mostly civilians, President Truman employed his win "truth weapon" the next day, stating, "[a] military base had been selected . . . 'because we wished in the first attack to avoid, as much as possible, the killing of civilians.'"[54] Nevertheless, that "truth" has failed to hold. "Hiroshima" symbolizes atrocity more than it does mere military engagement. And in addition to its evocation in connection with the drone killings of civilians, the "will-have-been" of Hiroshima is tied to another aspect of U.S. military strategy, the use of depleted uranium on the tips of bullets to help them pierce armored vehicles during the Iraq War. As one analyst summarizes the history of "dirty weapons," by 2007 there had been "61 years of uranium wars,"[55] and another suggests that the use radioactive ammunition in the Middle East will likely have claimed more lives than the atomic bombing of Hiroshima and Nagasaki.[56]

102   RESITUATING HIROSHIMA

ANOTHER CRITICAL CINEMATIC INTERVENTION[57]

When I watched Robert Greenwald's documentary *Unmanned: America's Drone Wars*, which provides an up-close view of the innocent civilian victims of drone strikes in Pakistan, the Hiroshima bombing flashed up yet again, especially because I was reminded of Masuji Ibuse's report about an initial reference of the targeted population of Hiroshima to the atom bomb as a "new weapon." In Greenwald's documentary, there is substantial footage of the effects of the "new weapon"—moving and still images of the carnage the weapon has produced among civilian noncombatants along with testimony of many who knew the victims of drone targeting. Especially notable is coverage of devastation to an important cultural practice. The documentary shows before and after footage of a Jirga assemblage, a peaceful meeting in which cultural conflicts are mediated in Pakistan. The Jirga was attacked by hellfire missiles, shot from a drone. Most of those assembled were killed. While anonymous U.S. officials are quoted to the effect that the assemblage was a terror-planning meeting (it was not the planning of a "bake sale," according to one), the documentary goes into the details of members of the Jirga participants with testimony from their relatives and from Pakistani officials familiar with the cultural practice. The testimony that Greenwald's documentary supplies constitutes a series of counter-biographies to the cynical necro versions used to justify targeted killings.

Two biographies are at the center of Greenwald's film. One is a brief autobiography narrated by Brandon Bryant (a former drone sensor), shown onscreen in close up as he recounts details of his unremarkable childhood, his decision to enter the air force (he wanted a reprieve from mounting student loans), and his position as a drone warfare operative, directing missiles against those designated as terrorists (the job involves "killing people" he is told). Remorseful by the time he has left the air force, he testifies to the arbitrariness of the targeting in which he was involved. Revisited later in the documentary, after Pakistani victims are shown and their relatives and friends testify onscreen to the misapprehensions that led to their targeting, Bryant recounts an episode of firing on and killing three men whose eligibility for eradication consisted only in the fact that they were walking around carrying rifles. In effect, as a drone sensor, Bryant was watching a documentary about deaths for which he was partly responsible in real time. The way he has been affected by his vocation as he recalls his witnessing of those onscreen deaths is registered on his face, as the camera zooms closer, creating what Deleuze calls an "affection image . . . the way in which the subject perceives itself, or rather experiences itself or feels itself, from the 'inside.'"[58]

The other most emphasized bio in Greenwald's documentary is of a 16-year-old high school student, Tariq Assiz, who is targeted and killed while in a car with his brother and cousins on their way to soccer team recruitment.

It becomes apparent that Tariq's CIA bio had thickened to the point where he was eligible for eradication. What data were available to constitute Tariq as a terrorist? As visuals of his movements and local testimony indicate, he attended a large public meeting in Islamabad in which tribal elders, Pakistani officials, other civic leaders, political candidates, and interested members of the public were present, primarily to share information about the drone killing of innocent civilians (e.g., one of Tariq's cousins) and to protest the drone program.

As the testimony of experts indicates, it is likely that an "informant" turned over Tariq's name to the CIA (for pay, as is the case with the CIA's informant practice). That information, along with the CIA's anthropological conceits, made a 16-year-old high school student, whose "crime" was the political activism of attending a public meeting, a victim of extrajudicial killing, a summary execution without a chance to testify about his intentions and behavior. Unlike what was available to the CIA and the rest of the targeting *dispositif* involved in the targeting decision, viewers of the documentary get to know this innocent high school student—a soccer player with good defensive talent; a youngster with a good sense of humor; a high school student admired by his teacher, Mr. Wali; and a politically energized citizen, prompted to get involved after a cousin dies in a drone attack.

Much of what the documentary conveys is done with images. In one scene, the camera closes in on a soccer ball, an important cultural object that functions in both Pakistani culture, in general, and in Tariq's filmed biography, specifically. As the sequence continues, the camera pulls back to show a large enough scene to include both the ball and a plane flying overhead. On one hand, there is extensive ethnographic information one can discern with interviews of people who knew the victims of drone attacks and can testify to the cultural practices on the ground (where the soccer ball sits; Figure 3.4). On the other

FIGURE 3.4
Soccer ball. Source: Robert Greenwald, *Unmanned: America's Drone Wars*, Brave New Films (2014).

is the distant anthropology of the CIA–military gaze, represented by a plane flying thousands of feet over the scene.

The documentary also supplies a similar juxtaposition; first, there is a landscape scene filmed from above through the surveillance lens of a drone; then, it is followed by a tracking shot on the ground as a local landscape is seen from a car window, representing Tariq's journey to the rally in Islamabad.

Ultimately in Tariq's case, as in the case of the documentary's other notable coverage of the drone attack on a "Jirga" (a democratic assemblage in which tribal elders gather with townspeople to settle local disputes) in the North Pakistan town of Datta Khel, the intelligence was misguided. As testimony and images show, within 40 minutes of the start of the meeting, drone attacks kill most of the participants, and subsequent interviews with Pakistani officials (e.g., the former ambassador to the United States) and the relatives of the victims indicate that a major cultural event was interpreted as a terrorist plot. Interspersed with the testimonies about the nature of the cultural event and the loss experienced by the relatives (mostly sons of tribal elders whose bodies were in fragments to the point where one son could distinguish his father's feet from his hands), are onscreen remarks by U.S. officials who dispense the administration's "truth weapons" to legitimate the murders—for example, "There's every indication that this was a group of terrorists, not a charity car wash in the Pakistani hinterlands" (tellingly, the anonymous official spokespersons are screening Pakistani culture through their own cultural practices). However irrational past wars may have been, the intelligibility demands involved in friend–enemy identification were relatively clear because the conflicts involved states versus states. In the case of the war on terror, ambiguities abound and arbitrary assassination decisions, based on sketchy information that constitutes individuals as enemies, are the rule.

Subjecting America's drone warfare to "a philosophical investigation," Gregoire Chamayou refers to "a crisis of intelligibility" because drone warfare defies the "established categories" that have hitherto been applied to warfare.[59] Chamayou's emphasis is on the way the new militarized gaze has constituted parts of the world as a hostile environment viewed through the lens of CIA anthropology and the resultant apparatuses constructed to implement their perspective. Robert Greenwald's documentary constitutes a return of that gaze. As the documentary shows, the implementation of that gaze has created precarious lives and the deaths of many innocents, while what the U.S. public hears are official lies—for example, CIA head William Brennan's at a press conference: "In the last year there hasn't been a single collateral death." Here is the documentary's main juxtaposition. On the day Tariq Assiz was murdered, an innocent 16-year-old high school student was murdered (as his high school teacher, Wali, points out onscreen). Cut to *The Washington Post*'s reporter Karen de Young: "I asked the CIA about the strike and they said no child was killed." The truth weapon remains a major part of the U.S.'s arsenal.

"ALL PLOTS TEND TO MOVE DEATHWARD"

The quoted heading belongs to the novelist Don DeLillo, who uses it more than once (e.g., in two of his novels *White Noise* and *Libra*), doubtless because he likes its ambiguity (all lives end in death, and so do the fictional ones he plots). For situating *my* plot, it is about the contingencies that mark innocent victims for death, as the U.S.'s employed killers (drone sensors and pilots) are brought into relationships with their victims (not only those selected for targeted assassination but also those in the vicinity who die as well). Greenwald's ethnographic subject, Brandon Bryant, found himself in his occupation as a result of economic privation, in his case a daunting accumulation of college loans. Although loans put temporality into economy, allowing one to defer debt, there remains a complex calculation about the viability of accumulating debt. One has to gauge a relationship between one's biological clock and the repayment period. Thus, although Bryant reports on liking to read comics that pitted good guys against bad guys, that binary was not what drove him to be a killer. Ambivalent from the beginning about his assignment, he found that the work turned out to be stressful. Richard Maxwell effectively captures the kind of stress visited on a Bandon Bryant: "Surveillance is tough work . . . working conditions can include any combination of the following: stress . . . irregular hours, and a heavy toll on private life." Moreover,

> [o]n top of the physical and psychological strain, a surveillance worker must also possess great self-disciple to control unproductive ethical impulses to look away, to perceive innocence instead of guilt, to see a friend not a foe, to accept the ineffable and resist the probable.[60]

Referring to how the task was characterized for him, "You kill people," Bryant says, "I worried about it; can I do this, can I pull the trigger (I'm actually not pulling the trigger; I'm guiding the missile in, but it's more or less the same thing"). Ultimately, Bryant was unable to "control unproductive ethical impulses." A grim-faced Bryant, brought back later in the documentary, reports an incident in which he guided a missile that hit three men carrying what appeared to be weapons in the mountains of Pakistan. Two are killed instantly, while a third is mortally wounded. Bryant recounts his death in graphic detail. He saw a pool of blood cooling on the ground as the victim rolled around in agony:

> We watched the guy turn the same color as the ground as he bled out. I could almost see his facial expression. I could almost see his mouth open, crying out. Maybe he cursed us, or maybe he asked Allah for forgives for us. Who knows what he said or thought. It wasn't pretty whatever it was. It was shock and trauma, and his ears were probably ringing. He was

bleeding out and he was in agony. I didn't know how to react. No one teaches you how to react; they teach you how to do it. They ignore the reaction part. I wished I never contributed to that.

CONCLUSION: ETHICAL SPACE AND THE SIGHT AND FRAMING OF DEATH

Tariq Aziz, the documentary's other significant biographical subject, did not get to provide his assessment of the arbitrariness of drone killing. The flagrant violation of his right to testify against the charges that led to his death warrant—a person eradicated on the basis of biographical whims—receive testimony from those who knew him: family members, a teacher, peace activists, and reporters. What we see of Tariq are photos of a smiling young man. The photos' appearances, at various moments in the documentary, constitute them as double events. In the context of their origin, they represent events of family and/or clan cohesion, moments of affective belonging. Their inclusion in Greenwald's composition of shots, images, and commentaries constitutes them as second events, in this case as counter-visions to what is seen through drone surveillance as an articulation of another "composition" (for the CIA what is seen is a function of how they compose the Pakistani lifeworld).[61] What do *we* see as viewers of the documentary? To borrow from Roland Barthes (on the temporality of the photo portrait of someone who has died), we "observe with horror an anterior future of which death is the stake."[62] Other victims, mostly nameless, whom the CIA's necro biographies have also transformed into future anteriors, appear anonymously as corpses. Their innocence is verified through the work of the journalist/photographer Noor Behram, who collected evidence in Waziristan of the civilian deaths, which, he says, "the CIA and U.S. government can't disprove" (his photos of the dead—many women and children—appear onscreen as he testifies).

Whereas Brandon Bryant offers an ethical position through his direct testimony, Robert Greenwald's documentary as a whole articulates an ethics through the montage of shots, images, and testimonies—for example, in the scene in which he juxtaposes an overhead, satellite-eye view of the landscape-as-space-for-targeting and the tracking shot of Tariq's journey from his village to a peaceful assembly in Islamabad. Jean-Luc Godard's suggestion, quoted earlier about *Hiroshima Mon Amour*, where he says that the aesthetic and moral aspects of the film coincide applies well here. Commenting on the coincidence of the aesthetic and ethical in film work, Marco Able suggests that literature and film (both fictional and documentary) "bear" what he calls "the *pedagogical* potential for activating an *ethical* mode of encounter with violence."[63] In light of the potential effects of Robert Greenwald's documentary film *Unmanned*, which challenges the violence of the drone *dispositif*'s role in the contemporary "war on terror," what Greenwald's documentary especially challenges is the drone's-eye view's relay of the security gaze. To give that challenge additional specificity, I want to heed Nasser Hussain's analysis of the phenomenology of a drone strike. Citing one of the drone program's military apologists (a retired colonel), he points out that a drone hovers for a while over its selected target, adding "oversight." The prolonged hovering produces a buzzing that terrorizes much of the population of Pakistan (as *Unmanned* attests). However, because drones operate only in a "visual economy," where sound is not available to the sensors and the rest of the drone *dispositif*, who have only vision, "the layers of supervision effectively evacuate the world of sound and the interpersonal reality that sound produces."[64] Moreover, the public perception of drone strikes arises from the phenomenology of the public point of view: "We have become too accustomed to seeing from the air, which violates all the familiar geometry and perspective of our mundane, grounded vision"[65] (which Greenwald's *Unmanned* supplies). The evacuation of sound, along with the lack of "grounded vision," is in part constitutive of what I have referred to elsewhere as "the weapons sublime"[66] (the problem of connecting one's local world of weapons production and deployment to the distant life-world of blurred boundaries between enemies and noncombatants). In effect, what Greenwald's documentary supplies is a counter-weapon. Borrowing from and reinflecting Walter Benjamin's enduringly relevant analysis of the power of a work of art, in his "The Work of Art in the Age of Mechanical Reproduction," I offer here a reinflection: "the work of art in the age of drones-eye vision," invoking especially Benjamin's notion of the "shock effect" of film-as-counter-weapon. Reflecting on the effect of the Dadaists, Benjamin wrote:

> From an alluring appearance or persuasive structure of sound the work of art of the Dadaists became an instrument of ballistics. It hit the spectator like a bullet. . . . Let us compare the screen on which a film unfolds with the canvas of a painting. The painting invites the spectator to contemplation; before it the spectator can abandon himself to his associations. Before the movie frame he cannot do so. No sooner has his eye grasped a scene than it is already changed. It cannot be arrested. This constitutes the shock effect of the film, which, like all shocks, should be cushioned by heightened presence of mind. By means of its technical structure, the film has taken the physical shock effect out of the wrappers in which Dadaism had, as it were, kept it inside the moral shock effect.[67]

Unmanned offers an encounter of technics. One associated with the weapons of war, the other the challenge of the technics of cinema. The perceptual violence of drone technology becomes shocking when encountered by the way the technology of cinema restores what drone perception evacuates. It brings us back to Hiroshima but with a notably different perspective on images of death. In the case of the Hiroshima bombing, the bomb itself created images of its victims; it had the only close-up view. In the case of drones, operators have to see what they are killing. The "new weapon" carries with it a different ethics of the image.

NOTES

1. Michael J. Shapiro, *Politics and Time: Documenting the Event* (Cambridge: Polity, 2016).
2. Kenzaburo Oe, *Hiroshima Notes*, trans. David L. Swain and Toshi Yonezawa (New York: Marion Boyars, 1995), 35.
3. See *Unforgettable Fire: Pictures Drawn by Atomic Bomb Survivors* (New York: Pantheon, 1977), 5.
4. Commentary and drawing by Yasuko Yamagata (age 49 at the time of the commentary) in Ibid., 52.
5. The quotation is from Roslyn Deutsche, *Hiroshima After Iraq: Three Studies in Art and War* (New York: Columbia University Press, 2010), 16.
6. The quotation is from a reading of Benjamin's concept of plastic temporality: Peter Fenves, *The Messianic Reduction: Walter Benjamin and the Shape of Time* (Stanford: Stanford University Press, 2011), 3.
7. Walter Benjamin, "Two Poems by Friedrich Hölderlin," in *Walter Benjamin: Selected Writing 1913–1926*, trans. S. Corngold (Cambridge, MA: Harvard University Press, 1996), 31,
8. Oe, *Hiroshima Notes*, 23.
9. The quotation is from Jonathan Boulter, *Melancholy and the Archive: Trauma, History and Memory in the Contemporary Novel* (New York: Bloomsbury, 2013), 11.
10. Deutsche, *Hiroshima After Iraq*, 10.
11. Jean Domarchi, "Hiroshima Notre Amour," *Cahiers du Cinema* 97 (1959), 63.
12. Quoted in Carol Mavor, *Black and Blue* (Durham: Duke University Press, 2012), 115.
13. *Ibid.*
14. The quotation is from Brent Steele, "Hiroshima: The strange case of maintaining (US) collective memory," Paper delivered at the 2011 annual meeting of the International Studies Association, 1.
15. Masuji Ibuse, *Black Rain*, trans. John Bester (New York: Kodansha, 2012 [originally published in 1969]), 77.
16. *Ibid.*, 44.
17. *Ibid.*, 282.
18. *Ibid.*, 168.
19. *Ibid.*, 171.
20. *Ibid.*, 211.
21. The quotation belongs to John Bester in his "Translator's Preface" to Ibuse's *Black Rain*, 6.
22. Ibuse, *Black Rain*, 149.

RESITUATING HIROSHIMA   109

23. Jean-Luc Godard, "Hiroshima Notre Amour," *Cahiers du Cinema* 97 (1959), 62.
24. Imre Kertesz, *Fatelessness*, trans. Tim Wilkinson (New York: Vintage, 2004), 165.
25. Mavor, *Black and Blue*, 117.
26. Deutsche, *Hiroshima After Iraq*, 21.
27. *Ibid.*, 16.
28. Chi-Hui Yang, "Q&A with Linda Hattendorf on 'The Cats of Mirikitani'," *Cinema Asian America*. On the web at: http://my.xfinity.com/blogs/tv/2013/08/01/cinema-asian-america-qa-with-linda-hattendorf-on-the-cats-of-mirikitani/.
29. The quotation is from Jacques Derrida, *Archive Fever: A Freudian Impression*, trans. Eric Prenowitz (Chicago: University of Chicago Press, 1995), 3.
30. Achille Mbembe, "The Power of the Archive and Its Limit," in *Refiguring the Archive*, eds. Carolyn Hamilton et al. (Dordrecht, Netherlands: Kluwer Academic Publishers, 2002), 19.
31. Derrida, *Archive Fever*, 3.
32. Gilles Deleuze, *Cinema 2: The Time-Image*, trans. Hugh Tomlinson (Minneapolis: University of Minnesota Press, 1989), 116.
33. Michael J. Shapiro, *Studies in Trans-Disciplinary Method: After the Aesthetic Turn* (London: Routledge, 2012), 25.
34. Jacques Rancière, *The Future of the Image*, trans. G. Elliot (New York: Verso, 2007), 55.
35. *Ibid.*, 53.
36. See Walter Benjamin, "Theses on the Philosophy of History," in *Illuminations* (New York: Schocken, 1968), 259.
37. Those numbers are reported in Sven Lindqvist, *A History of Bombing*, trans. Linda Haverty Rugg (New York: The New Press, 2001), 112.
38. Rob Nixon, *Slow Violence and the Environmentalism of the Poor* (Cambridge, MA: Harvard University Press, 2011).
39. Jill Bennett, *Empathic Vision: Affect, Trauma, and Contemporary Art* (Stanford: Stanford University Press, 2005), 67.
40. Slavoj Žižek, "Kate's Choice, Or the Materialism of Henry James," in *Lacan: The Silent Partners*, ed. Slavoj Žižek (New York: Verso, 2006), 290.
41. Jon Kertzer, "Time's Desire: Literature and the Temporality of Justice," *Law, Culture and the Humanities* 5: 2 (2009), 269.
42. Justin Erik Halldór Smith, "The Great Extinction," *The Chronicle Review*, On the web at: www.jehsmith.com/1/essays-for-the-chronicle-review.html.
43. John Hersey, *Hiroshima* (New York: Alfred A. Knopf, 1946), 96.
44. See, for example, Benjamin Medea, *Drone Warfare: Killing by Remote Control* (London: Verso, 2013) and Christian Enemark, *Armed Drones and the Ethics of War: Military Virtue in a Post-heroic Age* (London: Routledge, 2013).
45. See Gregoire Chamayou, "The Manhunt Doctrine," *Radical Philosophy* 169 (September/October, 2011), On the web at: www.radicalphilosophy.com/commentary/the-manhunt-doctrine.
46. *Ibid.*
47. *Ibid.*
48. See Michael J. Shapiro, *War Crimes, Atrocity, and Justice* (Cambridge: Polity, 2015), Chapter 3.

49. See Spencer Ackerman, "CIA Drones Kill Large Groups Without Knowing Who They Are," *Wired*, On the web at: www.wired.com/dangerroom/2011/11/cia-drones-marked-for-death/.

50. Robert Albro and Hugh Gusterson, "Do No Harm," in *C4!SA Journal*, 4/25/2012. On the web at: www.defensenews.com/article/20120425/C4ISR02/304250001/Commentary-8216-Do-No-Harm-8217-html.

51. Michel Foucault, *Society Must Be Defended*, trans. David Macey (New York: Picador, 2003), 54–55.

52. See the Stanford–New York University investigation: "Living Under Drones: Death, Injury, and Trauma to Civilians From US Drone practices in Pakistan, by the International Human Rights and Conflict Resolution Clinic of the Stanford Law School and the Global Justice Clinic of the NYU Law School," On the web at: http://livingunderdrones.org/.

53. Alice K. Ross, "Civilians Die in Reported Yemen Drone Strike as Weekend of Attacks Kill at Least 35," Projects. On the web at: www.thebureauinvestigates.com/2014/04/21/civilians-die-in-yemen-drone-strike-as-weekend-of-attacks-kills-at-least-35/.

54. The quotations are from Lindqvist, *A History of Bombing*, 112.

55. Leuren Moret, "From Hiroshima to Iraq, 61 Years of Uranium Wars," On the web at: www.globalresearch.ca/from-hiroshima-to-iraq-61-years-of-uranium-wars/594.

56. Sherwood Ross, "Radioactive Ammunition Fired in the Middle East May Claim More Lives than Hiroshima and Nagasaki," *Democratic Underground.com*. On the web at: www.democraticunderground.com/discuss/duboard.php?az=view_all&address=389x2314187.

57. The reading of the Greenwald documentary is drawn from my chapter "'Fictions of Time': Necro-Biographies," in Shapiro *Politics and Time: Documenting the Event*.

58. Gilles Deleuze, *Cinema 1: The Movement Image*, trans. Hugh Tomlinson and Barbara Habberjam (Minneapolis: University of Minnesota Press, 1986), 65.

59. *Ibid.*, 14.

60. Richard Maxwell, "Surveillance: Work, Myth, and Policy," *Social Text* 83 (Summer, 2005), 1.

61. Composition is in quotation marks because I am here inspired by Gertrude Stein's perspective on how what is seen is a result of a composition; see her "Composition as Explanation," On the web at: www.poetryfoundation.org/learning/essay/238702.

62. Roland Barthes, *Camera Lucida*, trans. Richard Howard (New York: Hill and Wang, 1982), 96.

63. Marco Abel, *Violent Affect: Literature, Cinema, and Critique After Representation* (Lincoln: University of Nebraska Press, 2007), 189.

64. Nasser Hussain, "The Sound of Terror: Phenomenology of a Drone Strike," On the web at: www.bostonreview.net/world/hussain-drone-phenomenology.

65. *Ibid.*

66. Shapiro, "'Fictions of Time': Necro-Biographies."

67. Walter Benjamin, "The Work of Art in the Age of Mechanical Reproduction," in *Illuminations*, ed. Hannah Arendt, trans. Harry Zohn (New York: Schocken, 1968), 238.

REFERENCES

Abel, Marco (2007) *Violent Affect: Literature, Cinema, and Critique after Representation*, Lincoln: University of Nebraska Press.

Ackerman, Spencer (2011) 'CIA Drones Kill Large Groups Without Knowing Who They Are,' *Wired*, at: www.wired.com/dangerroom/2011/11/cia-drones-marked-for-death/.

Albro, Robert and Gusterson, Hugh (2012) 'Do No Harm,' *C4!SA Journal*, April 25, 2012, at: www.defensenews.com/article/20120425/C4ISR02/304250001/Commentary-8216-Do-No-Harm-8217-html.

Barthes, Roland (1982) *Camera Lucida*, trans. Richard Howard, New York: Hill and Wang.

Benjamin, Walter (1968) 'Theses on the Philosophy of History,' in *Illuminations*, ed. Hannah Arendt, trans. Harry Zohn, New York: Schocken, pp. 253–264.

Benjamin, Walter (1968) 'The Work of Art in the Age of Mechanical Reproduction,' in *Illuminations*, ed. Hannah Arendt, trans. Harry Zohn, New York: Schocken, pp. 217–252.

Benjamin, Walter (1996) 'Two Poems by Friedrich Holderin,' in *Walter Benjamin: Selected Writing 1913–1926*, trans. Stanley Corngold, Cambridge, MA: Harvard University Press, pp. 18–36.

Bennett, Jill (2005) *Empathic Vision: Affect, Trauma, and Contemporary Art*, Stanford: Stanford University Press.

Boulter, Jonathan (2013) *Melancholy and the Archive: Trauma, History and Memory in the Contemporary Novel*, New York: Bloomsbury.

Chamayou, Gregoire (2011) 'The Manhunt Doctrine,' *Radical Philosophy*, 169, Sept/Oct, 2011, at: www.radicalphilosophy.com/commentary/the-manhunt-doctrine.

Deleuze, Gilles (1986) *Cinema 1: The Movement Image*, trans. Hugh Tomlinson and Barbara Habberjam, Minneapolis: University of Minnesota Press.

Deleuze, Gilles (1989) *Cinema 2: The Time-Image*, trans. Hugh Tomlinson, Minneapolis: University of Minnesota Press.

Derrida, Jacques (1995) *Archive Fever: A Freudian Impression*, trans. Eric Prenowitz, Chicago: University of Chicago Press.

Deutsche, Roslyn (2010) *Hiroshima After Iraq: Three Studies in Art and War*, New York: Columbia University Press.

Domarchi, Jean (1959) 'Hiroshima Notre Amour,' *Cahiers du Cinema*, No. 97, p. 63.

Enemark, Christian (2013) *Armed Drones and the Ethics of War: Military Virtue in a Post-heroic Age*, London: Routledge.

Fenves, Peter (2011) *The Messianic Reduction: Walter Benjamin and the Shape of Time*, Stanford: Stanford University Press.

Foucault, Michel (2003) *Society Must Be Defended*, trans. David Macey, New York: Picador.

Godard, Jean-Luc (1959) 'Hiroshima Notre Amour,' *Cahiers du Cinema*, No. 97, p. 62.

Hersey, John (1946) *Hiroshima*, New York: Alfred A. Knopf.

Hussain, Nasser (2013) 'The Sound of Terror: Phenomenology of a Drone Strike,' at: www.bostonreview.net/world/hussain-drone-phenomenology.

Ibuse, Masuji (2012) *Black Rain*, trans. John Bester, New York: Kodansha.

Japan Broadcast Company (1977) *Unforgettable Fire: Pictures Drawn by Atomic Bomb Survivors*, New York: Pantheon.

Kertesz, Imre (2004) *Fatelessness*, trans. Tim Wilkinson, New York: Vintage.

Kertzer, Jon (2009) 'Time's Desire: Literature and the Temporality of Justice,' *Law, Culture and the Humanities*, Vol. 5 (2), pp. 266–287.

Lindqvist, Sven (2001) *A History of Bombing*, trans. Linda Haverty Rugg, New York: The New Press.

Mavor, Carol (2012) *Black and Blue*, Durham: Duke University Press.

Maxwell, Richard (2005) 'Surveillance: Work, Myth, and Policy,' *Social Text*, Vol. 83 (2), pp. 1–19.

Mbembe, Achille (2002) 'The Power of the Archive and its Limit,' in *Refiguring the Archive*, eds. Carolyn Hamilton et al., Dordrecht, Netherlands: Kluwer Academic Publishers, at: https://sites.duke.edu/vms565s_01_f2014/files/2014/08/mbembe2002.pdf.

Medea, Benjamin (2013) *Drone Warfare: Killing by Remote Control*, London: Verso.

Moret, Leuren (2006) 'From Hiroshima to Iraq, 61 Years of Uranium Wars,' at: www.globalresearch.ca/from-hiroshima-to-iraq-61-years-of-uranium-wars/594.

Nixon, Rob (2011) *Slow Violence and the Environmentalism of the Poor*, Cambridge, MA: Harvard University Press.

Oe, Kenzaburo (1995) *Hiroshima Notes*, trans. David L. Swain and Toshi Yonezawa, New York: Marion Boyars.

Rancière, Jacques (2007) *The Future of the Image*, trans. G Elliot, New York: Verso.

Ross, Alice K. (2014) 'Civilians Die in Reported Yemen Drone Strike as Weekend of Attacks Kill at Least 35,' *Projects*, at: www.thebureauinvestigates.com/2014/04/21/civilians-die-in-yemen-drone-strike-as-weekend-of-attacks-kills-at-least-35/.

Ross, Sherwood (2007) 'Radioactive Ammunition Fired in the Middle East May Claim More Lives than Hiroshima and Nagasaki,' *Democratic Underground.com*, at: www.democraticunderground.com/discuss/duboard.php?az=view_all&address=389x2314187.

Shapiro, Michael J. (2012) *Studies in Trans-Disciplinary Method: After the Aesthetic Turn*, London: Routledge.

Shapiro, Michael J. (2015) *War Crimes, Atrocity, and Justice*, Cambridge: Polity.

Shapiro, Michael J. (2016) *Politics and Time: Documenting the Event*, Cambridge: Polity.

Yang, Chi-Hui (2013) 'Q&A with Linda Hattendorf on "The Cats of Mirikitani",' *Cinema Asian America*, at: http://my.xfinity.com/blogs/tv/2013/08/01/cinema-asian-america-qa-with-linda-hattendorf-on-the-cats-of-mirikitani/.

Žižek, Slavoj (2006) 'Kate's Choice, Or the Materialism of Henry James,' in *Lacan: The Silent Partners*, ed. Slavoj Žižek, New York: Verso, pp. 228–311.

SUGGESTED READING

For more analyses of the way the arts treat the Hiroshima bombing, see the Brad Evans and Keith Tester–edited special issue of *Thesis Eleven* published to mark the 70th anniversary of the bombing of Hiroshima and Nagasaki #129, August 2015, with additional articles by Keith Tester, Susan Neiman, Maja Zehfuss, Hiro Saito, Arne Johan Vetlesen, and Henry A Giroux.

CHAPTER **4**

"The Light of Reason"

INTRODUCTION: ECLIPSES

In this chapter I draw from an essay published in the journal *Political Theory*,[1] an engagement between Thomas Hobbes's canonical treatises—with most of the attention on his *Leviathan*—and Bela Tarr's film *The Werckmeister Harmonies* (2000; along with the literary version on which it is based, a chapter with the same title in Laszlo Krasznahorkai's novel *The Melancholy of Resistance*). It is hard to miss the connection between Hobbes's *Leviathan* and the Tarr–Krasznahorkai story because central to the film, which follows the literary narrative, is the entry into a Hungarian town of a circus tractor pulling a container with an enormous stuffed whale (a leviathan) for exhibition. However, once I viewed the film several times and reread Hobbes's *Leviathan* with attention to the figuration in his treatise, many subtler clues suggested that Tarr and his co-screenwriter, Krasznahorkai, had Hobbes in mind when they wrote the screenplay. The first clue that connects the treatise with Hobbes features eclipses. Early in *Leviathan* Hobbes refers to the fear evoked by unusual occurrences, such phenomena as "monsters or unusual accidents, as eclipses, comets, rare meteors, earthquakes, inundations, uncouth births, and the like, which they called 'portenta' and 'ostenta,' because they thought them to portend or foreshow some great calamity to come."[2] He goes on to disparage "prognosticators" who turn natural events, among which are "[e]clipses," into "auguries," which are "thought to portend, or foreshew some great Calamity to come," and adds, "So easy are men to be drawn to believe anything, from such men as have gotten credit with them; and can with gentleness, and dexterity, take hold of their fear, and ignorance."[3]

Krasznahorkai's literary version of "The Werckmeister Harmonies" begins with a scene in which an eclipse is both obliquely referenced and mimed. However, to set the stage for how the eclipse is contextualized, when it first appears in Krasznahorkai's Werckmeister story, we have to appreciate his sorting of

114 "THE LIGHT OF REASON"

diverse temporalities. The chapter begins with a long single-sentence description, full of diverse temporal references to the activities in a café:

> Since Mr. Hagelmayer, the proprietor of Pfeffer and Co, Licensed Victuallers of Hid Road . . . was usually longing for bed by this time and had begun to consult his watch with an ever sterner look on his face ("Eight O'clock, closing time, gentlemen!"), which meant . . . that he would shortly turn down the steadily purring oil-heater in the corner, switch off the light and, opening the door, usher his reluctant customers out into the unwelcoming icy wind beyond—it was no surprise to the happy and grinning Valuska . . . to be called upon, even encouraged to explain this business of "the erf and the mune", for this is what he had asked for last night, the night before and goodness knows how many nights before that, if only to distract the stubborn attention of the loud if sleepy landlord and allow for one last all-important spritzer.[4]

The sentence articulates and places in tension diverse perspectives on time. There is the proprietary time associated with opening and closing hours of the café (a concern of its grumpy proprietor, whose preoccupation is the rhythms of his sleeping and waking), the drinking times of the café's habitué's (always seeking to prolong their evening), and the cosmological time with which the character, Janos Valuska, is fascinated. He marvels at the order of the cosmos and is desirous of explaining its temporal rhythms, which he does by creating a celestial choreography with the bodies of the café's clientele (choosing one to play the sun and others to rotate around each other—the earth body around the sun and, simultaneously, the moon body around the earth).

In Tarr's film version the opening scene manages the clash of temporalities with an extended long take. Like the novel, the film features a contrast between the domestic rhythms of the café's opening and closing times and the celestial rhythms associated with eclipses. It begins with the camera doing an extended close up of the café's oven burner (Figure 4.1), which represents the materiality of the café's temporal rhythms; it provides the café's warmth during opening hours and is extinguished when the café closes.

After a close-up of the oven burner, we see the proprietor, Mr. Hagelmayer, creating the film story's first eclipse; he douses the fire with a pitcher of water in preparation for closing time. The camera then backs up to provide a framing shot of the entirety of the café's interior as its inebriated habitués stagger around. Shortly afterward, the choreography of drunken staggering is displaced by an imposed choreography by Valuska (Lars Rudolph), who enters near closing time. The drinkers, eager to prolong their evening, invite him to stage his cosmological play. Once he has the celestial structure operating (having the bar's patrons play a sun figure at the center, an earth figure circling

"THE LIGHT OF REASON" 115

FIGURE 4.1
Café oven. Source: Bela Tarr, *Werckmeister Harmonies*, Bela Tarr Productions (2000).

FIGURE 4.2
The celestial group. Source: Bela Tarr, *Werckmeister Harmonies*, Bela Tarr Productions (2000).

him, and a moon figure simultaneously circling the earth (Figure 4.2), he announces a celestial event, an eclipse. Describing it while choreographing it, he refers to a dark shadow that grows bigger so that soon only a narrow crescent of the sun can be seen.

116   "THE LIGHT OF REASON"

The scene proceeds slowly. Inspired by Krasznahorkai's long sentences, "Tarr's long take calls for a slow encounter with the material of narrative."[5]

While Valuska is announcing the dramatic event, he pushes the sun figure downward and has the rest of the celestial ensemble lower themselves in a representation of an eclipse. Then, while his celestial ensemble is lowered, he says (in both the novel and the film),

> The air gets suddenly colder "can you feel it?" the sky darkens and then all goes dark. The dogs howl, rabbits hunch down, the deer runs in panic . . . incomprehensible dusk, even the birds too are confused and go to roost, and then complete silence, everything is still . . . are the hills going to march off, will heaven fall upon us, will the earth open under us? We don't know for a total eclipse has come upon us.[6]

The camera then pulls back from the celestial grouping, with Valuska at the center saying, "But no need to fear; it's not over, for across the suns glowing sphere, the moon swims away and the sun again bursts forth." He then proceeds to lift the body of the sun character to an upright position once more and has the other figures stand as well to re-create the moving celestial choreography, as he says, "[T]he light and warmth again floods the earth." Similarly, the customers can expect that tomorrow they will be experiencing the warmth of the café from the relit oil burner, brought back into line, recovered from its closing-time "eclipse."

Valuska's intervention is an anachronism in that it brings back "solar time" in a modern period, which since the Renaissance has seen "social time" displacing solar time. Daniel Bensaid summarizes the shift: "From the Renaissance onward, social time supplanted solar time. The reassuring signs of the calendar and the uneven hours of the seasons were erased in indifferently divisible equal hours. Clocks and dials multiplied."[7] Although the celestial choreography scene is similar in both Werckmeister texts, where Krasznahorkai's novel explores the phenomenological depth of the characters who must cope with both expected and disturbing events, in Tarr's film, the camera shots themselves are events; they focus our attention on the discrete moments that emerge from Krasznahorkai's imagery instead of from his narrative. "[W]e argue," writes Steven Marchant perspicaciously,

> that what is achieved in the *Werckmeister* shot is inseparable from its being achieved in photography. The shot . . . is poorly understood when conceived as a representation, an act of looking or a window onto events, for the shot itself is an event—a photographic event.[8]

That cinematic style (like Krasznahorkai's literary style), which thinks in terms of discrete events or moments (a temporality the Greeks designated as *kairos* rather than in a traditional chronological sequence, which the Greeks designated as *chronos*), provides a frame for articulating what is effectively a critique of Hobbesian thinking by evoking the historical, visual, and temporal tropes that assemble the politics of the Hobbesian text. It is an approach that Foucault terms "eventualization," which eschews the legitimation of an order (Hobbes's preoccupation) and exposes relationships between knowledge and coercion (the political impetus of both Werckmeister texts).[9]

FILM FORM ECLIPSES NARRATIVITY

In addition to providing the contrast between the temporal rhythms of the café and that of the cosmos, simulating celestial dynamics in front of a stove and around a sun, respectively, the eclipse sets the tone for the rest of the film, which, through Tarr's cinematic play of light and dark, proceeds as a long shadow play. What the novel develops conceptually and figuratively, using an abundance of heliocentric tropes (which one finds as well in Hobbes's *Leviathan*), is manifested in the film with images enacted with a series of tonal choices, Tarr's plays of light and dark, which deliver much of the way the film thinks. "Images are closely related to concepts"[10] (as the filmmaker Harun Farocki puts it). Miming the eclipse, dark shadows cross lighted areas and dark figures pass before illuminated spaces and buildings, animating the visual moods that Krasznahorkai's light/dark-oriented tropes create in the literary version. In addition, the café scene's evocation of the "fear," to which Valuska refers, as he suggests that they can all be comforted by the certainty of the sun's return, is also central to Hobbes's rendering of the basis of communal coherence (in his case the basis for the implied contract legitimating centralized sovereign power). In the Werckmeister story, the reference to fear introduces a theme that is to arise after the characters in the novel leave the café and after the film narrative exits the confines of the café with them, to have the camera explore the small Hungarian town whose population is to be confronted with a fearsome chaos-inducing event.

THE COMPOSITIONAL STRATEGY

The unmistakable clues that suggest a Hobbesian framing of the Werckmeister story encouraged me to compose an essay (recast and somewhat rearranged here) in which I heed Hobbes's textual strategies to extract an aesthetic Hobbes, who provides the figuration with which Krasznahorkai and Tarr's screenplay challenges his political vision. It turned out that by reading the texts together (Hobbes's treatise with the film and book versions of the Werckmeister story), I was able to think *against* the political Hobbes by thinking *with* the aesthetic Hobbes. Moreover, from a methodological point of view, I could show how cinema and political theory can illuminate each other. It became evident as I watched the film and observed Hobbes's and Krasznahorkai's writing styles that Krasznahorkai and Tarr's literary/cinematic story, suffused with Hobbesian figuration, thinks both with and against Hobbes as it incorporates and reinflects aspects of Hobbes's treatise, especially his focus on the struggle between order and chaos.[11]

At the same time, just as Krasznahorkai's and Tarr's Werckmeister texts provide an innovative and critical way to read Hobbes, Hobbes's text provides a critical frame for an analysis of the political sensibilities in their literary and cinematic versions of the story. As is the case in the analyses in Chapters 1 and 3, the analysis here of the Tarr–Krasznahorkai film relies on the method of philopoesis, which Cesare Casarino applies to literary texts, the staging of an "interference" between philosophy, which features mainly concepts, and literary and cinematic texts, which are primarily assemblages of affects and percepts.[12] To elaborate the method once again and explicate its application in this chapter, I want to point out that although my emphasis is on what Casarino calls the "second type of interference," which occurs when "a practice slips imperceptibly into the domain of another practice," constituting an "interference . . . in which we witness a veritable becoming-philosophy of literature and a becoming-literature of philosophy,"[13] I also note the within-text, "first type of interference" he treats, which occurs when a practice "attempts to grasp from within its own domain and according to its own methods the defining features of another practice."[14] That type of interference is evident in the literary texts with which I am dealing—Hobbes's and Krasznahorkai's texts—both of which combine conceptual and aesthetic dimensions as they inter-articulate philosophical and literary effects. As a result, I include an extended analysis of Hobbes's aesthetic strategy.

While traditional treatments of Hobbes treatises focus on the logical structure of his political philosophy, it is evident that throughout *Leviathan*, "Hobbes often performs the unexpected, waxing and waning between logical and rhetorical, deliberative and exhortative writing."[15] And crucially, I insist much of the political sensibility one can derive from Hobbes's *Leviathan* yields itself with attention to Hobbes's style, especially his figuration, which has abundant resonances in the Krasznahorkai and Tarr versions of the Werckmeister story. Because much of my concern in this chapter (as in the rest of this pedagogical handbook) is on the intermediation of artistic media genres, I need to characterize the way a literary aesthetic is realized within a cinematic adaptation.

"THE LIGHT OF REASON" 119

LONG TAKES: LITERARY AND CINEMATIC

In two passages, one in Krasznahorkai's novel *War & War* (2006) and the other in his "Werckmeister Harmonies" chapter, there are literary equivalents of cinematic long takes, the first describing the sensations experienced by men and women observing the beauty of a flight attendant:

> The nipples delicately pressed through the warm texture of the snow-white starched blouse while deep *decollage* boldly accentuated the graceful curvature and fragility of the neck, the gentle valleys of the shoulders and the light swaying to and fro of the sweetly compact masses of her breasts, although it was hard to tell whether it was these that drew the eyes inexorably to her, that refused to let the eyes escape, or it was the short dark-blue skirt that clung to her hips . . . that arrested them; in other words men and women caught in the moment . . .—they stared quite openly, the men with crude, long-suppressed hunger and naked desire, the women with a fine attention to the accumulation of detail . . . dizzy with sensation but, driven by a malignant jealousy at the heart of their fierce inspection.[16]

The second is of the ugliness of a circus factotum, observed by Valuska:

> [H]is attention was drawn to a great mountain of flesh, well over six feet high, standing in the now clear "entrance" of the circus, a figure whose role was apparent not only from the fact that despite the intense cold he wore nothing but a dirty vest over his bulging and hairy torso (a "factotum" would in any case be expected to dislike the heat), but from his badly disfigured and generally squashed nose, the effect of which was not so much fierce as foolish, lending him an air of surprising innocence.[17]

The single-sentence passages are typical of Krasznahorkai's aesthetic; they dwell uninterruptedly on the embodied sensing of experience (the original Greek sense of aesthetics, *aisthetikos*). Krasznahorkai's aesthetic functions within what Jacques Rancière famously designates as the "aesthetic regime of the arts," a version of "novelistic realism" that offers "a fragmented or proximate mode of focalization, which imposes raw presence to the detriment of the rational sequences of the story."[18] Krasznahorkai's emphasis on physicality is also characteristic of Tarr's cinematic practice in which the lives of ordinary people are explored with lengthy long takes that emphasize the "physical experiences of his actors."[19]

Krasznahorkai's passage on beauty in his *War & War* is not articulated with the narrative thread, which follows the protagonist, Korin, a clerk archivist from a Hungarian town outside of Budapest who heads to New York to place a manuscript on the Internet so it will endure. In this novel there are no

120   "THE LIGHT OF REASON"

strong hints that Thomas Hobbes is a shadow presence, as he is more clearly in Krasznahorkai's *The Melancholy of Resistance*, in which his "Werckmeister Harmonies" chapter contains not only the Hobbes icon, a leviathan, but also other Hobbes figures, for example a prince whose presence is less important for his individual personhood than for how he serves as a reflective sounding board for the passions of everyman. But it is not implausible to read the title of *War & War* as inspired by Hobbes's famous designation of the state of nature in his *Leviathan* as a war of all against all. Another Hobbes hint is also available in *War & War* when the protagonist, Korin, describes both his own inner struggle and the experiences of a historically itinerate group whose exploits in wars are the subject of his found (or invented) manuscript, saying, "[T]here is only war and war everywhere . . ."[20] At a minimum, there are many indications of the influence of Hobbes's famous philosophical treatise embedded in much of Krasznahorkai's literary work, which renders the novels as philosophico-literary works whose mixing of conceptual and literary tropes exemplify what Casarino designates as the "first" modality of interference, the type of interference that occurs when a literary text creates "pure sensations of concepts," as it incorporates "the defining features of another practice" (in this case, the conceptual practices involved in political philosophy).[21]

That first modality of interference operates within Hobbes's text as well. Famously averse to metaphorical language—"[m]etaphors, and senseless ambiguous words, are like *ignes fatui*; and reasoning upon them is wandering amongst innumerable absurdities,"[22] he writes—the text is nevertheless replete with figural language, especially tropes involving, motion, light, and "reading" (the last his metaphor for understanding both oneself and others).[23] Moreover, Hobbes provides a metatextual guide to the reading of the text, suggesting that his treatise is both argumentatively conceptual (to encourage judgment) and reflectively literary (to suspend rash judgment). He sees as crucial to his argument both clear conceptual language (involving "severity of judgment") and "eloquence" (involving "celerity of fancy"), where the latter introduces a degree of ambiguity that suspends rapid closure on what is "Right and Wrong."[24] The combination of the two textual orientations must co-occur, Hobbes insists, because "Resolutions of men are rash, and their Sentences unjust . . . if there not be powerfull Eloquence, which procureth attention and Consent, the effect of Reason will be little."[25]

Significantly, *both* Hobbes and Krasznahorkai guide their readers with metatextual explications of their writing. Krasznahorkai's Korin, in *War & War*, explains the rationale for long sentences:

> There is an order in the sentences: words, punctuation, periods, commas all in place . . . and yet the events that follow in the last chapter may be characterized as a series of collapses . . . for the sentences have lost their reason, not just growing ever longer and longer but galloping desperately onward in a harum scarum scramble—*crazy rush.*[26]

"THE LIGHT OF REASON"   121

Given the fevered scramble that constitutes the consciousness of Krasznahorkai's Korin, the long, galloping sentences render the reader present to the modality of Korin's musings; the writing, as Krasznahorkai suggests, "draws us toward the consciousness of his archivist character."[27] Hobbes suggests a similar phenomenology of reading, offering a variety of suggestions about how to read *Leviathan*, among which is advice to the reader to "read thy self" in order to grasp "the similitude of the thoughts and Passions of one man, to the thoughts and Passions of another,"[28] and ultimately to understand the intellectual and emotional basis for "men" to yield to a sovereign authority. Thus, attention to an author's guidance about the consciousness-affecting writing style of a novel that is haunted by Hobbes turns our attention to Hobbes as a writer who was also attuned to the phenomenology of reading.

The intertextual resonances between Krasznahorhkai's and Tarr's Werckmeister texts and Hobbes's are even more pronounced. However, before I stage more of the engagement between "The Werckmeister Harmonies" and Hobbes's *Leviathan*, I want to rehearse the form-effects involved in the translation of Krasznahorkai's novelistic version (1998) into Tarr's film version. The Hobbes effects operate differently in the two different media genres. Whereas Krasznahorkai's version of the story employs a novelistic aesthetic—a plurality of perspectives articulated as multiple phenomenologies of (embodied) perception and as enactments in the form of "contending voices,"[29] clashing within a spatially bounded social field—Tarr's film articulates the characters' perspectives primarily with images and with variations in lighting while rehearsing the story's complex array of temporalities with long takes that constitute a cinematic articulation of Krasznahorkai's long sentences.

There is thus a striking homology between their aesthetics—long sentences, often encompassing entire paragraphs in the novel, and a cinematic style that uses long takes and relatively few cuts (Tarr favors the sequence shot and an emphasis on discrete events). By heeding the stylistic complicity of the novelist and film director with attention to novel–film translation and contrast, I extract from both a critical politics of temporality within which the story as written or animated becomes an appropriation and radical reinflection of Hobbes's *Leviathan*. Hobbes's text is also anchored by a temporal sequence, but it is one that is a mythic and wholly abstract "transformation of temporal consciousness,"[30] as citizens tacitly agree to move from a chaotic and fearful state of nature to a contracted, centralized state of lawful governance.[31] In contrast, both Werckmeister texts displace Hobbes's abstractions and idealized temporality (his imagined transfer of a mythic state of war to a mythic contract) with characters with diverse temporal allegiances, struggling within a concrete historically situated venue.[32] Yet the Werckmeister texts share with Hobbes a view of the social world as an arena of sensation and an emphasis on visuality. Like Krasznahorkai and Tarr, Hobbes was very much a visually oriented thinker. As Carl Schmitt suggests (in reference to Hobbes's frontispiece image

122   "THE LIGHT OF REASON"

in *Leviathan*), "[i]n the long history of political theories, a history exceedingly rich in colorful images and symbols, icons and idols, paradigms and phantasms, emblems and allegories, this leviathan is the strongest and most powerful image."[33] Drawing on Hobbes's imagery—the iconic leviathan and his many other visual tropes—the Werckmeister texts think within a Hobbesian aesthetic while challenging the historical prescience of his political commitments. They provide an incentive for recovering the thought worlds that frame both texts while at the same time giving us an opportunity to assess the contemporary value of Hobbes's famous treatise from an angle of vision that acutely critical cinema can offer.

A RETURN TO TARR'S *WERCKMEISTER HARMONIES*

Once Tarr's camera leaves Mr. Hagelmayer's café, the narrative turns to the arrival of a circus that plans to display the stuffed body of a huge whale and follows the narrative developed in Krasznahorkai's Werckmeister chapter. Rumors proliferate, and as the notice of the circus spreads, many assume that the circus organizers (and the enigmatic "Prince" who accompanies the circus) have an evil purpose. To cope with the disconcerting event, "[t]he frightened citizens cling to any manifestation of order they can find—music, cosmology, fascism."[34] Cryptic though that very brief summary may be, it captures the inter-articulated temporal aspects of the novel well. Krasznahorkai summons diverse historical frames and texts to articulate anxious and ultimately violent responses to perceived disorder, provoked by a threat to the coherence of the town's collective subjectivity by a "sublime" episode, an event involving something of enormous magnitude, identified in the description of the whale as "that innocent carcass vaster than imagination."[35] However, this sublime is unlike the Kantian version in which one takes comfort in realizing one's freedom, where (in Kant's words) one first experiences

> a feeling of inadequacy of [the] imagination for presenting the ideas of a whole, wherein the imagination reaches its maximum, and, in striving to surpass it, [but then] sinks back into itself, by which, however, a kind of emotional satisfaction is produced.[36]

In this case, emotional turmoil and violent acting out rather than satisfaction results.

In Krasznahorkai's novel, the impact of the sublime event is mediated by the diversity of temporal orientations in his collection of characters whose heterogeneous allegiances derive from diverse ontological pasts, each bringing

"THE LIGHT OF REASON" 123

longer-term temporalities into a confrontation with the present temporal rhythms of the small Hungarian town. Valuska's resistance to the fear that pervades the town is a result of his distraction from his immediate surroundings. His allegiance is to a cosmological reason, a deistic ontology in which the celestial order is an expression of a divine plan. While some in the town are attuned to local power arrangements—for example, a collaborative enterprise between an estranged wife, Tunde Eszter, and the chief constable who seek to exploit the turmoil and take control of the town—Valuska is a historical type who is a partisan of a celestial ontology. Preoccupied with eternal rather than contingent events, he seeks attunement to a changeless order. He desires "*rapture*" rather than power.[37]

The eponymous (Andreas) Werckmeister, embraced the same celestial ontology in which God's plan, manifested in the harmony of the celestial system, provides instruction for thinking/existing within the terrestrial domain. In his *Harmonologia Musica*, where he analyzes the harmonies of double counterpoint, Werckmeister turns to allegory:

> One such interpretive move in the *Harmonologia* hinges on a comparison between the movement of invertible counterpoint [a switching in the dominance of voices: A above B switched to B above A] and the motion of the planets, where cosmology and harmony are manifestations of the same universal principle [for Werckmeister viewed] . . . the constant motion of the heavens [as] . . . analogous to the perpetual revolution of the parts in a well-constructed piece of double counterpoint, whose inversions mirror the perfection of heavens and provide earthy beings with a glimpse of God's unending order, a prelude to the heavenly concert.[38]

The novel incorporates and re-inflects Werckmeister's invertible counterpoint with a contrast between its main two characters, Janos Valuska, and Gyorgy Eszter (Tunde's estranged husband), a learned musician at work revising Werckmeister's harmonic model by trying to adjust his piano (ultimately unsuccessfully) to a "natural" tuning. The two characters interact throughout the novel, for in addition to his role as a newsboy distributing a local newspaper, Valuska serves Eszter as a virtual valet, daily helping him retire for the night and arise each morning, and bringing him his lunch (despite his fixation on the eternal, Valuska's tasks are quotidian). Miming Werckmeister's invertible counterpoint, their relationship is contrapuntal. At times one or the other's radically different ontologies becomes the primary lens through which the spaces and events in the novel are viewed.[39] Those frames derive from venerable, incommensurate philosophical systems. Valuska's ontology harks back to antiquity, exemplified in Plato's *Timaeus*, where he has the celestial bodies materialize eternal time; they both mime eternity and provide

124 "THE LIGHT OF REASON"

the basis for measuring it. In Plato's words, "time was made in the image of eternal nature . . . All these bodies became living creatures, and learnt their appointed tasks."[40]

As Krasznahorkai's story suggests, because Valuska locates himself in the cosmological temporal order, he derives no messages from his immediate, terrestrial environment: "[D]isappointed in his desire to have the dizzying vaults of heaven constantly in view, [Valuska] had got used to staring at nothing but the ground beneath him, and consequently didn't actually 'see' the town at all."[41] In stark contrast, Eszter's perspective constitutes the major historical challenge to the cosmological ontology embraced by Valuska (and Werckmeister). He is a representative of what J. G. A. Pocock calls "the Machiavellian moment," the point (noted in the Introduction) at which people began seeing themselves as historical beings and thus as citizens of a city rather than as subjects of an eternal, heaven-centered cosmology.[42] A legacy of that "moment," Eszter's focus is on the (dis)order of the town—for example, a moment in which he tries (unsuccessfully) to establish the logic of its totality from its various physical elements; from the novel:

> His gaze took in the storm-lamps and the pillars covered in advertisements; he observed the bare tops of the chestnut trees and let his eyes run down both ends of the main road, seeking an explanation in terms of distance, size or discrepancy in proportions. But he found no answer there, so he tried to locate an axis that might impose some meaning on the town's ostensible disorder.[43]

Tarr's cinematic rendering of the Valuska–Eszter contrapuntal relationship is articulated in a key sequence, as a long take of the two walking through the town with two sensory effects on display. Marchant's description of the scene captures its implications of well:

> Janos and Eszter walking side-by-side into town, the two of them in step together, with the constant, steady sound of their heavy boots walking on changing surfaces accompanied by the low howl of the wind, the clank of billycans and the rustle of clothing (Figure 4.3). Held in close overlapping profile against a featureless background.[44]

The sound of their heavy boots (a sensation-based coding of the scene) is a preview of a later scene with a much louder sound, produced by the hundreds of boots of a fear-crazed mob that marches from the town square to a hospital to attack the patients. The novel and the film apply different sensory frames to the episode. In Krasznahorkai's novel version, "the two had to harmonize two ways of walking, two different speeds and indeed two different kinds

FIGURE 4.3
Valuska and Eszter walking. Source: Bela Tarr, *Werckmeister Harmonies*, Bela Tarr Productions (2000).

of incapacity"[45] (for Valuska had to hold up the relatively infirm Eszter and experiences the burden of his weight). In the film version, the other sensory aspect of the scene derives from the characters' differently aimed gazes. Tarr articulates their different ontologies during the long take of their walk by having Valuska's eyes cast mostly downward (a visual realization of Krasznahorkai's sentence: "Disappointed in his desire to have the dizzying vaults of heaven constantly in view, [Valuska] had got used to staring at nothing but the ground beneath him, and consequently didn't actually 'see' the town at all") and having Eszter's gaze aimed straight ahead, a visual articulation of Eszter's city focus (which in the novel's refers to his attempt "to locate an axis that might impose some meaning on the town's ostensible disorder"). Nevertheless, although the Platonic and Machiavellian systems illuminate the contrapuntal relationship between the two characters, it is Hobbesian political philosophy, Hobbesian skepticism and the Hobbesian aesthetic sensibility that apply more pervasively to the overall story.

Hobbes's political solution to anarchy is skepticism-driven. For Hobbes, how we are for each other is not provided by Valuska's resort, "an indubitable cosmological map according to which we place ourselves in the universe...."[46] "Averse" to any certainties about what is warranted as right and wrong, Hobbes promotes "the pursuit of peace rather than ... truth,"[47] a peace that he presumed could be achieved through a series of fear-inspired contractual

126   "THE LIGHT OF REASON"

commitments to a centralized authority. In Kraszanhorkai's "Werckmeister Harmonies," Gyorgy Eszter is his Hobbesian skeptic. Like Hobbes, he is a religious skeptic: "Better to keep silent . . . and not speculate about our late creator's no doubt exalted purposes," he thinks.[48] But unlike Hobbes, Eszter embraces no harmony-providing solutions, either musical or political, having discovered (contra Andreas Werckmeister) that there are no tuning solutions because there are no natural harmonies. Applying his skepticism equally to the social arena, he discerns no reliably peaceful order that would abrogate the chaos of interpersonal antagonism. As a result, he turns out to be prescient about the totalitarian policing consequences of the local project (led by his ex-wife, Tunde) to impose a police state-enforced political harmony. Through Eszter's discernments, Krasznahorkai's story tests Hobbes's political conceits in a contemporary Hungary that has experienced the totalitarian consequences of social peace-justifying, imposed orders.

DEFORMING HOBBES'S FEAR-INSPIRED MYTHIC CONTRACT

While Hobbes's approach to fear and its consequences is based on a series of singular mythic events—autonomous individuals agreeing to surrender their competitive proclivities in exchange for a sovereign's protection—Krasznahorkai and Tarr animate fear and its consequences as it possesses acting bodies. And notably, within the cinematic text, the fearful bodies are best understood as aesthetic subjects. Rather than a merely a psychological attribute, fear in Tarr's "Werckmeister Harmonies" translation is constituted by what it does to cinematic space and to a cinematically articulated mood (rendered through sounds and through light versus dark variations).[49]

While fear is central to the plot in both the novel and the film, the two texts treat it quite differently. As I have noted, Krasznahorkai's approach is phenomenological. His prose emphasizes the practices through which people make and seek to stabilize their worlds and the consequences for them of being faced with (or at least imagining) a disorder that is precipitated by a sublime event, the unanticipated arrival of an enormous whale (leviathan). In the novel collective fear is screened through Valuska's perspective. As he moves about the town, Valuska notices that

> [e]veryone he met was preoccupied by the notion of "the collapse into anarchy" . . . the "unpredictability of daily life" . . . this epidemic of fear was not born out of some genuine, daily increasing certainty of disaster but of an infection of the imagination whose susceptibility to its own terrors might eventually led to a catastrophe.[50]

"THE LIGHT OF REASON"   127

To manage the bridge between a literary text and a film, we have to heed the play of images. Thus in contrast with the way Krasznahorkai uses literary trope to model fear, Tarr translates fear cinematically by showing its sensory materialization with images and plays of light and dark, as a growing pervasive fear shapes the town's spaces of interpersonal relations, especially as they develop in the town square, where the interactions among bodies is becoming increasing frenetic. To emphasize the chaotic and darkly coded physical events as discrete moments, Tarr breaks them into fragments by ending each long take with a fade to white. However, it is the shadows that generate the way the cinematic mood articulates the chaotic emotional climate. Once Valuska leaves the café and heads to the home of Eszter, Tarr's shadow play generates repetitions of the temporary darkening caused by the eclipse that Valuska performs with the café's customers. First, there is a benign shadow; Valuska's shadow passes by the windows of Eszter's house, just before he enters. The next scene appears less benign. The circus's great stuffed whale arrives in the middle of the night. As a tractor pulls the whale's container along the street, an ominous-looking sequence of light sweeps across the buildings, which are then shown in darkness as it slowly moves down the street. The sequence mimes an eclipse as the tractor's headlights cast light on the buildings temporarily and then leave them in darkness. It is a sequence we see through Valuska's point of view while he is standing in the street (Figure 4.4). And in a later scene, an even more ominous play of shadows takes place. When the fear-crazed mob reaches the hospital,

FIGURE 4.4
Eclipse mimed on the building. Source: Bela Tarr, *Werckmeister Harmonies*, Bela Tarr Productions (2000).

128 "THE LIGHT OF REASON"

there is a sequence shot of their shadows passing by the high windows of the hospital's main room.

Rather than treating the inner lives of the townspeople (Krasznahorkai's approach), which yields their susceptibilities to mass panic and a violent acting out, Tarr figures the result by filming a play of light and dark, emphasizing the altered significance of shadows moving across lighted surfaces with eclipse-like extinctions of illuminated surfaces. And he supplements his shadow play with different levels of sound—for example, the moderate sounds of Valuska's and Eszter's boots as they walk across town together versus the loud sounds of the mob's boots in a long take of their march to the hospital (a phenomenon well captured by Elias Canetti who describes the rhythms of a rioting mob's feet: "a long stretch of time in which they continue to sound loud and alive").[51]

To return to the way the texts constitute a commentary on Hobbes's *Leviathan*, apart from the difference between their aesthetic forms—phenomenological versus imagistic and tonal—the fear problematic in both the novel and film is shaped by a deformation of Hobbes *Leviathan*. Certainly, the whale, a stuffed leviathan, is an unmistakable clue that Hobbes's text is being mined for concepts and images. However, there are also more subtle clues. At one point the novel, referring to Eszter's speculations, represents them as "the motions of his mind,"[52] which accords with the way Hobbes renders personhood—both body and mentality—as motion.[53] Hobbes was "obsessed by the idea of motion," which was central to his "science of politics," as C. B. Macpherson puts it.[54] Also, just as Hobbes privileges a monarchical model of sovereignty, a singular authority, the monarch's stand-in, the Prince is referred to in the novel as "the One."[55]

Most essential for the Hobbes effect in both texts is Hobbes's explanation for a fundamentally selfish humanity's turn to society ("Fear of death and wounds . . . [and] Feare of oppression disposeth a man to anticipate or to seek ayd by society").[56] It is the potential turmoil that selfishness (in the form of a desire for riches and power)[57] can engender that leads Hobbes to promote a singular authority in the form of a monarchy, which is figured in the frontispiece of his treatise. However, although Hobbes's monarch is a proto-text for the Prince in both Werckmeister versions, Krasznahorkai and Tarr "deform" that figure, resisting Hobbes's "figurative givens."[58] Rather than a unifying political figure, Krasznahorkai's Prince is among other things a "trickster," although "not merely."[59] Testifying to the shadow imagery that drives the film version, "Tarr, . . . [when] asked about the meaning of the film, [and] among other things about his perspective on the Prince,"[60] says (in English), "I haven't seen him. I have only seen his shadow."[61] Similarly Krasznahorkai has the Prince seem "[t]o emerge out of shadows of things where the conventions of the tangible world no longer applied, a place compounded of impossibility

"THE LIGHT OF REASON"   129

and incomprehensibility from which he radiated a magnetism so powerful that . . . his status far exceeded that of a freak in any circus side-show."[62]

Krasznahorkai's Prince serves as a combination of reflective background and sounding board, a figure that provokes projections of internal disorder, which Jacques Lacan famously theorized. The town's people (to borrow Lacan's words about identity anxiety) "throw back on the world the disorder of which [their] being is composed"[63] Unlike the Hobbesian sovereign, who draws the body politic into a coherent order, Krasznahorkai's and Tarr's texts invent a Prince who stands as a rebuttal to Hobbes's notion of the harmonizing effect of a centralizing sovereign. Rather than a sovereign composed of a legitimating set of singular decisions, the Werckmeister "Prince" is a trickster who provides no collective benefit. However, despite the reversals and contraries that Krasznahorkai and Tarr invent to discredit the historical relevance of the Hobbesian model of harmonizing governance, the aesthetic Hobbes has positive resonances with their story.

THE LITERARY AND CINEMATIC HOBBES: THINKING/WRITING WITH BODIES AND LIGHT

Hobbes's *Leviathan* was a dramatic (and controversial) departure from seventeenth-century treatises on the body politic. The physical tropes in Krasznahorkai's Werckmeister and images in Tarr's translation comport well with Hobbes's displacement of a prior historical ontology. Concerned with finding a solution to the political chaos of his century (notably the English civil wars), Hobbes replaced his century's entrenched divinely inspired model of a polity with an anatomical model in which the principal political operative, a unifying sovereign, represented as a large body, must humanize (make civil) the beastly existence of "men" who are effectively wolves to each other.[64] Resonating with Hobbes's imagery, Krasznahorkai's and Tarr's characters act out an animality, evinced rhetorically in the novel and imagistically in the film. For example, in the novel, Eszter at one point refers to his estranged wife, Tunde, as "that dangerous prehistoric beast from whom 'by the grace of God' he has separated long ago,"[65] while in the film Tarr has her creeping around cat-like as her conspiracy evolves. And most significantly, their Prince, unlike Hobbes's sovereign, brings out the beast in the men who assemble in the town square and ultimately rampage like a pack of wild animals as they rush to attack the town's hospital.

Also significantly, Hobbes's writing lends itself well to both Krasznahorkai's and Tarr's light-based imagery. Throughout *Leviathan*, a heliotropic metaphoricity is in evidence. "*Darkness* is [Hobbes's] controlling metaphor";[66] his entire fourth chapter is titled "Of the Kingdome of Darkness," and the light-versus-dark tropes are pervasive throughout the text (e.g., intelligibility for Hobbes functions through "perspicacious words," which constitute "the light of humane minds,"[67] while "spiritual darkness" derives from scriptural "misinterpretation").[68] And perhaps adding inspiration for the opening of Krasznahorkai's Werckmeister story, Hobbes figures failures of good sense as "darkness" in the form of "eclipses of reason."[69] Doubtless enhancing a suspicion that Hobbes inspires Krasznahorkai's story are various other references to eclipses in *Leviathan* as well. For example, recalling Valuska's remark about not fearing the eclipse, we can heed Hobbes's observation (quoted above) that people fear such phenomena as "monsters or unusual accidents, as eclipses, comets, rare meteors, earthquakes, inundations, uncouth births, and the like, which they called 'portenta' and 'ostenta,' because they thought them to portend or foreshow some great calamity to come."[70] Like Hobbes, Krasznahorkai makes abundant use of darkness tropes for emotions such as fear and for intelligibility in general as well—for example, at a point in which Eszter ticks off what he knows about the various characters in the town and deems the town a "whole breeding ground of dark stupidity."[71]

When we turn to the cinematic version of Werckmeister, we are encouraged to discover a cinematic Hobbes whose imagery has even stronger aesthetic resonances with the Werckmeister story. To figure a political philosopher's thought as cinematic requires an engagement between the thinker's phenomenological way of having/perceiving the world and the way that camera work renders a world. For example, in his reprise of David Hume's philosophy as cinematic (noted in the Introduction), Davide Panagia begins by describing how Hume saw his world: "David Hume lived in a world besieged by artifice. It surrounds and moves about him in a discontinuous array of successions and fluctuations."[72] Having situated Hume's world in that way, Panagia's proceeds to construct the cinematic character of Hume's impressions by elaborating the relevant dimensions of cinematic thinking. Similarly, inasmuch as for Hobbes the world is a dynamic of motion that confronts consciousness (also construed as motion), the most relevant aspect of cinematic thinking is the way the camera captures the dynamics of motion. And because Hobbes's textual strategy involves radically separating ecclesiastical and political forms of authority, the way a film incorporates the spaces of motion becomes relevant, especially the way cinematic editing manages the binary of what at any given moment is in the picture or frame versus not in the picture or outside the frame (even though it may exercise an effect on what is inside the frame).

Hence, a cinematic construal of the Hobbesian aesthetic becomes especially apparent if we heed Hobbes's rejection of the way a static version of intelligibility was constructed by the writers in antiquity for whom "forms or ideas are . . . eternal or immobile."[73] For Hobbes, intelligibility emerges from two kinds of motions, that of mind and that of the world of objects, resulting (as I have noted elsewhere) in a "co-motion" as mind-as-motion encounters the flux of the lifeworld, the kind of encounter that is the condition of possibility for ideas.[74] That temporal shift from immobility to motion as a model for thinking is homologous with Deleuze's analysis of the movement image in cinema. Deleuze points out that once the camera (as a technology of consciousness) was put in motion, cinema-as-thinking was liberated from stasis, opening itself to "a flowing-matter in which no point of anchorage nor center of reference would be assignable."[75]

To add to a cinematic construal of Hobbes, we can interpret an aspect of his textual strategy by heeding Noel Burch's analysis of what he calls "*Two different kinds of [Cinematic] space*," what is "on the screen" or "within the frame" and what is off-screen or "outside the frame." To apply that cinematic metaphor to Hobbes, we can note (as I suggested) the way he renders the deity's appearances in scriptures.[76] For Hobbes, God is effectively off-screen, appearing onscreen in the form of miraculous events—for example, as a vision "in the form of a burning bush that was not consumed."[77] God's onscreen presence (as it were) is achieved through the way "He" is summoned through a reading of the scriptures. As James Martel nicely puts it, "[t]he miracle lies in the way the phenomenon becomes 'read' as a symbol . . ."[78] God-as-writer does not shape the (mythic) political events to which Hobbes addressed himself. "His" presence exists through the scriptural reading of believers, who through their reading reenact the religious covenant that hovers behind the political contract. However, that onscreen presence must not be a result of multiple readings, which would endanger the interpretive consensus that Hobbes wants to promote.

For Hobbes, the God of scriptures achieves an onscreen presence or incarnation by being "personated" by historico-biblical figures—"first, by Moses . . . Secondly, by . . . Jesus Christ. . . . And Thirdly, by the Holy Ghost, or Comforter, speaking and working in the Apostles."[79] Just as he conjures a unity from a multiplicity in his political gloss on sovereignty, Hobbes turns religious sovereignty into a unity; those who personate God are a "Multitude of men," [who] are made One Person."[80] Hobbes's divine sovereign remains textually enigmatic; his off-screen existence in scripture becomes onscreen or present only to the extent that scripture is read because there are no direct revelations. For Hobbes, God is "Infinite" (and thus sublime). "No man can have in his mind an image of infinite magnitude . . . (for he is Incomprehensible)."[81] Nevertheless, Hobbes fashions a "textual obedience"[82] rather than licensing a plurality of perspectives on the law-giving intentions of "the One." As I have suggested, he expunges pluralistic reading by selecting out from scripture designated interpreters, for example, Moses, who becomes a "sole authorized reader"[83] of scriptures, bringing an off-screen God onscreen and at the same time unifying scriptural interpretation. It is through such authorization

132   "THE LIGHT OF REASON"

of a biblical hermeneutics that Hobbes's constitution of a divine sovereignty becomes homologous with his model of political sovereignty.

REPLURALIZING HOBBES'S UNITIES

If we recall Krasznahorkai's Prince, who is described as "the One," we observe a play on Hobbes's notion of composition, where both God and the sovereign are unities made through multitudes. And where Krasznahorkai has his townspeople ascribe magical powers to the circus's Prince, there is a play on Hobbes's treatment of the similarity of effects generated by both God's miracles and the conjuring of magicians, effects that "produce, hope, fear other passions, or conceptions in the hearer."[84] Similarly, Krasznahorkai's Prince, who

> seemed to emerge out of the shadows of things where the conventions of the tangible world no longer applied, a place compounded of impossibility and incomprehensibility [like Hobbes's God], . . . radiated a magnetism so powerful that . . . his status far exceeded that of a freak in any circus side-show.[85]

Through both narrative and form, Krasznahorkai's "One" creates disorder rather than the unified order, sensed by Valuska, who found his (the One's) words a "pitiless and wholly alien clangour . . . rendered all the more fearsome by the fact that they had been interpreted in piecemeal fashion by an intermediary whose grasp of Hungarian was less than perfect."[86] In short, the Prince's designated reader/interpreter (the Director) exacerbates rather than clarifies the words of "the One," whose "magnetism" is both compelling and chaos-inducing. Where Hobbes solves the centrifugal political effects of words ("Words have no effect, but on those who understand them")[87] by selecting privileged interpreters, for example, Moses, "God's Lieutenant,"[88] Krasznahorkai's invented characters derive wholly diverse implications from the Prince's incomprehensible words (which sound to Valuska's ear like "grumbling and chirruping").[89] The interpretive chaos occasioned by the Prince's verbally enigmatic existence helps to precipitate the violence of the town's multitude as their varying perspectives on what the Prince is about clash.[90]

While Valuska is perplexed by the words of "the One," Krasznahorkai's other protagonist, Eszter, having given up on natural harmony, sides with the novel's sensibility by appreciating interpretive chaos. The sublime event precipitated by the circus whale and the perplexing, incomprehensible words of the characters who accompany it merely confirm his newfound anarchistic outlook. He had ultimately realized that

> the present state of the area never had the slightest shred of meaning in the first place . . . as if the only order inherent in it was that it fitted it for

"THE LIGHT OF REASON"   133

chaos . . . desiring to take action against something that simply doesn't exist nor ever will exist . . . is not only exhausting . . . but quite pointless. . . . "Henceforth" he says, "I will abjure all independent and lucid thought as if it were the crassest stupidity."[91]

HOBBES ENTERS THE STORY, PERSONATED BY CIRCUS MANAGERS

Gyorgy Eszter's recognition of the chaos-inducing effect of a circus accompanied by "the One," resonates with the challenge that the Werckmeister story mounts to Hobbes's *Leviathan*. In addition to the operators—a whale, a prince, and fear—and the homologies between Hobbes's and the Werckmeister aesthetics (a similarity of the tropes that shape the Werckmeister and Hobbes's texts), which render "The Werckmeister Harmonies" a reinflection of and challenge to Hobbes's *Leviathan*, arguably Hobbes himself appears in the story, divided between the two characters who manage the circus. Doubtless drawing on the title of Hobbes's later text, *Behemoth*, Krasznahorkai's "Factotum," a "circus helper," is described physically as an "apparently sickly and overweight figure . . . an enormous *behemoth* [my emphasis] of a man . . ."[92] That reference engages precisely the reinflection of Hobbes's *Leviathan* that the Werckmeister story presents. The two monsters that Hobbes draws from the book of Job to fashion two treatises, a leviathan (Job 41:1–2, a huge sea creature) and a behemoth (Job 40:15–24, a huge land animal), signify the "peace-enforcing function of the state" and "civil war" (the "the anarchy brought about by religious fanaticism") respectively.[93] Providentially (for purposes of my analysis), in *Questions Concerning Liberty, Necessity, and Chance*, Hobbes suggests that "Behemoth against Leviathan" would make the proper title of a treatise challenging his *Leviathan*.[94] The "Werckmeister Harmonies" effectively enacts that challenge with an anarchy-provoking Prince, sponsored and encouraged by a behemoth, against the imperatives of the whale-harboring, peace-desiring Director.

Tellingly, in the conversation that Valuska overhears between the circus managers, the "Director" and the behemoth/"Factotum," the Director, concerned with the growing chaos in the street, is arguing that the disruptive Prince must not be allowed out in public:

> The title of Prince . . . was one I bestowed on him as a business decision! Tell him that I invented him! . . . I alone have the faintest conception of the world about which he plies lie upon outrageous lie.[95]

He then concedes to "let him out on one small condition. That he keeps his mouth shut"[96] (i.e., that like Hobbes's frontispiece, he functions as a silent

134 "THE LIGHT OF REASON"

image/symbol). The Director's claim to having invented the Prince comports with an aspect of Hobbesian deception, the disguising of his agenda (a tendency that Victoria Kahn has addressed).[97] James develops the implications of Kahn's position, noting, "Hobbes sees himself not as the subject of sovereignty, but . . . as the author of it," and

> [s]ince there is no "truth" to this authority, Hobbes sets out the project of creating this authority the only way he can, rhetorically. But of course Hobbes cannot do this openly; the realization that the sovereign authority is a rhetorical product (much less a product of one of its citizens, i.e., Hobbes) would be devastating to that authority. Hence Hobbes must disguise the fact that he is not describing but producing that authority by denouncing both his rhetorical talents . . . and his authority as an author, pretending to cede it to the sovereign.[98]

What is the implication of Krasznahorkai's Director (who has invented the Prince), revealing his authorship and refusing to cede authority? I suggest that it can be read as an indictment of the Hobbesian model of unitary sovereignty. Ultimately, it would seem that in rejecting the contemporary relevance of Hobbes's *Leviathan* to a fraught historical period of national and local politics in Hungary, Krasznahorkai's and Tarr's Werckmeister has three tricksters, the Prince his inventor, and his factotum/promoter (who insists "his public is out there waiting . . . and they are growing impatient").[99] Was Hobbes a trickster? Kahn's ingenious suggestion notwithstanding, the biographical and textual evidence would have us avoid a precipitous judgment. Certainly, Hobbes text deploys a rhetorical force aimed at persuasion. If we heed Berel Lang's oft-noted modes of philosophical writing—"expository," "performative," and "reflexive"[100]—we can identify Hobbes's aesthetic choice as mainly performative (in the sense that J. L. Austin famously explicated performative discourse, especially the persuasive or "perlocutionary" force of statements).[101] Hobbes enjoins a performative reader, not simply one "directed to an external reality for which his own presence is a matter of indifference" (the "expository" style) but also one who reads with a particular perspective on oneself, to "reenact what the author has done . . .,"[102] that is, to "read thyself." However, as is well known, "the reader" was not Hobbes's sole interlocutor. The rhetorical force of *Leviathan* is assiduously designed by an author/thinker who was faced with a complicated ideational constituency—of rulers, ecclesiastical authorities, and oppositional intellectuals.

To reconstruct how Hobbes responded to the complication, we can figure Hobbes as a radical, anti-ecclesiastical political theologian, whose textual strategy performs a delicate operation; he promotes a secular state, enabled by rendering the church's deity incomprehensible thereby keeping "Him" out

"THE LIGHT OF REASON"   135

of the picture or off-screen with the effect of freeing political authority from ecclesiastical authority.[103] Is Hobbes's strategy for radicalizing politics straightforwardly confrontational or strategically elliptical, that is, arcane/esoteric? On one hand, Hobbes is arguably more radical in his critique of religion than Spinoza. However, on the other, because he is "very rhetorical, and . . . more diplomatic,"[104] his text is less confrontational and, in various ways, indirect. Among other things, while not wholly renouncing a belief in scripture, Hobbes undertakes a critique of spiritualism in order to "secure an absolute unity for civil power," exercised "merely fictitiously," as Leo Strauss puts it.[105] Moreover, if we recognize that Hobbes was both rhetorically playful and cautious, operating in a contentious political environment within which he wrote, it is tempting to see much of the *Leviathan* as arcane. Carl Schmitt, referring to Hobbes's famous icon, makes that case:

> Because of Hobbes' psychological peculiarity, it is possible that behind the image of the Leviathan is hidden a deeper symbolic meaning. Like all great thinkers of his times, Hobbes had a taste for esoteric coverups. He said about himself that now and then he made "overtures" but that he revealed his thoughts only in part and that he acted as people do who open a window only for a moment and close it quickly for fear of a storm.[106]

However, Giorgio Agamben challenges Schmitt's reading of Hobbes's famous icon as arcane with a comprehensive archive-driven rebuttal that is impressive (if not wholly convincing). Agamben argues that inasmuch as Hobbes wanted to "put political philosophy for the first time on a scientific basis,"[107] esoteric evasion makes no sense. To make *his* case, Agamben does a hermeneutic reading of the frontispiece, pointing to several enigmas. He points out, for example, that the frontispiece is constructed as an optical illusion, influenced by Hobbes's investigations of optics. Although the existence of the many enigmas he treats might suggest (in opposition to his insistence that Hobbes was consistently direct) that Hobbes occasionally turned to esoteric subterfuge, I want to draw on some of his valuable insights about the text and the context of its construction rather than impugn his argument against Schmitt's position.

One enigma noted by Agamben helps to situate particularly well the Werckmeister engagement with Hobbesian concepts. Focusing on the image of the city in the frontispiece, Agamben adds a crucial temporality to Hobbes's treatise. He notes that, "with the exception of some armed guards and two very special figures situated close to the cathedral," the city "is completely devoid of its inhabitants (and he rejects the explanation "that the population of the city has been fully transferred to the body of the Leviathan").[108] Turning to Hobbes's *De Cive*, Agamben suggests that Hobbes himself clarifies the enigma

136   "THE LIGHT OF REASON"

by "distinguishing between people (*populous*) and 'multitude' (*multitudo*)".[109] For Hobbes, the "people" is "*single*"; it comprises "*one will*," and "reigns in the city," while "the citizens are the multitude."[110] To resolve what appears to be a paradoxical binary, which Hobbes produces in *De Cive*, Agamben offers a temporal solution: "The people is sovereign on the condition of dividing itself, of splitting itself into a 'multitude; and a 'people.'"[111]

That subtle temporal distinction inheres in what Hobbes "asserts in no uncertain terms in chapter 7 of *De Cive* . . . [that] at the very instant that the people choose the sovereign it dissolves itself into a confused multitude."[112] Accordingly, Agamben's suggestion is that for Hobbes, "[t]he people—the body political—exists only instantaneously at the point in which it appoints [quoting Hobbes] 'one Man, or Assembly of men, to beare their Person.'"[113] Agamben concludes therefore that the "the city is empty of inhabitants [because] . . . the multitude has no political significance; that it is what must disappear in order for the state to be able to exist."[114] The instantaneity that Agamben detects effectively doubles the temporality of Hobbes's mythic covenant to which I referred earlier; it follows the "transformation of temporal consciousness," which motivates agreement to the covenant, with a qualitative collective moment (the moment when the multitude becomes a people who have become subjects). That they are dissolved back into a multitude means that they can no longer displace sovereignty again ("cannot lawfully make a new Covenant") as Hobbes puts it in his *Leviathan*—hence his clarification of the paradoxical relationship between the people and the multitude.[115]

With that scenario in mind, Tarr's fades to white in the film version of *The Werckmeister Harmonies* take on a new significance, especially those fades ("dissolves" in film language) that take place after each scene of the crowd ("multitude") in the city square milling around the circus container. Tarr marks the endings of each of those scenes with a slow whiting out. And tellingly at the end of the film, we see Gyorgy Eszter walking through that now-empty square, which contains no people, only the ruins of the circus container and a collapsed leviathan.

CONCLUSION: "SOCIAL PEACE" AS REPRESSION

By noting the way Hobbesian thinking is reflected upon and animated by Krasznahorkai's and Tarr's characters, who disport themselves in the novel and film versions, respectively, we are encouraged to pay close attention to Hobbes's textual strategies, to what is perhaps best termed his politics of aesthetics. What then are the political implications of the way Hobbesian aesthetically oriented writing/thinking is rendered in two versions of Werckmeister story (ignoring Krasznahorkai's and Tarr's coy insistence that the story has

"THE LIGHT OF REASON"   137

no political referents). As I have implied, the primary political rejoinder is to Hobbes's drive to create a unitary, plurality-resisting political authority aimed at insulating the commonwealth from the chaos of a war of all against all. In their Werckmeister story, the effect of the Prince ("the One") is also depluralizing but not through a model of a series of covenants. It is rather a result of the exploitation of fear by a conspiracy to use the chaos created by the Prince to fill a political void with an authoritarian police state that mobilizes a military to surveil and punish ontologies of order that defy the order-demanding practices of the new regime. It is not much of an interpretive stretch to see that reinflection as a reference to that part of contemporary Hungarian political history that enfranchised authoritarian political leaders, who implemented strict censorship of diverse social, artistic, and political perspectives (alternative models of what constitutes a reasonable Hungarian modus vivendi or social peace). That outcome, mimed in the Werckmeister story by the policing power seized and implemented by Tunde Eszter and her associates, constitutes a challenge to the Hobbesian model of social peace. Instead of social peace, the result is violent repression as a spirit-deadening malaise descends on the town's main characters.

Ironically, it is the aesthetic Hobbes who supplies the figuration with which Krasznahorkai and Tarr's story challenges his political vision, making it possible (as I implied at the outset) to think against the political Hobbes by thinking with (implementing and adapting to literary and cinematic genres) the aesthetic Hobbes. In the Werckmeister story, Hobbes's rhetoric is rendered as animated rhetorical motion, as his tropes of motion, darkness, and light and his biblical monsters, the leviathan and behemoth, become the operating figures with which Krasznahorkai and Tarr allegorize a slice of Hungarian political history (likely the Mátyás Rákosi and János Kádár eras, 1948–1989, in which their leadership "personated" the Soviet leviathan)[116] that is recalcitrant to Hobbes's solution to the "war of all against all." At the end of the story, Tarr's film version uses the tropes of light and architecture to represent the policing of politically unacceptable ontologies. The last look at Valuska, shows him seated in a brightly lighted psychiatric hospital room, clad in a white hospital gown. "The light of (his version) of reason" no longer circulates. It has been quarantined in a "heterotopia."[117] And his contrapuntal friend, the contrasting, darkly dressed Eszter, who visits him the hospital, recounts how he, too, has been quarantined. He tells Valuska that he has been allocated a very small part of his former residence (a closed in summer porch), while his ex-wife and her police chief collaborator are occupying its main rooms. Eszter's anarchistic ontology of disorder has also been removed from its former place of practice. Ultimately, despite their claims that they are merely telling/filming a story, Krasznahorkai and Tarr offer a powerful politics of aesthetics.[118] Their literary and cinematic texts, which think both with and against Hobbes (incorporating

138   "THE LIGHT OF REASON"

much of Hobbes's aesthetic while challenging his political sensibility) prove to be worthy of the event(s) of contemporary Hungarian history.

NOTES

1. Michael J. Shapiro, "The Light of Reason: Reading the *Leviathan* with the Werckmeister Harmonies," *Political Theory* 45: 3 (February, 2016), 385–415.
2. *Ibid.*, 64.
3. Thomas Hobbes, *Leviathan*, ed. Richard Tuck (New York: Cambridge University Press, 1996), 65.
4. Laszlo Krasznahorkai, *The Melancholy of Resistance*, trans. George Szirtes (New York: New Directions, 1998), 65.
5. The quotation is from a description of another Krasznahorkai–Tarr collaboration: Janice Lee and Jared Woodland, "Apocalypse Withheld: On Slowness & the Long Take in Bela Tarr's *Satantango*," *Entropy*, online at: http://entropymag.org/apocalypse-withheld-on-slowness-the-long-take-in-bela-tarrs-satantango/.
6. Krasznahorkai, *The Melancholy of Resistance*, 73.
7. Daniel Bensaid, *Marx for Our Times*, trans. Gregory Elliott (New York: Verso, 2002), 72.
8. Steven Marchant, "Nothing Counts: Shot and Event in *Werckmeister Harmonies*," *New Cinema Journal of Contemporary* 7: 2 (2009), 137.
9. See Michel Foucault, "What Is Critique?" in *The Politics of Truth*, ed. Sylvere Lotringer (New York: Semiotext(e), 1997), 49.
10. Harun Farocki, "Workers Leaving the Factory," in *Senses of Cinema*, trans. Laurent Faasch-Ibrahim, Online at: http://sensesofcinema.com/2002/harun-farocki/farocki_workers/.
11. See Laszlo Krasznahorkai's, "The Werckmeister Harmonies," a chapter in his novel *The Melancholy of Resistance*, trans. George Szirtes (New York: New Directions, 1998). Bela Tarr's film version, entitled *The Werckmeister Harmonies*, with a screenplay on which Krasznahorkai collaborated, was released in 2000.
12. See Gilles Deleuze and Felix Guattari's chapter, "Percept, Affect, Concept," in *What is Philosophy?* trans. Hugh Tomlinson and Graham Burchell (New York: Columbia University Press, 1994), 163–199.
13. Cesare Casarino, *Modernity at Sea: Melville, Marx, Conrad in Crisis* (Minneapolis: University of Minnesota Press, 2002), xviii–xix.
14. *Ibid.*
15. The quotation is from Charles Cantalupo, *A Literary Leviathan: Thomas Hobbes's Masterpiece of Language* (Lewisburg: Bucknell University Press, 1991), 192.
16. Laszlo Krasznahorkai, *War & War*, trans. George Szirtes (New York: New Directions, 2006), 37.
17. Krasznahorkai, *The Melancholy of Resistance*, 87.
18. Jacques Rancière, *The Politics of Aesthetics*, trans. Gabriel Rockhill (New York: Continuum, 2004), 24.
19. The quotation is from Rose McLaren's treatment of the Tarr Aesthetic, "The Prosaic Sublime of Bela Tarr," *The White Review*, On the web at: www.thewhitereview.org/features/the-prosaic-sublime-of-bela-tarr/.

"THE LIGHT OF REASON" 139

20. Krasznahorkai, *War & War*, 203.
21. Casarino, *Modernity at Sea*, xviii.
22. Hobbes, *Leviathan*, 27.
23. On the metaphorical status of "reading" in Hobbes's text, see Gary Shapiro, "Reading and Writing in the Text of Hobbes's *Leviathan*," *Journal of the History of Philosophy* 18: 2 (1980), 147–157.
24. *Ibid.*, 399. See James Martel's turn to Paul De Man's analysis of rhetoric as suspensive and thus open to "vertiginous possibilities of referential aberration [quoting De Man's *Allegories of Reading*]," rather than aimed at mere persuasion: James R. Martel, "Strong Sovereign, Weak Messiah: Thomas Hobbes on Scriptural Interpretation, Rhetoric and the Holy Spirit," *Theory & Event* 7: 4 (2004), 13.
25. *Ibid.*, 389.
26. Krasznahorkai, *War & War* (New York: New Directions, 2006), 196.
27. See the interview with Krasznahorkai, On the web at: http://timesflowstemmed. com/2012/01/29/war-and-war-by-laszlo-krasznahorkai/.
28. Hobbes, *Leviathan*, 6.
29. The novel, in general, is famously characterized by M. M. Bakhtin as heteroglossic (containing many contending voices). See his "Discourse and the Novel," in *The Dialogic Imagination*, trans. Michael Holquist (Austin: University of Texas Press, 1981), Accordingly, Jacques Rancière refers to Krasznahorkai's story version in the novel as "polyphonic": *Bela Tarr, The Time After*, trans. Erik Berabek (Minneapolis: Univocal), 52.
30. The quotation is from Jose Brunner, "Modern Times: Law, Temporality, and Happiness in Hobbes, Locke, and Bentham," *Theoretical Inquiries in Law*, 8 (2007), 279.
31. As Charles Catalupo notes, "Hobbes writes as if the possibility of reality conforming to such political ideals is not even worth mentioning." See his "How to Be a Literary Reader of Hobbes's Most Famous Chapter," in *The Literature of Controversy: Polemical Strategy from Milton to Junius*, ed. Thomas Corns (London: Frank Cass, 1987), 73.
32. Nevertheless, as Deborah Baumgold insists, "There was always a place in Hobbes's theory for empirical facts of the Norman Conquest sort": Deborah Baumgold, "When Hobbes Needed History," in *Hobbes and History*, eds. G. A. G. Rogers and Tom Sorell (New York: Routledge, 2000), 32.
33. Carl Schmitt, *The Leviathan in the State Theory of Thomas Hobbes*, trans. George Schwab and Erna Hilfstein (Westport: Greenwood Press, 1996), 5.
34. Krasznahorkai, *The Melancholy of Resistance* (quotation on the back cover).
35. *Ibid.*, 94.
36. See Immanuel Kant, *Critique of Judgment*, trans. J. H. Bernard (Amherst: Prometheus Books, 2000), 88, 91.
37. I am taking the concept of rapture from Roberto Calasso's reading of the Vedas: *Ardor*, trans. Richard Dixon (New York: Farrar, Straus and Giroux, 2014), 20.
38. David Yearsley, *Bach and the Meanings of Counterpoint* (New York: Cambridge University Press, 2008), 20.
39. The Werckmeister-inspired contrapuntal relationship between the two characters (with reversing A over B and B over A) contrasts significantly with the way Hobbes constructs a dialogue between two characters, A and B, in his *Behemoth*. His interlocutors, A and B, are an adult and an adolescent, respectively, and rather than

140 **"THE LIGHT OF REASON"**

diverging ontologically, they complement each other, playing different intellectual roles—one (the younger) "steeped in theology" and the other (the older) in "history and law"—to provide an explanatory theoretical apparatus. What is telling is thus a contrast between a Hobbesian commitment to order creation and the Werckmeister suggestion that his mechanisms tend more toward chaos than order. The quotations are from Luc Borot, "Hobbes's *Behemoth*," in Rogers and Sorell eds. *Hobbes and History*, 139.

40. Plato, *Timaeus*, trans. Benjamin Jowett (Amazon Kindle edition, IAP, 2009), loc. 250.
41. Krasznahorkai, *The Melancholy of Resistance*, 77.
42. See J. G. A. Pocock, *The Machiavellian Moment: Florentine Political Thought and the Atlantic Republican Tradition* (Princeton: Princeton University Press, 2003).
43. Krasznahorkai, *The Melancholy of Resistance*, 126.
44. Marchant, "Nothing Counts: Shot and Event in *Werckmeister Harmonies*," 144.
45. Krasznahorkai, *The Melancholy of Resistance*, 134.
46. The quotation is from Samantha Frost, "Faking It: Thinking Bodies and the Ethics of Dissimulation," *Political Theory* 29: 1 (February, 2001), 32.
47. Quotations in *Ibid*.
48. Krasznahorkai, "The Werckmeister Harmonies," 103.
49. I am borrowing the idea that fear should be treated in terms of what it does to cinematic space from Leo Bersani and Ulysse Dutoit's reading of Jean Luc Godard's film *Contempt*. See Leo Bersani and Ulysse Dutoit, *Forms of Being* (London: BFI, 2004).
50. Krasznahorkai, *The Melancholy of Resistance*, 95–96.
51. Elias Canetti, Elias, *Crowds and Power*, trans. Carol Stewart (New York: Farrar, Straus and Giroux, 1984), 31.
52. Krasznahorkai, *The Melancholy of Resistance*, 95.
53. Hobbes, *Leviathan*, Chapter 5.
54. C. B. Macpherson, C. B. "Introduction," in Hobbes, *Leviathan*, 19.
55. Krasznahorkai, *The Melancholy of Resistance*, 154.
56. Hobbes, *Leviathan*, 162–163.
57. *Ibid.*, 139.
58. See Gilles Deleuze, *Francis Bacon: The Logic of Sensation*, trans. Daniel M. Smith (Minneapolis: University of Minnesota Press).
59. Krasznahorkai, *The Melancholy of Resistance*, 171.
60. I am translating the quotation from the Norwegian. See Christian Hokaas, "Ungarn: Werckmeister Harmonies," On the web at: http://jump-cut/jorden-rundt-pa-8--filmer-no-52-ungarn/.
61. *Ibid.*
62. Krasznahorkai, *The Melancholy of Resistance*, 171–172.
63. Jacques Lacan, "Aggressively in Psychoanalysis," in *Écrits*, trans. Alan Sheridan (New York: Norton & Co, 1977), 20.
64. For a treatment of this aspect of Hobbes's *Leviathan* and a review of the controversies it occasioned in its time, see Diego Rossello, "Hobbes and the Wolfman: Melancholy and Animality in Modern Sovereignty," *New Literary History* 43 (2012), 255–279.
65. Krasznahorkai, *The Melancholy of Resistance*, 110.

"THE LIGHT OF REASON"   141

66. The quotation belongs to Cantalupo, *A Literary Leviathan*, 196.
67. Hobbes, *Leviathan*, 26.
68. *Ibid.*, 345.
69. *Ibid.*, 379.
70. *Ibid.*, 64.
71. Krasznahorkai, *The Melancholy of Resistance*, 109.
72. Davide Panagia, *Impressions of Hume: Cinematic Thinking and the Politics of Discontinuity* (Lanham: Rowman & Littlefield, 2013), 1.
73. The quotation belongs to Gilles Deleuze, *Cinema 1* (Minneapolis: University of Minnesota Press, 1986), 4.
74. See Michael J. Shapiro, *Reading Adam Smith: Desire, History and Value* (Lanham: Rowman & Littlefield, 2000).
75. *Ibid.*, 57.
76. See Noel Burch, "Nana, or the Two Kinds of Space," in *Theory of Film Practice*, trans. Helen R. Lane (Princeton: Princeton University Press, 1981), 17.
77. Hobbes, *Leviathan*, 58.
78. Martel, "Strong Sovereign, Weak Messiah," 22.
79. Hobbes, *Leviathan*, 91.
80. *Ibid.*
81. *Ibid.*, 15–16.
82. The expression belongs to James R. Martel, *Subverting the Leviathan: Reading Thomas Hobbes as a Radical Democrat* (New York: Columbia University Press, 2007), 70.
83. *Ibid.*
84. Hobbes, *Leviathan*, 248–249.
85. Krasznahorkai, *The Melancholy of Resistance*, 171.
86. *Ibid.*, (loc 2779).
87. Hobbes, *Leviathan*, 249.
88. *Ibid.*
89. Krasznahorkai, *The Melancholy of Resistance*, 159.
90. That result, generated by Kraszanahorkai's narrative, is also inherent in the novel-as-form, which, as M. M. Bakhtin famously notes, is heteroglossic. The novel's many contending voices have a centrifugal effect, pulling away from a "verbal-ideological center": Bakhtin, "Discourse and the Novel."
91. Krasznahorkai, *The Melancholy of Resistance*, 188.
92. *Ibid.*, 85 (The Hobbes text is *Behemoth or The Long Parliament* (Chicago: University of Chicago press, 1990)).
93. The quotations are from Schmitt, *The Leviathan in the State Theory of Thomas Hobbes*, 21.
94. See Thomas Hobbes, *The Questions Concerning Liberty, Necessity, and Chance*, 704, ebook version at: www.WealthOFNation.com loc.
95. Krasznahorkai, *The Melancholy of Resistance*, 101.
96. *Ibid.*, 157.
97. See Victoria Khan, *Rhetoric, Prudence and Skepticism in the Renaissance* (Ithaca: Cornell University Press, 1985), 177.
98. Martel, "Strong Sovereign, Weak Messiah," 6–7.
99. Krasznahorkai, *The Melancholy of Resistance*, 105.

142 **"THE LIGHT OF REASON"**

100. Berel Lang, "Space, Time, and Philosophical Style," *Critical Inquiry* 2: 2 (Winter, 1975), 266.
101. See J. L. Austin, *How to Do Things with Words* (Cambridge, MA: Harvard University Press, 1962).
102. The quotations are from Lang, "Space, Time, and Philosophical Style," 271.
103. Conceiving the text in that way we can see a parallel textual strategy in Paul (as Jacob Taubes has famously interpreted his epistles). To summarize briefly, Taubes sees Paul's epistles as "polemical" and "revolutionary," aimed at inventing a radical Judaism—for example, Romans 13, which intermixes a section on obedience with one that promotes love as the fulfillment of the law": Jacob Taubes, *The Political Theology of Paul*, trans. Dana Hollander (Stanford: Stanford University Press, 2004), 53. However, with Roman surveillance in mind, Paul softens the revolutionary implications of his message to reassure the Romans. He states that "the present form of the world is passing away," which Taubes interprets as in effect saying, "there's no point in any revolution . . . for heaven's sake, don't stand out." Thus, Taubes construes Paul's theology as *political* in that it seeks to radicalize the Jewish religion while not alarming the Romans. Hobbes reverses the emphases. Although he, too, radicalizes religion, removing it from political relevance—chiefly by denying revelation—his main aim is to radicalize politics (*Ibid.*, 54).
104. The quotation is from Liu Xiaofeng, *Sino-Theology and the Philosophy of History*, trans. Leopold Lee (Brill Academic Publications, 2015), 54.
105. The quotations are from a reading of Leo Strauss's, *The Political Philosophy of Hobbes: Its Basis and Its Genesis* (Chicago: University of Chicago Press, 1963). See Timothy Burns, "Leo Strauss on the Origins of Hobbes's Natural Science," *Klesis – Revue Philosopique*, On the web at: www.revue-klesis.org/pdf/Strauss-8-Klesis-Burns-B.pdf.
106. Schmitt, *The Leviathan in the State Theory of Thomas Hobbes*, 26.
107. Giorgio Agamben, *Stasis: Civil War as a Political Paradigm*, trans. Nicholas Heron (Stanford: Stanford University Press, 2015), ebook loc. 345.
108. *Ibid.*, loc. 420.
109. *Ibid.*, loc. 453.
110. Agamben is quoting from *De Cive, Ibid.*
111. *Ibid.*, 473.
112. *Ibid.*, 493.
113. *Ibid.* (The inner quotations are from Hobbes, *Leviathan*, 120).
114. *Ibid.*, loc. 522.
115. See *Ibid.*, loc 508 and Hobbes, *Leviathan*, 97.
116. Among the historical moments that are likely referents for Krasznahorkai's and Tarr's oblique political commentary is an era beginning in the early communist period through the suppression of the 1956 uprising and for some time afterward, in which many Hungarian intellectuals were imprisoned and many others, for example, historians, "were 'eliminated in an administrative way' from historical journals and research posts at universities, the Hungarian Academy of Sciences, and Elsewhere" The quotation is from Antoon De Baets, *Censorship of Historical Thought: A World Guide, 1945–2000* (Westport: Greenwood Press, 2002), 256.
117. Psychiatric hospitals are among the heterotopias (spaces of otherness) to which Foucault refers as exiting on "the borderline" between "heterotopias of crisis" and "heterotopias of deviation." See Michel Foucault, "Of Other Spaces: Utopias

"THE LIGHT OF REASON" 143

and Heterotopias," trans. Jay Miscowiec. On the web at: www.vizkult.org/propositions/alineinnature/pdfs/Foucault-OfOtherSpaces1967.pdf.

118. For example, Tarr, who admits to having wanted at one time to be a philosopher, says in an interview about the film, "I never think about theoretical things when we are working" and that as for the theme of the film, "I just wanted to make a movie about this guy who is walking up and down the village and has seen this whale." See Fergus Daly and Maximilian Le Cain, "Waiting for the Prince – An Interview with Bela Tarr," *Senses of Cinema* 12 (February, 2001). On the web at: http://sensesofcinema.com/2001/feature-articles/tarr-2/.

REFERENCES

Agamben, Giorgio (2015) *Stasis: Civil War as a Political Paradigm*, trans. Nicholas Heron, Stanford: Stanford University Press.

Austin, J. L. (1962) *How to Do Things with Words*, Cambridge, MA: Harvard University Press.

Bakhtin, M. M. (1981) *The Dialogic Imagination*, Austin: University of Texas Press.

Baumgold, Deborah (2000) 'When Hobbes Needed History,' in *Hobbes and History*, eds. G. A. G. Rogers and Tom Sorell, New York: Routledge.

Bensaid, Daniel (2002) *Marx for Our Times*, trans. Gregory Elliott, New York: Verso.

Bersani, Leo and Dutoit, Ulysse (2004) *Forms of Being*, London: BFI.

Brunner, Jose (2007) 'Modern Times: Law, Temporality, and Happiness in Hobbes, Locke, and Bentham,' *Theoretical Inquiries in Law*, at: www7.tau.ac.il/ojs/index.php/til/article/viewFile/618/581.

Burch, Noel (1981) 'Nana, or the Two Kinds of Space,' in *Theory of Film Practice*, trans. Helen R. Lane, Princeton: Princeton University Press.

Calasso, Roberto (2014) *Ardor*, trans. Richard Dixon, New York: Farrar, Straus and Giroux.

Canetti, Elias (1984) *Crowds and Power*, trans. Carol Stewart, New York: Farrar, Straus and Giroux.

Cantalupo, Charles (1987) 'How to be a Literary Reader of Hobbes's Most Famous Chapter,' in *The Literature of Controversy: Polemical Strategy from Milton to Junius*, ed. Thomas Corns, London: Frank Cass.

Cantalupo, Charles (1991) *A Literary Leviathan: Thomas Hobbes's Masterpiece of Language*, Lewisburg: Bucknell University Press.

Casarino, Cesare (2002) *Modernity at Sea: Melville, Marx, Conrad in Crisis*, Minneapolis: University of Minnesota Press.

Daly, Fergus and Le Cain, Maximilian (2001) 'Waiting for the Prince – An Interview with Bela Tarr,' *Senses of Cinema*, No. 12, at: http://sensesofcinema.com/2001/feature-articles/tarr-2/.

De Baets, Antoon (2002) *Censorship of Historical thought: A World Guide, 1945–2000*, Westport: Greenwood Press.

Deleuze, Gilles (1986) *Cinema 1: The Movement Image*, trans. Hugh Tomlinson and Barbara Habberjam, Minneapolis: University of Minnesota Press.

Deleuze, Gilles (2005) *Francis Bacon: The Logic of Sensation*, trans. Daniel M. Smith, Minneapolis: University of Minnesota Press.

Deleuze, Gilles and Guattari, Felix (1994) *What is Philosophy?*, trans. Hugh Tomlinson and Graham Burchell, New York: Columbia University Press.

144 "THE LIGHT OF REASON"

Farocki, Harun (2002) 'Workers Leaving the Factory,' trans. Laurent Faasch-Ibrahim, *Senses of Cinema*, at: http://sensesofcinema.com/2002/harun-farocki/farocki_workers/.

Foucault, Michel (1967) 'Of Other Spaces: Utopias and Heterotopias,' trans. Jay Miscowiec, at: www.vizkult.org/propositions/alineinnature/pdfs/Foucault-OfOther Spaces1967.pdf.

Foucault, Michel (1997) 'What is Critique?,' in *The Politics of Truth*, ed. Sylvere Lotringer, New York: Semiotext(e), pp. 41–82.

Frost, Samantha (2001) 'Faking It: Thinking Bodies and the Ethics of Dissimulation,' *Political Theory*, Vol. 29 (1), pp. 30–57.

Hobbes, Thomas (1990) *Behemoth or The Long Parliament*, Chicago: University of Chicago Press.

Hobbes, Thomas (1996) *Leviathan*, ed. Richard Tuck, New York: Cambridge University Press.

Hobbes, Thomas (2005) *The Questions Concerning Liberty, Necessity, and Chance*, ebook version at: www.WealthOFNation.com.

Kant, Immanuel (2000) *Critique of Judgment*, trans. J. H. Bernard, Amherst: Prometheus Books.

Khan, Victoria (1985) *Rhetoric, Prudence and Skepticism in the Renaissance*, Ithaca: Cornell University Press.

Krasznahorkai, Laszlo (1998) *The Melancholy of Resistance*, trans. George Szirtes, New York: New Directions.

Krasznahorkai, Laszlo (2006) *War & War*, trans. George Szirtes, New York: New Directions.

Krasznahorkai, Laszlo (2012) 'Interview,' at: http://timesflowstemmed.com/2012/01/29/war-and-war-by-laszlo-krasznahorkai/.

Lacan, Jacques (1977) 'Aggressively in Psychoanalysis,' in *Écrits*, trans. Alan Sheridan, New York: Norton & Co.

Lang, Berel (1975) 'Space, Time, and Philosophical Style,' *Critical Inquiry*, Vol. 2 (2), pp. 263–280.

Lee, Janice and Woodland, Jared (2014) 'Apocalypse Withheld: On Slowness & the Long Take in Bela Tarr's *Satantango*,' *Entropy*, at: http://entropymag.org/apocalypse-withheld-on-slowness-the-long-take-in-bela-tarrs-satantango/.

Marchant, Steven (2009) 'Nothing Counts: Shot and Event in *Werckmeister Harmonies*,' *New Cinema Journal of Contemporary*, Vol. 7 (2), pp. 137–154.

Martel, James R. (2004) 'Strong Sovereign, Weak Messiah: Thomas Hobbes on Scriptural Interpretation, Rhetoric and the Holy Spirit,' *Theory & Event*, Vol. 7 (4), pp. 13–25.

Martel, James R. (2007) *Subverting the Leviathan: Reading Thomas Hobbes as a Radical Democrat*, New York: Columbia University Press.

McLaren, Rose (2012) 'The Prosaic Sublime of Bela Tarr,' *The White Review*, at: www.thewhitereview.org/features/the-prosaic-sublime-of-bela-tarr/.

Panagia, Davide (2013) *Impressions of Hume: Cinematic Thinking and the Politics of Discontinuity*, Lanham: Rowman & Littlefield.

Plato (2009) *Timaeus*, trans. Benjamin Jowett, Amazon kindle edition, IAP.

Pocock, J. G. A. (2003) *The Machiavellian Moment: Florentine Political Thought and the Atlantic Republican Tradition*, Princeton: Princeton University Press.

Rancière, Jacques (2004) *The Politics of Aesthetics*, trans. Gabriel Rockhill, New York: Continuum.

Rancière, Jacques (2013) *Bela Tarr, The Time After*, trans. Erik Berabek, Minneapolis: Univocal.

Rossello, Diego (2012) 'Hobbes and the Wolfman: Melancholy and Animality in Modern Sovereignty,' *New Literary History*, Vol. 43 (2), pp. 255–279.

Schmitt, Carl (1996) *The Leviathan in the State Theory of Thomas Hobbes*, trans. George Schwab and Erna Hilfstein, Westport: Greenwood Press.

Shapiro, Gary (1980) 'Reading and Writing in the text of Hobbes's *Leviathan*,' *Journal of the History of Philosophy*, Vol. 18 (2), pp. 147–157.

Shapiro, Michael J. (2000) *Reading Adam Smith: Desire, History and Value*, Lanham: Rowman & Littlefield.

Shapiro, Michael J. (2016) 'The Light of Reason: Reading the *Leviathan* with The Werckmeister Harmonies,' *Political Theory*, Vol. 45 (3), pp. 385–415.

Strauss, Leo (1963) *The Political Philosophy of Hobbes: Its Basis and Its Genesis*, Chicago: University of Chicago Press.

Taubes, Jacob (2003) *The Political Theology of Paul*, trans. Dana Hollander, Stanford: Stanford University Press.

Xiaofeng, Liu (2015) *Sino-Theology and the Philosophy of History*, trans. Leopold Lee Brill Academic Publications.

Yearsley, David (2008) *Bach and the Meanings of Counterpoint*, New York: Cambridge University Press.

SUGGESTED READING

For an analysis of Hobbes that heeds his light-versus-darkness tropes, see Devin Stauffer, *Hobbes's Kingdom of Light: A Study of Modern Political Philosophy* (Chicago: University of Chicago Press, 2018).

For Additional Studies of the Cinema of Bela Tarr, See

Andras Balint Kovacs, *The Cinema of Bela Tarr* (New York: Wallflower, 2013).

Thorsten Botz-Bornstein, *Organic Cinema: Film, Architecture, and the Work of Bela Tarr* (New York: Berghahn Books, 2017).

Emre Caglayan, *Poetics of Slow Cinema: Nostalgia, Absurdism, Boredom* (London: Palgrave Macmillan, 2019).

CHAPTER **5**

"Borderline Justice"[1]

INTRODUCTION: AN IMAGINED FUTURE

In contrast with the primary emphasis on time in Chapters 2 and 3, this chapter is extensively spatially as well as temporality oriented. It is concerned not only with layers of time but also with how cinema can illuminate the spatial practices associated with geopolitical border policing. Drawing on a chapter in my book on war crimes,[2] it is focused on the geography of the U.S.–Mexican border, beginning with a reading of Alex Rivera's film *Sleep Dealer* (2008), which imagines a future with an impermeable military-defended border wall between the United States and Mexico. I begin with Rivera's film because it is especially timely. During the presidency of Barack Obama (2009–2017), there was continual pressure in the American Congress for stronger security along the entire length of the U.S.–Mexican border. What had already been implemented and was left unrevised was The Secure Fence Act of 2006, in which higher barriers were extended along parts of the border combined with new policing collaborations among Immigration and Customs Enforcement (ICE), Drug Enforcement Agency (DEA), and Central Intelligence Agency (CIA) agents, working with Mexican police, and with new technologies of surveillance (including "Unmanned military aircraft").[3] Subsequently, campaigning with a promise to build a totally secure border wall (along with the fantasy that the Mexican government would be responsible for financing it) Donald Trump won the U.S. presidency with strong support from the part of the electorate that shared his antagonism toward the flow of undocumented Mexican border-crossers living and working in the United States. Although as I compose this chapter the Trump administration's plan for the wall has not been realized, in the future that Rivera's film constructs, it has been. In *Sleep Dealer*, the border is closed along its entire length and is policed with advanced surveillance and weapon delivery systems (including weaponized drones) managed by a private corporation located in San Diego. However, the secured border does not prevent Mexicans in Mexico from working in the United States. Through a futuristic technology, workers in Tijuana "the world's largest border town" (according to a sign one sees in the road upon entering the city) are fitted with nodes embedded in their flesh so that they can be turned into virtual biological robots that are jacked in as workers in the United States—as cab drivers, construction workers, and child-care nannies (indeed almost every occupational category)—while their physical bodies remain in Tijuana.

A voice-over in a high-tech, Fordist-looking factory, where assembly lines of workers are jacked into their virtual jobs (Figure 5.1), announces, "We give the U.S. what they've always wanted, all the work without the workers." In the future that *Sleep Dealer* constructs, U.S. corporate hegemony has created a virtual Bantustan in Tijuana. The worker recruitment and employment process are revealed by following one of the film's protagonists, Memo Cruz (Luis Fernando Pena), who has headed to Tijuana to earn money to aid his impoverished family. Prior to his arrival in Tijuana, the film opens in his small village of Santa Ana, where Memo and his family reside, deprived of free access to water because the Del Rio Corporation of San Diego has bought most of the land, has dammed up the nearby river, and charges an increasingly higher price for the water in their reservoir, which is secured by a fence and mounted weapons as well as by armed men who patrol its perimeter.

The militarization of the corporation's reservoir has turned the Cruzes' village into the abstract space of global capital flows, in contrast with the "lived space" of the Cruz family,[4] which is shown at the outset of the film as the family gathers for their late-afternoon meal. The contrast between a powerful corporate America and the Mexican families their enterprise has impoverished

FIGURE 5.1
Fordist factory. Source: Alex Rivera, *Sleep Dealer*, Maya Entertainment (2008).

is shown through images, for example, the towering building housing the Del Rio Corporation versus the squat buildings of the Cruz family enclave (Figures 5.2 and 5.3).

By way of a brief synopsis, Memo actualizes his dream of participating in a world beyond his village by hacking into global communications, including those of the Del Rio Corporation. At the beginning of the film narrative, he pauses in his hacking to join the family meal, during which he and his father have to break away and go through the degrading process of putting money in a machine at the barrier to the Del Rio Water Company reservoir to obtain water (under the watchful eye of armed surveillance). As they trudge home carrying their heavy water sacks, he says to his father, "Why are we still here?" His father, using an expression that locates an erased future in the present says, "Because here we had a future." The generational contrast is stark; while

FIGURES 5.2 AND 5.3
Del Rio Corporation and Casa Cruz. Source: Alex Rivera, *Sleep Dealer*, Maya Entertainment (2008).

"BORDERLINE JUSTICE"   149

Memo dreams of leaving the constricted lifeworld of his village, his father continues to celebrate what it has meant.

Shortly after Memo returns to his worldwide hacking, he stumbles into the Del Rio Corporation's communication network. His intrusion alerts the corporation, which locates Memo's position and sends a weaponized drone, piloted by one of their drone pilots, Rudy Ramirez (Jacob Vargas), who fires a missile, which locks onto Casa Cruz and kills Memo's father. Ramirez has already been living *his* dream as a virtual fighter pilot. Thereafter, the grieving and chastened Memo travels to Tijuana. However, at that point the film composition contains a forking path narrative.[5] While it is following Memo to Tijuana and recording his entry into the virtual working economy to deliver debilitating manhours, it cuts occasionally to Rudy, who has also been working virtually to deliver violence.

When Ramirez, who is represented as a heroic success story in one of the Del Rio Corporation's biographical commercials, learns about the atrocity he has committed, which he discovers because Luz Martinez (Leonor Varela), an aspiring writer and also a "coyotech," (who arranges Memo's employment by attaching the nodes he needs for the virtual work) has posted Memo's bio on her story blog, he decides to find Memo to make amends. He is ultimately able to connect with him with Luz's help. Meanwhile, Memo's part of the narrative shows the effects of the assembly line on the virtual Mexican workers. A Malthusian exhaustion is setting in, destroying the health of the workers jacked into their work venues in the United States. After a worker in Memo's virtual assembly line collapses and Memo realizes that he too is weakening (his energy is flowing from Tijuana to San Diego, where he is virtually helping to construct a building), he quits his job.

In contrast with virtualized manual labor is Luz's work in virtual space. Her storytelling blog ultimately emancipates Memo (with whom she had become romantically involved) once he and Rudy form an alliance to save Memo's water-deprived home village of Santa Ana. Rudy steals one of the Del Rio Corporation's drones and uses his piloting skill to blow up the dam that has cut off the water supply to Santa Ana. While coercive capitalism, using a virtual technology protected by its militarized policing *dispositif* has been pitting young men against each other, a benign and creative technology, storytelling has resisted the bio-violence of virtualized industry and has

> allow[ed] us to view [a life world] as a realm that is linked to neither nation nor race, and is characterized by a plurality of "incoherent" political actors . . . that "produce" innumerable stories . . . [yielding a] displaced notion of politics . . . [in] a related web of stories that cannot be subsumed under any higher concept.[6]

In the case of Luz, we must add *her* displacement to that "displaced notion of politics." In exile from her home state, she struggles to adapt to an unfamiliar place. Among other things, to be displaced is to be invited into an aesthetic experience, into a reorientation and reframing of one's sensible world. From the point of view of a radical politics, a displacement-engendered aesthetic experience disturbs authoritative distributions of social identity. In Jacques Rancière's apposite terms,

> [a]esthetic experience has a political effect to the extent that . . . it disturbs the way in which bodies fit their functions and destinations . . . It has a multiplication of connections and disconnections that reframe the relation between bodies, the world where they live and the way in which they are "equipped" for fitting it.[7]

With the politically acute, justice-creating effect of aesthetic approaches in mind, I go back to a past in which literature (specifically the novel) is a vehicle for political reflection, as the composition of the chapter incorporates another border story, one that has actually occurred.

POLICING ATROCITIES AND THE SPATIOTEMPORALITY OF THE NOVEL

In discussing the way literature contributes to a critical view of borders, I begin with a description of an encounter I have analyzed elsewhere.[8] The late Mexican writer Carlos Fuentes reported a conversation that took place while he and American friends were lost while on a driving trip in the Morelos region of Mexico. Assuming that the regional map had a unitary and stable set of addresses, he asked a local *campesino* the name of the village where they had stopped. The *campesino*'s reply astounded him: "That depends, we call the village Santa Maria in times of peace. We call it Zapata in times of war." On hearing the unanticipated answer, Fuentes was pushed to reflect on the plurality of temporal presences in the contemporary world. As he puts it, "the old *campesino*" possesses a knowledge that "most people in the West have assiduously ignored since the seventeenth century: that there is more than one time in the world, that there is another time existing alongside, above, underneath the linear calendars of the West."[9] Fuentes then turns to a reflection on the potential of his vocation as a novelist to capture the plurality to which he has been suddenly alerted. He asserts that his literary genre, the novel is especially attuned to multiplicity. It is the best vehicle for capturing a plurality of presences, the multiple spatiotemporal ways for people to be in the world. That multiplicity had been addressed decades earlier by another writer, Ernst Block, who remarked, "not all people exist in the same now."[10] While Block's observation hues closely to his ideational commitment—he was interested in the implications of the coexistence of multiple temporalities for dialectical materialism—Fuentes's focus is on literature, which he suggests can bring to presence

> our forgotten self [because] . . . the West, through its literature, internally elaborated a plurality of times in stark contrast to its external, chosen adherence to one time, the future-oriented time of progress . . . the novel is the literary form that, with most complexity, permits us to reappropriate time.[11]

Fuentes's writing effectively affirms his stated insights about the novel's perspicacity with respect to a temporal micropolitics. The assertions of individual sensibility that actually or potentially challenge macro-politics (the subject-forming codes of formal political institutions within national formations) are evident in his plots. Although this chapter ultimately embraces cinema as a genre especially well equipped to represent the spatiotemporal dynamics of borders, I first explore Fuentes's implementation of his claim about the multiplicity-representing capacity of novel by analyzing his observations about nations and temporality as they are articulated in his reflections on his home state of Mexico, in his last novel *Destiny and Desire*. In the novel, Fuentes's protagonists address the contemporary history of Mexico and animate his provocative observation, "Today the great drama of Mexico is that crime has replaced the state."[12]

As Fuentes's narrative surveys Mexico's varying national epochs, it begins in the nineteenth century, figuring the problem of justice by utilizing the typical way a novel aesthetically figures collective issues by exploring familial ones. His main protagonist, Josué, from a proletarian background, visits his friend Errol's privileged family, who live in a palatial home and exist, as the text puts it, "in the *have* column," while Josué "grew up in a gloomy house on Calle de Berlin." The comparison is then contextualized with reference to Mexico's "nineteenth century":

> When the country seemed to settle down after decades of upheaval (although it traded anarchy for dictatorship, perhaps without realizing it), the capital city began to spread beyond the original perimeter of Zocalo-Plateros-Alameda. The "colonias," as the new neighborhoods were called, chose to display mansions in various European styles.[13]

In contrast with Errol's class and territorial patrimony, Josué grew up in a crowded urban scene. Nevertheless, he implies that his class difference does

"BORDERLINE JUSTICE"

not yield a sense of envy and injustice. He reflects, "Now, how do you quantify familial possession or dispossession? People's opinion of the fair is based on whether they had a good time."[14]

As the novel proceeds, Fuentes implies that the state's governance has been about ensuring popular submission to structures of class privilege by managing the illusion that it governs a "democracy," where more realistically, "[t]he history of Mexico [up to the point where crime replaces the state] is a long process of leaving behind anarchy and dictatorship and reaching a democratic authoritarianism . . ."[15] And most significant, as Josué's lawyer friend, Sangines, tells him, "I grew up in a society in which society was protected by official corruption. Today . . . society is protected by criminals." He proceeds to provide an illustration drawn from recent history:

> Just yesterday . . . a highway in the state of Guerrero was blocked by uniformed criminals. Were they fake police? Or simply real police dedicated to crime? What happened on the highway happens everywhere. The drivers of the blocked buses and cars were brutally interrogated and pistol-whipped.[16]

Among the implications of Fuentes's observation that crime has replaced the state is the altered political geography the replacement implies. If we heed Nick Vaughan-Williams's suggestion that rather than fixed demarcations, state borders are a biopolitical process of inclusion and exclusion of modes of life (after Giorgio Agamben's binary, "bare," and thus expendable life versus politically qualified life), the conceptual issue becomes not merely one of a sovereignty-ordered biopower but a biopower that also results from the alternating struggles and collaborations between drug cartels and policing agencies.[17] The allies-versus-victims binary that the biopolitical contentions create result from the illicit policing-protected drug-trafficking enterprise. It is an altered mode of biopower that is elaborately illustrated through the fate of Laura Guerrero (Stepanie Sigman) in Gerardo Naranjo's feature film *Miss Bala* (2011), which I analyze later in this chapter.

That focus on "biopower," treated in Naranjo's film, is the primary impulse driving Fuentes's literary intervention into Mexico's narco politics. It is the kind of intervention that has been carried out often in popular culture texts, both literary and cinematic, which have exposed the complicity of law-enforcement apparatuses with the drug operations in Latin America.[18] Although Fuentes was well aware of the extent to which cross-border relations between the United States and Mexico have made significant contributions to the displacement of state authority by crime, his focus has been primarily on Mexico's internal dynamics. To refocus the issues, I turn to popular culture texts that expand the territory of the policing and crime *dispositifs*.

POPULAR CULTURE AND THE CROSS-BORDER POLICING *DISPOSITIF*

To situate the politics of Fuentes's intervention into the narco politics of the Mexican state, we have to move north and view aspects of the role of U.S. law enforcement in the "war on drugs." The novelist Don Winslow captures both the relevant historical moment and the diverse policing agents involved in exacerbating the gloomy picture that Fuentes provides. One of his characters, Ben, in his *Kings of Cool* (2012; one of four novels he has devoted to the U.S.–Mexico encounters involved in the policing of drug trafficking) describes the significant historical moment and thence the emergence of the key law enforcement players:

> Nixon declared the War on Drugs in 1973. Thirty-plus years later, billions of dollars, thousands of lives, and the war goes on, and for what? Nothing. . . . Well not nothing. . . . The antidrug establishment rakes in billions of dollars—DEA, Customs, Border Patrol, ICE, thousands of state and local antidrug units, not to mention prisons.[19]

Winslow's novelistic glosses on the war on drugs have operated within the genre of the exposé to challenge the official discourses within which the war on drugs, initiated during the Nixon presidency in the 1970s, has been promoted (by the antidrug establishment to which the passage refers).

Here I want to go back in time and expand the duration of the war on drugs with a brief genealogy of the interagency collaborations that have ultimately ended in the law enforcement apparatus that Winslow characterizes. Its source is a cinema archive that extends back historically to the mid-twentieth century. I initiate that genealogy with a cinematic text that combines documentary and noir genres to disclose a much earlier border policing *dispositif*, which was located in the U.S. Treasury Department, Anthony Mann's *T Men* (1947). The film begins with an interview with a fictional head of the U.S. Treasury Department, "Elmer Lincoln Hiram," who figures the "Treasury's strike force against crime" with a series of violent metaphors. There is the "Intelligence Unit," which "cracks down on tax violators"; there is the "Customs Agency" that regulates incoming products; there is its related "Border Patrol" arm that fights the smuggling of narcotics; there is also a "Secret Service Unit" that both guards the president and "ferrets out counterfeiters"; there is a "Tax Unit" devoted to uncovering bootleggers; and finally the "Coast Guard." Summing up the collective effect Hiram says, "These are the six fingers of the Treasury Department fist. That fist hits fair but hard."

"Fair but hard?" The narrative in Mann's *T Men* implies that the policing apparatus delivers an impartial justice. Mann replicates that perspective in his

154   "BORDERLINE JUSTICE"

later film, *Border Incident* (1949), in which U.S. and Mexican law enforcement agencies collaborate to end the violence and exploitation perpetrated on border-crossing Mexican agricultural workers, *braceros*. Nevertheless, *Border Incident*, also structured with Mann's documentary style, effectively exposes the conditions of possibility for border violence. After the voiceover at the outset of the film notes that "there is a vast army of farm workers . . . that comes from our neighbor to the South—from Mexico," the narration turns to a lesson in the moral economy that accompanies the political economy of California's agribusinesses. It distinguishes *braceros* that enter the United States with legal permits from those who enter illegally and are therefore exposed to bandits on both sides of the border. "It is this problem of injustice and human suffering about which you should know," says the voice-over.

As the film's pedagogy migrates into its drama, the action begins with an episode of violence. "Illegals," captured by bandits, are robbed and thrown into a bed of quicksand where they sink to their deaths. That event is followed by a scene in which policing agents from both the United States and Mexico arrive at a meeting for a planned collaboration, both to protect the legal border-crossing *braceros* and to prevent the victimization of the illegals. Well into the drama, after the American agent, Jim Bearnes (George Murphy) is killed by the Parkinson gang that has been preying on the border-crossers, the film ends with a shootout in which Bearn's Mexican counterpart, Pablo Rodriguez (Ricardo Montalban), is rescued and the Parkinson gang is vanquished. As was the case in Mann's earlier *T Men*, the policing apparatus (in this case, a binational one) hits "fair but hard."

However, the fairness ascribed to the binational policing initiative does not extend to Mann's filming style, which privileges a U.S. territorial imaginary. His film begins with an overhead shot of the canal on the border between the two countries and then surveys the rich and dense agricultural farms of California. Insofar as Mexico's value is represented, it is as a ragtag (often comical) collection of human capital, a migrating labor force from a territory that appears solely as a perilous terrain that the *braceros* must navigate. Shown in dark tones, the film's noir-oriented genre—"dark city streets" and "the ink shadows of a western setting"—yields a Mexico that courts death rather than productivity; its soil literally swallows "bandit" victims.[20]

There has been a more subtle treatment with a different political sensibility available since the mid-twentieth century, Orson Welles's *Touch of Evil* (1958), which stands out as a political event. It is a cinematic intervention that disrupts the model of historical time (a progressive United States and a retrograde Mexico) that had to that point characterized the way popular culture genres represented the ethico-political gulf between the two countries. A Deleuzean expression can serve as an effective critical account of what the film does: Welles's film "counter-actualizes" the cross-border experiences

"BORDERLINE JUSTICE" 155

interpreted in cinema history by mimicking and then reinflecting them to "double the actualization [in, for example, Mann's films and thereby] . . . to give the truth of the event[s] the only chance of not being confused with the only actualization . . . [and thus] to liberate [them] for other times."[21]

The radical departure from *Border Incident*'s political unconscious is evident in *A Touch of Evil*'s opening scene. While Mann's film begins with a "formal framing,"[22] an overhead shot of the river separating the United States and Mexico, followed by a panning shot of U.S. farmlands, with the effect of "represent[ing] the border as a demarcated boundary"[23] and reaffirming the significance of separated national entities (an agriculturally rich United states and a nearby labor pool that must cross jurisdictions), Welles's opening scene uses a tracking shot of a car crossing from Mexico to the United States. That sequence lends a critical ambiguity to the border effect; it "throws up a jumble of vanishing centers."[24] Moreover, a noir effect (dark tones throughout the film) in *A Touch of Evil* pervades both sides of the border, implying that, rather than being "fair but hard," policing agents are morally flawed in ways that render "justice" a result of the vagaries of poorly regulated policing agencies and the contingencies of encounter. Welles's protagonists are complex aesthetic subjects, especially Vargas (Charlton Heston in makeup that gives him a swarthy look), who mirrors Welles's decentering of territoriality by being a decentered character. With his two names, Miguel and Mike, he is a conflicted body, pulled centrifugally between desire and the law. He is, as Stephen Heath puts it (in his well-known frame-by-frame analysis of the film), "the name of desire" as the Mexican, Miguel, and "the law," as the American, Mike.[25]

Without going into elaborate plot details, we can observe that the film's political unconscious, unlike that immanent in Anthony Mann's two police procedurals, arguably shifts the problem of justice from the policing of particular crimes to the injustices of the U.S.'s neocolonial relationship with Mexico and more specifically to the violence of law enforcement, as "justice" is implemented in the border region.[26] And most significant, in contrast with Mann's two border films, Welles's divided characters, who articulate contradictions in both racial and sexual subject positions, fail to resolve conflicts, blur the line between good and evil, and function in a drama that leaves the relationship between law and justice disjunctive and unresolved.

In contrast with prior cinematic border treatments, Welles's film accomplishes the exposure of the corruption and crime complicity of policing agents. On the American side, Hank Quinlan's (Orson Welles) murderous and corrupt actions serve to erase the distinction between law breaking and law enforcement. After he has been killed and is found floating in waters between the United States and Mexico, his body not only effaces a rigid border separation with respect to crime but also, by mimicking the "wetback" with his corpse, blurs the distinction between the two forms of labor power, the *bracero* and the police detective.[27] The character on the Mexican side also has "a touch of evil." Although Vargas sees himself as one fighting corruption, he displays more interest in eliminating the corrupt, murderous Quinlan than in the civil rights of the Mexican defendant that Quinlan frames for a crime. Therefore, both main protagonists expose antagonistic features in both national societies and at the same time reveal the radical separation between the law and justice that Fuentes was to point out years later in his novelistic indictment of the way the Mexican state's militarization of law enforcement has amplified official complicity in criminal violence. However, to appreciate more fully the forces that radically separate the law from justice, we have to expand the force diagram well beyond the border area. For that purpose, I return to literature and engage Don Winslow's novel *The Power of the Dog* and Charles Bowden's hybrid text, *Dreamland*, which are well suited for that purpose.

THE POIESIS OF NARCO TRAFFICKING

Then two writers, the novelist Don Winslow and the journalist Charles Bowden, effectively capture the corrupt and violent practices of the U.S. law enforcement agents involved in the "war on drugs," the former with a novel and the latter with a hybrid text, an ethnography that is punctuated with drawings by Alice Leora Briggs and poetic renderings of the autobiography of the book's main informant. Both writers have been close to the violence of policing, Winslow as a private investigator and Bowden as an ethnographer interviewing both victims and perpetrators. They both evince what, Foucault famously designates as "fearless speech," *parrhesia:* "a kind of verbal activity where the speaker has a specific relation to truth through frankness, a certain relationship to his own life through danger, a certain type of relation to himself or other people through criticism."[28] Winslow's novel is an in-depth (literary narrative-oriented) inquiry into the U.S.'s "war on drugs," His *The Power of the Dog* links spaces and events whose interconnections tend to be evaded in official policy discourses. The novel opens in 1975, just after the U.S.'s ignominious withdrawal from Vietnam. Its literary geography comprises official corridors in Washington, D.C.; Manhattan's Hell's Kitchen; Tijuana and the deserts of the U.S. Southwest; the jungles of Latin America; and much of the California–U.S. border. At the same time, the novel maps the changing and fraught tensions between various agencies that constitute the U.S. justice *dispositif*—the CIA, DEA, and ICE (as well as some of their Mexican agency counterparts).

Briefly, the novel's protagonist, Art Keller is a former CIA agent who transfers to the DEA and likens his role in the "war on drugs" to his earlier war experience: "Except for the clothes, Art thinks, it could be Vietnam."[29] The

"BORDERLINE JUSTICE"   157

same subterfuge played out in Vietnam is in play across the Mexican border: "We Americans are just down here as 'advisers.'" Here's the novel's scenario, which matches the situation in the historical moment and place. It begins as Sinaloa's drug-trafficking hegemony is more or less accomplished and U.S. and Mexican agencies engage them: "The American war on drugs has opened a front in Mexico. Now ten thousand army troops are pushing through this valley near the town of Badiraguato, assisting squadrons of the Municipal Judicial Federal Police, better known as the *federales,* and a dozen or so DEA advisers like Art."[30]

The novel's drama displaces the abstractions one gets from policy discourses by mobilizing several realistic protagonists: Keller, the DEA advisor; his cynical DEA boss, Tim Taylor; Don Pedro Aviles, the head of the Sinaloa drug cartel; Miguel Angel Barrera, a would-be successor to control over the drug trade (and his nephews Adan and Raul); Sean Callan, a New Yorker from Hell's Kitchen and killer-for-hire who is ambivalently involved with mafia operators; a California woman/courtesan, Nora Hayden; and a Mexican archbishop, Juan Parada. And the narrative has temporal depth; it comprises over 30 years of Mexico's violent drug history, up to the post 9/11 period, during which not much has changed. The U.S. and Mexican policing agents remain complicit in atrocities while at the same time official pronouncements at the level of government in both countries perpetuate what Foucault has called a "truth weapon." As he poses the question, "[W]hat is the principle that explains history [and right]?" Foucault's answer is that it is to be found in "as series of brute facts" such as "physical strength, force, energy," in short in "a series of accidents, or at least contingencies." However, governments dissimulate the events of global violence by interpolating the use of raw force into implementations of rationality and right, and in a passage that captures the sense of how the two governments use their truth weapon, he writes of

> [t]he rationality of calculations, strategies and ruses; the rationality of technical procedures that are used to perpetuate the victory, to silence . . . the war . . . [and he adds that] given that the relationship of dominance works to their advantage, it is certainly not in their [the government's] interest to call any of this into question.[31]

The counter to the truth weapon is "critique . . . the movement by which the subject gives himself the right to question truth on its effects of power and question power on its discourses of truth."[32]

In Winslow's *The Power of the Dog,* much of the critique comes from the novel's literary geography. The players and forces Winslow sets in motion exist not only in the border zone but also in distant parts of the United States and Latin America. The effect is to show that the "border" is "as deep as it is wide."

158   "BORDERLINE JUSTICE"

Thereby the novel's intervention constitutes a challenge to the official "war on drugs" policy discourses that focus on walls and other controls situated on or very near the U.S.–Mexico border.[33] However, the novel's primary critique is constituted by the ways its protagonists/aesthetic subjects are involved less in a war in which narco traffickers are pitted against law enforcement agents than in a complex set of collaborations in which the alleged "law enforcement" functionaries aid and abet drug trafficking. In particular, the novel points out that in addition to the complicity of the mafia in the flow of drugs, the corrupt Mexican administration, along with collaborators in the U.S. intelligence agencies, engages in clandestine deals that fill the power vacuums and determine the differential levels of success among alternative trafficking operators rather than reducing the flows of drugs through Mexico to their largest clientele in the United States. In the novel (as a segment of the history of the cold war attests), some of the trafficking syndicates (the Barreras in the case of the novel, who are fictional representatives of one of the Sinaloa syndicates), manage to get a free pass from the U.S. intelligence agencies by providing weapons for U.S.-aligned counterinsurgency forces in Central America.

In the actual history of Washington-orchestrated covert intelligence and armed violence in the Americas, U.S. antidrug agencies, with the aim of supporting counterinsurgency operatives in Central America, went further than Winslow's novel suggests. In August 1996, an investigative report in the *San Jose Mercury News* (a series of articles titled "Dark Alliance") reported the appearance of cocaine on South-Central Los Angeles in the 1980s, a revenue-raising operation undertaken by the Nicaraguan Contras with U.S. intelligence agency assistance. A subsequent book elaboration by the reporter Gary Webb exposes the interconnections between American intelligence and the drug sales.[34] Although Webb's investigative report provides very credible evidence of the CIA–Contra collaboration in the drug sales, the CIA exercised *its* "truth weapon." A report resulting from an investigation led by the CIA Inspector General resulted in this frequently issued preface to all of Webb's findings about the connections: "No information has been found to indicate."[35] Among the most effective critical response to such official truth weapons is the Charles Bowden–Alice Leora Briggs collaboration, *Dreamland: The Way Out of Juarez.* The text is explicitly aimed at challenging the official truth weapons that promote the effectiveness of the war in drugs. Bowden notes, for example, that on the Mexican side of the war, "[p]residents come and go and pretend to be in charge."[36] And while both the United States and Mexico act as if they exercise effective sovereign power and that the war is either under control or being won, he sees through the disguises that are literally engraved in the landscape: "One nation is called the United States, the other Mexico. I find it harder and harder to use these names because they imply order and boundaries, and both are breaking down." The breakdown is such that, as Bowden puts it, he has to "try not to say the names," even as they continuously appear "right there on the maps and road signs."[37] As a result, he suggests that a critical view that can oppose the official truth weapons requires a different cartographic imaginary:

> This is a new geography, one based less on names and places and lines and national boundaries and more on forces and appetites and torrents of people. Some places, parts of Europe, island states here and there, remain temporarily out of play in this geography. But the Bermudas of the planet are toppling one by one. The waves wash up now into the most ancient squares by the most solemn cathedrals.[38]

Bowden points out that time, as well as space, must be rethought. The linear model of history as a progressive, justice-achieving dynamic in which lives are improved does not hold:

> We try to fit this into our notion of history and for centuries our notion of history has been progressive, that things get better, that an invisible hand guides us or invisible gods guide us, every generation lives better than the one before.[39]

How can one entertain such a model in the face of the proliferation of "little houses" where people are tortured and killed, he wonders.

Given the complicity of policing apparatuses in drug trafficking and murder, as illegal businesses employ police and federal agents, Bowden finds the discourses of crime and justice equally anachronistic:

> I must find a new language, one that avoids the empty words like justice and crime and punishment and problems and solutions . . . I can still say this side and that side. I can still say police and criminals. But the words are emptying out and the meaning is flowing down the *calles* and into the sewers.[40]

"This war I speak of cannot be understood with normal political language."[41] Bowden adds specifics along with his critique of policy languages. He points out, for example, that one U.S. policing agency, ICE, turns out to be especially callous:

> Between August 5 and January 14 twelve me were tortured, strangled, and buried at the quiet house, and ICE, a component of the new Department of Homeland Security, knew about the killings and did nothing . . . officially it was a sidebar detail in an investigation of the illegal smuggling of cigarettes . . . or a detail in an effort to penetrate the cartel. Or it was all about nothing.[42]

The most shocking specifics derive from Bowden's interviews with "Lalo," a former Mexican "cop" who had aspired to work for the CIA but chose instead to work as an assassin for two of the Mexican cartels after he failed to achieve his original ambition. Lalo also worked for both the DEA and ICE as well, agencies that protected him from U.S. prosecution for the crimes associated with his cartel services. The shock effect of Lalo's self-described resume is amplified by the way Bowden's text is partitioned; it is a pastiche of genres. The text has breaks captioned as "Lalo's Song," in which his words capture the grisly reality of the crime/policing collaborations in violence. A Bowden suggests, "His words catch the music of a new world that is being born."[43] In his first substantial song, Lalo reports on his drug-trafficking work after resigning from the federal highway police, moving cocaine with the help of a corrupt customs inspection agent and learning about the "executions" to settle drug-trafficking accounts.[44] Thereafter, most of his "songs" describe executions, many of which he arranged and carried out.

The text is also partitioned with drawings by Alice Leora Briggs, which interrupt the flow of the text with disjunctive images that juxtapose mundane, everyday-life scenes with death imagery. As a result, the text's montage effect introduces bizarre equivalences that shock the reader, turning his or her attention away from the simplicity of the objects treated and toward their contexts. It provides a sense of the bizarre realities hiding behind the official truth weapons of the war on drugs by mobilizing an aesthetic of shock in which "the object character of the artwork recedes entirely, and thus a radical diversion from what attracts . . . has been effectively achieved."[45]

Ultimately, as Bowden points out in his description of the new global geography of forces that has eclipsed the old world of geopolitical names, the violent world that his investigation and textual work reveal is but one space in a world in which official policies amplify the problems they purport to solve. After pointing out how North American Free Trade Agreement destroyed the old agricultural base of Mexico and thereby accelerated the drug-trafficking enterprises and how the "narc budget" increases in the United States have been accompanied by increases in drug use in the United States, accomplishing only a vast increase in the prison population, he writes, "[T]he only flaw in my notion is this: the Mexican war is simply part of a global breakdown, the shredding of traditional cultures by the machinery of trade"[46]

"NOTHING IS FAIR"

Bowden's insights are replicated and cinematically enhanced in Gerardo Naranjo's earlier-noted film *Miss Bala*. The film draws on a recent historical event, the arrest of the beauty queen Miss Sinaloa (Laura Zunega), who was discovered in a car with members of the Sinaloa drug cartel, along with a large cache of weapons and money in 2008 (specifically, "she was riding in one of two trucks, in which soldiers found a large stash of weapons, including two AR-15 assault rifles, 38 specials, 9mm handguns, nine magazines, 633 cartridges and US$53,000").[47] Whether Miss Sinaloa was a collaborator or merely a victim remains unclear. However, as Naranjo shifts the venue from Sinaloa to Baja California, he casts Miss Bala (Stephanie Sigman) as a victim whose misadventure unveils the cross-border network of narco trafficking, weapons transfers, and policing collaborations that constitute the contemporary drug-crime/justice *dispositif*.

"Nothing is fair" is a remark uttered by the organizer of the Baja California beauty contest, Luisa Janes (Leonor Vitoria). Although it is a response to Laura's remark, "It isn't fair," after she misses a rehearsal and is removed as a contestant (she had been delayed because she had to escape from a dancehall that had been invaded by a drug gang that killed many of the revelers), the remark has larger significance; it applies to the U.S.–Mexico war on drugs as a whole. At the time of the film's release the policy directing that "war," was the "Merida Initiative," a "partnership among the governments of the United States, Mexico, and the countries of Central America to confront the violent transnational gangs and organized crime syndicates" (afterward broadened to include the countries of the Caribbean), launched in 2007.[48] Despite the optimistic language of official policy discourse—"We have agreed with the Government of Mexico to work together in several of the most affected Mexican communities, including Ciudad Juarez," and "we are moving away from big ticket equipment and into an engagement that reinforces progress by further institutionalizing Mexican capacity to sustain adherence to the rule of law and respect for human rights"[49]—the death rate continued to escalate in Juarez (aka "Murder City") and the so-called security forces, as Bowden had pointed out, are among the major violators of "human rights."[50]

Like Bowden's investigatory texts, Naranjo's film evinces a critique that effectively challenges the "truth weapons" of official policy discourse. With his primary aesthetic subject, Laura Guerrero, he opposes the macropolitical frame that articulates the big lies of reasons of state and nation-to-nation initiatives of policy solidarity and cooperation with a micropolitical gloss in which a victim reveals the nature of the place in which "policy" is experienced. Although as I noted, Fuentes has argued that the novel is the ideal genre for reappropriating time in order to create a critical perspective, cinema is even more enabling with respect to a critical temporality. To create that critical temporality, Naranjo altered the sequence of the story on which the film is based. As I point out elsewhere, referring to "cinematic time," film is a "genre that is ideally suited to an 'epistemology of contingency' . . . because . . . cinema actualizes a contingent mode of time; through its 'yoking together of non-contiguous

162   "BORDERLINE JUSTICE"

spaces with parallel editing . . . cinema effects the 'disfiguration of continuous time.'"[51] In the case of *Miss Bala*, Naranjo states,

> We wanted to talk about the smuggling of weapons into Mexico, the death of a DEA agent [at the hands of] drug dealers and the beauty queen phenomenon. . . . Many of the stories were real but they didn't happen in that [particular] sequence of events. The license we took was to create a story where they could co-exist.[52]

The "license" to which Naranjo refers is constitutive of the contemporary cinematic aesthetic in which the "time image" dominates. Distinguishing that aesthetic (I repeat here quotations from earlier chapters), Deleuze opposes a "cinema of seeing" to a "cinema of action." In a cinema of seeing, he points out, "the viewer's problem becomes 'What is there to see in the image?' (and not now) 'What are we going to see in the next image?')."[53] However, although *Miss Bala* is a cinema of seeing rather than of action, the viewer trying to make sense of what he or she sees is put into the same situation as Laura. The way the film is shot with rapidly moving scenes and frequent cuts and juxtapositions renders Laura's and the viewer's seeing unclear. And, as Julia Peres Guimarães points out,

> [o]ne of the constant features of *Miss Bala* is a pervasive feeling of tension that muddles the spectator's sense of time. Even though scenes unfold chronologically, day and night clearly identified—the story takes place in no more than a couple of days—the lack of clear dialogues, the sub-dued lighting and sound effects a sense of discomfort (muffled car sounds, shooting, engines running, etc.) the audience never has a clear sense of what is happening to Laura.[54]

Neither Laura nor the viewers can anticipate what will happen next. The viewer experiences Laura's terror but is often not shown what is frightening. Naranjo states,

> I think the tension is built mostly in the viewer's mind. It was very impor-tant for us to not show the horrors but to put them on your head so you would recreate them. . . . The horror and the crime is something you don't see but you imagine.[55]

As Naranjo's statement suggests, much of the film's effect results from the two kinds of space it incorporates. Whereas a novel registers the forces on its subjects with the reach of its literary geography (e.g., Winslow's mapping of the war on drugs in his *The Power of the Dog*), a film works with images and

"BORDERLINE JUSTICE"   163

registers its effects by showing how what is within the frame and can be seen is often affected by what is unseen, exiting outside the frame. Noël Burch (whom I quote in Chapter 4) has put in this way:

> To understand cinematic space, it may prove useful to consider it as in fact consisting of *two different kinds of space:* that included within the frame and that outside the frame. For our purposes, screen space can be defined very simply as including everything perceived on the screen by the eye.[56]

In the case of *Miss Bala*, one kind of off-screen space is often brought into play when Laura leaves a room and the viewer has to await her arrival elsewhere while the camera remains momentarily behind; it is, as Burch puts it, a space in which

> a character reaches it by going out a door, going around a street corner, disappearing behind a pillar or behind another person, or performing some similar act. The outer limit of this . . . segment of space is just beyond the horizon.[57]

However, although many of the interactions of the two spaces are evoked by Laura's entries and exits from the frame, her cinematic odyssey as a whole reveals the larger geopolitical space within which the "war on drugs" is occurring. For example, while she is crouched, hiding in the shower of the nightclub as it is being invaded by the drug gang, we can hear one of the gang members say, "[F]ind the American." And when the gang loses its cache of ammunition, we hear a voice saying, "contact the Americans" (ultimately Laura is forced to travel to the United States with money taped to her body, to bring back the ammunition. A variety of signs expands the off-screen space to a "bi-national entanglement . . . the license plates are from California, the currency in dollars, the guns imported from across the border, and the principal drug market is the United States[, even as t]he carnage . . . remains in Mexico."[58] Thus, many of Naranjo's images of the places within the frame "open up a dimension wider than the 'plot' . . ."[59]

While Laura's spatial Odyssey implicates the macropolitical, binational connections involved in the narco trafficking and the reactive drug-war response, it is the suborned comportment of her body that registers the micropolitics of both (their coercive and violent effects on the everyday mundane lives of those who live in affected areas). The film opens in Laura's small, cramped house, which she shares with her younger brother and her father. In that opening there is not enough light for the audience to see her face clearly, and in the few moments where it might be possible, Laura is filmed mostly from the back, a cinematic statement to the effect that, in her dreary impoverished life, she has not yet risen above the threshold of special recognition. From behind her, we see her getting dressed for the first of many times. As it turns out, this is the *only* time that her dressing (or undressing) is voluntary.

Once she leaves the house, she is headed with her friend Suzu (Lakshmi Picazo) to enter the state of Baja California's beauty pageant (despite her father's prophetic warning that it is a dangerous environment to enter). When she signs up and takes her place among the other contestants, there is panning shot of the assembled hopefuls. What the viewer sees is a diorama of nervous and forlorn young women seeking an exit from their deprived and unhappy lives. Before she gets in that line, the abrupt, unfriendly organizer, Luisa (Leonor Vitorica), tells her she must get dressed in her contestant outfit. That gesture of control over Laura's bodily movements is merely the first of many such moments. Another immediately ensues as Laura and the rest of the contestants have to walk along a line drawn on the floor. Shortly thereafter, they are told to smile and utter a particular phrase, for example, "My name is Laura Guerrero, and my dream is to represent the beautiful women of my state" (here we get the first full-frontal shot of Laura, who hopes to exit from the dreary life in which she is seen primarily from the back in a darkened hovel of a house (Figure 5.4). That enforced remark, added to others that the contestants must make during the final contest (e.g., the eventual runner-up, Jessica Verdugo's [Irene Azuela] required speech is a complaint about the bad press her state gets), points to the way the contestants are enlisted as relays of the official truth weapon. In light of Fuentes's earlier-noted remark that crime has replaced the state, Naranjo takes that reality into the everyday-life sphere;

FIGURE 5.4
Laura wearing her crown. Source: Gerardo Naranjo, *Miss Bala*, Columbia Pictures (2011).

"BORDERLINE JUSTICE"   165

he sees his film as a challenge to official attempts to obscure that reality by show-ing something "unexplored: the secret life of panic, the way that crime invades the everyday and mentally corrodes people who are outside its actions."[60]

Shortly after registering for the contest, Laura is to experience that panic as she learns that the protocols controlling her bodily gestures and speech are minor compared to what she faces when she becomes a pawn of the drug gang. After she and Suzu become qualified contestants, they show up at a nightclub where the gang attacks. Although Laura had been allowed to escape after the head of the gang, Lino Valdez (Noé Hernandez) spotted her in the shower; she is later captured by the gang after she begs a transit policeman to help her locate Suzu, who has disappeared after the attack on the club. Instead of help-ing her, the cop turns out to be a collaborator with the gang and delivers her to them. Recognizing her from the club, they hustle her into a van, brutalize and threaten her, and leave her with a hood over her head with Lino, who is to decide her fate.

Throughout that sequence, Naranjo's rapidly moving camera gives the viewer the sense of the panic and confusion afflicting Laura as she is swept up in the gangs running battles with authorities. That cinematic style, along with the long takes, shows the way she is trapped by creating a sense of her claustrophobia, especially when the camera enters her cramped little home. After she has tried to run away, Lino and his gang occupy her house. Lino expels her father and her brother and forces her to share her bed after having demanded that she get undressed. In the household, Naranjo's visual language articulates the rhythms of light and dark that have altered Laura's domestic sphere, changing it from its day-to-day rhythms of domesticity to the rhythms of dominance and submission. As night turns into day (ambiguously as the play of light versus dark keeps switching), Lino prepares Laura for the delivery of money to the United States in order to acquire a new supply of ammunition lost during a police raid on the gang's hideout. Laure's trip to the U.S. side of the border reveals two levels of control and constraint, as well as the collection of agencies assembled to make narco trafficking possible.

The border policing is the first control; it is a place where typically "danger happens" because ordinarily, as "the boundary between inside and outside [where] the inside is safe, outside is danger."[61] However, in Laura's case, she is leaving one kind of danger behind and facing another, which the viewer sees from Laura's point of view, as on the way north, she passes through the border control in a taxi and responds to a question about the reason for her visit with the remark, "I'm going shopping." The same zoom/framing shot of the border is shown from her point of view on the way back, in heightened danger because she is driving a car full of the ammunition she has been forced to carry back from her "shopping trip." The second control is another instance of coercion over Laura's body. The "gringo" who cuts the tape around her waist and takes the money keeps demanding in a surly voice that she keep her hands on the wheel of the car. Although Laura's anxious journey is continuously onscreen, the viewer gets a sense of the network of apparatuses that are the conditions of possibility for the trafficking venture—the money taped to Laura, the taxi driver willing to take the risk, the pilot and plane used to fly her farther north, whoever has made the car available for her return trip, and all the persons involved in the United States who procure weapons and ammunition to sell to the traffickers, as well as the various officials and agencies that, either through incompetence or corruption, allow the transactions and the government agencies whose policy priorities direct insufficient attention to the problem.

Back at the beauty contest, we see a Laura who has become too traumatized to either smile or speak. When it is her turn to deliver the typical beauty-contest platitudes (her opponent, Jessica, who precedes her, says that the beautiful city of Baja deserves respect), she cannot make her voice work. She is crowned Miss Baja nevertheless because of the power of the drug-gang-policing apparatuses controlling her to make that happen. However, more coercive structures await. In the last venue where she is featured as the beauty queen, she is delivered to the military head of the antidrug initiative, General Duarte, at a hotel gathering, where Lino, who is now collaborating with the army, is pretending to set up an assassination but instead is setting up his own gang (although he, too, is betrayed and killed before the event is over). It is in the general's room that Laura is told to undress for the last time. When the general begins to caress her, she whispers to him that he is about to be murdered. He immediately tells her she must put her clothes back on. After the ensuing firefight in which both some gang members and some of the general's guards are killed, Laura becomes the prime sacrifice. The soldiers beat her up, television commentators (including Luisa, the beauty-contest coordinator) report her as a disgrace to Mexico as a narco-trafficking collaborator, and she is once again forced into a car and driven away. Bruised and battered, she is let out in a back-street warehouse district. As we see her for the last time, it is again from the back. She is the film's exemplary victim (doubtless representing the Mexican victims of the drug war as a whole). The view from behind her is a visual statement that she has now sunk below the level of recognition. Her moments of special recognition, which had been a contrivance of the main players in the duplicitous war, are over because her body is no longer useful capital for their nefarious projects.

Naranjo's film is a powerful attack on the official discourses of the "war on drugs." *His* weapons are what André Bazan famously calls "image facts" . . . "fragment(s) of concrete reality," which have the effect of freeing viewers from the dominant representations of state policy by allowing then to connect the fragments of image facts into a narrative coherence that gives the lie to the U.S.–Mexico truth weapons.[62] I want to note by way of locating Naranjo's style that, although his political sensibility is delivered with a cinematic aesthetic that is singular, it has some resonances with Pier Paulo Pasolini's cinematic politics. One way of construing that resonance is to see a Pasolini *interruptus* at work in the way Naranjo's camera moves. While, for example, Pasolini explored the dreary life worlds of the downtrodden classes living on the outskirts of a "Rome, Ringed by its Hell of Suburbs"[63] in his *Mama Rosa* (1962) with a lot of long takes and framing shots of desolate cityscapes and housing projects, Naranjo offers only brief glimpses of the more dreary venues of Baja California. Instead, he creates disrupting blurs of motion, as the actions of the narco-trafficking gang and their policing counterparts (who either oppose or assist their enterprise) disrupt even this mundane and oppressed parts of the lifeworld. We get glimpses of the Pasolini aesthetic, only to have it continually interrupted as Narranjo's camera captures rapidly moving bodies and vehicles (e.g., a fire fight between the gang and the police in which Laura is constantly threatened by the cross fire creates a charged and confusing atmosphere in a grim under-bridge urban scene, which ends when the gang escapes in a huge dump truck).

Having explored cinematic texts that effectively map the extent of the apparatuses involved in the war in drugs, while indicating their the effects on the everyday-life world in Mexico, I want to ascend to a theoretical reflection that theorizes justice by raising the question of where justice can be located in a war in which law enforcement is at least as responsible for atrocities as are the drug gangs and in a policy environment in which a new bantustanization is on the agenda.

JUSTICE?

Although it is clear that Laura's experience is traumatic, and her anxiety is palpable, the political force of her experience, as it emerges through her movement trajectory, is better understood if she is rendered as an aesthetic rather than as a psychological subject. By treating Laura as an aesthetic subject, we can look at the way the forces affecting her shape Naranjo's cinematic space, as she is forced to perform within many of the spaces that are the conditions of possibility for narco trafficking. Laura's movements etch the cartography of the drug trafficking and the policing process as they function both as an enterprise and as violent disruptions of much of Mexico's lifeworld. Although there is a manifest passivity in the way Laura reacts to her capture within the criminal/policing process, there is nevertheless a "political subjectivization" that she represents as a "subject of rights" (whose rights to free movement are abridged). She is the kind of political subject who "inscribe(s) the count of the uncounted," where the politics of subjectivity here is about the political

168   "BORDERLINE JUSTICE"

qualification of those regarded as unqualified.[64] Thus, although Laura herself is passive, Naranjo's film is active. Effecting a political subjectivization of its protagonist, it uses the force of his cinematic art to allow Laura to rise above the level of recognition, not only as one who achieves notoriety by winning a beauty contest but also as one who stands for the uncounted within the political discourses of the war on drugs. While generally beauty contests can create instant recognition for those who are largely unnoticed within a system of the social exchange of recognition, in this case, the film adds contingency to that kind of recognition event by framing it within a historical moment when extra-state forces are impinging on the society, creating panic, quiescence, and the breakdown and/or corruption of justice-implementing agencies whose personnel collaborate with crime organizations.

Official proclamations to the contrary, in the "war on drugs" (as the beauty contest coordinator, Luisa, says in an earlier quotation), "nothing is fair." The problem to contemplate then is to how to conceive justice, given the facts of complicity between the justice *dispositif*, constituted by the official war on drugs, and the crime *dispositif*, as it unfolds in the process of narco trafficking. Inasmuch as my focus has been on the diverse apparatuses that are the vehicles of the trafficking and policing, I want to summon the relevant methodological insight provided by Michel Foucault's remarks on *dispositifs* in his lectures under the title of *The Birth of Biopolitics*, where he begins with some remarks on his "choice of method," suggesting,

> instead of deducing concrete phenomena from universals, or instead of starting with universals as an obligatory grid of intelligibility for certain concrete practices, I would like to start with the concrete practices and, as it were, pass these universals through the grid of these practices.[65]

A focus on the policing practices involved in the war on drugs highlights the injustices. Given the vagaries of policing and the arbitrariness of the way states and their implementing agencies determine licit versus illicit commodities and warrants for their transfers, it turns out that in the war on drugs, "nothing is fair," both in terms of what becomes an object of coercive control and in terms of the extent to which there is protection of the rights of those who live in areas where the drug war is ongoing. Agencies that might otherwise concern themselves with justice-as-fairness, pursue a "justice" that takes the form of violent confrontation.

Are there other options? There is one nation-state, Bolivia, which much to the chagrin of U.S. policing agencies, resists the model of justice-as-a-war-on-drugs. In contrast with a series of Mexico presidents, whose militarization of the policing function has accelerated the death rate in the Mexican drug war, is Bolivian president Evo Morales's approach. His weapon is "coca licensing" rather than the militarization of the policing function.[66] The context for Morales's approach is the historical subordination of Bolivia's indigenous population whose cultural practices and interests, prior to Morales's presidency, were neglected. Although they had begun to achieve some recognition within a neoliberal development economic paradigm before Morales assumed the presidency, there was no recognition of the moral economy within which many of them worked as coca farmers. Pre-Morales governments continued to participate in the global antidrug initiatives.

After taking office in January 2006, Morales introduced a different "borderline justice," one based on a different governmentality. In terms of the "borderline," he sharply distinguished coca from its manufactured by-product, cocaine. And in terms of his altered governmentality, rather than continuing with the prior model in which all citizens were regarded as the same political subjects, he focused on the fault lines within the Bolivian society that have historically created different interests and alternative moral economies between the Euro-Hispanic and indigenous populations.[67] In effect, Morales turned back the clock to delink coca from contemporary commodity flows and reenfranchise (pre–global capitalist) relationships that had shaped Bolivian society:

> A three-century interregional Spanish colonial coca leaf trail traversed what is now Peru, Bolivia, Chile, and Northern Argentina, largely for mine workers and other hard laborers. It predated the creation of a global taste and market for coca, which only started with the French luxury commodity drink *Vin Maraini* in 1863 and later industrialized during the German medicinal *kocain* boom of 1884–1887.[68]

Intervening in the drug-war protection racket, where states have sought to have fiscal control over commodity flows, in 2009, Morales kicked out the agents of the U.S.'s DEA and arrested the former head of the Bolivian antinarcotics police (on trafficking charges). Those moves were coupled with a strict licensing law applied to coca growing, which has led to drop in coca production of 12 to 13 percent along with a drop in the violent crimes that are "the bloody byproduct of American-led measures to control trafficking in Colombia, Mexico and other parts of the region."[69] Although Bolivia under Morales still criminalizes cocaine, it recognizes coca leaf as a traditional medicine/stimulate, chewed by a large percentage of the indigenous population. Registering thousands of growers in the Chapare region, the government limits plantings to make sure of equal access to the product (as well as a fair level of income for growers) while containing its use in trafficking. Without the violence associated with the American paramilitary model, the Morales government has eradicated many acres of coca without anything like the levels of violence that the antidrug war in Mexico has produced: "A government report said that 60 people were killed and more than 700 wounded in the Chapare from 1998–2002 in violence related to eradication."[70]

"Fair but hard?" Finally, to return to the line from the film narrative in Mann's *T Men*, which implies that the policing apparatus delivers an impartial justice. I want to consider briefly the flaws in the ever-popular rationalistic approach by justice of liberal constitutionalists such as John Rawls and Ronald Dworkin. In his famous (continually adjusting) account of justice as fairness,[71] Rawls privileges a political liberty in which each person would want to be in a society in which he or she has an equal right to a basic liberty that would apply to all and in which social and economic inequalities are in an arrangement that should be to everyone's advantage and are connected to positions and offices that are equally available to all citizens. In addition, committed to a Kant-inspired model of public reason, Rawls embraces a democratic imaginary in which equality amounts to an arithmetic sum such that in matters of justice there is an "inexhaustibility of representation"—anyone can be added to the list of those participating in the justice-related deliberation.[72] In effect, Rawls "talks like a state." In his later writings, he argues that justice as fairness is political rather than metaphysical and is evoked in debates about "constitutional matters."[73]

Dworkin perpetuates a similar classical liberal model of justice in which equality is the central concept and a political arithmetic is the primary analytic. At the center of his model is an ahistorical "ethical individual," who should be given an equal opportunity. As I have noted,

> Dworkin reduces political equality to the opportunity individuals have to express their political preferences. His failure to recognize the power of discourse is evident in his articulation of the seemingly unproblematic premise that "people have . . . political preferences"[74] [whereas] . . . It is more politically perspicuous to say that political preferences have people. By privileging subjective agency as his primary model of political enactment, Dworkin bars access to the entrenched models of political intelligibility [the talk of the state] available to subjects.[75]

With a version of politics that opposes the Rawls/Dworkin political imaginary that sustains their liberal model of justice, Jacques Rancière provides a critique of

> the typical political arithmetic within which everyone is a subject before the law or has a political preference to be counted along with others. In contrast to "the arithmetic of shopkeepers and barterers" . . . Rancière speaks of "a magnitude that escapes ordinary measurement," a "paradoxical magnitude" that escapes a logic that equates the equality of anyone at all with anyone else.

Rancière's version of politics is well suited to the acts of subjectivization inherent in Naranjo's film *Miss Bala* and President Morales's new governmentality. For Rancière, politics is an event in which an action by a part that is uncounted makes an appearance that challenges "the system that creates modes of subjectivization by reordering the significance of the bodies and spaces within which they function." Naranjo's Laura and Morales's indigenous coca growers are lent justice by being allowed to rise above the threshold of visibility in challenges to the commodity-oriented "racial state" in Morales's case and to the drug-control apparatuses of the drug-war state in Naranjo's. Morales challenges the lawmaking violence that divides licit versus illicit drugs. Naranjo challenges the biopolitical/legal order of division of politically qualified versus unqualified bodies. I give Jacques Derrida the last words in this chapter: "Justice as law is never exercised without a decision that *cuts*, that divides."[76]

NOTES

1. "Borderline Justice" is in quotation marks because the title is inspired by an essay on Orson Welles's film *A Touch of Evil*: See Donald Pease, "Borderline Justice/States of Emergency: Orson Welles' *Touch of Evil*," *The New Centennial Review* 1: 1 (2001), 75–105.
2. Michael J. Shapiro, *War Crimes, Atrocity, and Justice* (Cambridge: Polity, 2015).
3. See Reece Jones, *Border Walls: Security and the War on Terror in the United States, India, and Israel* (New York: Zed Books, 2012), 110.
4. The distinction between abstract and lived space belongs to Henri Lefebvre. See his *The Production of Space*, trans. Donald Nicholson-Smith (Malden: Blackwell, 1991).
5. On forking-path film narratives see Chapter 5, "The Art Cinema as a Mode of Practice," in *Poetics of Cinema*, ed. David Bordwell (New York: Routledge, 2007).
6. The quotation is from Olivia Guaraldo, *Storyline, History and Narrative from an Arendtian Perspective* (Jyvaskyla, Finland: SoPhi 63, 2001), ii.
7. Jacques Rancière, "Aesthetic Separation, Aesthetic Community: Scenes from the Aesthetic Regime of Art," *Art & Research* 2 (1), On the web at: http://artandresearch.org.uk/v2n1/ranciere.html.
8. See the most recent references in Michael J. Shapiro, *Studies in Trans-Disciplinary Method: After the Aesthetic Turn* (London: Routledge, 2012), xv, 25.
9. Carlos Fuentes, "Writing in Time," *Democracy* 2 (1962), 61.
10. Ernst Block, "Nonsynchronism and the Obligation to its Dialectics." Trans. Mar Rotter [originally published in 1932] *New German Critique* 11 (Spring, 1977), 22.
11. *Ibid.*72.
12. Carlos Fuentes, *Destiny and Desire*, trans. Edith Grossman (New York: Random House, 2011), 382.
13. *Ibid.*, 41.
14. *Ibid.*
15. *Ibid.*, 382.
16. *Ibid.*

172 **"BORDERLINE JUSTICE"**

17. See Nick Vaughan-Williams, *Border Politics: The Limits of Sovereign Power* (Edinburgh: Edinburgh University Press, 2009). The bare life–versus–politically qualified life binary is developed in Giorgio Agamben, *Homo Sacer: Sovereignty and Bare Life*, trans. Daniel Heller-Roazen (Stanford: Stanford University Press, 1998).

18. This is especially the case in crime novels. See, for example, Andrew Pepper, "Policing the Globe: State Sovereignty and the International in the Post-9/11 Crime Novel," *Modern Fiction Studies* 57: 3 (Fall, 2011), 401–424.

19. Don Winslow, *Kings of Cool* (New York: Simon & Schuster, 2012), 174.

20. The quotations are from Jonathan Auerbach's reading of the film in his *Dark Borders: Film Noir and American Citizenship* (Durham: Duke University Press, 2011), 131.

21. The quotation is from Gilles Deleuze, *The Logic of Sense*, trans. M. Lester (New York: Columbia University Press, 1990), 182.

22. Auerbach, *Dark Borders*, 131.

23. The quotation is from Elena Dell'Agnese, "The US–Mexican Border in American Films," *Geopolitics* 10: 2 (2005), 217. She provides, in her words, a good summary of the "connotations that the American film industry has given to cross-border experience over the years."

24. The quotation is from Gilles Deleuze, *Cinema 2* (Minneapolis: University of Minnesota Press, 1989), 142.

25. Stephen Heath, "Film and System, Terms of Analysis," *Screen* 16: 1–2 (1975), 93.

26. I say "arguably" because there are two different but equally compelling positions on the political force of the film. Homi Bhabha offers a colonial critique version (see his "The Other Question: Difference, Discrimination and the Discourse of Colonialism," in *Literature, Politics and Theory*, eds. Francis Barker et al. [London: Methuen, 1986], 148–172), while Michael Denning sees historically specific reference to Welles's activism in issues taken up by the "cultural front." See his *The Cultural Front: The Laboring of American Culture in the Twentieth Century* (New York: Verso, 1996), 401.

27. My interpretation is edified by Donald E, Pease's reading the film: "Borderline Justice," 89.

28. Michel Foucault, *Fearless Speech*, ed. Joseph Pearson (New York: Semiotext(e), 2001), 19.

29. Don Winslow, *The Power of the Dog* (New York: Alfred A, Knopf, 2005), 9.

30. *Ibid.*, 10.

31. Michel Foucault, *Society Must Be Defended*, trans. David Macey (New York: Picador, 2003), 54–55.

32. Michel Foucault, "What Is Critique?" in *The Politics of Truth*, trans. Lysa Hochroth and Catherine Porter (New York: Semiotext(e), 2007), 47.

33. The quotations are from Mat Coleman, "A Geopolitics of Engagement: Neoliberalism, the War on Terrorism, and the Reconfiguration of the US Immigration Enforcement," *Geopolitics* 12: 3 (2007), 627.

34. Gary Webb, *Dark Alliance: The CIA, the CONTRAS, and the CRACK COCAIN EXPLOSION* (New York: Seven Stories Press, 1998).

35. See the release by the CIA's Office of Inspector General, Investigations Staff, "Overview: Report of Investigation. On the web at: www.cia.gov/library/reports/general-reports-1/cocaine/overview-of-report-of-investigation-2.html.

"BORDERLINE JUSTICE" 173

36. Charles Bowden and Alice Leora Briggs, *Dreamland: The Way Out of Juarez* (Austin: University of Texas Press, 2010), 2.
37. *Ibid.*, 6.
38. *Ibid.*, 138–139.
39. *Ibid.*, 152.
40. *Ibid.*, 12.
41. *Ibid.*, 58.
42. *Ibid.*, 43.
43. *Ibid.*, 14.
44. *Ibid.*, 21.
45. The quotation is from Rudolphe Gasche's explication of Walter Benjamin's concept of shock "Objective Diversions: Some Kantian Themes in Benjamin's 'The Work of Art in the Age of Mechanical Reproduction,'" in Andrew Benjamin and Peter Osborne eds., *Walter Benjamin's Philosophy: Destruction and Experience* (New York: Routledge, 1994), 195.
46. Bowden and Briggs, *Dreamland*, 76.
47. "Miss Sinaloa 2008 Laura Zuniga Arrested in Mexico," *Herald Sun*, On the web at: www.heraldsun.com.au/news/victoria/beauty-shopping-for-trouble/story-e6frf7lx-1111118404718.
48. The quotations are from testimony by Roberta S. Jacobson, Deputy Assistant Secretary, Bureau of Western hemisphere Affairs, to the U.S. House of Representatives Committee on Foreign Affairs, publishes as "U.S.-Mexico Security Cooperation: Next Steps for the Merida Initiative," *U.S. Department of State: Diplomacy in Action*, On the web at: www.state.gov/p/wha/rls/rm/2010/142297.htm.
49. *Ibid.*
50. See Charles Bowden, *Murder City: Ciudad Juarez and the Global Economy's New Killing Fields* (New York: Nation Books, 2011).
51. Michael J. Shapiro, *The Time of the City: Politics, Philosophy and Genre* (London: Routledge, 2010), 40. The internal quotes are from Mary Ann Doane, *The Emergence of Cinematic Time* (Cambridge, MA: Harvard University Press, 2002), 19 and 194.
52. "Miss Bala: Gerardo Naranjo Interview," *Film*. On the web at: www.sbs.com.au/films/movie-news/899515/miss-bala-gerardo-naranjo-interview.
53. Gilles Deleuze, *Cinema 2: The Time Image*, trans. H. Tomlinson and R. Galeta (Minneapolis: University of Minnesota Press, 1989), 272.
54. Julia Peres Guimaraes, "Cinema and the Official United States Discourse on the 'War on Drugs': The Film *Miss Bala*," Masters Dissertation in International Relations at The Pontifical Catholic University of Rio de Janeiro, September, 2012.
55. "Miss Bala: Gerardo Naranjo interview.
56. Noël Burch, *Theory of Film Practice* (Princeton: Princeton University Press, 1981), 18.
57. *Ibid.*
58. The quotations are from Harley Shaiken, "Holding a Mirror to Mexico," *Berkeley Review of Latin American Studies* (Fall, 2011/Winter, 2012). On the web at: http://clas.berkeley.edu/publications/review/index.html.
59. The quotation is from Roger Cardinal, "Pausing Over Peripheral detail," quoted in Elena Gorfinkel and John David Rhodes, "Introduction: The Matter of Places,"

174   "BORDERLINE JUSTICE"

in *Taking Place*, eds. Elena Gorfinkel and John David Rhodes (Minneapolis: University of Minnesota Press, 2009), xiii.

60. The novelist/essayist Juan Villoro writing about the film—quoted in Elizabeth Malkin, "In the Crossfire of the Mexican War in Drugs," *The New York Times*, On the web at: www.nytimes.com/2012/01/15/movies/gerardo-naranjos-miss-bala-reflects-mexican-drug-war.html?src=recg.

61. The quotations are from Emma Haddad, "*Danger Happens at the Border*," in *Borderscapes*, eds. Prem Rajaram and Carl Grundy-Warr (Minneapolis: University of Minnesota Press, 2007), 119.

62. See André Bazin, *What Is Cinema?* Vol 2, trans. Hugh Gray (Berkeley: University of California Press, 1971), 37.

63. This is a Pasolini quote, heading a chapter in John David Rhodes, *Stupendous Miserable City: Pasolini's Rome* (Minneapolis: University of Minnesota Press, 2007), 17.

64. The quotations and conceptual orientation here draw on Jacques Rancière's analysis of rights subjects in "Who Is the Subject of the Rights of Man," *The South Atlantic Quarterly* 103: 2/3 (Spring/Summer, 2004), 305.

65. Michel Foucault, *The Birth of Biopolitics*, trans. G. Burchell (New York: Palgrave, 2008), 3.

66. See William Neuman, "Coca Licensing Is a Weapon in Bolivia's Drug War," *The New York Times*, On the web at: www.nytimes.com/2012/12/27/world/americas/bolivia-reduces-coca-plantings-by-licensing-plots.html?pagewanted=all&_r=0.

67. For a summary of the Morales difference, see Robert Albro, "Confounding Cultural Citizenship and Constitutional reform in Bolivia," *Latin American Perspectives* 37: 3 (May, 2010), 71–90.

68. Paul Eliot Gootenberg, "Talking Like a State," in *Illicit Flows and Criminal Things*, eds. Willem van Schendel and Itty Abraham (Bloomington: Indiana University Press, 2005), 106.

69. Neuman, "Coca Licensing Is a Weapon in Bolivia's Drug War."

70. *Ibid.*

71. See the original formulation in John Rawls, *A Theory of Justice* (Cambridge, MA: Harvard University Press, 1981) and his subsequent "Justice as Fairness: Political Not Metaphysical," *Philosophy and Public Affairs* 14: 3 (Summer, 1985), 223–251.

72. For a good commentary on this aspect of the Rawlsian liberal imaginary, see Davide Panagia, *The Poetics of Political Thinking* (Durham: Duke University Press, 2006), 80–81.

73. John Rawls, *Political Liberalism* (New York: Columbia University Press, 1993), 240.

74. Ronald Dworkin, *Sovereign Virtue: The Theory and Practice of Equality* (Cambridge, MA: Harvard University Press, 2000), 17.

75. Michael J. Shapiro, *Methods and Nations: Cultural Governance and the Indigenous Subject* (New York: Routledge, 2004), 23.

76. Jacques Derrida, "Force of Law," in *Deconstruction and the Possibility of Justice*, eds. Drucilla Cornell, Michael Rosenfeld and David Gray (New York: Routledge, 1992), 24.

REFERENCES

Agamben, Giorgio (1998) *Homo Sacer: Sovereignty and Bare Life*, trans. Daniel Heller-Roazen Stanford: Stanford University Press.

Albro, Robert (2010) 'Confounding Cultural Citizenship and Constitutional reform in Bolivia,' *Latin American Perspectives*, Vol. 37 (3), pp. 71–90.

Auerbach, Jonathan (2011) *Dark Borders: Film Noir and American Citizenship*, Durham: Duke University Press.

Bazin, André (1971) *What is Cinema?*, Vol. 2, trans. Hugh Gray, Berkeley: University of California Press.

Bhabha, Homi (1986) 'The Other Question: Difference, Discrimination and the Discourse of Colonialism,' in *Literature, Politics and Theory*, eds. Francis Barker et al., London: Methuen, pp. 148–172.

Block, Ernst (1977) 'Nonsynchronism and the Obligation to its Dialectics,' trans. Mark Rotter [originally published in 1932], *New German Critique*, No. 11, pp. 22–38.

Bordwell, David (2007) *Poetics of Cinema*, New York: Routledge.

Bowden, Charles (2011) *Murder City: Ciudad Juarez and the Global Economy's New Killing Fields*, New York: Nation Books.

Bowden, Charles and Briggs, Alice Leora (2010) *Dreamland: The Way Out of Juarez*, Austin: University of Texas Press.

Burch, Noël (1981) *Theory of Film Practice*, trans. Helen R. Lane, Princeton: Princeton University Press.

Coleman, Mat (2007) 'A Geopolitics of Engagement: Neoliberalism, the War on Terrorism, and the Reconfiguration of the US Immigration Enforcement,' *Geopolitics*, Vol. 12 (3), pp. 607–634.

Deleuze, Gilles (1989) *Cinema 2*, trans. Hugh Tomlinson and Robert Galeta, Minneapolis: University of Minnesota Press.

Deleuze, Gilles (1990) *The Logic of Sense*, trans. M. Lester, New York: Columbia University Press.

Dell'Agnese, Elena (2005) 'The US-Mexican Border in American Films,' *Geopolitics*, Vol. 10 (2), pp. 204–221.

Denning, Michael (1996) *The Cultural Front: The Laboring of American Culture in the Twentieth Century*, New York: Verso.

Derrida, Jacques (1992) 'Force of Law,' in *Deconstruction and the Possibility of Justice*, eds. Drucilla Cornell, Michael Rosenfeld and David Gray, New York: Routledge, pp. 3–67.

Doane, Mary Ann (2002) *The Emergence of Cinematic Time*, Cambridge, MA: Harvard University Press.

Dworkin, Ronald (2000) *Sovereign Virtue: The Theory and Practice of Equality*, Cambridge, MA: Harvard University Press.

Foucault, Michel (2001) *Fearless Speech*, ed. Joseph Pearson, New York: Semiotext(e).

Foucault, Michel (2003) *Society Must Be Defended*, trans. David Macey, New York: Picador.

Foucault, Michel (2007) 'What is Critique?,' in *The Politics of Truth*, trans. Lysa Hochroth and Catherine Porter, New York: Semiotext(e), pp. 41–82.

Foucault, Michel (2008) *The Birth of Biopolitics*, trans. G. Burchell, New York: Palgrave.

176 **"BORDERLINE JUSTICE"**

Fuentes, Carlos (1962) 'Writing in Time,' *Democracy*, Vol. 2 (1962), pp. 59–73.

Fuentes, Carlos (2011) *Destiny and Desire*, trans. Edith Grossman, New York: Random House.

Gasche, Rudolphe (1994) 'Objective Diversions: Some Kantian Themes in Benjamin's "The Work of Art in the Age of Mechanical Reproduction",' in *Walter Benjamin's Philosophy: Destruction and Experience*, eds. Andrew Benjamin and Peter Osborne, New York: Routledge, pp. 183–204.

Gorfinkel, Elena and Rhodes, John David eds (2011) *Taking Place*, Minneapolis: University of Minnesota Press.

Guaraldo, Olivia (2001) *Storyline, History and Narrative from an Arendtian Perspective*, Jyvaskyla, Finland: SoPhi.

Heath, Stephen (1975) 'Film and System, Terms of Analysis,' *Screen*, Vol. 16 (1–2), pp. 91–113.

Jones, Reece (2012) *Border Walls: Security and the War on terror in the United States, India, and Israel*, New York: Zed Books.

Lefebvre, Henri (1991) *The Production of Space*, trans. Donald Nicholson-Smith, Malden: Blackwell.

Malkin, Elizabeth (2912) 'In the Crossfire of the Mexican War in Drugs,' *The New York Times*, at: www.nytimes.com/2012/01/15/movies/gerardo-naranjos-miss-bala-reflects-mexican-drug-war.html?src=recg.

Neuman, William (2012) 'Coca Licensing Is a Weapon in Bolivia's Drug War,' *The New York Times*, at: www.nytimes.com/2012/12/27/world/americas/bolivia-reduces-coca-plantings-by-licensing-plots.html?pagewanted=all&_r=0.

Panagia, Davide (2006) *The Poetics of Political Thinking*, Durham: Duke University Press.

Pease, Donald (2001) 'Borderline Justice/States of Emergency: Orson Welles,' *Touch of Evil, The new Centennial Review*, Vol. 1 (1), pp. 75–105.

Pepper, Andrew (2011) 'Policing the "Globe" State Sovereignty and the International in the Post-9/11 Crime Novel,' *Modern Fiction Studies*, Vol. 57 (3), pp. 401–424.

Rajaram, Prem and Grundy-Warr, Carl eds. *Borderscapes*, Minneapolis: University of Minnesota Press.

Rancière, Jacques (1992) 'Politics, Identification, and Subjectivization,' *October*, Vol. 61, pp. 58–64.

Rancière, Jacques (2004) 'Who is the Subject of the Rights of Man,' *The South Atlantic Quarterly*, Vol. 103 (2/3), pp. 297–310.

Rancière, Jacques (2008) "Aesthetic Separation, Aesthetic Community: Scenes from the Aesthetic Regime of Art,' *Art & Research*, Vol. 2 (1), at: http://artandresearch.org.uk/v2n1/ranciere.html.

Rawls, John (1981) *A Theory of Justice*, Cambridge, MA: Harvard University Press.

Rawls, John (1985) 'Justice as Fairness: Political not Metaphysical,' *Philosophy and Public Affairs*, Vol. 14 (3), pp. 223–251.

Rawls, John (1993) *Political Liberalism*, New York: Columbia University Press.

Rhodes, John David (2007) *Stupendous Miserable City: Pasolini's Rome*, Minneapolis: University of Minnesota Press.

Shaiken, Harley (2011) 'Holding a Mirror to Mexico,' *Berkeley Review of Latin American Studies*, at: http://clas.berkeley.edu/publications/review/index.html.

Shapiro, Michael J. (2004) *Methods and Nations: Cultural Governance and the Indigenous Subject*, New York: Routledge.

Shapiro, Michael J. (2010) *The Time of the City: Politics, Philosophy and Genre*, London: Routledge.

Shapiro, Michael J. (2012) *Studies in Trans-Disciplinary Method: After the Aesthetic Turn*, London: Routledge.

Shapiro, Michael J. (2015) *War Crimes, Atrocity, and Justice*, Cambridge: Polity.

Vaughan-Williams, Nick (2009) *Border Politics: The Limits of Sovereign Power*, Edinburgh: Edinburgh University Press.

Webb, Gary (1998) *Dark Alliance: The CIA, the CONTRAS, and the CRACK COCAIN EXPLOSION*, New York: Seven Stories Press.

Winslow, Don (2005) *The Power of the Dog*, New York: Alfred A, Knopf.

Winslow, Don (2012) *Kings of Cool*, New York: Simon & Schuster.

SUGGESTED READING

For More on the Connection Between Cinema and the US-Mexican Border, See

Peter Andreas, *Border Games: The US-Mexico Divide* (Ithaca: Cornell University press, 2009).

Jose Carlos Lozano, "Film at the Border: Memories of Cinema Going in Laredo Texas," *Memory Studies* 10:1 (2017), 35–48.

Marcus Power and Andrew Crampton eds., *Cinema and Popular Geo-Politics* (New York: Routledge, 2007).

CHAPTER **6**

A Bi-City Cinematic Experience

INTRODUCTION: AT THE BERLINALE

Following an experience as a juror on the Peace Film Prize jury at the Tromsø International Film Festival in 2005 (the TIFF), I attended the much larger Berlin film festival, "The Berlinale," in February 2007 in order to understand better the way film festivals operate when they are large and complex. The Berlinale attracts not only many more film attendees than the TIFF, numbering in the thousands compared with the hundreds attending the TIFF, but also a more extensive variety of films and more film-related practitioners: directors, producers, marketing people, and so on. In short, it is a much larger "cinematic heterotopia"[1] than the one in Tromsø, and it takes place in a much larger and more populated urban venue. The 2007 Berlinale I attended had "more than 19,000 accredited professionals from 127 countries, including 4,000 journalists came to the festival. Over ten days, the Berlinale saw about 430,000 cinema visits, and a record 220,000 tickets were sold . . ."[2]

Among the films I watched at the Berlinale was Yau Nai-Hoi's *Eye in the Sky*, a detective thriller set in present-day Hong Kong. Along with the inspiration of the film was the inspiration of the city venue in which I watched it. The viewing situation yielded a homology between my way of experiencing the film and the festival as a whole. Just as I was continuously involved in timing my movements to manage my film attendance within the incessant kinesis of the city of Berlin (bodies and vehicles moving rapidly here and there and a rush of urban impressions at every moment), so was one of the film's main protagonists, the head of a theft ring, Chan Chong-Shan (Tony Leung Ka-fai), who was orchestrating his gang's thefts.

As a result, the essay that is the basis of this chapter intermediates my film viewing with my experience of Berlin. It is an intermediation that is especially compelling because, among other things, both the city locus of my viewing and the city in the film are newly reconfigured. Berlin, by then a relatively recently unified national capital after a significant political reorientation, is, like Hong

A BI-CITY CINEMATIC EXPERIENCE   179

Kong, heavily populated with moving bodies at all hours and is full of large corporate and government buildings as well as many global commodity franchises. And significantly, both cites had recently undergone dramatic change. Berlin's reconfiguration, like Hong Kong's, had taken place in a highly politicized context—in Berlin's case, an attempt at an architecture that promotes the value of an open civil society, manifesting a "democratic transparency."[3] The architecture of the New Berlin faced the issue of "how to make a credible Berlin out of a city with no consensual idea of itself and no common history beyond a negative one."[4] For example, needing to efface the Berlin imaginary of Hitler's architect, Albert Speer, whose Berlin design was on a north–south axis, the new government sector is topologically oppositional; it runs on an east–west axis.[5] While the architectural solution in the case of Berlin was oriented toward reordering the nature of Germanness, Hong Kong had also been involved in an identity problematic, its relationship with Chineseness, which intensified after the handover from British to Chinese control in July 1997.

The political problematic surrounding the creation of the new Hong Kong involves a different kind of erasure. Hong Kong's transition was a movement from a colonially controlled "emporium" to a modern (still-colonial) global city. It was in Ackbar Abbas's terms, a movement to a "colonial space of disappearance," where "disappearance" is intrinsic to contemporary culture insofar as Hong Kong culture defies the traditional binaries—for example, the embodiment of an East–West hybridity through which it has been historically represented.[6] Shaped by the "long good-bye" to British control and the preparation for China's reclaiming of the city-state, Hong Kong's architecture is a combination of the old and the new. As a perennial "intersection of spaces" with a long history of a changing ethnoscape, as well as changing loci of power and control, Hong Kong has had a "floating identity," which articulates well with its fluvial situation.[7] As one commentator aptly puts it,

> [t]he local is experienced as a field of instability, discontinuity, and exclusiveness that transforms any available models of culture. . . . This elusive, translated local can come to presence, paradoxically, only when it is going to become extinct with the possible disappearance of its former lifestyle after the 1997 handover.[8]

One aspect of Hong Kong's local culture that speaks to this paradox is enacted in the Clifton Ko film *Chicken and Duck Talk* (1988) in which the film narrative treats the threat to a traditional local restaurant run by Danny Poon of expanding global food franchises, such as McDonald's and Kentucky Fried Chicken, situated in close proximity to his establishment. Animating a classic story (originally in novel form), it "portrays a post traditional Hong Kong where established cultural values are challenged by market logic."[9] The film expresses an aspect of Hong Kong food culture precisely at a moment when it is threatened with disappearance as Hong Kong has faced a tension between cultural commitments and economic forces. Its

> postmodern urban landscape not only maps culture and power; it also maps the opposition between markets—the economic forces that detach people from established social institutions—and place—the spatial forms that anchor them to the social world, providing the basis of a stable identity.[10]

Apart from what is revealed in commentaries on Hong Kong identity, which point out how culinary culture has been central to Hong Kong's connection with Chineseness, it should be noted that across the range of cultural modalities, what is threatened with disappearance is relatively recent. It was not until the mid-1960s that "Hong Kong's historically migrant society harbored a majority native-born population."[11] What is local or native, and thus what is "Hong Kong culture," has a short historical trajectory, even though much of Hong Kong culture partakes, in varying degrees, of southern Chinese culture. The instability of Hong Kong's ethnoscape and cultural practices is paralleled by its architecture. Hong Kong's "architecture of disappearance"[12] defies a history of representational binaries applied to the city-state because the city combines sites of selective cultural preservation—for example, "the Hong Kong Cultural Center on the site of the old Hong Kong railway terminal" (ibid.)—along with culturally indistinguishable structures—for example, signature buildings by architects with global credentials (among other things, like Berlin, Hong Kong has a new I. M. Pei building). Most significant for purposes of this analysis, Hong Kong cinema articulates Hong Kong's complex spatial history, emphasizing a variety of scopic regimes from alternative perspectives. In general, as Abbas has pointed out, Hong Kong cinema has responded to the "space of disappearance,"[13] articulated as an intersection of imperialism and globalism, with images and narratives that explore that conflicted space. More specifically, contemporary Hong Kong cinema reflects a spatial history through the ways in which it focuses alternatively on the city's vernacular and global architectures.[14] All that is explored in Yau Nai-Hoi's *Eye in the Sky*. However, before offering my reading of the film, I need to situate the complexities of my viewing experience.

PERIPATETIC FILM VIEWING

To elaborate my viewing situation, as one among thousands of film attendees, I was a cinema-focused tourist negotiating both large and small spaces in a complex urban venue. Occasionally on public transportation but mostly on foot

A BI-CITY CINEMATIC EXPERIENCE   181

in the city, I was what Walter Benjamin famously refers to as "a kaleidoscope equipped with consciousness."[15] I was experiencing the kind of fragmented perceptual apparatus that reflects the shocks delivered by the city's hyper-stimulating environment (as Benjamin notes such shocks are also delivered by film, which formalizes the shocks of the city's sensorium).[16]

As for the two spaces, first, I was situated in Berlin as a whole, a city that no longer conformed to its expected imaginary because its recent reconstruction had effaced most of the visible legacy of its Cold War history. Gone was the Berlin Wall as well as much of what else had been the cityscape around Potsdamer Platz, the main festival site. That city center, which had once been in the eastern sector of the formerly divided Berlin and for years since had been primarily a construction site, was now a thriving commercial center with theaters, shops, and restaurants, containing an architecture that is reminiscent of the Potsdamer Platz of the 1920s and 1930s—a busy square that serves as "a major transport hub that contain[s] numerous bars, cafes and cinemas"[17] but owes nothing to its recent past. The historical instability of Berlin's built environment is paralleled by what one analyst euphemistically calls "a certain fragility of national identity,"[18] owed largely to a past from which Berliners, like most contemporary Germans, would have liked to distance themselves. However, the ongoing contention over architectural choices at the time indicated that however citizens might have wished to distance themselves from a shameful national past, Berliners remained engaged in a "proliferation of, and struggle over, alternative futures."[19]

Second, as a film festival attendee, I was more frequently located in a smaller version of the city, the "cinematic heterotopia," carved out of the larger city, a space that the Berlinale creates for 10 days every year, consisting of a film center that houses the marketing booths, an information and ticket center where festival attendees queue to register, obtain a bar code (depending on one's status among multiple possibilities), and obtain film tickets for which one's codes indicates eligibility; several designated theaters for the screenings; and a few shuttle vehicles that run between the film center and the other Berlinale venues. Both the space of Berlin as a whole and the smaller cinematic version imposed timing and coping demands. From the outset of my arrival, to move about the city I needed to manage the bus, U-Bahn (subway), and S-Bahn (metro railway) routes, first to get to my hotel and thereafter, as the days of my attendance transpired, to match the film administration and theater map with my city map in order to secure my film attendance preferences and get to the theaters.

There is a theoretically pregnant homology between my experience of Berlin and my cinema spectatorship. My travel around the city involved me in what Giuliana Bruno calls "site-seeing," which I had to articulate with my film viewing. Inasmuch as cinema enacts moving spaces, film viewing invites one

182   A BI-CITY CINEMATIC EXPERIENCE

into a "kinetic affair" that has a striking resemblance to what is experienced in walking the city streets.[20] To move from the city streets to the theaters, a shift from voyageur to voyeur, is thus to transition from one kinetic experience to another. Specifically, in the case of the Hong Kong film I am analyzing, the locus of my film viewing connected a mobile consumption of Berlin with an experience of a cinematically represented dynamic Hong Kong.

Moreover, as I have suggested my viewing experiences of the two cities, one through my own movement and other onscreen, engaged me with cities that still bore the signs of dramatic transfers—the transfer of the capital from Bonn to Berlin and the transfer of Hong Kong from Britain's to China's control. In effect, as my viewing involved a transition from the Potsdamer Platz of the new German capital to a theater with a film treating the recently transferred Hong Kong, I was moving from one recently reoriented city square to another: "The screen," as Paul Virilio puts it, has become "(since the beginning of the twentieth century . . . the city square)."[21]

While certainly the dramas involved in the transfers of the two cities inflected the inter-articulation of my walking and viewing, the management of two examples of dense urban stimuli (the city of Berlin and a cinematically delivered Honk Kong) evokes yet another conceptual framing, which Roland Barthes renders as an urban erotics. Addressing the effects of one's movement from the city streets to the film theater, he writes, "The movie auditorium condenses the 'modern eroticism' of the big city."[22] Two aspects of history therefore introduce temporal imaginaries that compete with the "eroticism," the desire-driven aspects of one's cinematic experience. There is both a cinema history, which affects one's film viewing in Berlin and a geopolitical history that haunts contemporary Berlin. With respect to the former, in consuming cinema in Berlin, one is participating in a historical trajectory of a city–cinema articulation in which Berlin has famously participated from early in the twentieth century. The pioneering cinematic treatments of Berlin are Walther Ruttmann's *Berlin: The Symphony of a Great City* (1927) and Dziga Vertov's *Man with a Movie Camera* (1929). As those films testify, from early in its development in Berlin cinema displayed "a structural affinity" with the city. As "a darkened chamber typically located at the heart of the big city [it] provided the space where modernity negotiated and tried to come to terms, both cognitively and affectively with its contradictory impulses of repression and revelation, transparency and obscurity."[23]

However, for me the transitions from street to theater at the Berlinale were only smoothly articulated sensually and conceptually. As a bottom-feeder at the festival (one with a barcode that restricted access to those films shown to the mass of attendees and not to films restricted to persons with professional credentials), I was moving about in a temporary "society of control," where access is regulated by codes.[24] The barcode on the badge I received when I registered allowed me to obtain the program booklet. Thereafter, it had to be scanned, both when I sought to obtain tickets and when I entered the theaters. On one hand, the divided Berlin of the Cold War had been constituted pervasively as a society of control, and aspects of that former control remain part of Berlin's geopolitical framing. Reflecting an irrepressible past that still marks the city, close to the main festival sites was the famous Cold War barrier between the east and west sectors of the city, Checkpoint Charlie, now a preserved space of historical memory that is open to all as a tourist site. On the other hand, paralleling the historical checkpoint were the Berlinale checkpoints, a smaller and temporary society of control, managed by the bureaucracy of the Berlinale, which distinguished the eligible from the noneligible for each film.

That dual spatial situation I was negotiating—one with vestiges of a former control and one with temporarily implemented controls—was also articulated with a dual temporality; the historical city of Berlin, which had been recently (and radically) transfigured, primarily to effect an overcoding of Germany's wars (both hot and cold), contained a brief cinematic event in a space with a long temporal trajectory. Both temporalities challenged my imagination and coping strategies. I had not only to appreciate the historical depth of city sites but also to focus on the short-term timing of my movements: rising and breakfasting early enough to avoid long lines at ticket counters (where one's only chance for a ticket required an appearance at least 48 hours ahead of the film's showing) and then showing up early enough to get a preferred seating section in the theater. At the same time, I was consuming the historical city, timing both public transportation as well as festival-connected shuttles to move about the city in order to eat, shop, and visit historical and cultural sites. With respect to both, the Neue Nationalgalerie helped me become acquainted with aspects of Berlin's past. That particular site turned out to provide a resource for my reflections on the relationship between the historic space of the city and the temporary space of the festival, as well as on the identity differences between Berlin and Hong Kong. Moving through the art museum's exhibition rooms, I encountered Ernst Ludwig Kirchner's (1914) eponymous painting of an early version of the Potsdamer Platz (Figure 6.1). Having wondered how that city center, now fundamentally redesigned and rebuilt to be dominated by large emporiums of consumption—for example, the new, massive Sony Center—must affect those who remember both the pre-war and Cold War versions. Kirchner created an image of the place as it must have been experienced by residents and visitors in the early part of the twentieth century. His version of Potsdamer Platz captures an essential experience of modern urban life and at the same time resonated with my city and festival experiences. The bodies in the Platz manifest the typical kinetic energy of city dwellers in motion. There are various elegantly attired pedestrians in close proximity and in brisk walking postures. Their positioning and directional orientations display a studied indifference to each other. For example, the two women in the foreground, in very close proximity and caught in mid-stride on a circular pedestal-like section of pavement, are oriented obliquely to each other.

FIGURE 6.1
Kirchner Potsdamer Platz image. Source: Ernst Ludwig Kirchner, *Berlin Street Scene*, Neue Galerie, Berlin.

Kirchner's urban images capture two primary aspects of modern life. First, the kinetic energy in his urban paintings anticipates the cinema–city relationship. Like Ruttmann and Vertov, whose documentaries captured Berlin's dynamism, Kirchner's Berlin scenes reflect the hyperkinetic feeling that the city conveyed to him. As he put it (speaking about himself in the third person),

> [h]e discovered that the feeling that pervades a city presented itself in the qualities of the lines of force (Kraftlinien). In the way in which groups of persons configured themselves in the rush, in the trams, how they moved, this is how he discovered the means to capture what he had experienced.[25]

Kirchner's rendering remains contemporary. Despite massive changes in the configuration of the Potsdamer Platz, the essential urban demands of the Berlin of the early twentieth century have remained in force in the early twenty-first century. Contemporary Berlin, like other urban venues, continues to require an effort at interpersonal indifference in situations of close interpersonal proximity.

Given the cinematic quality of Berlin's moving energy and the need for one to manage its temporal rhythms while maintaining the posture of indifference in close proximity that belongs to city-dwellers, the city habitus of my film viewing was like the situation in the opening scene of the film that most captured my attention at the festival, the previously mentioned crime story set in a heavily populated and bustling contemporary Hong Kong.

Eye in the Sky

In Yau Nai-Hoi's *Eye in the Sky* what is central to the crime plot is a set of competing scopic regimes, two systems of surveillance, enacted by a theft ring, on one hand, and the Investigative Bureau (IB) of the Hong Kong police, on the other. As their contest operates within and seeks to manage the spaces and temporal rhythms of the city, the viewer is invited into a dynamic cityscape, which comes to life through the moving bodies that the film mobilizes. The film's opening displays the more venerable aspects of the urban experience captured in Kirchner's painting of Berlin's Potsdamer Platz, demands on urbanites for indifference in the midst of a crowded urban peoplescape. The film begins with a vertical panning shot of the new Hong Kong, aimed initially at tall buildings before it slowly descends toward the street, where the focus is on moving traffic. The camera then zooms in on a bus, which stops to pick up a man, whom we later learn is Chan Chong Shan, the head of a theft ring.

After this initial sequence, the opening scene proceeds with a striking resemblance to Samuel Fuller's classic Cold War noir thriller *Pickup on South Street* (1953), which begins with an exterior shot of a moving subway in New York and then takes the viewer inside a subway car, where a typical urban transportation scenario is underway. All the passengers in the car, including the protagonists—a federal agent, Zara (Willis B. Bouchey); a police captain, Dan Tiger (Murvyn Vye); and their suspect, "Candy" (Jean Peters), whom they think is giving military intelligence to communists—maintain a feigned indifference to their fellow riders, even though some of them are intimately connected (which becomes evident later in the film narrative; Figure 6.2). Their studied

FIGURE 6.2
McCoy and Candy on metro car. Source: Samuel Fuller, *Pickup on South Street*, Twentieth Century Fox (1953).

air of distraction is underscored when a pickpocket, Skip McCoy (Richard Widmark), manages to steal Candy's wallet with no one noticing until the theft is accomplished. Zara and Tiger rush toward the closing doors, too late to pursue McCoy.

The scene on the Hong Kong bus mimics Fuller's scene. Chan Chong Shan takes a seat next to a young woman, an undercover constable Ho Ka-Po (Kate Tsui), who it turns out is involved in crime-surveillance training. She and Shan avoid eye contact as Shan proceeds to don his glasses and work on a Sudoku puzzle book, while she, (code name) Piggy, closes her eyes momentarily and appears to be concentrating on the music from an iPod plugged into one ear (Figure 6.3). She steals a glance at a man feigning sleep several seats away and across from her. He turns out to be Sergeant Wong Man Chin, aka "Dog Head" (Simon Yam), her undercover police surveillance mentor, who is tailing her to evaluate her competence. Thus, *Eye in the Sky*'s opening scene, like *Pickup on South Street*'s, introduces the viewer not only to the main protagonists but also to a typical urban *mise-en-scène*, people moving about the city in crowded proximity while maintaining an air of mannered indifference to each other.

The two films' surveillance regimes, operating within different historico-political frames and venues, hark back to the initial literature of detection,

FIGURE 6.3
Piggy and Shan on bus. *Source:* Yau Nai Hoi, *Eye in the Sky*, Milkyway Image Ltd. (2007).

A BI-CITY CINEMATIC EXPERIENCE 187

which emerged in the nineteenth century along with the "immense human traffic of the centripetal metropolis."[26] However, their storylines treat different issues. While the political frame in *Pickup on South Street* is the anticommunist hysteria of the 1950s, the micropolitics of crime that frames *Eye in the Sky* emerges from attention to the forces shaping the rapidly changing postcolonial Hong Kong, which had become a global city dominated by the banking, accounting, and legal services (along the many other aspects of dense commercial activity that characterizes such cities). While the images in *Eye in the Sky* eventually capture those realities, the film's narrative progression, following from the scene on the bus, articulates the beginning of one of the film's narrative threads, a becoming professional of a new recruit, a narrative genre known as the *roman d'éducation*. Constable Ho Ka-Po, aka "Piggy," is learning to be an effective detective.

After the three principals, Shan, Piggy, and Dog Head, leave the bus, all seemingly headed in different directions, Piggy ends up in a restaurant, where Dog Head also enters after surreptitiously following her through the streets. Piggy and Dog Head's eventual quarry, Shan, heads in precisely the opposite direction from Dog Head's heading, after leaving the bus directly behind him. He walks through the city as the camera tracks the kinetics of moving pedestrian traffic on the sidewalks and vehicular traffic on the streets. He then moves through a shopping arcade, past some upscale shops, and finally up a ramp that affords a view from a high perch where he prepares his surveillance of the local scene around the jewelry store that his gang is about to rob. At this point, the film narrative has proceeded within what David Bordwell identifies as a "forking-path plot," a film narrative that "proceeds from a fixed point" (in this case, the stop at which the protagonists leave the bus) and heads off in "mutually exclusive lines of action."[27] While Shan heads off to manage a robbery and Piggy and Dog Head proceed in a different direction that ends in a rendezvous in connection with their policing vocation. However, their paths will ultimately intersect, as is the case with many "forking-path plots, because the cohesion of such plots are appointments," for example, deaths or other forms of consummation.[28]

In *Eye in the Sky*, the intersection of the paths will occur when Piggy's path leads to Shan's capture and killing. Shan's catastrophe at this intersection also involves a competence issue, in his case the incompetence of some of his gang members, who violate Shan's timing codes because they cannot defer gratification (they linger past Shan's specified duration for the robbery, three minutes, in order to grab more gems).

Significantly, what drives the two paths or action trajectories are professional commitments, one kind that succeeds (the police's) and another that fails (the gang members'). Bearing in mind the complexities that constitute Hong Kong's unusual historical situation, the two sets of commitments reflect much of the way the film reveals Hong Kong's relatively singular micropolitics. Vocational commitments are unusually strong forms of allegiance in a city that has had an unstable civic identity and solicits little by way of national allegiance. As a result, vocations have more identity weight than they have in places where national and civic allegiances have more traction. Indeed, in the case of Hong Kong, the policing vocation has been unusually important from the colonial to the postcolonial period. As one history of Hong Kong policing observes, "[t]he Hong Kong police survive as guardians of the territory's political stability and cultural identity."[29] In addition, inasmuch as Hong Kong is effectively a city-state, the policing identity has special cultural authority because it "also doubles as national defense."[30] Moreover, as is evident in the film, the policing establishment is now on the cutting edge of technical sophistication. "Their ubiquitous officers, vehicles, technological devices, and architectural sites . . . represent their postcolonial authority."[31]

To return to Shan's path, after he leaves the bus, his situation resonates with the previously described regimen of my Berlinale experience. Shan's task at this juncture in the film narrative is one of timing the rhythms of the city to manage an event. At the point at which his men arrive in a car, mask their faces, and enter the store, Shan sets his stopwatch to three minutes and begins scrutinizing the area around the store, while the camera swings around, showing two of his gang members who remain outside the store to surveil the surroundings from street level. The dramatic event of the robbery (the gang members inside smash cases, grab jewels, and threaten store employees) activates the rest of the film narrative, even as much of the film's focus and significance is a nonnarrative treatment of modern Hong Kong's lifeworld. In this sense, Yau's *Eye in the Sky* conforms to what Jacques Rancière refers to as the contemporary "aesthetic regime of the arts," which abandons "the primacy of the narrative over the descriptions" and employs "a fragmented or proximate mode of focalization, which imposes raw presence to the detriment of the rational sequences of the story."[32]

Apart from the forking-path plot in which the film's drama is activated, two persistent images of contemporary Hong Kong constitute the primary descriptive gloss on the city early in the film, both based on the ways in which Hong Kong is saturated with modern technologies. Although Shan's stopwatch is the only visible piece of technology involved in the robbery (apart from his gang's weapons), it is evident that the gang has also used devices to map and time of city traffic. Knowing the patterns, they use a truck, to follow the robbers' car, and block the road so that when the robbers emerge from the store, they can escape while police vehicles are blocked. At the same time that the robbery is in progress, Dog Head and Piggy make use of a different technology, their cell phones. Once they have met in the restaurant and Dog Head has allowed Piggy to pass her test to become a new recruit to the IB (after closely questioning her on the details of what she has witnessed on the bus and thereafter), they

A BI-CITY CINEMATIC EXPERIENCE   189

arrive at the police station. There, Piggy is introduced to her new colleagues. However, the interpersonal encounters the viewer observes appear less significant than the technological displays at the station—advanced computer and video-feed technologies used to surveil the entire city. The film's shots enhance the surveillance thematic by emphasizing the densely saturated surveillance environment of Hong Kong.

As the Shan gang's robbery is developing, the camera occasionally pans upward to show surveillance cameras both on the street, aimed at pedestrian and vehicular traffic, and in stores, aimed at customers. And some of the shots of the characters simulate the lenses of surveillance cameras. As the film cuts back and forth between the robbery dynamic and the education and professionalization of Piggy, the viewer is introduced to the vagaries of the two intimately connected vocations, crime and policing. The characters within both of these inter-articulated milieus are shown sharing two aspects of their respective practices, which are often in tension with each other—eating and surveillance. Eating in the cases of both the policing and crime personnel (on which the camera focuses frequently throughout the film) turns out to compete with the primary aspects of their vocational tasks. The pervasive scenes of eating, at all times of the day and night, reflect the singular nature of Hong Kong's culinary culture. Once Dog Head finishes eating in the restaurant where he and Piggy first meet, they enter the police station, which is abuzz with news of the robbery, as various department personnel are working with computers and surveillance videos. At one point, without warning. the process of viewing and information sharing is suspended while one of the heads of the crime unit pauses to eat his soup, after announcing that it is "time for soup."

Meanwhile, one of the Shan gang, "Fat Man," whose job it is to survey the street and watch out for police, is shown eating continuously. The first shots of Fat Man show him eating food off a skewer as he stands in a strategic position in the street outside the jewelry store. Then at a crucial moment during the robbery, he looks through the window of a 7-Eleven convenience store and sees a man eating chicken off a bone, which he has obviously purchased within the store (Figure 6.4). Impulsively, Fat Man rushes into the store and buys a piece of chicken. While he is in the store, the viewer sees a surveillance camera recording him swiping his "Octopus card" to make the purchase (a card available from vending machines that can be used for transportation and small purchases throughout the city). That gesture turns out to be the fatal mistake that ultimately leads to the capture of Shan and his gang. It is a sequence that later helps the police to identify Fat Man as part of the robbery, and at the same time, it reflects two aspects of Hong Kong, one singular and one shared with all modern cities.

First, with regard to the shared dimension, as William Leach has pointed out, three technologies have combined historically to provoke consumer

FIGURE 6.4
Fat Man. Source: Yau Nai Hoi, *Eye in the Sky*, Milkyway Image Ltd. (2007).

desire: color, glass, and light. An advertising trade journal *Signs of the Times* from which Leach quotes speaks to the intended effects of the century-long development of the pervasive store windows and neon signs that Yau's camera focuses on continually: "Electrical advertising is a picture medium. Moreover it is a color medium; still again, electrical advertising is a medium of motion, of action, of life, of light, of compulsory attraction."[33] Leach goes on to note the way in which those technologies, incorporated into the modern store, effectively divided consumer classes in the early twentieth-century American city, a division that applies well to contemporary Hong Kong, with its upscale stores on the one hand and its open market stalls on the other. Reliance on glass for display had several significant consequences. "it contributed to the formation of a new culture of class—that is, it helped to demarcate more clearly the affluent from the poorer buying public. . . . Glass also closed off smell and touch, diminishing the consumer's relationship with the goods." At the same time, it amplified the visual dimension of experience, transforming the already watching city person into a potentially compulsive viewer.[34]

Fat Man's capitulation to an eating impulse at a crucial moment during the robbery therefore articulates the summons that technologies have participated in for over a century all over the globe, albeit with something singular about Hong Kong's culinary culture. Certainly, the provocation of eating impulses is endemic to the modern city, which has witnessed "the penetration of food services into almost every other leisure site."[35] However, continual eating at all hours and often while standing and walking is more culturally specific. Although it is not wholly peculiar to Hong Kong, it is very much a Hong Kong

A BI-CITY CINEMATIC EXPERIENCE 191

cultural signature. A brief comparison with the culinary culture of Italy should suffice to highlight the distinctiveness of Hong Kong's eating practices. Donna Leon captures the Italian culinary habitus well in her Venice crime stories. For example, in her *Willful Behaviour*, her perennial main character, Police Commissioner Guido Brunetti, engages in highly scheduled, elaborate, and slowly savored meals. The relevant sequence begins one day at "a little before twelve" as Brunetti is "beginning to think longingly of lunch."[36] When he finally makes his way home for lunch (as is his habit throughout the stories in which he is featured), he sits down to a very elaborate repast, prepared by his wife, Paola:

> In keeping with the changing season, Paola had risotto di zucca and into it at the last minute had tossed grated slivers of ginger, its sharp bite softened to amiability by the chunk of butter and the grated Parmigiano that had chased it into the pot. The mingled tastes drove all dread of Raffi's music [his son's annoying compact disc] from Brunetti's mind, and the chicken breast grilled with sage and white wine that followed replaced that music with what Brunetti thought must be the sound of angels singing.[37]

Brunetti drinks a glass of Chardonnay with the meal and follows his main course with a Braeburn apple and a thin slice of Montasio cheese, accompanied by a glass of Calvados.[38]

In contrast to the timing and savoring central to the Italian culinary culture, Hong Kong eating, which is pervasively shown in Hong Kong films, is rapid and virtually continuous. That eating habitus is in keeping with the frenetic pace of other dimensions of an urban lifeworld in which temporal boundaries hardly exist. For example, "the bright light of Hong Kong at night" can be "contrasted with rural China where evenings [are] covered with darkness."[39] It should be noted as well that food consumption in Hong Kong cinema tends to stand in for desire, *tout court*. For example, in Wong Kar-Wai's *Chungking Express* (1994), Eros is radically entangled with eating, as expressed in the soundtrack when Dinah Washington sings, "It's heaven when you find romance on your menu."

In *Eye in the Sky*, one of the most significant eating scenes takes place at the theft ring's warehouse hideout. The robbery has seemingly succeeded, despite a violation of Shan's three-minute robbery protocol. One of the men says that he had tarried beyond the three minutes because, as he puts it, "I wanted more," making it evident that his desire for more loot, like Fat Man's food lust, had threatened the enterprise. Shan points this out and admonishes his headman for not controlling the maverick gang member who had dangerously delayed their exit from the store. At that point, a furious fight breaks out and threatens to become lethal when Shan grabs a meat skewer and holds it to the maverick's throat. The close-up camera shot of the skewer at the throat

192 A BI-CITY CINEMATIC EXPERIENCE

is not its first appearance. It is shown earlier in a close-up shot, (in a long take) as it is being used to impale a chicken part about to be barbecued. The skewer's dual iconic role becomes evident as the scene develops. After the argument and fight end, one of the men looks out the window and notices an attractive young woman removing her clothes while standing near her window, in full view from the gang's point of observation. The viewer calls attention to the scene for the rest of the gang. They all stare, while the camera cuts back and forth between the woman undressing and the rapt faces of the voyeurs, until the mood and focus are suddenly aborted as one of the men shouts, "Let's barbecue!" At this point, the skewer is once again returned to its primary purpose. Seemingly the moment of erotic desire has been displaced by a different kind of Eros.

However, more significantly, the sequence foregrounds the pervasive tension that Hong Kong shares with other cities in which distracting stimuli and almost infinite possibilities for consumption are readily available. Shan, like the police officials in Hong Kong's IB, has to manage group tasks in the face of desire-provoking distractions. Both organizations must pit codes against desire—policing codes, on one hand, which Dog Head incessantly imparts to Piggy, and robbery protocol codes, on the other, which Shan attempts to impose on his gang. While the two fraught pedagogies are unfolding in parallel, as the film cuts back and forth between them, the film's *mise-en-scène* is thinking well beyond the normative codes that organize the tasks of the two organizations. By the time the second planned heist is about to go down, Shan discerns—again from a high perch overlooking the targeted jewelry store—that the police are closing in. He had begun as usual by setting his watch to time the robbery process but has ultimately to abort it and then to evade the police by rushing away from his perch on foot, taking a circuitous path through the city's back alleys. Heeding not only the close timing required for robberies but also the time images that operate as the framing of Hong Kong as a whole has made it apparent that the city incorporates many layers of time which for the viewer emerge through the operation of "cinematic time," a mode of temporality that highlights the contingencies of encounter.[40]

As for the temporalities in *Eye in the Sky*, from the point of view of the cops-and-robbers theme, which carries the film's dramatic narrative, the timing issues are specific to managing robberies successfully on the one hand and to catching the culprits on the other. Both are managed while competing with the temporal rhythms of bodily demands, specially hunger, as both the gang and the policing organizations are shown perpetually eating, mostly rapidly to avoid interfering as little as possible with their vocational demands. Within these task-related temporal problematics, what must be timed are the dynamics of entering and leaving a jewelry store, the intervals of police surveillance in the vicinity of the robberies, and the interval between the police being alerted to a robbery and

A BI-CITY CINEMATIC EXPERIENCE   193

their convergence on the scene. While timing issues of the robbery and the IB's attempts at apprehension are shown with cuts back and forth between the two groups, there are other ways in which the filming provides deeper levels of historical time.

Hong Kong historical time is conveyed with time images that are interspersed within the drama and are conveyed with action or "movement images."[41] The initial time images are enacted with vertical panning shots, which are introduced before robberies and before each mobilization and pursuit by the IB policing unit. The vertical panning shots of the tall buildings deliver up the modern Hong Kong in which much of the architecture reflects the differential prosperity between those who profit from the city's status as a key node in global exchanges versus those restricted to local commerce conducted mostly in street stalls.[42] However, when Shan makes his escape on foot through the city, and when Dog Head, Piggy, and the rest of the IB crime unit fan out through the city on foot and in an unmarked van, the framing, tracking, and panning shots—all within a street-level, horizontal plane—deliver up a vernacular Hong Kong in which local stores, street vendors, and open-market enterprises exist alongside the more posh, global franchises that are targeted by criminal gangs.

The time images in Yau's film are not simply the indirect aspects of time that result from 'action-images." They are direct time images or "chronosigns," which derive from the mode of time-consciousness created by the camera's director-imposed mode of narration.[43] Significantly, the Hong Kong that was leased to Britain for 99 years emerges in both images and names during the vehicular chase, when after the second robbery is aborted, Dog Head and colleagues track the movements of Shan and his gang. Having recognized that there is a man behind the gang, the IB police unit gives him the name "The Hollow Man," a reference to T. S. Eliot's poem *The Hollow Men*. That sobriquet articulates with their hybrid speech, which intermixes English words with a Hong Kong Cantonese dialect, an indication that British culture continues to participate in contemporary Hong Kong.

Throughout the film, the legacy of British hegemony is readable in a city that is mapped by Shan's and the IB's movements. Racing through the city, while receiving reports from the station by those monitoring surveillance cameras, the policing trajectory informs us of street names through which Shan has passed. Here, the moving camera captures a city that is, like many major cities, historically dynamic. For example, writing of Paris, which he refers to as "*la ville qui remue*, the city that is always on the move," Walter Benjamin points out that nevertheless, the city retains some aspects of stasis through its street names, which "preserve the name of a landed proprietor . . . the movement of the streets [is thus constituted as] the movement of names"[44]

194   A BI-CITY CINEMATIC EXPERIENCE

Similarly, in the Hong Kong of *Eye in the Sky*, the continual displacement of historical provenances with new structures and expanding commerce nevertheless preserves vestiges of historical proprietary control. The metropolitan transit stations and streets passed in the IB police's pursuit of Shan—Jordan MTR (Mass Transit Railway) station, Nathan Road, Aberdeen Street, Staunton Street, Lyndhurst Terrace, and Pottinger Street—preserve the names of former British proprietors of the city-state. Yet it is clear that Hong Kong, like the Paris observed by Benjamin, is in constant transformation. Like all global cities, it is continually shaped by the forces of global commerce.

The film's drama thus operates with an action temporality within the larger historical one. Simultaneous with the time images of the contemporary and historical Hong Kong is the vocational time allocated to Piggy's character. In her first encounter with Dog Head, early in the film narrative, when he accosts her and says he recognizes her, Piggy fails to maintain her cover by the hesitation in her denials of the identification that Dog Head is insisting on. Late in the film, there is a moment of referential montage; Shan, who has the same keen visual memory as the IB policing operatives, repeats Dog Head's earlier test as he accosts her in an eating establishment and insists that he recognizes her as someone who has been following him. This time Piggy does not blow her cover, even though Shan knows that she is lying. And in yet another pair of repeated scenes, Piggy first fails to stick to her mission. Instead of following protocol and maintaining her pursuit of the suspect (Shan), she stops to help a downed policeman, However, later, as the film's climax approaches, she acts more professionally, managing to leave a badly wounded Dog Head (who has been slashed in the neck by Shan) to continue her pursuit.

Once Piggy is again on task, her newfound ability to focus leads to the death of Shan (who gets *his* neck slashed on a large fishhook while running from a tactical squad). Her successful pursuit ends the gang's threat to local commerce and signals the promise of an effective career in law enforcement. However, in some ways we learn more from the impediments to Piggy's ultimate success. Because the main cops-and-robbers drama in *Eye in the Sky* proceeds in Hong Kong's commodity and media-saturated environment, we are able to observe an articulation between two aspects of Hong Kong's participation in a modernization process, which is well described by Jonathan Crary. First, it is evident that Hong Kong shares in the global modernizing process that involves "a ceaseless and self-perpetuating creation of new needs, new products, and new consumption," and second are the rapid changes in "perceptual modalities," which are also produced by a modern capitalism that has increasingly "undermine[d] any stable or enduring structure of perception."[45] Given "the emergence of a social, urban, psychic, industrial field, increasingly saturated with sensory input," attention has become one of modernity's primary

A BI-CITY CINEMATIC EXPERIENCE   195

problems. As Crary summarizes it, we can regard "one crucial aspect of modernity is a continual crisis of attention."[46]

Crary's observations speak directly to the notable moments of distraction in the film, two of which I have already noted with respect to *Eye in the Sky*'s robbery and policing tasks. One is Fat Man's sudden desire for a piece of chicken, which distracts him from his surveillance of the street during the robbery. Another is a distraction created by a street food and trinket seller, who interferes with the surveillance task of one of the police's street operatives, and another is the distraction created by the mortally wounded policeman, whose condition distracts Piggy from her pursuit of one of the crime culprits. However, while a shared need for the thieves and police to watch and time the rhythms of the city from panoptic vantage points is central to the film's drama, at the same time the film displays a more general aspect of modernity, the ways in which the multiple desire-provoking stimuli of the modern city inhibit or interfere with attention-demanding projects. Georg Simmel's famous account of the psychic demands that the modern city levies on its inhabitants, especially for those unused to coping with an urban sensorium, remains influential:

> The rapid crowding of changing images, the sharp discontinuity in the grasp of a single glance, and the unexpectedness of onrushing impression. These are the psychological conditions which the metropolis creates. With each crossing of the street, with the tempo and multiplicity of economic, occupational and social life, the city sets up a deep contrast with small town and rural life with reference to the sensory foundations of modern life.[47]

However, we have to modify Simmel's formulation in two ways to apply it to *Eye in the Sky* and attain a political grasp of the management of the city's hyperstimulating sensorium. The first alteration requires a shift from a psychological to an aesthetic idiom so that the film's characters become aesthetic rather than psychological subjects. As I have noted in previous chapters, treating cinematic subjects not as static entities with fixed personalities but as mobile beings with multiple possibilities for becoming shifts our attention from the motivational forces of individuals, that is, from psychic subjectivity to aesthetic subjectivity, which enables us to discern the ways that characters' interactions and trajectories of movement articulate spatiotemporal frames. Leo Bersani and Ulysse Dutoit enact such a conceptual shift in perspective in their reading of Jean-Luc Godard's film *Contempt* (1963), a film treating a couple that becomes estranged when the wife Camille (Bridget Bardot) changes her affect toward her husband, Paul (Michel Piccoli), from love to contempt. They point out that Godard's concern is not "the psychic origins of contempt" but "its effects on the world," a concern that is articulated through film form, specifically through "what contempt does to cinematic space . . . how it affect[s] the visual field within which Godard works, and especially the range and kinds of movement allowed for in that space."[48] Similarly, what a critical, politically oriented reading of Yau Nai-Hoi's *Eye in the Sky* can provide is not primarily insight into the motivations of robbers and police detectives but into the way that both robbery and policing render a cinematic articulation of the spatial history and temporal rhythms of Hong Kong.

The second shift requires us to modify Simmel's general ascription of the mental life of the city by recognizing that different characters face different levels of demand for stimulus management and a general rendering of the city as legible. In *Eye in the Sky*, the costs of inattention weigh heavily on the personae involved in robbery and in policing Furthermore, inattention has different consequences depending on a character's level in each hierarchical organization. Moreover, an appreciation of the different implications attentiveness to signs and stimuli has for different situations types can lead us to a more general consideration of the micropolitics of contemporary global cities. For example, the consequences of ignoring surveillance technologies can produce disastrous consequences for illegal aliens and bad, but less disastrous, ones for shoplifters. And if, instead of focusing on illegal acts and structures of policing, one instead treats levels of estrangement within the city, we can access a kind of micropolitics of everyday life that pertains to Hong Kong, Berlin, and all global cities.

Sensitive to the micropolitics of adjustment afflicting immigrants in large global cities, the artist Krzysztof Wodiczko has invented technological prostheses for them to wear. One is an "alien staff," which resembles a biblical shepherd's rod. It carries a video monitor at its top that runs visuals and voices of the carrier's biography. The device is meant to overcome the anonymity of the immigrant as well as to disrupt the practices of inattention that distance people from each other in public space. As Wodiczko puts it, "[a]s the small image on the screen may attract attention and provoke observers to come very close to the monitor and therefore to the operator's face, the usual distance between the stranger and the observer will decrease."[49] Whatever may be the ultimate effects of the interactions provoked by Wodiczko's various devices, his approach to modern urbanism articulates a recognition of the differential costs of urban attentiveness and inattentiveness. If we return to the specific problematic that *Eye in the Sky*'s cops-and-robbers scenario portrays, we are encouraged to ascend to an identity problematic that afflicts Hong Kong as a whole and consider a collective identity issue, the problem of Chineseness. That issue becomes apparent if we recognize that for all the dynamics that *Eye in the Sky*'s *mise en scène* lends to Hong Kong—the changes evident in the city's built environment, its culinary practices, global commercial outlets that seem

A BI-CITY CINEMATIC EXPERIENCE   197

to be displacing the traditional street commerce, and the ongoing hide-and-seek dramas involving robbery and policing—there are significant aspects of cultural resistance accompanying those dynamics.

To retrieve that cultural resistance, we can recast the two culinary events to which I have referred, one in which policing is interrupted when a police captain says that it is "time for soup" and the other when the gang's fighting ends with the injunction "Let's barbecue," as moments in which a traditional Chinese culinary habitus remains in a city that is otherwise too drawn into global commerce to provide time and space for traditional Chinese culture. Once we discern such moments of arrest in an otherwise hyperkinetic drama and setting, we have to question what it is that is being policed by Hong Kong's IB unit. Recalling the earlier quotation about the importance of policing in a rapidly shifting Hong Kong, that "the Hong Kong police survive as guardians of the territories' political stability and cultural identity," Yau's *Eye in the Sky* ascends from a crime story involving simply a politics of crime and punishment to a politics of cultural governance with the IB police unit as the primary governing agent.

Clearly, the police are significant players with respect to the subject of governance. However, to discern the object or the *what* of that governance, one has to recognize the peculiarities of Hong Kong's relationship with Chineseness. As Kwai-Cheung Lo characterizes it,

> Hong Kong's Chineseness is a site of performative contradictions. Its existence is simply a living and contingent contradiction, in the sense that the city's culture both exaggerates and negates Chineseness in the vicissitudes of its sociopolitical milieu [as a result] Hong Kong culture operates as an articulation of "transitional Chineseness."[50]

Accordingly, the role of policing in Hong Kong is to maintain Hong Kong's status as, in Lo's terms, "the master signifier of the Chinese nation."[51] Within such a context, crime becomes a signifier that exceeds its threat to the commercial enterprises it preys upon. As Lo points out, the Hong Kong enclave, with its notorious drugs, prostitution, and gangs, among other things, has been regarded by the governmental leadership in China as an affront to "traditional Chinese moral values." And as a representative of the bad and corrupt vis-à-vis the good of the mainland, Hong Kong has served to reinforce China's moral identity with its very transgressions.[52]

Thus, the policing response to the Shan gang's robberies can be construed as a policing-while-highlighting of the rampant anti-Chineseness that constitutes Hong Kong's difference from mainland China. The film's presentation of the need for a surveillant policing in Hong Kong serves as a warrant of Chineseness, giving an extended (if ironic) meaning to the sense in which the cinematic

198 A BI-CITY CINEMATIC EXPERIENCE

representations of Hong Kong's police (and Shan's gang, for that matter) serve to protect Chinese cultural identity, even as it shows that culture is in a state of transition. Yau's crime story therefore devolves into a complex cultural governance story and encourages, once again, a reflection on the intercity cinematic experience with which my analysis begins, because politics in contemporary Berlin is very much about cultural governance, which, in the case of Berlin, involves how to represent Germanness.

CONCLUSION: BACK TO BERLIN

While *Eye in the Sky*'s foregrounding of policing and its scenes of Hong Kong's culinary culture speak to a politics of Chinese identity, cultural governance in my viewing venue, Berlin, is articulated through the arts, in general, and architect, in particular. While contemporary Hong Kong cinema is one of the primary genres within which the city's Chinese identity is thought and negotiated, especially since the transfer from British to Chinese control,[53] the negotiation of Berlin's participation in the issue of Germanness has been centered on the architectural projects though which Berlin has sought to transcend its infamous past. Given that collective identity involves the temporal projections of memory and further that the cogency of such projections requires visible markings, the creation of the New Berlin has proceeded with the presumption that "memory is built."[54] As a result, the process of designing the built environment of the city has involved a "negotiated politics of memory,"[55] which has intensified in Berlin since the Berlin Wall came down and the capital was transferred to Berlin from Bonn. Indeed, as Andreas Huyssen puts it, "there is no other western city that bears the marks of twentieth century history as intensely and self-consciously as Berlin."[56]

While Hong Kong architecture often proceeds through the establishment of monuments to its past—for example, the declaration as a monument of Flagstaff House, once a British military headquarters and now a museum—Berlin's architecture is self-consciously antimonumental. As Huyssen suggests, the historical distancing impetus of contemporary Berlin architecture proceeds within the binary of the visible–invisible so that the built environment articulates a progressively oriented history of space.[57] Thus, debate over how to shape the New Berlin has been focused on superseding the past and convincing Germany, as well as the rest of the world, that the new Germanness is emancipated from previous versions. Ultimately therefore my viewing situation—watching the rapidly mutating, hyperkinetic Hong Kong of Yau's *Eye in the Sky* while situated in a rapidly and self-consciously changing Berlin—provoked a consideration of modes of cultural governance in the modern global city and the genres through which they are articulated.

NOTES

1. The expression, "cinematic heterotopia" belongs to Victor Burgin, *The Remembered Film* (London: Reaktion Books, 2004), 7.
2. The quotation is from the festival site at: www.berlinale.de/en/archiv /jahresarchive/2007/01_jahresblatt_2007/01_Jahresblatt_2007.html.
3. See Jane Kramer, "Living with Berlin," *The New Yorker*, July 5, 1999, 84–92.
4. *Ibid.*, 58.
5. On that result see Michael Z. Wise, "The New Berlin: Expressing Government Power with Pomposity," *The New York Times*, On the web at: www/com/yr/mo/ day/art;leisure/berlinarchitecture.htm.
6. The quotations are from Ackbar Abbas, "Hong Kong: Other Histories, Other Politics," *Public Culture* 9: 3 (1997), 293–313.
7. Akbar Abbas, *Hong Kong: Culture and the Politics of Disappearance* (Minneapolis: University of Minnesota Press, 1999), 294–295.
8. Kwai-Cheung Lo, *Chinese Face/Off: The Transnational Popular Culture of Hong Kong* (Champaign, IL: University of Illinois Press, 2005), 99.
9. Lisa Tyler and Michael Hoover, *City on Fire: Hong Kong Cinema* (New York: Verso, 1999), 174.
10. The quotation is from Sharin Zukin, "Postmodern Urban Landscapes," in *Modernity and Identity*, eds. Scott Lash and Jonathan Friedman (Cambridge, MA: Blackwell, 1992), 223.
11. Karen Fang, "Britain's Finest: The Royal Hong Kong Police," in *After the Imperial Turn*, ed. Antoinette Burton (Durham: Duke University Press, 2003), 297.
12. Abbas, "Hong Kong: Other Histories, Other Politics," 66.
13. *Ibid.*, 16–17.
14. See Abbas, *Hong Kong: Culture and the Politics of Disappearance*, 308.
15. Walter Benjamin, "On Some Motifs in Baudelaire', in *Illuminations*, trans. Harry Zohn, (New York: Schocken, 1968), 175.
16. *Ibid.*
17. The quotation is from a website on the history of the Potsdamer Platz. See http:// aviewoncities.
18. Simon Guy, "Shadow Architectures: War, Memories, and Berlin's Futures," in *Cities, War and Terrorism: Towards an Urban Geopolitics*, ed. S. Graham (Cambridge, MA: Blackwell, 2004), 77.
19. *Ibid.*
20. See Giovanna Bruno, *Atlas of Emotion: Journeys in Art, Architecture, and Film* (New York: Penguin, 2002), 15–17.
21. Paul Virilio, *The Aesthetics of Disappearance* (New York: Semiotext(e), 1991), 25.
22. The Barthes quotation, from his *The Pleasure of the Text* (1973), is taken from Burgin, *The Remembered Film*, 33.
23. The quotation is from Carsten Strathhausen, "Uncanny Spaces: The City in Ruttmann and Vertov," in *Screening the City*, eds. Tony Fitzmaurice and Mark Shiel (New York: Verso, 2003), 17.
24. On the relationship of codes to societies of control, see Gilles Deleuze, "Postscript on Societies of Control," *October* 59 (Winter, 1992), 3–7.
25. The excerpt is a translation from Kirchner's diary (Tagebuch) quoted in Charles W. Haxthausen, "A New Beauty: Ernst Ludwig Kirchner's Images of Berlin," in

Berlin: Culture and Metropolis, eds. C. W. Haxthausen & H. Suhr (Minneapolis: University of Minnesota Press, 1990), 67.

26. Edward Dimendberg, *Film Noir and the Spaces of Modernity* (Cambridge, MA: Harvard University Press, 2004), 25.

27. David Bordwell, "Film Futures," *SubStance* 31: 1 (2002), 89.

28. *Ibid.*, 94.

29. Fang, "Britain's Finest: The Royal Hong Kong Police," 293.

30. *Ibid.*, 303.

31. *Ibid.*, 301.

32. Jacques Rancière, *The Politics of Aesthetics*, trans. Gabriel Rockhill (New York: Continuum, 2004), 24.

33. William Leach, *Land of Desire* (New York: Pantheon, 1993), 47.

34. *Ibid.*, 62–63.

35. Gill Valentine and David Bell G., *Consuming Geographies: We Are Where We Eat* (New York: Routledge, 1997), 130.

36. Donna Leon, *Willful Behavior* (New York: William Heinemann, 2002), 13.

37. *Ibid.*, 66.

38. *Ibid.*

39. Eric Kit-Wai Ma, "Consuming Satellite Modernities," *Cultural Studies* 15: 3–4 (2001), 447.

40. For that kind of cinematic discernment see Mary Ann Doane, *The Emergence of Cinematic Time* (Cambridge, MA: Harvard University Press, 2002).

41. On the movement image, see Gilles Deleuze, *Cinema 1*, trans. Hugh Tomlinson and Barbara Habberjam (Minneapolis: University of Minnesota Press, 1986).

42. In an analysis of the key services provided by "world cities" in the age of globalization, Hong Kong scores very high (only below New York and London) when total services scores on accountancy, banking/finance, and law are summed. See Peter Taylor, "World Cities and Territorial States Under Conditions of Contemporary Globalization," *Political Geography* 19: 1 (2000), 5–32.

43. On that distinction see Gilles Deleuze, *Cinema 2: The Time Image*, trans. Hugh Tomlinson and Robert Galeta (Minneapolis: University of Minnesota Press, 1989).

44. The quotation is from Walter Benjamin's "Notebook P" of his Paris project. I have taken the passage from Samuel Weber's discussion of Benjamin's Paris: Samuel Weber, "'Streets, Squares, Theaters': A City on the Move – Walter Benjamin's Paris," *Boundary 2* 30: 1 (2003), 22–23.

45. Jonathan Crary, *Suspensions of Perception: Attention, Spectacle, and Modern Culture* (Cambridge, MA: MIT Press, 1999), 45.

46. *Ibid.*, 47.

47. Georg Simmel, "The Metropolis and Mental Life," in *The Sociology of Georg Simmel*, ed. Kurt H. Wolff (New York: Free Press, 1950), 410.

48. Leo Bersani and Ulysse Dutoit, *Forms of Being: Cinema, Aesthetics, Subjectivity* (London: British Film Institute, 2004), 6.

49. Krzysztof Wodiczko, *Critical Vehicles* (Cambridge, MA: MIT Press, 1999), 104.

50. Lo, *Chinese Face/Off*, 4.

51. *Ibid.*, 6.

52. *Ibid.*

A BI-CITY CINEMATIC EXPERIENCE 201

53. See, for example, Anne Tereska Cieko, "Hong Kong: Cinematic Cycles of Grief and Glory," in *Contemporary Asian Cinema*, ed. Anne Tereska Cieko (New York: Berg Publishers, 2006), 169–181.
54. Karen E. Till, *The New Berlin: Memory, Politics, Place* (Minneapolis: University of Minnesota Press, 2005), 17.
55. *Ibid.*
56. Andreas Huyssen, *Present Pasts: Urban Palimpsests and the Politics of Memory* (Stanford: Stanford University Press, 2003), 51.
57. *Ibid.*, 7.

REFERENCES

Abbas, Ackbar (1997) *Hong Kong: Culture and the Politics of Disappearance*, Minneapolis: University of Minnesota Press.

Abbas, Ackbar (1997) 'Hong Kong: Other Histories, Other Politics,' *Public Culture*, Vol. 9 (3), pp. 293–313.

Benjamin, Walter (1968) 'On Some Motifs in Baudelaire,' in *Illuminations*, trans. Harry Zohn, New York: Schocken, pp. 155–200.

Bersani, Leo and Dutoit, Ulysse (2004) *Forms of Being: Cinema, Aesthetics, Subjectivity*, London: BFI.

Bordwell, David (2002) 'Film Futures,' *SubStance*, Vol. 31 (1), pp. 88–104.

Bruno, Giovanna (2018) *Atlas of Emotion: Journeys in Art, Architecture, and Film*, New York: Penguin.

Burgin, Victor (2004) *The Remembered Film*, London: Reaktion Books.

Cieko, Anne Tereska (2006) 'Hong Kong: Cinematic Cycles of Grief and Glory,' in *Contemporary Asian Cinema*, ed. Anne Tereska Cieko, New York: Berg Publishers, pp. 169–181.

Crary, Jonathan (1999) *Suspensions of Perception: Attention, Spectacle, and Modern Culture*, Cambridge, MA: MIT Press.

Deleuze, Gilles (1986) *Cinema 1*, trans. Hugh Tomlinson and Barbara Habberjam, Minneapolis: University of Minnesota Press.

Deleuze, Gilles (1989) *Cinema 2: The Time Image*, trans. Hugh Tomlinson and Robert Galeta, Minneapolis: University of Minnesota Press.

Deleuze, Gilles (1992) 'Postscript on Societies of Control,' *October*, Vol. 59, pp. 3–7.

Dimendberg, Edward (2004) *Film Noir and the Spaces of Modernity*, Cambridge, MA: Harvard University Press.

Doane, Mary Ann (2002) *The Emergence of Cinematic Time*, Cambridge, MA: Harvard University Press.

Fang, Karen (2003) 'Britain's Finest: The Royal Hong Kong Police,' in *After the Imperial Turn*, Antoinette Burton, Durham: Duke University Press, pp. 293–307.

Guy, Simon (2004) 'Shadow Architectures: War, Memories, and Berlin's Futures,' in *Cities, War and Terrorism: Towards an Urban Geopolitics*, ed. Stephen Graham, Cambridge, MA: Blackwell, pp. 75–92.

Haxthausen, Charles W. and Suhr, Heidrum eds. (1990) *Berlin: Culture and Metropolis*, Minneapolis: University of Minnesota Press.

Huyssen, Andreas (2003) *Present Pasts: Urban Palimpsests and the Politics of Memory*, Stanford: Stanford University Press.

Kit-Wai Ma, Eric (2001) 'Consuming Satellite Modernities,' *Cultural Studies*, Vol. 15 (3–4), pp. 444–463.

Kramer, Jane (1999) 'Living with Berlin,' *The New Yorker*, July 5th, pp. 84–92.

Leach, William (1993) *Land of Desire*, New York: Pantheon.

Leon, Donna (2002) *Willful Behavior*, New York: William Heinemann.

Lo, Kwai-Cheung (2005) *Chinese Face/Off: The Transnational Popular Culture of Hong Kong*, Champaign: University of Illinois Press.

Rancière, Jacques (2004) *The Politics of Aesthetics*, trans. Gabriel Rockhill, New York: Continuum.

Simmel, Georg (1950) 'The Metropolis and Mental Life,' in *The Sociology of Georg Simmel*, ed. Kurt H. Wolff, New York: Free Press.

Strathhausen, Carsten (2003) 'Uncanny Spaces: The City in Ruttmann and Vertov,' in *Screening the City*, eds. Tony Fitzmaurice and Mark Shiel, New York: Verso, pp. 15–40.

Taylor, Peter (2000) 'World Cities and Territorial States under Conditions of Contemporary Globalization,' *Political Geography*, Vol. 19 (1), pp. 5–32.

Till, Karen E. (2005) *The New Berlin: Memory, Politics, Place*, Minneapolis: University of Minnesota Press.

Tyler, Lisa and Hoover, Michael (1999) *City on Fire: Hong Kong Cinema*, New York: Verso.

Valentine, Gill and Bell David G. (1997) *Consuming Geographies: We Are Where We Eat*, New York: Routledge.

Virilio, Paul (1991) *The Aesthetics of Disappearance*, New York: Semiotext(e).

Weber, Samuel (2003) 'Streets, Squares, Theaters: A City on the Move – Walter Benjamin's Paris,' *boundary 2*, Vol. 30 (1), pp. 17–30.

Wise, Michael Z. (1999) 'The New Berlin: Expressing Government Power with Pomposity,' *The New York Times*, at: www/com/yr/mo/day/art;leisure/berlinarchitecture.htm.

Wodiczko, Krzysztof (1999) *Critical Vehicles*, Cambridge, MA: The MIT Press.

Zukin, Sharin (1992) 'Postmodern Urban Landscapes,' in *Modernity and Identity*, eds. Scott Lash and Jonathan Friedman, Cambridge, MA: Blackwell, pp. 221–247.

SUGGESTED READING

For More on Hong Kong Cinema, See

Petra Rehling, "Beyond the Crisis of the 'Chaotic Formula' of Hong Kong Cinema," *Inter-Asian Cultural Studies* 16:4 (2015), 531–547.

Jason Siu, "Screening Stereotypes: An Analysis of Female Police Officers in Contemporary Hong Kong Films," *Conference of the International Journal of Arts and Sciences* 6:1 (2013), 463–477.

C. M. Yau ed., *At Full Speed: Hong Kong Cinema in a Borderless World* (Minneapolis: University of Minnesota Press, 2005).

CHAPTER 7

The Phenomenology of the Cinema Experience

INTRODUCTION: *PSYCHO* REMAKES

In the Introduction I reviewed the enduring effect of "the moment of psycho," as Alfred Hitchcock's cinematic aesthetic, in which "bloodletting, sadism, and slaughter [came to be] taken for granted,"[1] and left a legacy reflected in (among other films) Roman Polanski's *Repulsion* (1965) and David Lynch's *Blue Velvet* (1986). Here, in order to treat the complications and mediations involved in cinematic reception (which includes not only watching films but also writing about them), I begin with a focus on another aspect of the Hitchcock legacy, remakes of his *Psycho*, one I have treated elsewhere, Gus Van Sant's frame-by-frame remake of the film (his *Psycho* [1998]), and Douglas Gordon's *24 Hour Psycho* (1993), an installation at the Museum of Modern Art, which slowed down Hitchcock's version to approximately 2 frames a second from its original 24. The effect of Gordon's remake is made especially palpable in a Don DeLillo novel in which one of his protagonists views it a number of times (a text I treat below).

Van Sant's film received an abundance of negative reviews, one of which was William Rothman's, which neglected the nuances of repetition and quotation and concerned itself solely with content. Rothman complained that his *Psycho* imaginary had been violated by casting choices and changes in the dialogue: "Vince Vaughan pales in comparison to Anthony Perkin's 'boy next door quality'" and "'the dialogue doesn't adhere to the original screenplay at several quintessential moments.'"[2] Concerning herself with film form—specifically the impact of quotation on the viewer—Chelsey Crawford provides a different, more appreciative, and conceptually nuanced reflection on Van Sant's remake. Invoking Mikhail Iampolski's concept of cinematic quotation she writes, "The quote is a fragment of the text that violates its linear development and derives the motivation that integrates it into the text from outside the text itself'" and goes on to reflect on how cinematic quotation can affect reception: "The quotation interrupts the linearity of the text because it fractures the *mind* [my emphasis] of the viewer—causing her or him to enact an alternate, yet simultaneous, mode of thought."³ Like so much of Van Sant's cinematic corpus, his *Psycho* remake is more about thinking than about entertainment. James Naremore, in a famously negative review of the film, admits as much, referring to Van Sant's *Psycho* remake as a "metafilm [that] . . . reveals a good deal about Hitchcock's specific achievement."⁴ Certainly among what Van Sant's innovative film form achieves is attributable to his color-coding of Hitchcock's black-and-white version (Figure 7.1). The effect is not only to reorder the salience of the film's original details (e.g., the rivulets of red blood running down the shower drain, which emphasize the wasting of a life) but also to broaden the associations of the film's detailing of the moment of death (e.g., Van Sant's interspersing of time-lapse clouds, colored in "blue-greys" that match "the rapidly receding strands of colour in the extreme close-up of Marion's iris dilating at the point of unconscious").⁵ His remake provides valuable insights into the available tools—chromatic narrative strategies, among others—of cinematic composition for those whose writing projects seek to connect cinema with political thinking.

Nevertheless, in focusing on the critical effect of cinematic gestures (by Van Sant, among others) that "fracture the mind of the viewer" (or at least involve it), it is crucial to recognize that not all viewers have the same "mind." As Rudolph Arnheim pointed out, while images are perceptual objects whose compositions contain "various dynamic centers . . . generated by the work itself," the sense derived from visual compositions are also "contributed by mechanisms inherent in the viewer's own behavior," for example, the "directionality imposed on the visual field."⁶ However, the cinema–viewer interaction exceeds the mechanisms of perception. Cinematic reception derives both from the way viewers have been situated in the lifeworld (in Martin Heidegger's

FIGURE 7.1
Van Sant's *Psycho* victim. Source: Gus Van Sant, *Psycho*, Universal Picture (1998).

THE PHENOMENOLOGY OF THE CINEMA EXPERIENCE   205

terms, their "situation" or "factical life experience")[7] and from the history of their cinema experience, to which, thanks to contemporary technologies, they have easy access. This latter part of the film viewer's "situation" is elaborately analyzed in Victor Burgin's commentary on cinematic memory. In his *The Remembered Film* he points out that whereas once the recovery of instances from a remembered film was possible only if the film returned to a theater near you, contemporary technologies of video reproduction and streaming make it possible now to recover recalled fragments from former viewing experiences almost immediately.

Exploring that effect, Burgin rehearses it with an example from one of his own viewing experiences in which his reception was enhanced by contrasting two films that allowed him to move from particular scenes to a theoretical conclusion. In the first scene, a woman climbs a path toward the camera as the camera adopts a variety of locations to position her in a landscape (from Tsai Ling-Liang's *Vive L'Amour*, 1994). In the second scene, which the first scene evokes for Burgin, there is a long shot of a woman entering the frame, while thereafter the camera positions her in the landscape from various locations (Michael Powell and Emeric Pressburger's film *Canterbury Tales*, 1944). Because the first scene reminded him of the second, Burgin was able to replay them and see them as an antithesis: "town and country, old world and new, East and West."[8] He thus moved from his memory-aided cinematic experience to a theoretical insight, aided by contemporary technology.

Burgin's conceptual remix strategy is effectively enacted in Christian Marclay's video installation *The Clock* (2010). It is a 24-hour video that draws on cinema history as it inter-articulates clips from thousands of films. An analogy can help us appreciate one of its primary effects on the viewer. The development of a unitary sightline or focal point, one of the innovations in Renaissance paintings, had the effect of anchoring the viewer in a position that gave the painter's scene its primary theme (e.g., centering the viewer in front of the painting's main character). The anchoring effect in Marclay's video is temporal. During the moments when the video is punctuated by scenes that show watches and clocks, the times they display match the time of the viewing (Figure 7.2). As a result, viewers are anchored in their own time, ushered into introspection on their present world as they are viewing a trajectory of cinematic pasts.

The other major effects of Marclay's *The Clock* are a function of the many interventions of the filmmaker: "re-editing, reframing, repetitions, stopping and slowing,"[9] a cinematic rhythm that confronts viewers with discrete segments that break concentration and mount a challenge to comprehension. Because the viewer of *The Clock* is deprived of a coherent narrative, the relevant question that arises is about the kind of comprehension that Marclay's video encourages. For that, we can recur to the model that Burgin supplies in his

FIGURE 7.2
One of Marclay's clocks. Source: Christian Marclay, *The Clock*, White Cube Gallery (2010).

autobiographic account of his own viewing moment of the two films from which he derives a series of antitheses.

Marclay's cuts and juxtapositions repay a similar kind of attention. The video is composed of shots of "time keepers," attached to "numerous motif clusters."[10] For example, at one point, a clip shows several nurses dancing with newborn babies in their arms, swaddled in blankets. That clip, punctuated by shots of clocks, is followed by clips of bodies wrapped in various textiles: sheets, blankets, bandages, and so on, one of which is a sheet-covered dead body. What the viewer therefore apprehends inferentially is the time-based materiality of wrapping as it operates at various stages of the life cycle. Similarly, many juxtaposed clips show people rapidly moving about in automobiles at moments when they are hurrying to meet deadlines. Here, the inference suggested is about automobility's role in the multiple temporalities of the lifeworld.

While the juxtapositions that Burgin's insights and Marclay's video enact draw on a cinematically framed historical duration that technology collapses, allowing for a virtually simultaneous comparison and inter-articulation of films from different eras, a deeper conceptual appreciation of the phenomenology of that kind of viewing experience requires us to recognize the durational character of the viewing subject as well (which is incorporated to an extent in Marclay's video by the simultaneity of viewing and watch and clock times). However, viewers exist in extended durations. As Henri Bergson has famously pointed out, *subjects* are durations. Consequently, the apprehension of events, cinematic or otherwise, is inflected by the recollection of one's own

THE PHENOMENOLOGY OF THE CINEMA EXPERIENCE   207

extra-cinematic "factical life experience." If we heed what Gilles Deleuze calls "Bergsonism," we must regard

> the body [as] something other than a mathematical point . . . it is the recollections of memory that link . . . instants to each other and interpolate the past in the present. . . . It is therefore memory that makes the body something other than instantaneous and gives it a duration in time.[11]

However, rather than merely taking that statement as an important insight about the cinematic experience, we need to follow a situated, rather than abstract, subject to witness an encounter of durations, that of the subject's life experience and the temporal layers of the film being encountered. For that, I turn to the promised example from a Don DeLillo's novel, his *Point Omega*, in which the durational aspect of a cinematic subject is located in a narrative that conveys some of the particulars of his cinematic reception.

DeLillo himself is an exemplar of the cinematic subject his novel invents. In a commentary on one of his early stories, "The Uniforms" (1970), an adaptation of the Jean Luc Godard film *Weekend*, DeLillo describes his viewing experience and subsequent novelistic adaptation of the film:

> I consider this piece of work a movie as much as anything else. Not my movie, however. No, the work is an attempt to hammer and nail my own frame around somebody else's movie. The movie in question is "Weekend," made of course by the mock-illustrious Jean-Luc Godard. After seeing this film for the first and only time, I walked the two miles or so from the theater where it was playing to the monochromatic street I live on and immediately set to work *remaking* [my emphasis] what I'd seen and heard . . . I guess I was just trying to find one small way in which literature might be less rigid in the sources it uses. Thousands of short stories and novels have been made into movies. I simply tried to reverse the process.[12]

In contrast with DeLillo's rapid appropriation of Godard's *Weekend* is his *Point Omega* in which he provides a much more patient film viewer, one who spends hours exposing himself to the Douglas Gordon *24 Hour Psycho* installation in New York's Museum of Modern Art. Thoroughly cinematic throughout, the novel effectively features three films. In addition to Gordon's *24 Hour Psycho* is a second unrealized film in preparation by one of the novel's protagonists. His fictional filmmaker, Jim Finley, has planned a documentary that would film the reclusive former war planner Richard Elster talking about his two years at the Pentagon during President George Bush's "War on Terror" (I treat that planned documentary comparatively later in this chapter). The third film is constituted by Delillo's writing style (his "The Uniforms" is not

208   THE PHENOMENOLOGY OF THE CINEMA EXPERIENCE

his only "movie"). Like the style in many of his stories, *Point Omega* is pervasively cinematic as it explores a contrast between urban life and the slowness of a desert environment "out beyond cites and scattered towns."[13] Elster had "exchanged all that [his Washington, D.C., life] for space and time."[14] After Finley visits and experiences Elster's desert location, it evokes the contrast for him that it had for Elster. They experience its contrast with the rapid buzz of images in Washington, D.C. (Elster), and Manhattan (Finley).

DeLillo's cinematic effects operate allusively as well, for they contain a variety of Hitchcockian moments. For example, after Elster's daughter Jessie visits—an "otherworldly" woman from New York whose intervention disrupts the Finley–Elster dyad and arouses Finley's libido—she disappears in the desert, never to be found. That part of the story calls to mind the Hitchcock mystery thriller *The Lady Vanishes* (1938). Moreover, Finley, although sexually drawn to Jessie, makes no attempt at seduction; he remains a voyeur. During her presence in the house, he "watch[es] her with the same uneasy intentness as the unnamed man watching Janet Leigh in *Psycho*."[15] That stance has two Hitchcockian resonances; it connects the mode of reception of Finley with that of the character whose posture, continually watching Gordon's *24 Hour Psycho* bookends the section involving Finley, and it recalls Hitchcock's personality as described by his interviewer, the French filmmaker Francois Truffaut. Noting that "Louis-Ferdinand Celine divided people into two categories, the exhibitionists and the voyeurs," Truffaut says, "Hitchcock belongs in the latter category. He is not involved in life; he merely contemplates it."[16]

Doubtless, however, the primary way that Hitchcock inhabits the novel-as-film is in the scenes in which Gordon's remake is described from the point of view of the unnamed character's viewing situation, introduced at the beginning the novel:

> There was a man standing against the north wall, barely visible. People entered in twos and threes and they stood in the dark and looked at the screen and then they left. Sometimes they hardly moved past the doorway, larger groups wandering in, tourists in a daze, and they looked and shifted their weight and then they left. There were no seats in the gallery. The screen was free-standing, about ten by fourteen feet, not elevated, placed in the middle of the room. It was a translucent screen and some people, a few, remained long enough to drift to the other side. They stayed a moment longer and then they left. The gallery was cold and lighted only by the faint gray shimmer on the screen. Back by the north wall the darkness was nearly complete and the man standing alone moved a hand toward his face, repeating, ever so slowly, the action of a figure on the screen.[17]

THE PHENOMENOLOGY OF THE CINEMA EXPERIENCE   209

That mode of reception, made possible by the Gordon's slowing down of the film narrative, allows the character to both contemplate and mime the film's details: "Every action was broken into components so distinct from the entity that the watcher found himself isolated from every expectation."[18] Not swept up in dramatic action, he has time to indulge his capacity to see:

> He watched Anthony Perkins reaching for a car door, using the right hand. He knew that Anthony Perkins would use the right hand on this side of the screen and the left hand on the other side. He knew it but needed to see it and he moved through the darkness along the side wall and then edged away a few feet to watch Anthony Perkins on this side of the screen, the reverse side, Anthony Perkins using the left hand, the wrong hand, to reach for a car door and then open it. But could he call the left hand the wrong hand? Because what made this side of the screen any less truthful than the other side?[19]

Ultimately, DeLillo's novel challenges the Hitchcock aesthetic. When he describes his character wanting "to forget the original movie or at least limit the memory to a distant reference, unintrusive" and as feeling "like someone watching a film," DeLillo is likely describing both himself and his reader. In appreciation of Gordon's remake, DeLillo is revising Hitchcock and is making his reader feel as if he or she is watching a film. What then constitutes the primary nature of the revision? Recalling Deleuze's analysis of a cinema of action (discussed in earlier chapters)—in which, as Deleuze puts it, the viewer is asking him- or herself, "What are we going to see in the next image?"[20]—we can locate precisely the kind of reception that Hitchcock sought. Suggesting that the literary version closest to the way his films invite reception is the short story, Hitchcock says his aim is to create "suspense, which is the most powerful means of holding onto the viewer's attention. It can be either the suspense of the situation or the suspense that makes the public ask itself, 'what will happen next?'"[21] As I also noted in earlier chapters, Deleuze contrasts a "cinema of seeing" to a (Hitchcockian) cinema of action. In a cinema of seeing, "the viewer's problem becomes 'What is there to see in the image?, [not] 'What are we going to see in the next image?'"[22] Inasmuch as seeing details more than anticipating sequences is the focus of DeLillo's viewer of *24 Hour Psycho*, the sections on the reception of the film make it evident that Gordon's *Psycho* remake turns Hitchcock's film from a cinema of action to a cinema of seeing. That altered effect is exemplified in these moments of the viewer's reception of Gordon's slowed down *Psycho*: "The nature of the film permitted total concentration and also depended on it. The film's merciless pacing had no meaning without a corresponding watchfulness, the individual whose absolute alertness did not betray what was demanded. He stood and looked,"[23] and "[i]t takes close

210 THE PHENOMENOLOGY OF THE CINEMA EXPERIENCE

attention to see what is happening in front of you. It takes work, pious effort, to see what you are looking at."[24]

DeLillo's novel-as-film as a whole is seeing/experiencing oriented; his composition thinks about the relationship between slowness and seeing, in general, primarily through the way it describes the altered temporality that his characters, Elster and Finley experience in Elster's desert retreat, a space with a temporality that matches the slowness of Gordon's *24 Hour Psycho*. For Elster, the altered time sense is a difference between the intense interactions he has had among "the fantasists" on "[t]he third floor of the E ring at the Pentagon," which he has "exchanged . . . for space and time. . . . There were the distances that enfolded every feature of the landscape and there was the force of geologic time, out there somewhere, the string grids of excavators searching for weathered bone."[25] As he explains to Finley, "Time slows down when I'm here. Time becomes blind. I feel the landscape more than see it. I never know what day it is. I never know if a minute has passed or an hour. I don't get old here"[26] That time sense strikes Finley similarly: "There were no mornings or afternoons. It was one seamless day," he reports.[27] Elster remarks that "this is what he wanted, to feel the deep heat beating into his body, feel the body itself, reclaim the body from what he called the nausea of News and Traffic. This was desert, out beyond cities,"[28] and in a conversation with his daughter, he explains what's different in the desert from the "minute-to-minute reckoning" one experiences in cities:

> It's all embedded, the hours and minutes, words and numbers everywhere, he said, train stations, bus routes, taxi meters, surveillance cameras. It's all about time, dimwit time, inferior time, people checking watches and other devices, other reminders. This is time draining out of our lives. Cities were built to measure time, to remove time from nature.[29]

DeLillo thus doubles the concept of slowness. It is articulated both in his treatment of his viewer's experience of Gordon's *24 Hour Psycho* and in his other characters' experience of the desert.

SLOWNESS

Through both form and content, DeLillo's *Point Omega* theorizes cinematic reception. One aspect of that theorization has DeLillo in agreement with Hitchcock, who insisted that in cinema, the image is more important than the film's dialogue. Hitchcock argues that a character's persona and mood should be conveyed visually: "The substance of a scene is not the dialogue."[30] Accordingly, he suggests that the silent film is the exemplar of cinematic perfection:

THE PHENOMENOLOGY OF THE CINEMA EXPERIENCE   211

"In the final era of silent movies, the great film-makers . . . had reached something hear perfection. The introduction of sound, in a way, jeopardized that perfection."[31] DeLillo has his viewer of *24 Hour Psycho* second Hitchcock's view of cinematic perfection: "He understood completely why the film was projected without sound. It had to be silent. It had to engage the individual at a depth beyond the usual assumptions, the things he supposes and presumes and takes for granted."[32]

Another important cinematic pedagogy that DeLillo's novel imparts is about the way "slow movies"[33] *intensify* the involvement of the viewer:

He wanted complete immersion . . . wanted the film to move even more slowly, requiring deeper involvement of eye and mind, always that, the thing he sees tunneling into the blood, into dense sensation, sharing consciousness with him. Norman Bates, scary bland, is putting down the phone. . . . The man separates himself from the wall and waits to be assimilated, pore by pore, to dissolve into the figure of Norman Bates, who will come into the house and walk up the stairs in subliminal time, two frames per second, and then turn toward the door of Mother's room.[34]

While there are many exemplars of cinematic slowness, the Russian director Andrei Tarkovsky stands out because he both thematizes and implements that slowness cinematically. Noting that he practices a cinematic aesthetic that privileges what he calls a "long take style," Tarkovsky (as I quote him in the Introduction) points to what it gives the viewer "an opportunity to live through what is on screen as if it were his own life, to take over the experience imprinted in time on the screen," whereas, he argues, a montage style with rapid cuts "deprives the person watching the screen of the prerogative of film . . . film's impact."[35] (Later in the chapter, I redeem the critical effect of the cuts and juxtapositions belonging to the montage style.)

Tarkovsky's privileging of the slowness effect, a long-take style that he juxtaposes to his compatriot, Sergei Eisenstein's use of montage, anticipates a difference that the era of video has brought about and is realized in Douglas Gordon's *24 Hour Psycho*. Lutz Koepnick provides an analysis of the way video has changed cinematic reception:

Though early video artists did not shy away from capturing harrowing experiences, their medium necessitated a new way of thinking about the relationship between form and content and hence about how moving images could and should communicate the substance of traumatic histories . . . video no longer automatically associated the cut with both accelerated and shocking structures of temporality. The rigor of form

THE PHENOMENOLOGY OF THE CINEMA EXPERIENCE

no longer carried predictable content; the cut lost its formerly privileged status as a means of grafting the conditions of modern life quasi-directly onto the physiological receptors of the viewer.[36]

Situating the reception effect of Gordon's *24 Hour Psycho*, he adds:

> Gordon's revised version of his 1993 Hitchcock film, 24 Hour Psycho Back and Forth and to and fro (2008), slow-motion images . . . serve the purpose of intensifying the viewer's viewing, not simply in the sense of sharpening our awareness for things normally left unnoticed, but of allowing us to explore the indeterminate space between represented time and the real time of our viewing.[37]

VIEWING AND LIVING

As commentaries on the most critical effect of a slow cinematic style suggest, it allows for an "intensification of viewing" and thereby restores what typical modes of perception tend to evacuate. However, *perception* is a small part of the phenomenology of viewing. Moments of viewing (films, videos, television broadcasts) are situated in a lifeworld of needs, desires, and everyday demands that compete for attention. For example, recognizing that moving images of endangered and precarious lives evoke denial as much as concern, Tobias Hecht offers the observation that what tends to hold people's attention are attempts to extract something positive from everyday life rather than to contemplate something painful and disturbing:

> The thought that hundreds of thousands of children are at this very moment wasting away from kwashiorkor is incompatible with good coffee or even a few minutes of window-shopping. How can we enjoy a Brahms clarinet sonata when a woman is being raped in a prison somewhere—as one surely is—or an elderly person is dying alone? What we prefer to deny is coincident with erotic poetry and the bouquet of an Australian Pinot Noir. Denial is by turns protective and corrosive, inevitable and unforgiveable, human and inhumane. It is a failing, it would seem, that permits us some leeway in which to live without the full benefit or devastation of perception.[38]

Zadie Smith's narrator in her story *The Embassy of Cambodia* makes a similar point, noting that although the people of "Willesden" (the embassy's suburban location) feel uneasy about having the Cambodian Embassy in their suburb,

THE PHENOMENOLOGY OF THE CINEMA EXPERIENCE 213

they fail to engage in lengthy reflection about the violent episode (the Cambodian genocide) for which the embassy is a material reminder:

> We [the residents of Willesden] were surprised by the appearance of the Cambodian Embassy. . . . It is not the right sort of surprise somehow [However] . . . the fact is if we followed the history of every little country in this world . . . we would have no space left in which to live our own lives or to apply ourselves to necessary tasks.[39]

Apart from the way the stress of managing one's lifeworld exhausts attention spans is the short time span of broadcast media's coverage of global violence. Milan Kundera captures the temporality of that media effect with a fictional moment of television viewing. At one point in his novel *Slowness* the narrator, who is traveling with his wife, remarks that their stay in a chateau "coincides with the period when, every day for two weeks [the television news media] showed the children of an African nation, whose name is already forgotten, ravaged by war." The children appear "thin, exhausted, without strength to wave away the flies walking across their faces."[40] Later in the novel, when the images are no longer being carried by the television networks, the narrator remarks that "the situations history stages are floodlit only for the few minutes" and continues:

> No event remains news over its whole duration, merely for a quite brief span of time, at the very beginning. The dying children of Somalia whom millions of spectators used to watch avidly, aren't they dying any more? What has become of them? Have they grown fatter or thinner? Does Somalia still exist? And in fact did it ever exist? Could it be only the name of a mirage?[41]

As Kundera's narrator points out, the impressions left by stark images of suffering carried in news media have too brief an exposure to have a lasting effect on peoples' conceptual and empathic attunements to violence.

DOCUMENTING EVENTS

Here, I want to juxtapose a medium with a more extended temporal trajectory than that of television journalism, the video documentary, and focus initially on one that challenges television's hegemonic control over the presentation of global violence. In his *Dial H-I-S-T-O-R-Y* (1997), a film (or, more properly, a video assemblage) about the history of airplane hijackings as portrayed by television media, Johan Grimonprez intersperses his film with voice-over passages from DeLillo's novels, *White Noise* and *Mao II*, more pervasively the latter in which DeLillo's character, a writer, laments the terrorists' hijacking of his cultural role as an arbiter of collective consciousness. Although with respect to the object of his video, Grimonprez's *Dial* is about a plane hijacking, the way the film as form works makes it more about the way media, especially television, has appropriated/invented the meaning of plane hijacking. What is at stake, according to Grimonprez, is control over the meaning of catastrophic events. As he puts it in an interview about the video, "every technology invents its own catastrophe. TV technology has reinvented a way to look at the world and think about death"[42] (Figure 7.3). Grimonprez sees himself as one contending with television media, which has hijacked the events of hijacking. To challenge TV journalism's hegemonic interpretive position, he brings them into his video to demonstrate how what they do is turn a catastrophic event into a sensational commodity for media consumption. Using a montage style with cuts and juxtapositions, he decenters their role in the events. Depriving them of their role as the main media protagonists, he constructs a mixed-media narrative to challenge mainstream television media's ownership of events.

Grimonprez's hybrid cinematic text bears comparison with the genre-bending textual practice in the video film work of Péter Forgács, who supplies a collage of decades of footage from Hungarian and Dutch home movies, compiled and rearticulated with segments of news reports of historical events, music, and occasional voice-overs to renarrativize historical moments—in his case, the "periods of extraordinary upheaval and cultural loss—World official history ... [in order to have] us understand that time does not unfold through a [single] collective narrative."[43] Similarly, Grimoprez rearticulates a history of

FIGURE 7.3
A Grimonprez television still. Source: Johan Grimonprez, *D.I.A.L History*, Zap-O-Matik (1997).

THE PHENOMENOLOGY OF THE CINEMA EXPERIENCE 215

plane hijackings, with that variety of archived film segments—in his case, non-chronologically arranged television coverage of plane hijacking between 1931 and 1996, composed of footage from CNN and ABC news archives, which he then intersperses with images from cartoons, advertisements, propaganda and Hollywood films, segments from didactic videos (which are reminiscent of the documentary film work of Harun Farocki), and his own home movies.

Crucially for purposes of my focus on the phenomenology of the cinema experience, Grimonprez's method is not a slowing down to intensify the viewer's apprehension of images. Instead, it is more akin to the remixing that constitutes Christian Marclay's *The Clock*. It bears comparison with DJs working with turntables, engaged in cutting practices that mix together disparate musical segments to rearticulate musical history and reorder the prominence of alternative musical moments. Remixing challenges the control over the communication of sound by a small group of entrepreneurs that have dominated musical commerce. In the form understood as "regenerative remix," remixing disrupts traditional musical temporality, reordering the salience of historically developed musical moments. Instead of pandering to consumption, the regenerative impulse seeks with a practice of "cut/copy and paste," to elevate and add nuance to cultural forms that have been commoditized.[44] The montage effect that Grimonprez shares with Forgács and other remix practitioners, such as Marclay, involves the disruption of narrative expectation rather than the intensification of identification with the persons and objects in his film.

Grimonprez's cinematic method with which he surveys and remixes the contexts of plane hijackings is responsive to his view that "[t]he plane is a metaphor for history [because] it is transgressive, always on the move between several countries, between several homes."[45] However, Gimonprez's main concern is not simply the plane's historical role as articulated in the genealogy of hijacking episodes; it is concerned rather with a different aspect of the events. His film video is about meta-mediation, about how hijacking has, as I have suggested, been hijacked by televisual media's, that is, about the capture of hijacking events. Staging a battle between the filmmaker and television journalism, he mounts a cinematic challenge that "counter-actualizes" the way television journalism invents the meaning of plane hijacking.

To appreciate the cinematic renarrativization that Grimonprez enacts we have to appreciate as well the situation within which TV journalism creates its events. Television journalism's approach to imposing the boundaries that constitute events operates within a complex apparatus that includes desk editors, reporters, photographers, and so on, all involved in structured assignments to produce a product oriented toward commercial consumption. As a voice-over in Grimonprez's film says, "[n]othing happens until it is consumed." What is produced is "news" that results from a process of time-pressured production and circulation. As a result what emerges is "by no means the property of the event" but is, rather, a function of how news sources are organizationally managed to compete in a situation of a need for rapid production and circulation in order to hold its viewers.[46] In contrast, Grimonprez's splicing and zapping, which creates repeated moments within continually altered contexts, is organized to dissolve boundaries and open the event to critical political reflection. To alert the perspective of the viewer to that difference, Gimonprez curates a different way of having history while imposing a curatorial task on the viewer with a film that mimics the zapping practices of viewers with remotes in their hands. His film video therefore conforms to the way television technology has (in his words) "replaced our conventional models of perception and experience."[47] The viewers are left to try to reorganize what Grimonprez's zapping disorganizes, as he throws back at them a work of rapid editing that mimics and thus contends with their editing/zapping role. However at the same time, by emphasizing the way television journalism appropriates each hijacking event (e.g., in scenes that cut from the footage of the event to swarms of television journalists and cameramen pursuing the hijackers), the film is a counter actualization of definitive modes of the narrativized comprehension that television creates rather than merely an alternative object of commercial consumption meant to close the process of coming to terms with the event.

Importantly, Grimonprez competes with the television media *within* his film. For example in his footage of the Lod Airport massacre in Jerusalem, 1972, we see the perpetrator, Kozo Okamoto, on trial in Tel Aviv, with media shots of his courtroom persona, wearing headphones and in handcuffs, while guards manage his movements with restraining equipment—the typical media approach to the event, focusing on the implements of capture and control framed within the scene of the trial. What Grimonprez adds are Okamoto's words, which carry the event beyond the claustrophobic courtroom protocols; onscreen is his metaphorical rendering of his act in which he sees himself bound to his victims, a poiesis of terrorism: "We Red Army soldiers wanted to become stars of Orion. It calms my heart to think that all the people we killed will be stars in the sky. As the revolution goes on how the stars will multiple." To put it conceptually, Grimonprez's film video is shaped by a politically nuanced "chronotope" (M. M. Bakhtin's term for the way literary genres articulate temporality).[48] Suggesting that "[h]istory is always happening between places. . . . It is only afterwards that the structures of power consolidate it into a text, an image, a TV series, a narrative," Grimonprez puts a particular history of terrorism—plane hijacking—on the move again within an altered temporal trajectory in order to allow for different readings and show that no one version can ultimately capture an event. "History," he states, "is read differently by different people."[49] The temporality of Grimonprez's video reenactments, with their incessant interruptions that create thinking spaces, face viewers with a situation in which what is available to cognition is "continually breached."[50]

THE PHENOMENOLOGY OF THE CINEMA EXPERIENCE   217

The viewer is forced to think because the signposts that encourage familiar forms of recognition are destabilized.

DOCUMENTING EVENTS: INTENSITY VERSUS DISRUPTION

In order to compare and contrast slow movies that summon intense viewing with those that break concentration, I return to the second film in DeLillo's *Point Omega*, the filmmaker Finley's planned documentary, a biopic of the fictional disaffected former war planner, Richard Elster, and contrast the film form Finley plans to use with that of Errol Morris's biopic of Robert McNamara, *The Fog of War: Eleven Lessons from the Life of Robert McNamara* (2003). Although there are no hints in DeLillo's novel that Finley's planned documentary is meant to feature an anti-McNamara type, his Elster comes across as one nevertheless. As for kind of cinematic experience the Finley film is meant to create, the hints are available in the description of viewing of the novel's first film, Gordon's *24 Hour Psycho* watched by an anonymous viewer.

Doubtless DeLillo's description of his nameless character's viewing experience of Gordon's *24 Hour Psycho* is meant as a model for the way Finley's documentary is meant to be viewed, with an intense scrutiny of each detail— for example, "He [the nameless viewer] found himself undistracted for some minutes by the coming and going of others and he was able to look at the film with the *degree of intensity that was required*" (my emphasis),[51] this:

> The less there was to see, the harder he looked, the more he saw. This was the point. To see what's here, finally to look and to know you're looking, to feel time passing, to be alive to what is happening in the smallest registers of motion. Everybody remembers the killer's name,[52]

and finally this:

> It takes close attention to see what is happening in front of you. It takes work, pious effort, to see what you are looking at. He was mesmerized by this, the depths that were possible in the slowing of motion, the things to see, the depths of things so easy to miss in the shallow habit of seeing.[53]

Equally important for how the documentary is to be experienced is the nature of the subject of the biopic, one who contrasts dramatically with Morris's subject, McNamara:

> [T]he life he'd left behind, more than two years of living with the tight minds that made the war. . . . There were the risk assessments and policy

THE PHENOMENOLOGY OF THE CINEMA EXPERIENCE

papers, the interagency working groups. He was the outsider, a scholar with an approval rating but no experience in government. He sat at a table in a secure conference room with the strategic planners and military analysts. He was there to conceptualize, his word, in quotes, to apply overarching ideas and principles to such matters as troop deployment and counterinsurgency.[54]

Finally, there is the matter of how Finley's documentary is to be framed and filmed. Here is Finley's description of the approach:

> "No plush armchair with warm lighting and books on a shelf in the background. Just a man and a wall," I told him. "The man stands there and relates the complete experience, everything that comes to mind, personalities, theories, details, feelings. You're the man. There's no offscreen voice asking questions. There's no interspersed combat footage or comments from others, on-camera or off." "What else?" "A simple head shot." "What else?" he said. "Any pauses, they're your pauses, I keep shooting." "What else?" "Camera with a hard drive. One continuous take." "How long a take?" "Depends on you."[55]

The "Depends on you," remark sets up a profound difference between Elster's fictional intended documentary and another "unavowed fiction" Errol Morris's *The Fog of War* because in Morris's biopic, McNamara is effectively deprived of control over his story. I am referring to Morris's documentary as "unavowed fiction," heeding Jacques Rancière's argument that even texts that are intended as nonfiction have to be composed and are this, like (what he refers to as) "avowed fiction," i.e., are shaped by an imposed temporal structure: "the forms of unavowed fiction at work in politics, social science or other theoretical discourses [are] . . . obliged to construct what is at the heart of any fictional rationality but easily can be presupposed in the forms of unavowed fiction: time, which means the form of coexistence of facts that defines a situation and the mode of connection between events that defines a story."[56]

Thus, the difference between the planned Elster documentary and Morris's McNamara biopic is not between fiction and nonfiction but between one that is an unedited long take and one that is heavily edited. As Finley remarks, referring to his one competed film, a documentary of Jerry Lewis charity telethon,

> [t]he film was all Jerry, pure performance, Jerry talking, singing, weeping, Jerry with his ruffled shirt open at the collar, bow tie undone, a raccoon flung over his shoulders, Jerry inviting the nation's love and wonder at four in the morning, in closeup, a crew-cut sweating man in semidelirium, a disease artist, begging us to send money to cure his afflicted children.[57]

THE PHENOMENOLOGY OF THE CINEMA EXPERIENCE 219

In contrast with such an invitation to identify intensely with the documentary's subject is Morris's practice of editing around his subject in a way that imposes sets of spatiotemporal contexts (in this case, the security crises and wars in which McNamara has been a decision maker), depriving the subject of control over his biography and at the same time creating aesthetic breaks that interrupt the narrative McNamara seeks to impose. At the same time, that filming strategy prevents viewers from identifying with the self-understanding of the McNamara subject.

As was the case with the planned biopic of DeLillo's fictional filmmaker, Finley, Morris's McNamara biopic explores the relationship between autobiography and history. While Finley's subject, Elster, is situated as a participant in President Bush's War on Terror, Morris takes McNamara through his various roles from World War II through the Cold War and Cuban Missile Crisis to the Vietnam War, with an emphasis on his service as secretary of defense during the Vietnam War under Presidents Kennedy and Johnson. The discursive context that inspires Morris's film is McNamara's attempts—first through autobiography and then through a return to Vietnam to renegotiate the war experience with his former adversaries—to clarify and legitimate his government service. McNamara's later years were marked by a commitment to offering a pedagogy about war by reflecting on and illuminating retrospectively his policy-making role during the Vietnam War. His turn from autobiography (1995)[58] to dialogue was an attempt to solicit assent to that pedagogy from the Vietnamese decision makers (who resisted his interpretation that "misunderstanding has contributed to the war).

While McNamara's return failed to produce the level of resolution-through-dialogue for which he had hoped, it doubtless seemed to him that the documentary format, in which he produces long monologues in response to queries from someone with whom he has no history, gives him free reign to elaborate his purchase on the "eleven lessons from the life of Robert McNamara" that organize the flow of the documentary, and thus allows him to impose the kind of resolution he seeks on his and the United States' Vietnam experience. Doubtless, he expected effectively to lift the 'fog of war' with lucid and progressive thinking. But such documentaries merely give the interviewee the illusion of personal control over meaning-making. Reviewer Roger Ebert refers to the documentary's presentation of McNamara's lessons as "his thoughts . . . as extrapolated by Morris."[59] However, extrapolation is hardly the appropriate analytic. McNamara's "thoughts" do not exhaust the narrative space of the documentary. Morris's camera work—the ways in which he frames the speaking McNamara and the cuts and juxtapositions of his editing, as McNamara's words are interspersed with historical, archival footage and taped conversations (along with the contrapuntal tenor of Philip Glass's musical score)—creates a conflicting, dysnarrative challenge to McNamara's accounts.

220 THE PHENOMENOLOGY OF THE CINEMA EXPERIENCE

Rather than lifting the fog of war (McNamara's oft-stated intention), the form of Morris's documentary, which challenges McNamara's verbalized accounts with an assemblage of voices, scenes, and sounds, offers conflicting perspectives on what it is that constitutes the fog. The documentary is a drama that creates a context that threatens the sense-making of its protagonist. As I have suggested while referring to Ranciere's blurring of the boundary between fiction and nonfiction, documentaries should not be radically distinguished from feature films. As Michael Renov points out, the

> documentary's use of high or low camera angles, close-ups which trade emotional resonance for spatial integrity, the use of telephoto or wide-angle lenses which squeeze or distort space, the use of editing to make time contract, expand or become rhythmic . . . [are all effects that] . . . documentary shares [with] . . . its fictional counterpart.[60]

Morris's documentary begins with perverse intrusions on an aesthetically pleasing scene, in this case a seascape. A serene ocean setting is the background for sailors scrambling on a battleship as weapons are loaded into firing positions. And as the weapons—and fighting-despoiled land—and seascapes are shown, the camera cuts to historical footage in which McNamara is shown at a press briefing. His weapon in this instance is a pointer, aimed at a map as he addresses the media with an air of supreme confidence, a confidence that he maintains decades later at the beginning of his interview with Morris. He begins by as stating that he remembers exactly where the conversation had left off. As was the case while he addressed the media during the Vietnam War, McNamara seems assured that his words and gestures will make their way through the media without reinflection or recontextualization. However, immediately after McNamara expresses his sense of control over the interview and proceeds to state his major theme—that rationality is not sufficient, that leaders can make mistakes that kill people—the assemblage of shots and sounds imply a different set of forces at work. As the documentary's historical footage is shown in rapid cuts and juxtapositions, Philip Glass's contrapuntal musical score contains clashing musical voices that match the rapidity of the montage.

Here as elsewhere in the documentary, the music doubles the disharmony between McNamara's and the film's meaning-making. The Glass score has two reinforcing effects on the disjuncture between McNamara's meaning-making and the documentary's. First, the contrapuntal music conveys alternative, conflicting voices that contrast with McNamara's confident monologue. Second, the speeded tempo reinforces the kinetic kaleidoscopic montage, which, along with the music's dark tonalities, suggests that the speed of events is part of a dangerous dynamic well beyond the control of the rationality and proportionality that are the primary tropes of McNamara' s account. Glass's use of counterpoint, as opposed to melodic or lyrical harmonies, effectively reinforces Morris's disruption of the rationalistic talk that emanates from the defense establishment's habitual discourse (manifestations of what DeLillo's Elster called "tight minds"). Counterpoint introduces ironies that are conceptually disruptive, in contrast with pleasant melodies that reinforce habitual patterns of thought. As Glass notes, his music is influenced by Samuel Beckett, whose writing delivers shocks to habitual forms of intelligibility. Accordingly, his music "denies habitual patterns of expectation."[61] Moreover, Glass's score, which displays the quickening emotional tempo he found in Beckett's plays, provides an emotional counterpoint to the cool and methodical tone in McNamara's monologues. Doubtless, however, the most powerful disruptions to McNamara's control of his story in the documentary are visual. Two aspects of Morris's documentary filming wrest control over meaning-making and reinflect the interpretations one can derive from McNamara's accounts. The first, most obvious, and more familiar meaning-making effect of the documentary is achieved through the editing process. While documentary evidence belies some of McNamara's accounts, especially his self-positioning as one reluctant to endorse military action during the Cuban Missile Crisis and during the military escalation in Vietnam during Lyndon Johnson's presidency, it is the form of the film, the cuts to archival footage and taped conversations that disturb or alter the contexts that McNamara uses to frame his claims. Two brief examples of the most significant challenges to McNamara's perspective on his role should suffice. First, under the rubric of "Lesson 2: Rationality Will Not Save Us," McNamara asserts the limits of rationality, noting that the world was saved from an all-out nuclear war by luck, because all the relevant decision makers were rational. But here his discourse is wholly geopolitical. In explicating this lesson (as well as in other segments of the film), he argues that what was at risk was the existence of "nations," by which he means sovereign states. Juxtaposed with his remarks, however, are scenes of populations. The viewer is shown fast-forwarded panning and tracking shots of pedestrians in dense urban venues, a blur of moving crowds. At such moments, McNamara's reasons of state, his macro-level, geopolitical focus, effectively evacuate vulnerable civilians from his scenario, while, in juxtaposition, Morris's editing brings them back, foregrounding the human lives rather than the "nations" that McNamara says were at risk.

Nevertheless, in the segment treating "Lesson 4: Proportionality Should Be a Guideline in War," McNamara evinces an awareness of the slaughter of civilian populations, admitting, in the case of the fire-bombing of civilian populations in Japan, for example, that he was "part of the mechanism that in a sense recommended it." While here, as elsewhere, McNamara's discourse is primarily logistical, Morris's editing situates the mechanisms that deliver violence from a perceptual and technologically mediated distance: meetings of the Joint Chiefs, military planning sessions with maps and charts, teletyped messages, numbers rather than bombs raining down on landscapes, and scenes of industrial production and the fitting out of weapons, alongside scenes of the devastation caused by the bombing: cities destroyed and heaps of burned and maimed bodies in burned-out landscapes. The juxtapositions make McNamara's career of logistical distance bizarre and insensitive to the human costs to which his war planning disproportionately contributed (as Morris's images point out, for they show many scenes of McNamara in planning sessions at many levels of executive and military decision making). And they make his vocabulary and grammar—especially when he frequently resorts to the passive voice in this segment—distancing as well. In short, much of the editing process of the documentary changes what McNamara renders as a necessary evil (McNamara's Lesson 9 is "To Do Good, You Have To Do Evil") into an evil, followed by its legitimation as necessity.

Although Morris's, editing carries much of the burden of the documentary's interpretation of the consequences of McNamara's (former and current) perspectives, there is another, more subtle aspect of the camera work that wrests control from McNamara's responses and monologues. Despite a filing structure in which Morris's interrotron—aimed directly at its speaking subject—allows McNamara to make eye contact with his interlocutor and thus to look directly at the viewers, he is rarely in the center of the frame. The decentering of McNamara is a large part of what I have termed the dysnarrative flow of the documentary (Figure 7.4). Morris's camera offers us a body that is recalcitrant to the story it is telling. A McNamara who wants to fill the entire space of the narrative fails to command and fill the frame. He is often shown off to one side and cut off so that one sees him from just below the neck to only part of his head.

FIGURE 7.4
McNamara off-center. Source: Errol Morris, *The Fog of War*, Sony Pictures (2003).

THE PHENOMENOLOGY OF THE CINEMA EXPERIENCE   223

The dysnarrative effect of Morris's continual repositioning of the McNamara body comports with the critical effect of some feature films in which bodies are positioned to resist narrative complicity. As the film theorist Vincent Amiel points out, in classic cinema the tendency was "to utilize the body as a simple vector of the narrative, abandoning its density for the exclusive benefit of its functionality," but more critically oriented directors offer a body that is not an "instrument in the service of narrative articulation."[62] Lest there be any doubt about the semiotic effect of the way he distributes McNamara's body around the frame—cutting more at some moments (especially when McNamara is being the least self-disclosing) and less at others, but rarely allowing him a centered and full-bodied exposure—Morris's epilogue seals the effect. At the end of the film, as McNamara is called to account, Morris asks him if he feels "responsible," even "guilty," about his contribution to the enormous loss of life in Vietnam. While McNamara, now seated behind the wheel of a Ford, refuses to answer the question, he is more radically cut than at any previous moment. First, only part of his head and one eye is in the frame; then, his whole face is available but only in the car's rear-view mirror. For McNamara, as he states toward the end of the interview, the "fog of war" is merely war's complexity, the large number of variables one must consider and manage. Morris's filming suggests however that the fog is elsewhere; it exists among other places in the lens through which McNamara saw and continues to see the world (as emphasized in the last shots of McNamara's face—the only ones taken from an oblique angle—in which the most centered element is one lens of his eyeglasses. Ultimately, the overriding conclusion about his tenure as secretary of defense that McNamara wants to emphasize derives from the contrast he sees between what he calls the success of the Kennedy administration's actions during the Cuban Missile Crisis and the Johnson administration's failure to terminate the Vietnam War before huge casualties occurred. He ascribes the success of the former to "empathy"—the ability, in his words, "to get inside the other person's skin"—and the failure of the second to lack of empathy.

It is clear from his writings, as well as from his remarks in Morris's documentary, that empathy for McNamara is not an ethical concept. Rather, it is a perception of one's enemy's motives and intentions. The conceptual armament with which McNamara treats the 'Other' is of a piece with his general tendency to regard the world through a strategic lens. From his perspective, insofar as he has accumulated debts during his career, they are to the people he served in government, not those that were the target of his government's war policy.

However, there is another way to approach one's debts, an alternative to McNamara's perspective on responsibility and to the persistence of the militarized lens through which the U.S. perpetually sees its "enemies." It is a turn to critical literature (DeLillo's strategy). Here, I want to emphasize the particular strategy of a Canadian professor of literature, Claude Mark Hurlbert, who

THE PHENOMENOLOGY OF THE CINEMA EXPERIENCE

teaches Iraqi literature in order to overcome the alienation of his students from a people who are represented as, alternatively, fanatic and enigmatic by the militaries and the media of Western powers. Hurlbert draws on the work of Bill Readings to locate the question of our obligation to "explore the nature of our incalculable obligations to others," which Readings renders as a "network of obligations" that emerges when we can appreciate "singularities," the "unique aggregates of historically specific characteristics existing within webs or relations to other singularities."[63] Hurlbert's and Readings's attention to one's debts to otherness contrasts markedly with McNamara's empathy, which is a management tool rather than an ethical disposition. The fogging effect of the policy discourses within which McNamara constructed the enemy/other continued to allow him to remain comfortably at home with himself, in radical contrast with the Richard Elster, whom DeLillo invents. An ethical regard, as Emmanuel Levinas has famously enjoined, allows the other to remain a respected stranger, "who disturbs the being at home with oneself."[64] What is revealed when Morris's documentary lifts the fog of McNamara's strategic thinking is the absence of a self-reflective sense of responsibility to those who turned out to be the victims of the policies that he helped to put in place. A lyrical passage from novelist Arundhati Roy's novel *The God of Small Things* fits the sense of this revelation and provides an apt conclusion. Morris's *The Fog of War* serves to "nudge [McNamara's] hidden morality from its resting place and make it bubble to the surface and float for a while. In clear view, for everyone to see."[65]

NOTES

1. David Thomson, *The Moment of Psycho: How Alfred Hitchcock Taught America to Love Murder* (New York: Basic Books, 2010), 67.
2. The quotations are from Chelsey Crawford, "The Permeable Self: A Theory of Cinematic Quotation." *Film-Philosophy* 19: 1 (2015), 30 (in which she is quoting from Rothman's review).
3. Crawford, *Ibid.*, 107, quoting Iampolski, *The Memory of Tiresias: Intertextuality and Cinema* (Berkeley: University of California Press, 1998).
4. James Naremore, "Remaking *Psycho*," *Hitchcock Annual* (1999), 6, On the web at: http://jamesnaremore.net/wp-content/uploads/2018/07/Remaking Psycho.pdf.
5. The quotations are from Catherine Constable, "Reflections on the Surface: Remaking the Postmodern with Van Sant's *Psycho*," in *Adaptations in Contemporary Culture: Textual Infidelities*, ed. Rachel Carroll (London: Bloomsbury, 2009), 31.
6. Rudolph Arnheim, *The Power of the Center* (Berkeley: University of California Press, 1982), 37.
7. See Martin Heidegger, "Methodological Introduction: Philosophy, Factical Life Experience, and the Phenomenology of Religion," in *The Phenomenology of Religious Life*, trans. Mathias Fritsch and Jennifer Anna Gosetti-Ferencei (Bloomington: Indiana University Press, 2010), 3–13.

THE PHENOMENOLOGY OF THE CINEMA EXPERIENCE   225

8. Victor Burgin, *The Remembered Film* (London: Reaktion Books, 2005), 59.
9. The quotation is from Catherine Fowler, "*The Clock*: Gesture and Cinematic Replaying," *The Journal of Cinema and Media* 54: 2 (Fall, 2013), 227.
10. The quoted expressions are from a commentary on Marclays *The Clock*: Eli Horwatt, "On *The Clock* and Christina Marclay's Instrumental logic of Appropriation," *Framework: The Journal of Cinema and Media* 54: 2 (2013), 209.
11. The quotation is from Gilles Deleuze, *Bergsonism* trans. Hugh Tomlinson and Barbara Habberjam (New York: Zone, 1991), 25–26.
12. Don DeLillo, "The Appendix" to his "The Uniforms," in *Cutting Edges: Young American Fiction for the '70s*, ed. Jack Hicks (New York: Holt, 1973), 533.
13. Don DeLillo, *Point Omega: A Novel* (New York: Scribner, 2010), 17.
14. *Ibid.*, 18.
15. I am quoting from James Lasdun's review of the novel, "Point Omega by Don DeLillo," On the web at: ps://www.theguardian.com/books/2010/feb/27/don-delillo-point-omega.
16. Francois Truffaut, *Hitchcock*, Revised ed. (New York: Simon and Schuster, 2015), ebook Loc. 343.
17. DeLillo, *Point Omega*, 3.
18. *Ibid.*, 7.
19. *Ibid.*, 4.
20. Gilles Deleuze, *Cinema 2: The Time Image*, trans. Hugh Tomlinson and Robert Galeta (Minneapolis: University of Minnesota Press, 1989), 272.
21. Hitchcock in conversation with Truffaut: Truffaut, *Hitchcock*, ebook loc 1069.
22. Deleuze, *Cinema 2*, 272.
23. DeLillo, *Point Omega*, 4.
24. *Ibid.*, 13.
25. *Ibid.*, 18.
26. *Ibid.*, 23.
27. *Ibid.*, 36.
28. *Ibid.*, 17.
29. *Ibid.*, 44.
30. Truffaut, *Hitchcock*, loc. 258.
31. *Ibid.*, loc. 905.
32. DeLillo, *Point Omega*, 6.
33. "Slow Movies" is in quotations because among the emerging analyses of slow cinema is Ira Jaffe's, *Slow Movies: Countering the Cinema of Action* (New York: Wallflower, 2014).
34. DeLillo, *Point Omega*, 115–116.
35. Andrei Tarkovsky, *Sculpting in Time*, trans. Kitty Hunter Blair (Austin: University of Texas Press, 2012), 183.
36. Lutz Koepnick, *On Slowness: Toward an Aesthetic of the Contemporary* (New York: Columbia University Press, 2014), ebook loc. 3203.
37. *Ibid.*, loc 3216.
38. Tobias Hecht, "Denial: A Visit in Four Ethnographic Fictions," in *Crumpled Paper Boat*, eds. Anand Pandian and Stuart McLean (Durham: Duke University Press, 2017), 131.
39. Zadie Smith, "The Embassy of Cambodia," *The New Yorker*, February 11 and 18, 2013, 89–91.

THE PHENOMENOLOGY OF THE CINEMA EXPERIENCE

40. Milan Kundera, *Slowness* (London: Faber and Faber, 1996), 12.
41. *Ibid.*, 79.
42. Catherine Bernard, "Supermarket History: An Interview with Joan Grimonprez," On the web at: www.johangrimonprez.be/main/interviews_DH_st4.html.
43. The quotation is from Kaja Silverman, "Waiting, Hoping Among the Ruins of All the Rest," in *Cinema's Alchemist: The Films of Péter Forgács*, eds. Bill Nichols and Michael Renov (Minneapolis: University of Minnesota Press, 2011), 96.
44. The quotation (and much of my understanding of remix as method) belongs to Eduardo Navas, *Remix Theory: The Aesthetics of Sampling* (New York: Springer, 2012), 65.
45. See Catherine Bernard, "Supermarket History: AN Interview with Johan Grimonprez," On the web at: www.johangrimonprez.be/main/interviews_DH_st4.html.
46. See Dorothy Smith, "On Sociological Description: A Method from Marx," *Human Studies* 4 (1981), 332.
47. Johan Grimonprez in an interview with Hans Obrist, On the web at: http://archive.constantvzw.org/events/e11/en/jg.html.
48. See M. M. Bakhtin, "Forms of Time and of the Chronotope in the Novel," in *The Dialogic Imagination*, trans. Caryle Emerson and Michael Holquist (Austin: University of Texas Press, 1981), 84–258.
49. Interview with Grimonprez in Bernard, "Supermarket History."
50. I am borrowing the phrase from Eben Wood in a version of his reading of Grimonprez's *Dial H.i.s.t.o.r.y*, On the web at: www.johangrimonprez.be/main/Film_DIALHISTORY_Story_6.html.
51. DeLillo, *Point Omega*, 3.
52. *Ibid.*, 5.
53. *Ibid.*, 13.
54. *Ibid.*, 18.
55. *Ibid.*, 21.
56. Jacques Rancière, "Fictions of Time," in *Rancière and Literature*, eds. Grace Hellyer and Julian Murphet (Edinburgh: Edinburgh University Press, 2016), 26.
57. DeLillo, *Point Omega*, 25.
58. See Robert S. McNamara, *In Retrospect: The Tragedy and Lessons of Vietnam* (New York: Times Books, 1995).
59. See Roger Ebert, "Striding Through the Fog of 20th-Century Wars," *Honolulu Advertiser*, February 27, 2004, 32.
60. Michael Renov, *Theorizing Documentary* (New York: Routledge, 1993), 3.
61. Helen Tworkov, "Interview with Philip Glass," in *Writings on Glass*, ed. Richard Kostelanetz (New York: Schirmer, 1997), 319.
62. Vincent Amiel, *Le Corps au cinema: Keaton, Bresson, Cassavetes* (Paris: Presses Universitaires de France, 1998), 2.
63. See Claude Mark Hurlbert, "'From Behind the Veil': Teaching the Literature of the Enemy," *The Canadian Modern Language Review* 60: 1 (September, 2003), 56 and Bill Readings, *The University in Ruins* (Minneapolis: University of Minnesota Press, 1995), 185.
64. Emmanuel Levinas, *Totality and Infinity*, trans. Alphonso Lingus (Pittsburgh: Duquesne University Press, 1969), 39.
65. Arundhati Roy, *The God of Small Things* (New York: Random House, 1997), 35.

REFERENCES

Amiel, Vincent (1998) *Le Corps au cinema: Keaton, Bresson, Cassavetes*, Paris: Presses Universitaires de France.

Arnheim, Rudolph (1982) *The Power of the Center*, Berkeley: University of California Press.

Bakhtin, M. M. (1981) 'Forms of Time and of the Chronotope in the Novel,' in *The Dialogic Imagination*, trans. Caryle Emerson and Michael Holquist, Austin: University of Texas Press, pp. 84–258.

Bernard, Catherine (1998) 'Supermarket History: An Interview with Johan Grimonprez,' at: www.johangrimonprez.be/main/interviews_DH_st4.html.

Burgin, Victor (2005) *The Remembered Film*, London: Reaktion Books.

Constable, Catherine (2009) 'Reflections on the Surface: Remaking the Postmodern with Van Sant's *Psycho*,' in *Adaptations in Contemporary Culture: Textual Infidelities*, ed. Rachel Carroll, London: Bloomsbury, pp. 23–33.

Crawford, Chelsey (2015) 'The Permeable Self: A Theory of Cinematic Quotation,' *Film-Philosophy*, Vol. 19 (1), pp. 105–123.

Deleuze, Gilles (1989) *Cinema 2*, trans. Hugh Tomlinson and Robert Galeta, Minneapolis: University of Minnesota Press.

Deleuze, Gilles (1990) *Bergsonism*, trans. Hugh Tomlinson and Barbara Habberjam, New York: Zone Books.

DeLillo, Don (1973) '"The Appendix" to "The Uniforms",' in *Cutting Edges: Young American Fiction for the '70s*, ed. Jack Hicks, New York: Holt, p. 533.

DeLillo, Don (2010) *Point Omega: A Novel*, New York: Scribner.

Fowler, Catherine (2013) '*The Clock*: Gesture and Cinematic Replaying,' *The Journal of Cinema and Media*, Vol. 54 (2), pp. 226–242.

Hecht, Tobias (2017) 'Denial: A Visit in Four Ethnographic Fictions,' in *Crumpled Paper Boat*, eds. Anand Pandian and Stuart McLean, Durham: Duke University Press, pp. 130–144.

Heidegger, Martin (2010) 'Methodological Introduction: Philosophy, Factical Life Experience, and the Phenomenology of Religion,' in *The Phenomenology of Religious Life*, trans. Mathias Fritsch and Jennifer Anna Gosetti-Ferencei, Bloomington: Indiana University Press, pp. 3–13.

Horwatt, Eli (2013) 'On *The Clock* and Christian Marclay's Instrumental Logic of Appropriation,' *Framework: The Journal of Cinema and Media* Vol. 54 (2), pp. 208–225.

Hurlbert, Claude Mark (2003) '"From Behind the Veil": Teaching the Literature of the Enemy,' *The Canadian Modern Language Review*, Vol. 60 (1), pp. 55–68.

Iampolski, Mikhail (1998) *The Memory of Tiresias: Intertextuality and Cinema*, Berkeley: University of California Press.

Jaffe, Ira (2014) *Slow Movies: Countering the Cinema of Action*, New York: Wallflower.

Koepnick, Lutz (2014) *On Slowness: Toward an Aesthetic of the Contemporary*, New York: Columbia University Press.

Kundera, Milan (1996) *Slowness*, London: Faber and Faber.

Lasdun, James (2010) 'Point Omega by Don DeLillo,' at: ps://www.theguardian.com/books/2010/feb/27/don-delillo-point-omega.

228   THE PHENOMENOLOGY OF THE CINEMA EXPERIENCE

Levinas, Emmanuel (1969) *Totality and Infinity*, trans. Alphonso Lingus, Pittsburgh: Duquesne University Press.

McNamara, Robert S. (1995) *In Retrospect: The Tragedy and Lessons of Vietnam*, New York: Times Books.

Naremore, James (1999) 'Remaking *Psycho, Hitchcock Annual*,' at: http://james naremore.net/wp-content/uploads/2018/07/RemakingPsycho.pdf.

Navas, Eduardo (2012) *Remix Theory: The Aesthetics of Sampling*, New York: Springer.

Rancière, Jacques (2016) 'Fictions of Time,' in *Rancière and Literature*, eds. Grace Hellyer and Julian Murphet, Edinburgh: Edinburgh University Press, pp. 1–31.

Readings, Bill (1995) *The University in Ruins*, Minneapolis: University of Minnesota Press.

Renov, Michael (1993) *Theorizing Documentary*, New York: Routledge.

Roy, Arundhati (1997) *The God of Small Things*, New York: Random House.

Silverman, Kaja (2011) 'Waiting, Hoping Among the Ruins of All the Rest,' in *Cinema's Alchemist: The Films of Péter Forgács*, eds. Bill Nichols and Michael Renov, Minneapolis: University of Minnesota Press.

Smith, Dorothy (1981) 'On Sociological Description: A Method from Marx,' *Human Studies* Vol. 4, pp. 313–337.

Smith, Zadie (2013) 'The Embassy of Cambodia,' *The New Yorker*, at: www.newyorker. com/magazine/2013/02/11/the-embassy-of-cambodia.

Tarkovsky, Andrei (2012) *Sculpting in Time*, trans. Kitty Hunter Blair, Austin: University of Texas Press.

Thomson, David (2010) *The Moment of Psycho: How Alfred Hitchcock Taught America to Love Murder*, New York: Basic Books.

Truffaut, Francois (2015) *Hitchcock*, revised ed., New York: Simon and Schuster.

Tworkov, Helen (1997) 'Interview with Philip Glass,' in *Writings on Glass*, ed. Richard Kostelanetz, New York: Schirmer, pp. 319–321.

Wood, Eben (2007) 'Grimonprez's *Dial H.i.s.t.o.r.y*,' at: www.johangrimonprez.be/ main/Film_DIALHISTORY_Story_6.html.

SUGGESTED READING

For More on the Phenomenology of Film Reception, See

Pier Paolo Pasolini, "The Cinema of Poetry," in *Heretical Empiricism*, trans. Ben Lawton and Louise K. Barnett (Bloomington: Indiana University Press, 1988), 167–237.

For More on Film Remakes, See

Constantine Verevis, *Film Remakes* (Edinburgh: Edinburgh University Press, 2006).

K. Loock and C. Verevis, *Film Remakes, Adaptations and Fan Productions: Remake/ Remodel* (London: Palgrave Macmillan, 2012). by K. Loock (Editor), C. Verevis (Editor)

Anat Zanger, *Film Remakes as Ritual and Disguise: From Carmen to Ripley* (Amsterdam: Amsterdam University Press, 2011).

Afterword

The Phenomenology of Watching and Writing

RESEARCH PROTOCOLS

Because much of the instructional approach in this book has been based on showing rather than saying (each chapter is meant as an exemplary political theory–cinema articulating composition), some important things about the method of inquiry that have been implied in the analysis thus far need to be addressed more fully and explicitly. For that purpose, I am reprising a section in my 2012 *Studies in Trans-Disciplinary Method* book, where I reflected on the research protocols in a methods text that was part of my graduate student training. After reproducing what the authors referred to as the "major steps in research—

> 1) A statement of purpose is made in the form of *formulating the problem* (my emphasis). 2) A description of the study design is given. 3) The method of data collection is specified. 4) The results are presented. 5) Frequently, there follows a section on conclusions and interpretation[1]

I noted that most of the research handbook's coverage was devoted to steps 2 through 5 and called attention to the lack of "sustained attention to the historical context of inquiry, for example the methodological concern with why particular problems emerge at particular historical moments."[2] Certainly the importance of that "methodological concern" remains relevant in this investigation. It is treated in the Introduction, where I refer to the significance of "events" that mark important breaks in the histories of philosophy, political theory, and cinema. Here, however, I want to point to a different concern that is also unaddressed in the mid-1960s' methods book whose protocols I have reproduced. That book's research agenda presumes a writing subject with no experiential duration, "an isolated epistemological subject that must somehow leap out of itself into a relation with the world."[3]

230 AFTERWORD

Rather than a timeless blank slate, prepared to look at a world of problems, register them, then narrate a context to execute a research design, the theorist-as-writing-subject dwells in a lived experiential duration. To borrow from a quotation in Chapter 7, more than "a mathematical point," he or she is a body with "memory . . . recollections . . . that link . . . instants to each other and interpolates the past in the present." Applied to inquiring subject/theorists, the methodological injunction (which I am here adding to the ones I offered in Chapter 1) is that one is always already involved in inquiry before formulating a specific problem to elucidate and pursue. What is neglected in traditional empiricist research instruction is the phenomenology of the *preparation* for the composing experience, which I illustrate by returning to a film I have analyzed elsewhere, Stephen Frears's *Dirty Pretty Things* (2002). In my treatment of the film, I suggested that, among other things, *Dirty Pretty Things* is a story of bodies and buildings.

The film drama opens and closes at one of London's Heathrow International Airport's terminals where, at the outset, Okwe (Chiwetel Ejiofor), a Nigerian refugee and medical doctor (working illegally without a valid passport and visa), is soliciting passengers for the cab he drives during the day and is working as desk clerk in the fictional Baltic Hotel in the evenings (where much of the film drama takes place). In the conclusion, he is again at Heathrow to see his friend Senay (Audrey Tautou), a Turkish refugee, off as she departs for the United States. In between, the film story is set in motion when Okwe discovers a human heart clogging a toilet in one the Baltic Hotel's room. He subsequently learns that the hotel manager, Senior Juan, is running an illegal organ harvesting and trafficking enterprise in the room at night. Although Okwe and Senay ultimately defeat Senior Juan's attempt to obtain and market Senay's kidney in return for a passport (Okwe takes over the operation and harvests Senior Juan's instead, after drugging him), to illustrate the phenomenological predicates of my writing strategy, I want to focus on another seemingly minor character, Okwe's friend Guo (Benedict Wong), a mortician working for the city who continually explains to Okwe the forces shaping the interpersonal relations in which he is situated. For example, in response to Okwe's report about his discovery of a human heart stuck in a hotel toilet, he reminds Okwe about his vulnerability as an illegal immigrant, saying, "Okwe, you are nothing, you have nothing . . . just help the people you can." And later in the film drama, as Okwe and Senay's relationship becomes emotionally fraught, Guo explains to Okwe something that Okwe has not perceived: that Senay is in love with him.

Having to make sense of Guo's role and articulate my analysis of it with the rest of the composing process, which is centered on a reading of the film, I discovered that I was prepared. I was able to draw on two aspects of my experiential archive (reading and film watching): theoretical treatments of aesthetic subjects and cinematic moments, respectively. For the former, I recalled and enlisted Gilles Deleuze's observations about a figure in the painter Francis

AFTERWORD   231

Bacon's canvasses that is peripheral to the main theme, a character that Deleuze refers to as an "attendant" (a "spectator" who "seems to subsist, distinct from the [main] figure").[4] As I had summarized that role in an earlier investigation, "Deleuze sees the attendant as a provider of facticity of the scene, or in his words, 'the relation of the Figure to its isolating place,' or 'what takes place.'"[5] In order to adapt the attendant function from painting to cinema, and thus needing an illustration, I recalled a striking moment in Louis Malle's film *Pretty Baby* (1978), which I narrated as follows:

> [It's] a film whose plot involves the transition of a young girl, raised in a New Orleans bordello, from childhood to the vocation of a prostitute. In keeping with the bordello's tradition of an elaborate ceremony for the transition, the 12-year-old 'virgin,' Violet (Brook Shields), is auctioned off in a setting that bears a startling resemblance to a slave auction. After being carried into the main sitting room om a large pallet, Violet stands on a small raised platform as the bidding progresses . . . the camera lingers for some time [a long take] on the face of Professor (Antonio Fargas), an African American piano player in the bordello, who until the moment of the bidding had seems to share in the celebratory spirit of the occasion.[6]

I designated the "Professor" as an attendant who, in that moment, was reinflecting the facticity of the scene by placing it in a comparative context. No longer the mere coming out of a prostitute to her vocation, the moment recalls an earlier one in which bodies are commodities. The Professor's role as an attendant translates the scene from an isolated episode to "a history of coercion, when humans were turned into exchangeable things in slave markets."[7]

The point of my extended illustration is that I had ready at hand both a conceptual strategy and a cinema example. I drew from an experiential archive that had been built from reading theory and watching films. Simply put, to compose an essay, one needs material to bring to the analysis. When you consume theoretical, literary, and visual texts—reading and watching, respectively—you are preparing yourself to draw on those texts. The reading experiences that precede a particular inquiry constitute what I want to call *proto inquiry*. In reading and watching, you are involved in inquiry-ready self-fashioning as a theorist and writer.

THE EXPERIENCE OF INQUIRY

One way to put the methodological issue is our need to recognize our habitual inattention. As Samuel Beckett puts it, "life is habit . . . a succession of habits," and as he famously figures it as a problem, "[h]abit is the ballast that chains the

232   AFTERWORD

dog to his vomit."[8] Beckett's remark performs the problem as well as stating it; his mixed metaphor inhibits the habitual reading process in which one moves on to consume the next sentence; its jarring juxtapositions force the reader to think rather than scan. What I am therefore suggesting is that critically oriented interpretive work requires a phenomenology that implicates and disrupts the analyzing subject. However, I want to add that it is too facile to refer simply to an "analyzing subject" because the inquiry-initiating assumptions about one's subjectivity as a thinker/analyst can be effectively disrupted in the writing process. Among those who have addressed themselves to that kind of phenomenology is Michel Foucault, who, in conversation about what he refers to as an "experience-book," says that when he writes, he seeks to transform himself, "not to think the same thing as before."[9] Writing practices, he says, should be regarded in the same way as philosophical practices; they are practices of "the self on the self."[10] As the conversation proceeds, Foucault juxtaposes his self-changing approach to writing with the conventional phenomenological approach to subjectivity, which he says, "tries to grasp the significance of daily experience in order to reaffirm the fundamental character of the subject."[11] Rejecting that approach and identifying with a phenomenology of writing he ascribes to "Nietzsche, Blanchot, and Bataille," he conceives the purpose of the writing "task" as one of "'tearing' the subject from itself in such a way that it is no longer the subject as such, or that it is completely 'other' than itself . . . a 'desubjectifying undertaking.'"[12] Foucault's approach yields yet another methodological injunction. Be prepared to be afflicted by your investigation, for example, to discover incoherence in your self-understanding.

I close with an illustration of my first cinematic affliction (with which I want to issue one last methodological injunction). In, 1961when I was an undergraduate student at Tufts University in Medford, Massachusetts, I used to travel to nearby Cambridge to watch foreign films at the Brattle Street movie theater (what one now calls an "art-house" theater). The first one I watched there affected my experience of myself. It was Ingmar Bergman's twenty-first feature film, *The Virgin Spring* (1960). Up to that point, my filmgoing experiences had issued no ethico-political challenges or occasions for serious introspection. My prior film viewing had been primarily the western and the crime story genres, which featured "the good the bad and the ugly" in ways that solicited relatively unambiguous judgments. *The Virgin Spring* stunned me. Because I was used to action films, which had me continually anticipating the next moment in dramas in which good characters vanquished bad ones, its slowness, which had the camera lingering on faces in ways that transcended individual personality, disrupted my habitual mode of reception. That effect, a "long-take style," which I describe in the Introduction and Chapter 7 as characteristic of the Russian film director Andrei Tarkovsky's films, "gives the viewer [as I quoted him] an opportunity to live through what is on screen as

AFTERWORD   233

if it were his own life, to take over the experience imprinted in time on the screen."[13] In short, doing political theory with cinematic texts should include attunement to the world in which the inquiry takes place in ways that disrupt the attunement one has with oneself. That commitment to vulnerability opens one to seeing and thinking differently.

NOTES

1. Claire Selltiz et al., *Research Methods in Social Relations* (London: Methuen, 1965), 9.
2. Michael J. Shapiro, *Studies in Trans-Disciplinary Method: After the Aesthetic Turn* (London: Routledge, 2012), 4.
3. I am quoting Anthony Curtis Adler, *Celebricities: Media Culture and the Phenomenology of Gadget Commodity Life* (New York: Fordham University Press, 2016), 14.
4. Gilles Deleuze, *Francis Bacon: The Logic of Sensation*, trans. Daniel W. Smith (Minneapolis: University of Minnesota Press, 2003), 14.
5. Michael J. Shapiro, *Cinematic Geopolitics* (London: Routledge, 2009), 100. The inner quotation is from *Ibid.*, 60.
6. Shapiro, *Cinematic Geopolitics*, 100–101.
7. *Ibid.*, 101.
8. Samuel Beckett, *Proust* (New York: Grove Press, 1957), 8.
9. Michel Foucault, *Remarks on Marx: Conversations with Duccio Trombadori*, trans. R. James Goldstein and James Cascaito (New York: Semiotext(e), 1991), 27.
10. Michel Foucault, *The Government of Self and Others: Lectures at the College De France 1982–1983*, trans. Graham Burchell (New York: Palgrave Macmillan, 2010), 255.
11. *Ibid.*, 31.
12. *Ibid.*
13. Andrei Tarkovsky, *Sculpting in Time*, trans. Kitty Hunter Blair (Austin: University of Texas Press, 2012), 183.

REFERENCES

Adler, Anthony Curtis (2016) *Celebricities: Media Culture and the Phenomenology of Gadget Commodity Life*, New York: Fordham University Press.
Andrei Tarkovsky (2012) *Sculpting in Time*, trans. Kitty Hunter Blair, Austin: University of Texas Press.
Beckett, Samuel (1957) *Proust*, New York: Grove Press.
Claire Selltiz, Claire, et al. (1965) *Research Methods in Social Relations*, London: Methuen.
Deleuze, Gilles (2003) *Francis Bacon: The Logic of Sensation*, trans. Daniel W. Smith, Minneapolis: University of Minnesota Press.
Foucault, Michel (1991) *Remarks on Marx: Conversations with Duccio Trombadori*, trans. R. James Goldstein and James Casciato, New York: Semiotext(e).
Foucault, Michel (2010) *The government of Self and Others: Lectures at the College De France 1982–1983*, trans. Graham Burchell, New York: Palgrave Macmillan.
Shapiro, Michael J. (2009) *Cinematic Geopolitics*, London: Routledge.
Shapiro, Michael J. (2012) *Studies in Trans-Disciplinary Method: After the Aesthetic Turn*, London: Routledge.

Name Index

Adorno, Theodor W. 5, 19n23
Agamben, Giorgio 135–136, 142n107, 142n110, 152, 172n17
Agee, Arthur (athlete) 63, 69, 71
Agnew, Ray (athlete) 52–54, 56–57, 59–62
Aichele, George 14, 21n69
Amiel, Vincent 223, 226n62
Amin, Ash 37, 48n30
Antonioni, Michelangelo 12–13, 20n61
Arnheim, Rudolph 204, 224n6

Bacon, Francis (painter) 27–28, 47n5
Bakhtin, M. M. 139n29, 141n90, 226n48
Bardot, Bridget (actor) 8, 195
Barthes, Roland 2, 18n5, 106, 110n62, 182, 199n22
Bazin, Andre 6, 19n26, 174n62
Behram, Noor 106
Benjamin, Walter 17, 19n40, 20nn46–47, 21n88, 53, 71, 75n4, 78n73, 108n7, 109n36, 110n67, 181, 193–194, 199n15
Bennett, Jill 97, 109n39
Bensaid, Daniel 116, 138n7
Berenson, Marisa (actor) 66, 69
Bergson, Henri 45, 49n47, 206
Bersani, Leo 8, 19n30, 140n49, 195, 202n48
Bertolucci, Bernardo 8–9
Blanchot, Maurice 46, 49n49, 232
Bordwell, David 171n5
Bouchey, Willis B. (actor) 185

Bowden, Charles 156, 158, 161, 173n36, 173n46, 173n50
Briggs, Alice Leora 156, 158, 160, 173n36, 173n46
Burch, Noël 141n76, 163, 173n56
Burgin, Victor 199n1, 199–n22, 205, 225n8
Bush, President George W. 99

Canetti, Elias 128, 140n51
Casarino, Cesare 14, 21n70, 31, 47n13, 118, 120, 138n13, 139n21
Celine, Louis-Ferdinand 208
Césaire, Aimé 46–47, 49n52
Chamayou, Gregoire 104, 109n45
Chandler, Raymond 36
Coleridge, Samuel Taylor 35
Conan Doyle, Sir Arthur 36
Conley, Tom 29, 47n7
Cossa, Frank 66, 77n61, 77n63
Crary, Jonathan 70–71, 78n72, 194–195, 200n45
Crawford, Chelsey 203, 224nn2–3
Cuarón, Alfredo 11, 20n55

Deleuze, Gilles 2–3, 10–11, 13–16, 18n3, 18n11, 20n49, 20n51, 20nn53–54, 20n62, 20n66, 21nn71–74, 27, 31, 39, 45, 47n3, 47n6, 47nn11–12, 47n14, 48nn32–33, 49n48, 57, 63–66, 69, 72, 77nn41–43, 77n46, 77n48, 77n52, 77nn57–58, 77n65, 77n67, 78n79, 96, 102, 109n32, 110n58, 131,

138n12, 140n58, 141n73, 154, 162, 172n21, 172n24, 173n53, 199n24, 200n41, 200n43, 207, 209, 225n11, 225n20, 225n22, 230–231, 233n4
DeLillo, Don 105, 203, 207–211, 214, 217, 219, 221, 223–224, 225nn12–13, 225n15, 225n17, 225n23, 225n32, 225n34, 226n51, 226n57
Derrida, Jacques 30, 40, 47n9, 48n22, 48n36, 95, 109n29, 109n31, 171, 174n76
Deutsche, Rosalyn 81–82, 85, 93–94, 108n5, 108n10, 109n26
Dick, Philip 10
Dubuffet, Jean 36, 48n28
Duras, Marguerite 81, 86, 89, 92–93, 98
Dürrenmatt, Friedrich 38
Dutoit, Ulysses 8, 19n30, 140n49, 195, 200
Dworkin, Ronald 170, 174n74

Ebert, Roger 219, 226n59
Elias, Norbert 60, 76n34
Elphick, Michael (actor) 28
Eisenstein, Sergei 17, 211
Eliot, T. S. 193
Eysenck, H. G. 5

Flusser, Vilém 40, 48n38
Ford, Henry 43
Ford, John 26
Foucault, Michel 2–3, 18n6, 18nn8–9, 30, 41–42, 46, 47n8, 49n40, 49n49, 57–59, 63, 76n23, 76nn26–27, 101, 110n51, 117, 138n9, 142n117, 156–157, 168, 172n28, 172nn31–32, 174n65, 232, 233nn9–10
Freeman, Mike 52–54, 56, 75n2
Fuentes, Carlos 150–153, 156, 161, 164, 171n9, 171n12
Fuller, Samuel 185–186

Gates, William (athlete) 63, 69, 71, 74
Gilbert, Peter 62
Glass, Philip 219–221
Godard, Jean-Luc 8, 18n4, 34, 90–91, 96, 106, 109n23, 140n49, 195–196, 207

Gordon, Douglas 203, 207–212, 217
Greenwald, Robert 102, 104–107, 110n57
Grimonprez, Johan 214–216, *214*, 226n42, 226n45, 226n47, 226nn49–50
Guattari, Felix 2, 10–11, 18n3, 20n48, 20n51, 20n54, 21n73, 47n12, 64, 77n43, 138n12
Guimarães, Julia Peres 162, 173n54

Hammett, Dashiell 36
Huizinga, Johan 60, 76n33
Hussain, Nasser 107
Hattendorf, Linda 81, 94–97, 99
Hayes, Lester (athlete) 61
Hecht, Tobias 212, 225n38
Heidegger, Martin 20n65, 58, 76n21, 204, 224n7
Hernandez, Noe (actor) 165
Herzog, Werner 34, 44
Heston, Charlton (actor) 155
Hitchcock, Alfred 4, 13, 34, 203–204, 208–212, 225n21
Hitler, Adolph 43, 46–47, 179
Hobbes, Thomas 113, 117–118, 120–122, 125–126, 128–138, 138n3, 139nn22–24, 139n28, 139n39, 140nn53–54, 140n56, 140n64, 141n67, 141n77, 141n79, 141n84, 141n87, 141n94, 142n103, 142n113, 142n115
Hölderlin, Friedrich 85
Holmes, Oliver Wendell 70, 78n71
Holmes, Sherlock 36
Honig, Bonnie 1, 18n1, 26–28, 47n2
Huizinga, Johan 60, 76n33
Hume, David 12, 130
Hurlbert, Claude Mark 223–224, 226n63
Huyssen, Andreas 198, 201n56

Ibuse, Masuji 87–89, 91, 97, 100, 102, 108n15, 108nn21–22
Iampolski, Mikhail 203, 224n3

James, Steve 62
Johnson, President Lyndon 221

NAME INDEX 237

Jordan, Michael (athlete) 62, 77n39
Joravsky, Ben 62
Joyce, James 45

Kádár, János 137
Kafka, Franz 39, 48n34
Kahn, Victoria 134
Kant, Immanuel 3, 27, 31–34, 41, 48n18, 53–59, 61, 63–64, 70, 75nn6–7, 75n9, 76n10, 76n12, 76nn18–19, 76n22, 122, 139n36, 170
Kanze, Hideo (actor) 82
Kennedy, President Jack 219, 223
Kermode, Frank 12
Kertesz, Imre 31–32, 47n15, 92, 109n24
Kirchner, Ernst Ludwig 183–185, 199n25
Kluge, Alexander 13, 17, 20n63, 21n87
Knight, Easmond (actor) 29
Ko, Clifton 179
Koepnick, Lutz 211, 235n36
Kolbowski, Silvia 85–86, 93–94, 98, 98
Kracauer, Siegfried 17, 22n90
Krasznahorkai, Laszlo 113, 116–119, 120–122, 124–130, 132–134, 136–137, 138nn4–6, 138n11, 138nn16–17, 139n20, 139nn26–27, 139n29, 139n34, 140n41, 140n43, 140n45, 140n48, 140n50, 140n52, 140n55, 140n59, 140n62, 140n65, 141n71, 141n85, 141n89, 141n91, 141n95, 141n99, 142n116
Kubrick, Stanley 65–67, 69, 75n3
Kundera, Milan 213, 226n40

Lang, Berel 142n100, 142n102
Leach, William 189–190, 200n33
Leigh, Janet (actor) 4, 208
LeMay, Curtis (General) 39
Leon, Donna 191, 200n36
Leung Ka-fai, Tony (actor) 178
Levinas, Emmanuel 224, 226n64
Ling-Liang, Tsai 205
Lo, Kwai-Cheung 197, 199n8, 200n50
Lucarelli, Carlo 6–7, 19n25
Lynch, David 4, 203
Lyotard, Jean-François 12, 20n64, 48n17

Machiavelli, Nicolo 4
Mann, Anthony 153–155, 170
Mann, Thomas 41–42, 49n41, 49n44
Marchant, Steven 116, 124, 138n8, 140n44
Marclay, Christian 205–206, 206, 215, 225n10
Marso, Lori J. 1, 18n1, 26–28, 47n2
Martel, James R. 131, 139n24, 141n78, 141n82, 141n98
Marx, Feeder 62
Maxwell, Richard 105, 110n60
Mbembe, Achille 95, 109n30
McNamara, Robert S. 217–224, 222, 226n58
Morales, President Evo 168–169, 171, 174n67
Morris, Errol 217–224
Mussawir, Edward 16, 21n81
Mussolini, Benito 6, 9

Nai-Hoi, Yau 178, 180, 184, 196
Naranjo, Gerardo 152, 160–168, 171
Naremore, James 204, 224n4
Nietzsche, Friedrich 15, 30–31, 33–34, 36, 48n21, 57, 76n20, 232
Nixon, President Richard 153
Nixon, Rob 97, 109n38

Obama, President Barack 81, 100, 146
Oe, Kenzaburo 83, 108n2, 108n8
Okada, Eiji (actor) 86
O'Neill, Ryan (actor) 67

Padura, Leonardo 37, 48n31
Panagia, Davide 1, 12, 20n59, 130, 141n72, 174n72
Pasolini, Pier Paulo 14, 20n62, 21n69, 167, 174n63
Pena, Luis Fernando (actor) 147
Perkins, Anthony (actor) 4, 209
Peters, Jean (actor) 185
Picazo, Lakshmi (actor) 164
Piccoli, Michel 8, 195
Pippen, Scottie (athlete) 62
Plato 38, 123–124, 140n40
Pocock, J. G. A. 3, 18n12, 124, 140n42

NAME INDEX

Poe, Edgar Allen 45
Polanski, Roman 4, 203
Powell, Michael 205
Pressburger, Emeric 205

Rákosi, Mátyás 137
Rancière, Jacques 5, 17, 18n4, 19n21,
22n91, 34, 48n23, 96, 109n34, 119,
138n18, 139n29, 150, 170–171,
171n7, 174n64, 188, 200n32, 218,
220, 226n56
Rawls, John 170, 174n71, 174n73
Readings, Bill 224, 226n63
Renov, Michael 220, 226n43, 226n60
Resnais, Alain 81, 86, 89, 93–94, 96, 98
Riva, Emmanuel (actor) 86
Rivera, Alex 146
Robbe-Grillet, Alain 14
Rokeach, Milton 5
Rossellini, Roberto 9, 13, 21n67
Rothman, William 203, 224n2
Roy, Arundhati 226n65
Rushd, Ibn (aka Averroës) 38
Ruttmann, Walther 182, 184

Salcedo, Doris 97
Sandell, Jillian 72, 78n77
Savalas, Telly (actor) 43
Schmitt, Carl 121, 135, 139n33,
141n93, 142n106
Shindo, Kaneto 82, 89
Sigman, Stepanie (actor) 152, 161
Simmel, Georg 195–196, 200n47
Smith, Adam 11–12
Smith, Zadie 212, 225n39
Speer, Albert 179
Spinoza, Baruch 135
Strauss, Leo 135, 142n105

Tarkovsky, Andrei 11, 17, 21n86, 34,
45, 211, 225n35, 232, 233n13
Tarr, Bela 113–114, 116–119, 121,
126–129, 136–137, 138n5, 138n11,
142n116, 143n118
Thackeray, William Makepeace 65–66
Thomson, David 4, 18n16, 224n1
Thrift, Nigel 37, 48n30
Trier, Lars von 1, 26–47, 48n27,
49n50
Truffaut, Francois 208, 225n16,
225n21, 225n30
Trump, President Donald 100, 146
Tsui, Kate (actor) 186

Van Sant, Gus 203–204, 204, 224
Varela, Leonor (actor) 149
Vaughan, Vince (actor) 203
Vaughan-Williams, Nick 152, 172n17
Vertov, Dziga 182, 184
Virilio, Paul 70–71, 78n68, 182,
199n21
Vitoria, Leonor (actor) 161
Vye, Murvyn (actor) 185

Webb, Gary 158, 172n34
Welles, Orson 154–155, 171n1,
172n26
Wells, Jerold (actor) 35, 43
Wagstaff, Christopher 9, 19n28, 19n31,
19n38, 21n67
Werckmeister, Andreas 123, 126
Widmark, Richard (actor) 186
Winslow, Don 153, 156–158, 162,
172n19, 172n29
Wodiczko, Krzysztof 196, 200n49

Yam, Simon (actor) 186

Subject Index

aesthetics: Bazin on 6; Benjamin on 9–10, 17; Bersani and Dutoit on 8; breaks 219; Deleuze and Guattari on 10; in DeLillo 217; in Fuentes 150–153, 156, 161; Hitchcock's 4, 34, 203–204, 208–212; in Hobbes 117–118, 120–122, 125–126, 128–138; Krasznahorkai's 116–119, 120–122, 124–130, 132–134, 136–137; literary 118; Lucarelli's 6–7; and morality 90; Mussawir on 16; in Naranjo 152, 160–168, 171; Neorealist 7, 9, 12–13; Pasolini's 14, 167; politics of 7, 9, 96, 137; Rancière on 5, 17, 34, 96, 119, 150, 170–171, 188, 218, 220; of shock 10, 17, 107, 160; subjects 26, 126, 155, 158, 195, 230; in Tarkovsky 11, 17, 34, 45, 211, 232; in Tarr 116–119, 121, 126–129, 136–137; in von Trier 1, 26–47

architecture: Berlin's 178–184, 198; Hong Kong's 178–180, 196–198; Mussolini and 9; in Tarr's *Werckmeister Harmonies* 136

autobiography: in Bowden and Brigg's *Dreamland* 156, 158; Derrida on 30, 40, 95, 171; and history 219; McNamara and 217–224; necro-100, 106; in von Tier's *The Element of Crime* 26–27, 29, 37–38

cartography: in Bowden and Brigg's *Dreamland* 156, 158; Conley on 29; In Naranjo's *Ms. Bala* 152,

160, 162–163, 171; in von Trier's *The Element of Crime* 26–27, 29, 37–38

clichés: Deleuze on 2–3, 10–11, 13–16, 27; Honig and Marso on 1, 26–28; in von Trier's *The Element of Crime* 26–27, 29, 37–38

colonial/colonialism: Bolivia's experience of 168–169; in border films 155; Césaire on 46–47; Foucault on 2–3, 30, 41–42, 46, 57–59, 63, 101, 117, 156–157, 168, 232; Hong Kong's experience of 180, 182, 185, 198; in von Trier's *The Element of Crime* 26–27, 29, 37–38

critique: Bowden on 156, 158, 161; film form as 39–40; Foucault on 30, 41–42, 57–59, 117, 156–157; in Hobbes 117–118, 120–122, 125–126, 128–138; of Hobbes 118, 120–122, 128, 131, 133–136, 138; in Kant 31–34, 41, 53–59, 170; Machiavelli's 4; in Naranjo's *Ms. Bala* 152, 160, 162–163, 171; Rancière's of rationalism 34, 119, 170; in von Trier's *The Element of Crime* 26–27, 29, 37–38; Winslow's 156–158, 162

documentaries: DeLillo's fictional 105, 207–211, 214, 217, 219, 221, 223–224; Greenwald's 102, 104–107; Hattendorf's 81, 94–97, 99; Morris's McNamara 217–219

240   SUBJECT INDEX

enlightenment: critique of in von Trier's *The Element of Crime* 26–27, 29, 37–38; Foucault on 2–3, 30, 41–42, 46, 57–59, 63, 101, 117, 156–157, 168, 232; Kant on 3, 27, 31–34, 41, 53–59, 61, 63–64, 70, 122, 170

ethics: Able on 106; Aristotle on 34; of attention 97; in Bergman's *The Virgin Spring* 232; Dworkin on 170; Godard on 34, 90–91, 96, 106; in Greenwald documentary 102, 104–107; Ibuse's reflections on 87–89, 91, 97, 100, 102; in Hattendorf's *The Cats of Mirikitani* 81, 94, 96; in *Hiroshima Mon Amour* 81, 85–86, 89–90, 93–94, 98, 106; Kant on 31–34, 170; in Kertesz's novel 31–32, 92; in Kolbowski video 85–86, 93–94, 98; Levinas on 224; of modernity 72; in Morris 's documentary 217–224; re War crimes 16, 146; in Salcedo works 97

fascism 5, 8–10, 122

fiction: Able on 106; Carlo Lucarelli's 6–7; detective 6, 36; in documentary 106, 218; Don Delillo's 105, 203, 207–211, 214, 217, 219, 221, 223–224; Imre Kertesz's 31–32, 92; Philip Dick's 10; Rancière on 5, 17, 34, 96, 119, 150, 170–171, 188, 218, 220; William Makepeace Thackery's 65–66

genealogy: of narcotics prevention policy 153; of plane hijacking 214–216; of sporting experience 59–61

history: of atrocity 81, 92, 94, 97, 101, 149; autobiography and 219; Benjamin on 9–10, 17, 53, 71, 181, 193–194; Berlin's 178–184, 198; of bombing 81–83, 85–93, 95–97, 99–102, 108, 221–222; cinema and 1, 118; of cinema 2, 4–6, 31; of cold war 158, 181; Deleuze on philosophical 2–3, 10–11, 13–16, 27, 31, 39, 45, 57, 63–66, 69, 72, 96, 102, 131, 154, 162, 207, 209,

230–231; Derrida on 30, 40, 95, 171; of drug war 163, 166, 168–169, 171; of forms 14, 31; Foucault on 2–3, 30, 41–42, 46, 57–59, 63, 101, 117, 156–157, 168, 232; genealogical 2; Geopolitical 182; German 46; Hong Kong's 178–180, 182–194, 196–198; Hungarian 138; Huyssen on 198; Kant on 3, 31–34, 41, 53–59, 61, 63–64, 70, 122; in Kolbowski video 85–86, 93–94; Kundera on 213; Mann on 41–42; Marclay on 205–206, 215; of Mexico 151–152; musical 215; of plane hijacking 214–216; of political theory 3, 9, 229; politics of 17; (Adam) Smith on 11–12; Thackeray on 65–66; of weapons 99–108

justice: aesthetics and 150, 155; anthropology of 16; Bolivia's approach 168–169; in borderline film narratives 169, 171n1; Bowden on 156, 158, 161; Derrida on 30, 40, 95, 171; Dworkin on 170; as fairness 168, 170; Fuentes on 150–153, 156, 161, 164; methodology for 16; Mussawir on 16; Rancière on 17, 96, 150, 170–171; Rawls on 170; redemptive 98; temporality of 97; in von Trier's *The Element of Crime* 26–27, 29, 37–38; Winslow on 153, 156–158, 162

metaphor(s): Aristotle on 34; Beckett's 221, 231; Burch's cinematic 131; Deleuze's drama 13–16; Grimonprez on 214–216; Hobbes's 120–122, 125–126; Kant's 31–34, 41, 53–59; in (Anthony) Mann's *T Men* 153–154; Nietzsche on 15, 30–31, 33–34, 36, 232; Rancière on 34, 119; in von Trier's *The Element of Crime* 26–27, 29, 37–38

painting(s): Antonioni's use of 12–13; Benjamin on painting *versus* film 71; Deleuze on Bacon's 2–3, 10–11, 13–16, 27; Kirchner's Postdamer

SUBJECT INDEX 241

Platz 183–185; in Kubrick's *Barry Lyndon* 65–70; Renaissance 205
political theory 1–3, 5, 9–12, 14, 17–18, 26, 46, 83, 118, 122, 229, 233
power: air (in Smithsonian narrative) 85; of archives 95; arrangements in Tarr's *Werckmeister Harmonies* 113, 122, 126, 136; bio- (Agamben) 135–136, 152; of cinema 27; civil (in Hobbes) 135; Deleuze on "power of the false" 66; desire for (in Hobbes) 123, 128; of discourse 170; Foucault on 2–3, 41–42, 46, 57–59, 63, 117, 156–157; Kant on mentality's 33, 41, 56, 170; labor (in Welles's *A Touch of Evil*) 154–155; loci of 179; magical in Tarr's *Werckmeister Harmonies* 132; map of 180; modality of in the twentieth century 2; in Naranjo's *Ms. Bala* 152, 160, 162–163, 171; policing in Tarr's *Werckmeister Harmonies* 137; political 3; *versus* rapture 123; sovereign 2, 117, 158; of sport's temporalities 56, 59; structure of in eighteenth century 70, 74; structures of 216; Virilio on 70–71, 182; in von Trier films 1, 26, 27, 31, 34, 36, 41; of work or art (Benjamin) 107

space(s): abstract 147; academic 74; of Berlin 178–184, 198; Bowden on 156, 158, 161; of Chinese culture 197; cinematic 8, 126, 163, 167, 196; cinematic heterotopia 178, 181, 199n1; colonial 179; of contestation 95; non-contiguous 161; estate 65, 77n55; of disappearance 179; ethical 106; gallery 97; historical 29, 30, 33; of historical memory 183; history of 198; of Hong Kong 178–180, 182–194, 196–198; indeterminate 212; inner (in von Trier protagonist) 40, 41; illuminated 117; of interpersonal relations 127; juridical 16; lived 147, 171n4; of living 71; of motion 130; moving 181; narrative 219; negotiating large *versus* small 180; of negotiation 198; off-screen

163; organization of 61; practices of 67; privileging of time over (in Deleuze) 64; public 41, 55, 56, 196; representational 72; of retreat 210; social 71–72, 78n76; temporary 183; thinking 216; virtual 149
subjects/subjectivity: aesthetic 6–7, 16, 26, 33, 41, 87, 126, 155, 158, 161, 167, 195, 230; becoming 15; biographical 106; cinematic 195, 207; cognitive 40; collective 16, 122; and concepts 15; contingencies of 15, 16; as contrivance 16; cosmological 123, 124; Deleuze's 2–3, 10–11, 13–16, 27; DeLillo's fictional 217; durational 16; epistemological 26, 229; ethnographic 105; formation of 15, 16; Foucault's 2–3, 30, 41–42, 46, 57–59, 63, 156–157, 168, 232; of governance 197; grammar of 15; Hobbes's sovereign 134; Kant's 3, 27, 31–34, 41, 53–59, 61, 63–64, 70, 122, 170; legal 187; Morris's (documentary) 217–219; as observers 12; Oe's 83; political 167, 169; post-traumatic 85; psychological 30, 167, 195; racial 155; Rancière's 17, 34, 119, 150, 170–171, 218, 220; representational activity of 54; of rights 167; sexual 155; situated 207; speaking 222; stable 16; transcendental 31; unstable 15; value of 66; viewing 206; writing 229, 230

textuality 1–2, 12, 18, 42, 117, 120, 130–131, 134, 136, 160, 214

value: of African American bodies 52, 62, 70, 98; Benjamin on 9–10, 17; of civil society 179; cultural 60, 179; Deleuze on 100; economic 61; exhibition 108; Foucault on 57–59, 63, 156–157; of heritage 66; Kant on 27, 53–59, 61, 63–64, 70, 122, 170; politics of 64; of mobility 74; moral 197; Nietzsche on 15, 30–31, 33–34, 36, 57; ritual 71; in (Adam) Smith 11–12; and time 52, 64, 65, 72, 75n1

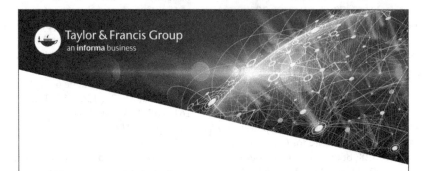

Taylor & Francis eBooks

www.taylorfrancis.com

A single destination for eBooks from Taylor & Francis with increased functionality and an improved user experience to meet the needs of our customers.

90,000+ eBooks of award-winning academic content in Humanities, Social Science, Science, Technology, Engineering, and Medical written by a global network of editors and authors.

TAYLOR & FRANCIS EBOOKS OFFERS:

- A streamlined experience for our library customers
- A single point of discovery for all of our eBook content
- Improved search and discovery of content at both book and chapter level

REQUEST A FREE TRIAL
support@taylorfrancis.com